PICKFORD

PICKFORD

—

THE·WOMAN·WHO MADE·HOLLYWOOD

—

EILEEN·WHITFIELD

THE UNIVERSITY PRESS OF KENTUCKY

Publication of this volume was made possible in part by
a grant from the National Endowment for the Humanities.

Published by The University Press of Kentucky
Scholarly publisher for the Commonwealth,
serving Bellarmine College, Berea College,
Centre College of Kentucky, Eastern Kentucky University,
The Filson Club Historical Society, Georgetown College,
Kentucky Historical Society, Kentucky State University,
Morehead State University, Murray State University,
Northern Kentucky University, Transylvania University,
University of Kentucky, University of Louisville,
and Western Kentucky University.

Editorial and Sales Offices: The University Press of Kentucky
663 South Limestsone Street, Lexington, Kentucky 40508-4008

01   00   99   98   97   5   4   3   2

Library of Congress Cataloging-in-Publication Data
are available from the publisher.

Printed and bound in Canada

ISBN 0-8131-2045-4

To my mother, Lily Duerkop,
and my late father, John Duerkop

CONTENTS

ACKNOWLEDGMENTS

I would like to thank the Canada Council, the Ontario Arts Council, and the Toronto Arts Council for their generous financial aid. Without their support, I would never have been able to write this book. I am equally grateful to my publishers, Macfarlane Walter & Ross, for commissioning the manuscript (and waiting so long for its arrival). I'd also like to thank my editor, Barbara Czarnecki, as well as Liba Berry and Rosemary Shipton for additional editorial input, Sara Borins, Paul Woods, and the book's designers, James Ireland Design Inc. Last but not least, I thank my agents, Lee Davis Creal, Linda Turchin, and Jan Whitford, of Westwood Creative Artists.

The assembly of a life is a daunting project. In Pickford's case, that life was lived in the glare of celebrity journalism. This makes scholarship all the more crucial, as research gives context to the half-truths, lies, and occasional insights of popular legend. All the more reason, I believe, to express my gratitude to those who helped me navigate the myriad press accounts of Pickford's career. I am also grateful to those who helped me pinpoint her life through public documents, and to those who supplied me with reels of film – not only Pickford's movies, but those of Sarah Bernhardt, Eleanora Duse, Marguerite Clark, Douglas Fairbanks, D. W. Griffith, Mary

Miles Minter, Jack and Lottie Pickford, Olive Thomas, and others.

I was privileged to interview Pickford family members Douglas Fairbanks Jr., Letitia Fairbanks Smoot, Lucile Fairbanks Crump, John Mantley, and Buddy Rogers. I thank them all for their grace, trust, and candor. I regret that Roxanne Monroe chose not to be interviewed, but I am grateful to Nicholas Eliopoulos for sharing his taped interview with her. The Reverend Malcolm Boyd and Roger Seward gave me eloquent interviews regarding Pickford's later life. In addition, I thank William Bakewell, Lina Basquette, Robert Blumofe, Bartine Burkett, Margaret Bush, Gaylord Carter, Marguerite Champion, C.B. Charles, Maxine Elliott Hicks, Eleanor Keaton, Charles Kiel, Douglas Kirkland, Harry Lewis, Rheba Lutz, Gerald Pratley, Daniel Taradash, Tony Thomas, and Coy Watson, all of whom shared thoughts and observations.

Two scholars have contributed immeasurably to this book. Kevin Brownlow not only answered my endless queries but gave me unqualified creative support. Most important, it is owing to his books and documentaries that I first became fascinated by the silents, and by Pickford in particular. Brownlow opened my eyes to an art form I hadn't known existed, and this is a precious gift indeed.

Robert Cushman, curator of photographs at the Academy of Motion Picture Arts and Sciences, was one of the first film scholars to realize the significance of Pickford's contribution to film. Since 1989 he has patiently shared with me his near-endless knowledge of Pickford's life, guided me through the Academy's vast Mary Pickford collection, and held me to accuracy's highest standards. His alertness and advice and even our occasional disagreements have been key to this biography's realization.

In the course of my studies, I relied on the expertise of many librarians and archivists. I owe a great debt to the staffs of the Margaret Herrick Library of the Academy of Motion Picture Arts and Sciences, Los Angeles (Sam Gill, Patrick Stockstill); the Archives of the City of Toronto; the Archives of Ontario, Toronto; the Special Collections library at Boston University (Karen Mix); the Brooklyn Historical Society; the CBC Radio Archives, Toronto (Gail Donald); the First Church of Christ, Scientist, Boston (Robert Warneck); the Motion Picture Study Room (Paolo Usai, Francisco Gonzalez, and Edward Stratman) and the Richard and Ronay Menschel Library (Barbara Schaefer) of George Eastman House,

Rochester, New York; the Kansas City Library, Nebraska (Patricia Christie); the Motion Picture Reading Room, Library of Congress, Washington (Kathy Loughney, Madeline Matz); the Marine Museum of the Great Lakes, Kingston, Ontario; the Mary Pickford Company, Los Angeles (Elaina B. Archer and Keith Lawrence); the Metropolitan Toronto Reference Library; the film department of the Museum of Modern Art, New York (Nancy Bates, Eileen Bowser, Stephen Higgins, Charles Silver); the National Archives of Canada, Ottawa (Sylvie Robitaille); the Billy Rose Theater Collection and Robinson Locke Collection at the New York Public Library for the Performing Arts (Donald Fowle); the Olathe Public Library, Kansas (Cindy McAdam); the Shubert Archive, New York (Maryann Chach); and the United Church Baptismal Archives, Toronto.

For further guidance, I am indebted to film scholars Tino Balio, Ben Brewster, and Tom Gunning. Robert Birchard, Marc Wanamaker, and the staff of the Academy of Motion Picture Arts and Sciences let me view an avalanche of Pickford photos, which contained their own special revelations. The wisdom and moral support of biographers Cari Beauchamp and Betty Lee also proved invaluable. I could not have completed my work without researchers Belinda Bruce, John and Elizabeth Guice, Jon Gundersen, and Ruth S. Lyons – all of whom did meticulous work from blurred, microfilmed sources. Ian Mutsu advised me on Pickford's popularity in Asia. Risa Shuman of TVOntario, in Toronto; and Cynthia Avila, Yvonne Craig, Roberta Hanlen, Maria Rudolph, and especially Bart Williams, in Los Angeles, provided leads to many Pickford and silent-film sources. In New York City, I received invaluable support from actress Patricia Hicock and actor/director Philip Galbraith, as well as research advice from Dusty Mortimer-Maddox. And special mention must be made of the indefatigable Christel Schmidt, who not only aided my research but, through her love for Pickford – and familiarity with the Pickford cache at George Eastman House – provided both knowledge and a lift to the heart.

My research in Los Angeles would have been impossible without the ideas, advice, and pure commitment of Susan Oldfield, who not only shares my love of silent film but gives new meaning to the terms generosity and friendship. More support for my efforts was offered by the guests at

Toronto Life magazine's Photograph Fundraising Party. This astonishing event taught me much about kindness. Indeed, while writing this book, I received the love and encouragement of my family, as well as friends both new and old. For fear of leaving someone out, I will not list them name by name. I only hope that, because they are so close to me, they know who they are, and how deeply I thank them. This book is, in many ways, their creation.

PROLOGUE

No one knows when she began to think it, but she said it in 1931: Mary Pickford, one of the greatest performers on celluloid as well as a pioneer of silent film, planned to burn her life's work. The more than 190 titles, spanning the beginnings of dramatic silent movies from 1909 to the dawn of talking pictures, revealed the same compelling figure – a small woman, only five feet tall, with an almost magnetic effect on the camera. The figure appeared in many guises: as a newlywed, a flirt, a convent girl, a young mother. She was a temptress, a scheming murderess; she sized men up with her hands on her hips, swooned in their arms, or delivered a sturdy kick to their backsides. Often her face and melancholy eyes were framed by byzantine patterns of ringlets or hair pulled back from a tranquil forehead. But such outward frailty belied an inner toughness; this madonna could handle a snake, a whip, or a rifle and hurtle a chair at a would-be rapist. She might materialize as a Cockney, a Spaniard, a citizen of Japan, an Inuit, a native of India, or a native American. Her startling performances as children stole the limelight from her other roles, but all of Mary Pickford's work reveals an uncanny insight into behavior, expressed with

1

subtlety and nuance. Indeed, she changed the nature of acting, deserting the grand, artificial style of turn-of-the-century theater for a simple, direct connection to the camera. Her decision to burn this precious work shocked her friends, who insisted the movies were not hers to demolish.

"Why not?" asked Pickford, a forthright woman who produced as well as acted in many of her films. "I made them."

In her heart she knew the reasons. Mary Pickford's importance encompassed more than the sheer scale of her talent. She was the first great film celebrity, a popular icon known as "Little Mary" and "America's Sweetheart." Viewers loved her with an abandon difficult to grasp in our fickle era. Dizzy journalists called her presence "a flash of sunlight across a dark room, a white moth glimmering in the dusk," and praised "her tender human sympathy, her utter sweetness." In 1918 critic Julian Johnson invoked "the spirit of spring imprisoned in a woman's body" and compared her to "the first child in the world." In 1915 poet and philosopher Vachel Lindsay, after viewing Pickford in Cecil B. DeMille's *A Romance of the Redwoods*, directed his readers to the Art Institute of Chicago, where he claimed Mary's reflection could be found among Botticelli's muses. Scholar Edward Wagenknecht, whose open letter to the actress appeared in the *Chicago Tribune* in 1955, wrote with the benefit of hindsight: "We who loved you were . . . much simpler people than the sophisticates who go to the movies nowadays, and you meant more to us than anybody can mean to them. We accepted you without question or analysis; we adored you in the honest simplicity of our hearts."

Her fans *were* simple – swept up by the public romance with film, which was then in its early, most heady stages. Mary's first film director, D.W. Griffith, had transformed the motion picture camera from a creatively exhausted toy to the springboard of an art with unlimited potential. When Pickford joined him in 1909, the confluence of their talents alone created films that entranced the public. When Pickford married actor Douglas Fairbanks in 1920, she was probably the best-known woman in the world, perhaps the most famous who had ever lived. At first she asked for unprecedented fees and the right to approve all aspects of production; later she decided to produce films herself. Applying a financial acumen that stunned male colleagues, the actress reconciled art

2

and business in polished films that drew huge crowds. Today her films record the image not only of Hollywood's first female mogul but of a woman aggressive before her time, and of popular filmgoing taste for two decades.

But the public's whims were Mary's downfall. She guessed correctly that silent films, pushed off the screen by talking movies, would soon become a curiosity. Indeed, for many who view them today, such movies – often cracked and corroded with age – seem to be artifacts from an impenetrable, distant world. The absence of dialogue in the silents demanded that filmmakers shape their work with an appropriate sensibility, one to which viewers no longer relate. Performing in silents was a specialized art. Actors who were trained in the theater coped with the intimate lens of the camera by reducing the grand gestures of the stage, adding naturalism and, paradoxically, mime for clarity. Pickford suffered a most human fear: that modern viewers would find her work ridiculous.

"I can't imagine any worse Hades," Pickford remarked in the 1930s, "than to have to go and look at ten-year-old films of myself." The films became twenty, thirty, and forty years older, and time only stiffened her resolve. Pickford told her third husband, actor and musician Buddy Rogers, "When I go, my films go," and she specified her plans in a codicil to her will. Then she faded from public life – and almost entirely from view, rarely leaving the rooms of Pickfair, her elegantly rambling Hollywood home. Once the Buckingham Palace of the film world, Pickfair was the chosen playground of figures as diverse as the Earl of Mountbatten, Albert Einstein, and Charlie Chaplin. Known as America's second White House, the estate high atop the Los Angeles hills had embodied not only the silent-movie culture but the hope and ebullience of America during the 1920s.

But as time went on, Pickfair became a fortress. By 1966 its chatelaine was a recluse; she took to bed, stating that she had worked all her life and wished to spend the rest of it reclining. For a while Rogers insisted that he or the chauffeur take his wife for an occasional drive through the outside world (meaning Hollywood, Los Angeles, or Beverly Hills). But these tours left her shaken, and the actress was soon ushered back to Pickfair. There her bedroom door was closed to almost all. Access was granted to a tiny circle, including her stepson, Douglas Fairbanks Jr., and silent-film actress Lillian Gish, Pickford's intimate friend since they were children.

Gish and others argued hard against Mary's bonfire, but for years the cause seemed hopeless. Mary Pickford had lost the belief that her silent-film performances were art and, by doing so, had lost the last vestige of herself.

1

—

FOR CHARLOTTE'S SAKE

"A spirit stronger than myself has always whipped me to action," Mary Pickford explained to a reporter at the age of almost forty. "It was as though some outside force lashed me from one step to another." The spirit – which inspired a streak of self-assertiveness unexpected in women born in the days of the corset – could be traced, she suggested, to her "fiery ancestors." And her memoirs reveal that the fire in Pickford's clan often came from women.

Her maternal grandmother, the sharp-tongued Catherine Faeley, was born about 1851 in Tralee, a small, pretty town in County Kerry, Ireland. Catherine's father was a miller; her religion was whip-cracking, firebrand Catholicism. When Catherine was young, she would supposedly stride into local brothels and confront the whores, demanding, "Does your mother know about this thing?" If the harlots told her they were too ashamed, Catherine thundered back that they *should* be ashamed. Then she softened: "God is on the side of every penitent sinner." If the whores were Catholic, Catherine pressured them to have their children baptized and often drove her quarry to church to see a priest. Sometimes the prostitutes burst into tears. Pickford wryly called this "Grandma's contribution to God" and described Grandma Hennessey as "the warrior in the family." In 1917

Pickford drew closely on her Hennessey grandmother for *The Pride of the Clan*, a silent film in which her character, whip in hand, decides to fill the pews of an empty church. Cowed, an entire village scuttles before her, as well as a few startled geese and pigs.

During one of Ireland's frequent famines, the Faeleys obtained free passage to Canada for the warrior Catherine. (They probably acquired it through the British government, which made such offers to needy Irish.) For her daughter's debut in the Canadian wilds, Catherine's mother stopped a peddler and bought two lengths of cotton. From these she produced two handsewn dresses. Catherine, who was accustomed to hand-me-downs, danced ecstatically in her finery, finding a wall outside the house where she pranced in partnership with her shadow. A child next door watched this exhibition, then asked what on earth Catherine Faeley was doing. "Oh faith," she laughed. "Sure, and I'm not going to stop now till I make a show of meself with clothes." This statement quickly entered Pickford family lore. Mary later described it as a "cherished heirloom," and in 1915 she reprised Catherine's shadow dance in *Fanchon the Cricket*, another silent film.

Catherine met John Pickford Hennessey in Quebec. He was also an immigrant from Tralee, but they never would have met had they stayed in Ireland. Hennessey was of the middle class, which kept themselves strictly apart from the farmers, including small capitalists like the Faeleys. When Mary's great-grandmother Hennessey heard of her son's alliance with Catherine, she denounced the marriage and swore not to speak to John as long as she lived. And according to Pickford, she kept her promise.

"I don't know where I got this ham blood in me," Mary later said idly to a reporter. Then she caught herself and burst out, "Yes, I do!" John Hennessey, who worked in Toronto in the postal service, loved the theater so much he was usually the first in line to enter. But Catherine, a side-splitting mimic in private, outwardly disapproved of stage shenanigans. Her husband convinced her to join him at the theater on one occasion. Catherine took her seat but was obviously on the edge of it. When a fire engine passed with its clattering horses and alarms, she ran hysterically up the aisle and hurried on to the Hennessey household, which she felt sure had gone up in flames. Naturally, everything was in order, except perhaps Grandfather Hennessey's evening. "Never again," declared Grandma

Hennessey, "will I pay good money to make a fool of myself watching other people making fools of themselves." She never attended a stage performance by Mary Pickford, or by Lottie or Jack, Mary's thespian siblings.

Mary's paternal grandmother, Sarah Key Smith, was short, barrel-shaped, and humorless. Mary remembered her in mourning (Sarah's husband died in 1890), wearing black silk over stiff violet petticoats, hands sheathed in black gloves, clutching a black beaded bag. Matching this daunting ensemble was a black bonnet trimmed with tiny violets. The hat only made Grandma Smith more awesome. Later Mary recalled that the rustle of that majestic silk was enough to send her skittering through the house in fear.

A British-born Methodist who attended the same Toronto church until her late eighties, Sarah Smith practiced a chilling austerity. But though her religion condemned the theater, Grandma Smith made an exception when nine-year-old Mary appeared in *Uncle Tom's Cabin* in Toronto. Who knows; she may have liked it (the play, after all, is overtly Christian). In 1913 she tried again, attending a film called *In the Bishop's Carriage*. It starred Mary Pickford, now a celebrated actress. The title led Grandma Smith to believe that the movie dealt with Christian subjects. Instead, she saw Pickford escape from a poorhouse, fall in with a thief, and use a bishop's carriage to escape police. At one point Mary wore a brief ballet costume. The sight of her granddaughter's bare legs and arms sent Sarah Smith, like Grandma Hennessey before her, hurtling up the aisle.

Joseph Smith, whom Sarah married, was born in Liverpool, then brought to Canada as an infant. According to legend, his family entered the Dominion in triumph, negotiating the St. Lawrence River in the comfort of their own ship. But soon this apparent wealth was squandered; meeting the needs of twelve children drained the money, and Mary believed they made bad investments. Many Smiths decided to remain near Kingston, in eastern Ontario; others straggled on to Toronto. No one knows how Pickford's grandmother and the impoverished Joseph met, or when or where they married. But it was probably in Toronto, about 1890, that their twenty-two-year-old son John Charles met, fell in love with, and married Catherine Hennessey's daughter Charlotte.

She was sometimes known as Elsie Charlotte: twentyish, slender, with large, tender eyes, a firm chin, and masses of blue-black hair – practical, witty, and high-spirited, as well as accomplished in the womanly arts (she could pull forty yards of lace into a ruffle). When she met John Charles, she was living cheek by jowl with her older sister, Lizzie, Lizzie's husband, William Watson (a banjo teacher), and Grandma Hennessey, a widow since 1882. Charlotte paid her own way; in 1889 she had worked as an upholstery machinist, and two years later she declared herself an expert in piano covers.

It must have seemed a charming match. John Charles Smith was slight, with golden-brown hair that sprang up in ripples and a drooping mustache. Charlotte kept her feet on the ground to balance her husband's flights of fancy – and indeed, he was dreamy and impractical. Simply put, John Charles couldn't hold a job. Before his marriage, he made a trip to Alberta and returned with a drawl and a cowboy hat, spinning dreams of pulling up stakes and ranching. He also ran a candy counter, tended bar, and worked as a printer. Mindful of the erratic family cash flow, he even put aside his Methodist principles one night and helped some stagehands strike a set. In the next few years the Smiths, who now had Grandma Hennessey with them, followed the Watsons around the city, moving almost every year and living down the block, around the corner, or across the street. There is no clear reason for such gypsy behavior, unless, being short on rent, both families were attempting to elude the bill collectors. Or they simply may have been always in search of cheaper rooms, or larger rooms – the Smiths, at least, needed a cradle handy.

The birthdate of Gladys Louise Smith was properly registered as April 8, 1892. She was nearly named Sarah, for Grandma Smith, but "Gladys" was suggested by Lizzie Watson, who was then in the thrall of a popular novel and thought the name of its heroine romantic. The name Mary Pickford was attached to Gladys when she later went to work on the Broadway stage.

A second daughter, Lottie, was born in June 1893, if one accepts Mary's claim that Lottie was her junior by fourteen months; John (known as Jack) was probably born in 1895. But these births were never registered, and Pickford played fast and loose with dates. For instance, she insisted – and made everyone believe – she was born in 1893, a fib she began as a child actress. Youth is important to theatrical children; the younger the child, the more precocious and the easier to dote upon. Shaving off a year stressed

Mary's prodigy status. Lottie, too, as an adult, often changed her age for journalists. In the process the actress got younger and younger, until she had a birth year of 1896. This, incidentally, is the year of Jack's birth in the records of Toronto's Grace Street School, which he briefly attended in 1906. He was born, he told the registrar, on August 18 – but the boy, like his sisters, may have lied.

The greater lie governing this family's life was John Charles's unacknowledged drinking problem. Alcoholism may run like poisoned groundwater through the generations; in addition, it may often be denied by the people it affects. John Charles Smith's alcoholism is a matter of rumor, not fact, but the alcoholism that later infested, then ravaged all his children forms a deeply suggestive pattern. The children of alcoholics live in a quagmire of emotions, combining love and fear of the ailing parent with an aching need for his approval. They may overempathize toward those they perceive as the drunkard's victims. And their wish to replace the drunken parent by bearing his responsibilities turns them into mini-adults and perfectionists. Sadly, their anxiety and stress is capped by a horror of causing pain to other people. As Mary grew, she displayed these empathetic traits with textbook precision.

When she was a child, her emotions were especially fervent. Mary loved her Aunt Lizzie with abandon. In her memoirs she introduces her just as a child would: Lizzie Watson is simply *there*, unexplained, a satellite in Mary's world. She also turns up in intimate contexts: putting Mary to bed and getting her up the next morning, reading the newspaper over breakfast, scolding and advising Charlotte, holding Mary, petting her. Mary remembered Aunt Lizzie slipping her arm around her one evening as the child sat on the curb and pondered. Mary had already taken her place in family legend by confronting her Methodist Sunday-school teacher and demanding why God allowed Hell to exist. "Why doesn't He kill the devil," she reasoned, "so I wouldn't be a bad little girl any more and have to go to the hot place?"

She was haunted, in her early years, by thoughts of death. Mary even grew frightened of the prayer "Now I lay me down to sleep," which hinted at dying in the dead of night. And somehow the details of Dante's "Inferno" had slipped into her nightmares. In response, she developed an obsession with knowing where she came from; not biologically, but "back there" – a place that was easier, whole and right. All would be revealed, the child decided, if she thought about it hard enough. To help herself concentrate, she hid behind the drapes or crawled beneath the kitchen table, pulling down the tablecloth like a curtain. "I want to go back," she thought, "but where do I begin?" This was not a game; Mary turned to these thoughts in the midst of depression. The tendency puzzled her years later because outwardly, her three-year-old days were happy; their very simplicity made them special.

She was born at 211 University Avenue – a flat, featureless building that has since been torn down. (Today a plaque stands nearby to mark the actress's birth.) Its location was among the most enchanting in the city, for the thoroughfare was elegantly planned on the model of the stately, sheltered lanes that led to Oxford and Cambridge. Homes were allowed on the east side only, giving families like the Smiths a view of rows of flowering chestnuts, specially brought from the United States and the first such trees to appear in Toronto. They shaded the sidewalks and grassy boulevards, scattering petals, nuts, and leaves. Maple trees were also in view, turning a deep, brilliant red in the autumn. In spring there were intoxicating lilacs.

Strollers followed University to the expanses of Queen's Park, the site of the provincial parliament building. Here they mingled at leisure on the lawns. Little Mary was among them, clinging like a monkey to the iron fence that surrounded parliament, watching the regiments parade. To the end of her life, she loved kilts and bagpipes. A Canadian-Scots regiment reduced her to tears, as could almost any company of soldiers. She also remembered, with startling clarity, drinking water from a public fountain: the feel of the chain, the cup, the water.

There were other, more ladylike amusements for Mary and her siblings, such as taking the air on the belt-line trolley. The trolley, the pride of the Toronto street railway, offered a showcase of the city, passing the horticultural gardens, the stores, and especially the mansions. On summer Sundays the car filled with mothers, babies, and the Smith children, enjoying the breezes – while Grandma Smith, who opposed the operation of transit on the Sabbath, sat on a citizens' committee to stop them. Or Mary took the ferry to Hanlan's Point, on an island a mile across Lake Ontario. It boasted, as well as endless parkland, a merry-go-round that Mary rode, almost falling off her horse in an effort to grasp the gold ring of the harness. Other days she would visit High Park, four hundred acres of grassland where she once braved the perilous toboggan runs. She sped down the slopes on a garbage can lid until she collided with a group of boys and shot from her improvised sled into a snow pile. Mary preferred the park in summer, when she could wade daintily through bluebells.

John Smith found a job in the late 1890s with the Niagara Steamship company, working as a purser on the holiday steamers that sailed between Toronto and Lewiston, New York. It must have been pleasant, open-air work; the paddle steamer traveled at a fast clip, marking departures and arrivals with the toot of a whistle or jingling bells. Travelers visited Smith's snack bar, walked the covered deck, or basked in the breeze at the open rail. One day, according to his daughter, Smith made his way below deck and struck his head – hard – on a dangling pulley. The blow caused a blood clot on the brain. Six months later, on February 11, 1898, John Charles died of a cerebral hemorrhage.

Here happy memories end abruptly.

"I can close my eyes now and hear that scream of Mother's at the moment my father passed on," wrote Pickford. Here is her story – her own cherished heirloom.

She arrived at the bedroom and gazed about, watching events unfold as if she were in the middle of a dream. To Mary, her father appeared to be sleeping. Yet beside his remote, still form, her gentle mother was a horrifying vision. She was beating her head against the wall, cutting herself, shrieking. Her blue-black hair streamed past her waist and down her dressing gown, only partly concealing her bloody face. Charlotte stared through these frightening tresses without recognizing Mary in the doorway. In a heartbeat the image, with its violence and disorder, penetrated Mary's being. Lizzie hurried upstairs, grasped the situation, gathered up her niece, and took her to her own room. There, while other Watsons tended Charlotte, Lizzie rocked the stunned child to sleep. The next morning Lizzie carried Mary, still befuddled, to the dining room for breakfast. As they passed the master bedroom, Lizzie turned the child's head away – a kind gesture, but one that had the wrong effect. Images of the previous night returned in a dark flood, and this time Mary understood their meaning. Rather than eating, the child spent breakfast jammed between the serving table and the wall, wailing full-throttle for her father.

It's a heartrending story, and it's almost true. John Charles Smith did not die at Mary's house — or if he did, the house was not his home. Three years before, he had deserted the family.

City directories show the separation. In 1895 John Charles left Charlotte for a home on Avenue Road (his job, at this point, was tending bar). Charlotte's shock must have been severe, for the desertion left her at sea: no steady income, two daughters (still toddlers), and Jack either on the way or still a small baby. Last but not least, she had her mother in tow — and Grandma Hennessey was growing increasingly frail and would soon be partly paralyzed.

Charlotte did what any woman would have done — at least in those days — and declared herself a widow. Like many of the genteel poor, she was fervently concerned with appearances. Lacking material goods or bloodlines, they had only decent reputations and manners to indicate "propriety" — the civilized behavior that signaled one's status above the slums. John Charles's abandonment would have caused her not only anguish but humiliation. But widowhood imbued her with purity, courage, and importance; it even gave John Charles these attributes. Still, five-year-old Mary sensed the truth. Women of the period, she remembered later, "lived with husbands they loathed. The children knew the father and mother hated each other." And when a husband came home drunk, the long-suffering wife would "draw her mouth a little tighter" and endure. But equally strong in her memory were impressions of her father's charm, the poignancy of early death, and Charlotte's grief. Gradually Mary let this view prevail and cast John Charles as the family saint, his flaws lost in blameless, sacred mist.

Indeed, the moment of her father's death was the core around which Mary's life evolved. And Charlotte's scream had inspired not only shock but a stab of recognition. The events confirmed her intuitions: that the world was a vulnerable, uncertain place, one in which families, and people, could be wounded.

Now, seared by the image of her mother's grief, Mary became hypersensitive to the fragility of happiness. When others suffered, Mary, as well as feeling sympathy, empathized, feeling other people's pain, or the way she imagined them to feel it. This tendency must have been useful for an actress, but it also caused Mary pain in her personal life. She centered her concern on her family. A mother's sob, a sister's glare stayed etched in her mind as an agonizing tableau of a hurt she had witnessed or believed she had caused. In her effort to protect her loved ones, Mary Pickford held herself to ideals of behavior she seldom applied to other people. And she suffered a magnified sense of guilt, which led her to confess, years later, that she couldn't remember having liked herself. Many memories of her childhood are really confessions of actions that, in her mind, seemed reprehensible.

She stole – only once, on a mischievous impulse. She was six, buying birdseed in a pet store, when she found herself distracted, then entranced by a goldfish. Mary grabbed the "flashing bit of sunlight," scampered home, and breathlessly flung her pet into the toilet bowl. Rather than darting and flicking, it floated. Suddenly Mary realized what she'd done: not only swiped, but killed. And her mother, who took particular pride in the fact that her children would never steal, could devastate her eldest with a single look. Rather than face those reproachful eyes, Mary waited twenty years before confessing all to Charlotte.

In the decorating style of the era, Charlotte propped a sketch of John Charles on an easel in the parlor, draping the picture with tasseled yellow silk. And every morning she curled Mary's yellow hair by applying water and turning the tresses around her fingers. She must have praised their beauty, too, for now Mary tried this technique on the tassels, hoping to surround her father's image with ringlets. After an afternoon of work, the tassels drooped in stringy little tangles. Charlotte was furious at the damage and gave the wrong daughter, Lottie, a spanking. Mary watched, thunderstruck with guilt, and could still remember in her sixties the look of outraged pain on Lottie's face.

Worse, she believed she had offended her mother by showing John Charles too much affection. Mary had idolized him, and it showed. Probably because of his frequent unemployment, John Charles spent more time with the children than Charlotte, who, like most women of her day, was consumed with the backbreaking tasks of Victorian housework. Later Pickford lamented that John Charles's job as a stagehand had given "those graceful hands of his" blisters — almost as if she herself bore the scars.

She longed to be his favorite, but Lottie was. It all began, thought Mary, when Charlotte, exhausted after childbirth, listlessly complained that the child was female. "She's a beautiful baby!" cried John Charles, as he gazed at the one-day-old, ten-pound bundle. Soon he gave Lottie a boyish nickname; she became, teasingly, "my Chuckie baby." Chuckie looked eagerly up the street for her father's return every evening, running toward the streetcar when she saw him alight and arriving at full gallop in his arms. Mary, who longed for John Charles's approval, tried to compete by playing hard to get, edging up to her father primly or holding back till he approached her. Later she harshly reproached herself for hurting John Charles and being jealous. After all, she reasoned, she was often in the spotlight because of illness.

Throughout her childhood, Pickford suffered diphtheria, tuberculosis, and pneumonia — any one of which might have killed her — as well as nervous conditions, colds, and night sweats. All were excellent reasons for avoiding school. Not only were childhood diseases rampant, but there were few effective treatments. (Charlotte tried folk cures, such as rubbing an ointment of goose grease, onions, and meal into Mary's skin. This, she believed, drew poisons from the body.) Schools were reluctant to readmit sick students and set up elaborate tests for them. After diphtheria, for instance, a child was allowed to attend school only after he produced two negative throat cultures, obtained and tested a day apart, and approved by the ministry of health. Often all the Smiths were quarantined with Mary, bringing on another sickness: cabin fever.

The sick child in the darkened room, surrounded anxiously by family, possessed an almost romantic appeal for the Victorians. But though she may have enjoyed the attention, Mary became a bit disgusted by her own retirement to the bedroom; "spoiled and pampered," she remarked in her memoirs. One day the drama reached its height when a Catholic priest, who had heard that Mary had diphtheria, paid a visit. "You cannot come in," Charlotte told him at the door. "We're quarantined." Then, hearing that the child had not been baptized (Charlotte and John Charles had feared offending their parents if they chose the wrong religion), the priest strode past her and improvised the rite at Mary's bedside. This thrilled Grandma Hennessey, who beamed in the background.

She nearly died, wrote Mary, on four occasions. Indeed, the doctor who pulled her through – a George B. Smith – was such a constant presence in the household that the Smiths began calling him "Little G.B." In return, the doctor (who had also attended John Charles on his deathbed) fell hard for the large-eyed, wistful Mary and discussed adopting her with Charlotte. G.B. was wealthy, married, and childless. And if she moved from Smith to Smith, little Gladdie could even keep her surname. But G.B. did not gain himself a daughter; instead, his action capped events that created an indestructible bond between Mary Pickford and her mother.

"When Father died," wrote Pickford, "I realized, with a strange and frightening suddenness, that Mother was alone." This awareness may have started at her father's funeral, when adults held Mary up to kiss the corpse goodbye. In that moment she tried to memorize her father's features: "Father had been such a handsome man and Mother adored him." She was determined to keep his image in her memory, not for her own sake but for her mother's. For Charlotte.

Mary was pierced by Charlotte's plight: no husband, no savings, three children, and an invalid mother to support. And at first, her father's death rendered Charlotte helpless. "After a very sad time, we were all dispersed," Pickford recalled years later. "My brother was in one house, my sister in another, and I in another. I don't know where my poor old grandma was. Because Mother – well . . ." Here she groped for words. "She was so terribly upset about my father's death she wanted nothing to do with anyone she'd ever known." Charlotte emerged from her state of shock when Jack fell ill: "She realized then she had no time for sorrow," remembered Mary in a reverent voice. "And so we were reunited."

One of Charlotte's first acts was to baptize the children – all Protestant, in honor of her Methodist husband (apparently, Mary, the sole child to be baptized a Catholic, was a doubly committed Christian). Then Charlotte turned to her old talent, sewing, and made ends meet by making homemade dresses for three dollars apiece. One night Pickford laid her doll aside and came to the sewing table. "Mama, have you next month's rent, and money for the coal?" "No, darling," Charlotte answered, "but don't worry, we'll get [it] somehow."

Mary, dreadfully upset, ran off and wrapped herself in the red chenille drapes in the hallway. There Lizzie, who seemed to be everywhere, found her. After listening to Mary weep, Lizzie confronted Charlotte. Pickford's version of the scene seems drawn from bad domestic drama:

> LIZZIE: (*in kitchen*) Lottie, you've just got to stop letting that child hear those things!
> CHARLOTTE: (*bent over the sewing machine*) What things?
> LIZZIE: That you don't have money for food or rent....
> CHARLOTTE: Oh, Lizzie, I didn't mean to say it; I was so busy and distracted. How dreadful!
> LIZZIE: She's getting thinner and paler every day, and worrying about money isn't going to help her get any better.
> MARY: (*peering out from behind some drapes*) Mother was never caught off her guard again!

Lizzie had a point: Charlotte's answer was careless. But it suggests a need for someone, even a young child, to encourage her. In Mary, Charlotte found a susceptible listener in whose mind she made a symbiotic imprint. After her father's death, Mary fused her emotions and values with her mother's. At the same time she idolized her; once she joked lightly that she almost broke the First Commandment for her. No other mother did so much or loved as much, in Mary's view. She stitched and restitched clothes, for instance, updating dresses for Mary and Lottie with handmade lace or dignifying old hats with ribbon. Turning dresses inside out or attaching one bodice to another skirt was the custom of poor folk, but never mind: Mary was dazzled by Charlotte's ingenuity. If she woke in the night, she often heard the hum of the sewing machine – a comfort, as well as a reminder of her mother's commitment and sacrifice. By day, she would sit at her mother's feet, nestled inside the sewing machine cover, pretending to sail a boat across the ocean. An older and more anxious Mary stood beside the sewing machine to steady the lamp as Charlotte's aching feet pumped the treadle.

The Smith tradition of women warriors was confirmed when Charlotte, in fine form, confronted Miss Adams, principal of the Louisa Street School and a nightmarish figure of Mary's childhood. Mary and Lottie spent slapdash mornings bathing themselves and dressing alone, then trotting off to school unsupervised (usually Charlotte had gone to work).

When the Smiths came to class late one winter morning, they received a tough lecture from Miss Adams. The next day they rushed up the street in hysteria, stumbling in after the bell rang. "The next time you are late," said Miss Adams severely, "the devil will send a big black wagon for both of you, and you will never see your mother again."

The girls gaped, struck by this agonizing vision, then ran pell-mell out the door, leaving their hats, coats, and leggings in the schoolroom. Shocked, teeth chattering, they slithered downhill on the snow toward home. Charlotte, by chance, had returned to the house when the girls fell through the doorway. They gasped out the story, throats rough and aching. Charlotte calmed them, took them back to school, and asked Miss Adams to repeat her speech. The principal did it proudly, adding that the girls deserved a thrashing.

Charlotte's eyes could take on a glinty stare when she wished, and they glinted now. Miss Adams would not lay a hand on her children. She, Charlotte Hennessey Smith, would not allow it. In fact, she was going to the board of education to lodge a complaint that very moment. Charlotte was better than her word; she withdrew her daughters from school, bought textbooks, and taught them, when she found time, at home. Unfortunately, the devil story gave Mary nightmares, causing her to sleep so badly that doctors ordered her back to the sickroom. Charlotte nursed her there, as she did Lottie when her second child fell ill with typhoid fever. To Mary, her mother was an angel of mercy, one who not only favored her but poured her heart out to the girl as though her eldest were an adult.

Mary became her mother's partner, alter ego, adviser, and crutch. She felt no need to play with other children. She isolated herself with Charlotte. Mary's immersion was so complete that she became a little mother, seeing Lottie and Jack not as her sister and brother, not even as other children, but as *her* children, hers and Charlotte's, to be washed and scolded. Lottie and Jack soon let Pickford know what they thought of this arrangement; they called her "the Policeman," "the Czarina," and "the Big Stick." Surprisingly, "Miss Perfect" didn't make the list, as Pickford hated to see them get dirty and hounded them constantly on the subject. Inevitably, Jack and Lottie stopped thinking of Mary as a child and began to see her as an authority figure. Sometimes Charlotte did the same. She liked to tumble and tussle with Jack and Lottie on the floor, but if Mary saw them, Charlotte stood up and straightened out, looking guilty. Probably Charlotte feared a lecture. But Mary insisted that Charlotte did this because she knew Mary worried for her safety; indeed, she was morbidly frightened of losing her mother, sometimes sobbing herself to sleep at the idea of Charlotte's unexpected death. Even her happiest moments were marred when the certainty of Charlotte's loss passed through her like a shock wave. Meanwhile, Jack and Lottie formed a band against them; Lottie, in particular, was deeply hurt by Mary's claim on their mother's attention. This made an even stranger knot of the family's already skewed configuration.

Sometimes, as she worried, fussed, and bossed, Mary sensed she was missing something vital: the world of play with other children, the carefree moments any child enjoys. She knew these things while her father was alive and still felt them, fleetingly, when on her bike. In the years of her childhood, the bicycle craze had an air of revolution; ladies abandoned their corsets to ride them, sometimes wore divided skirts, and met their lovers unchaperoned. Soon Toronto was crowded with bicycle shops. Mary could rent a bike for ten cents and ride without a care in the world, pedaling steadily with her short legs and her yellow hair flying out behind her. When Charlotte announced she would buy her a bicycle on her eighth birthday, Mary tried to refuse it. (Charlotte bought it anyway.) Though Mary loved riding her bike alone, she felt more pleasure when her mother rode beside her – more, Mary claimed, than she later derived from her first Rolls-Royce.

Mary's unity with Charlotte became complete through the efforts of George B. Smith to adopt her. When she first heard G.B.'s offer, Charlotte quickly declined, a response that brought out the nag in Lizzie, who had had a similar chance with a wealthy couple and felt Charlotte had no right to stand in Mary's way. Somewhat browbeaten, Charlotte agreed, dressed her eldest in her best frock, and boarded the streetcar for G.B.'s residence. The house, which boasted a stained-glass window in the hallway, proved to be wealthy and tasteful, with a charming white chintz bedroom set aside for Mary. But the child found other matters more important: Would she have ice cream? Would she have a pony and cart? Would she have chicken every day? Charlotte listened, unnaturally quiet, as G.B. and his wife assured her daughter that all such luxuries would be provided.

Waiting for the homebound streetcar, Mary bubbled over with pleasure, grandly planning to share the pony and cart with Jack and Lottie, and to push plates of delicious chicken across the table to Grandma Hennessey and Charlotte. Charlotte immediately corrected her. Here Pickford's memory was diamond-sharp; she always recalled the moment when Charlotte kneeled down in the grass, gazed in her eyes, and told her, in the shadow of the chestnuts, that if she chose to live with the Smiths, she would not be Charlotte's child any longer. Mary "felt a terror clutching at my heart. 'Mama,' I said, 'don't you want me any more?'" Charlotte began to cry, a blow from which Mary never fully recovered. "I'll always want you, darling, but I can't give you the pony and cart, and I can't give you chicken and ice cream every day." Mary was appalled. "I don't want to be Dr. Smith's little girl and I don't like ponies and I want to go home with you, Mama!" Now Mary cried, too, and they shared Charlotte's handkerchief. Pathos – yet the scene rings true. Indeed, it revealed pure grit in Mary: "A determination was born in me the day of our visit to Dr. Smith that nothing could crush: I must try to take my father's place in some mysterious way, and prevent anything from breaking up my family."

She felt she must somehow seal the family up, making it into an impregnable cell against the forces that might destroy it. The family was a citadel, a stronghold of values – work, blind loyalty, and devotion – that would make its members invulnerable. In fact, early members of Hollywood society called the Smith clan the Four Musketeers ("all for one and one for all"), with some amusement. There was nothing funny about it to Mary, who shouldered the family cause with focus and ruthless efficiency, despite ingratitude on several sides. With spectacular success she unleashed her ambition and dragged the Smith family in its wake. Mary Pickford was not the family martyr. Instead, she was tenacious, single-minded, determined, uncomplaining, uncompromising – a fanatic.

2

—

EVANGELINE

Shortly after John Charles's death, Charlotte readied the master bedroom for rental. A series of single women lived there till 1899, at which point Charlotte, with trepidation, allowed a married couple named Murphy to rent it. She made the decision after a council on propriety attended by Grandma Hennessey and Lizzie; a widow who rented to a man – even a married man – courted scandal. And Murphy's profession was déclassé. He worked as a stage manager in the theater.

The tale, as told by Mary, seems a bit too grand. At this time Charlotte was living next door to the Watsons in a house on Orde Street. Probably the Smiths, the Watsons, and the theater people were all boarders, none of them in a position to be too choosy about their neighbors. But Charlotte's alarm at rubbing elbows with "theatricals" was typical. Most decent citizens thought show folk were lowlifes. Early in the Victorian era, theaters – with the exception of those hosting learned entertainments such as opera – were rowdy, even combative places. The working-class audience let off steam by rioting over ticket prices, throwing food at the actors, or stopping the action to demand a different play. Even as audience behavior improved, the status of the performers did not. Victorians treasured the institutions of family and a fixed address, and many assumed that actors, whose profession made them footloose, were by nature stray cats and villains.

Actresses were, if anything, more tainted. They first appeared in the British theater in 1660, glittering like exotic birds, each hoping to ensnare a rich, blue-blooded lover. The reputations of these Nell Gwyns clung to actresses for decades. In the 1890s the middle class celebrated women as the shining light of the home, not the stage. And the church had condemned the theater for centuries. Pickford maintained that if her father had lived, he would never have let her appear onstage. Charlotte, too, thought the concept unwholesome. Yet there were talented women displaying themselves before the footlights. Toronto produced little home-grown theater, but American and European tours passed through, bringing such international celebrities as Minnie Maddern Fiske, Ellen Terry, Sarah Bernhardt, and Madame Modjeska. Several rungs down the cultural ladder were the beauty Lillie Langtry, in the teasingly titled *The Degenerates*, and an up-and-coming showgirl named Anna Held, who sported a thirty-thousand-dollar costume in *The French Maid*, a pre-Follies Ziegfeld attraction.

Acrobats, animal acts, and magic paid the rent at Toronto's vaudeville houses. One could also see "flickers," the earliest generation of silent movies, shown as an act on the vaudeville program or in makeshift curtained rooms on Yonge Street, Toronto's main thoroughfare. The films offered glimpses of anything that moved – waterfalls, bicycles, policemen, babies. But the Smiths were oblivious to such entertainments. And Charlotte was shocked when Mr. Murphy asked if the girls might join the cast of a play he was stage-managing called *The Silver King*.

"I'm sorry," Charlotte replied, indignant, "but I will never allow my innocent babies to associate with actresses who smoke.... The thought of those infants making a spectacle of themselves on a public stage!"

The Cummings Stock Company, where Murphy worked, was the tenant at Toronto's Princess Theatre. This dignified building, on King Street near modern Toronto's theater district, was the first public structure in the city with electric lights. It also housed an art gallery, banquet hall, reception rooms, drawing room, and ballroom. Two balconies circled the auditorium, which sat over fifteen hundred people. A few watched the stage from the hush of boxes, dramatically trussed and draped with curtains.

The company in residence was somewhat more ragtag. For several seasons, Cummings actors had flooded the city with melodrama, the most popular type of drama on the continent, alongside adventure (*The Prisoner of Zenda*), sentimental fantasies (*Little Lord Fauntleroy*), musicals, and an occasional assault on Shakespeare. To create a stock company such as this, an actor/manager (here, Robert Cummings) would rent a theater for a season and choose the cast, almost always Americans. Cummings not only produced and directed but starred in the hiss-the-villain roles. Actors, who were hardy and self-sufficient, created their own costumes, wigs, and makeup, ruining their backs as they patched old dresses and craning their necks as they pinned up curls. Most were happy to have the work, which was fairly secure throughout the season and, most important, stationary. Most acting jobs involved touring the country. A resident company, in which actors bought stock, offered forty weeks in one location and a sense of permanence, which they treasured.

"I respect your misgivings, Mrs. Smith," said Murphy, "but will you do me a favor before you make a final decision?... Come backstage with us tonight. I assure you that professional people are no different from any others. They are good, bad, and indifferent like the rest of the world. This happens to be a very happy and respectable group of actors and actresses who have been together for a long time."

Charlotte agreed to make the trip backstage and found the group (no doubt forewarned) on their best behavior. Some were charming, and some – more surprising still – were married. This set Charlotte thinking. Money was still desperately needed in her household. Murphy offered eight dollars a week for Mary's talents and – here accounts contradict one another – either eight or somewhat less for hiring Lottie, who would play a smaller role than her pretty sister. Charlotte weighed money against propriety, no doubt noting that the genteel Princess was only a few minutes' walk from her home. And her "innocent babies" would be tainted with stagecraft for only a week. In the end, propriety took a back seat to money, and Mary and Lottie were enlisted. And so was Charlotte, who supplied "sob music" by sitting in the wings and playing "Now the Day Is Over" on the organ.

Throughout her life Pickford claimed she began her career when she was five years old – a pretty story and, as usual when her age was concerned, a pretty cheat. On January 8, 1900, when she opened in *The Silver*

King, Pickford was nearly eight years old, and Lottie was six. Still, both were remarkably young to work, though Mary had a keen desire to begin. She had once leaned her cheek against Charlotte's knee and asked her how many years she must wait before she could contribute to the family income. Charlotte made her hold up ten chubby fingers. Even earlier, as a toddler, Mary had marched past Grandma Hennessey, armed with a hammer and a grim expression, intending to smash an errant nickel from between two keys of Charlotte's upright piano.

A memory of her father involved the first money to pass from his hand to hers. John Charles stood beside his daughter and told her to open her tiny hands. Then he slipped her seventy-five cents, his total earnings for work that evening. Pickford felt what she called the "lure of money": the coins lay in her hands like jewels. With a superb instinct, she handed the precious cash to Charlotte. The children would repeat this ritual for years. All monies earned were passed on to their mother, who kept their wages in one purse, thus underscoring their merged identities.

Acting offered a way for Mary to ease Charlotte's burdens, contribute income, and substitute for John Charles. Pickford realized from the start that the roles she performed — frequently an orphan, in fact or spirit — played on her own feelings for her missing father. "If there are any who believe that a child forgets in a day, look at me and learn that the memory of childhood unhappily is longer. I did not forget him in a day. I never forgot him, and the plays in which I appeared as a child unfortunately had the lines to remind me of my loss."

Melodrama underlined other lessons. Pickford identified with the poor, with victims; so did melodrama, in spades. Aimed at the working class, the form filled the theater with characters still known today, if only through parody. These included dead, alcoholic, or absent fathers, wolves and landlords at the door, virtuous wives, and angelic children. The plays spilled over with toddlers suffering life-threatening illnesses. Often a child was torn from his mother's arms and thrown into the poorhouse. But other children were stiff-upper-lip types who cooked, and cleaned, and spouted wisdom, all the while shivering in their threadbare clothes.

For spice, melodrama loved the wicked. Officially the form condemned them, but not before underlining their glamour. This was a major source of audience satisfaction. Usually the villain was well-bred, with a mustache, cape, and manners, and a doomed woman somewhere to adore him. Sometimes she was also evil – red shoes often gave her away – but out of respect for her sex, the role was labeled "an adventuress." But the villain met his match in the saintly mother, whose modest beauty always moved him. She also stirred murderers, pirates, gamblers, madmen, vampires, and rich cads. In 1976 James L. Smith described her perils:

> Helpless and unprotected, broken-hearted and alone, she staggers through the windy wood, prairie wild or city snow, pursued by human bloodhounds armed with daggers, tomahawks or warrants for her immediate arrest. She may be auctioned as an octoroon or buried in an avalanche, tied senseless to the railway track or stranded on a sea-girt rock with big waves lapping round her ankles.... Doting mothers fret for her, angry fathers turn her out of doors, and avaricious bailiffs eject her from the mortgaged garret she has made her home. And then there are pathetic angel children, who cry for bread when she is penniless, ask artlessly if Grandmamma has gone to heaven yet, and always want a good-night kiss from Daddy when he's doing six months' hard labour for the villain's crime.

Add to the suffering of the mother, the absent father, and the noble children the subconscious force of the stage itself, a magnified area filled with colors, over-large objects, and actors with huge and painted features, and imagine their effect on a sensitive child. Melodrama demanded that the stage effects be at least as sensational as the story. As Mary continued on the stage, she stood among rolling dioramas, trapdoors, and simulated acts of God – earthquakes, volcanic eruptions, and rainbows. These effects would seem primitive today: porcelain moons, red streamers for fire, confetti snowflakes, and cardboard waves. But they thrilled the turn-of-the-century audience and made the stage resemble a child's toyland. The theater, wrote Mary, "was my playhouse. It was my nursery. It was my school." Three of the scripts in which she appeared are considered melo-dramatic classics: *The Silver King*, *Uncle Tom's Cabin*, and *East Lynne*. They moved their intended viewers deeply – and also Mary, who found that each play nudged her developing conscience.

The Silver King, by Henry Arthur Jones, premiered in London in 1882 and proved a dramatic staple for decades. (The title refers to the hero's windfall when he invests in a silver mine.) Jones exploited all the elements of melodrama, but without ghoulish excess; the heroine's greatest humiliation is kneeling to beg before the landlord. Though its literary value is paper-thin, the play is tightly wound and abounds in fearlessly theatrical conventions – soliloquies, apostrophes, asides. The result was about four hours of pumping adrenaline.

Mary played the touching role of Ned, the hero's dying son. (Little girls often played little boys, and sometimes little boys played girls.) True to melodramatic tastes, Jones used children to twist a knife in the hearts of their parents. When Nelly, the heroine, finds her jobless, charming, and soused husband in a bar, she bursts out: "Oh, Will, I have just put our little Cissy and Ned to bed and they have said 'God bless our dear father!'" Later, penniless and abandoned, Nelly calls to Ned: "Sleep on, my darling boy! You are happier so. You do not feel you are hungry, and you do not tear your poor mother's heart by begging for the food she has not to give."

But Mary – who, as an adult, was trapped in roles depicting compassionate women – preferred her second part in the play, a character with no redeeming virtues: "a *nasty* little girl," she remembered with relish. As schoolchildren (one of them played by Lottie) spill onto the stage, Cissy, the sweet and grave daughter of the hero, approaches a group and pleads, "Let me play with you!" Mary, as "Big Girl," stamps her foot and commands: "Don't speak to her, girls; her father killed a man!" The children obediently fall into line behind Mary's little martinet and exit.

Mary's role, minuscule as it is, contains a desirable element: focus. For one moment on the stage, her bossy little snob is the center of attention. An actor's first experience on stage – especially as the center of attention – can produce a daunting body shock: the yawning black hole of the proscenium (in this case, looming sixty-five feet above Mary), the intensity of light saturating the skin, the palpable sense of an unseen crowd. It is an environment that touches the extrovert in some and reduces others to near paralysis. On opening night the atmosphere was also charged with the presence of the second contingent that Canada was sending to the Boer War; the soldiers had chosen *The Silver King* as their farewell amusement before departure for South Africa. The mood throughout the theater was electric.

Mary was excited but not afraid. She enjoyed standing before a crowd and was far from threatened when they looked at her. Acting often satisfies a need for display, one through which a solitary, private person may manipulate and mingle with others. In a play's best-acted moments, the exchange between crowd and performer is close and unguarded. To a child (and to many an adult) this intimacy translates into love – the stage as a kind of perpetual bear hug. No doubt Mary wallowed in it. She even felt creative release and indulged in a sudden improvisation. As the plot races to its close, Nelly and her husband hold an urgent conversation. Mary was directed to play inconspicuously with some toys. All very well, but she built her toy blocks into a pyramid and then sent them crashing to the floor with a toy horse. This startled the actors and produced a laugh.

Pickford was elated; the fleeting attention felt as intense as an ovation. That is, until the stage manager told her sharply what stealing a scene meant: taking the focus from those who deserved it, and usually doing it upstage, behind them, so the theft goes unnoticed by the actors. Mary deflated like a pricked balloon and carried the lesson – and her guilt – for a lifetime.

After eight performances *The Silver King* folded. Stock actors led exhausting lives, rehearsing one five-act script by day while presenting another five-act script at night. They appeared in a new play every week and were forever learning sheaves of dialogue. Mary and Lottie, who were not company members, departed when *The Silver King* closed; the rest stayed on till the company disbanded. This came earlier than expected. A dwindling box office took its toll. In the spring the actors assembled at the theater, only to discover that Cummings and presumably their paychecks had mysteriously disappeared. Probably penniless, the cheated actors straggled toward home to await casting season in New York.

In Toronto, Gladys Smith also made some plans. During rehearsal and her time onstage, she had watched Maggie Quinn, the featured girl of the company. Maggie, as the heroine's daughter, Cissy, seemed to have endless, eloquent dialogue, while Mary, as Ned, stood without a speech. Mary made a mental note that she could play Cissy as well as anyone. Soon she was standing in front of a mirror, admiring herself and imitating Maggie

Quinn. This competitive spirit, combined with her sense of freedom in the footlights, may have led to the drama of the horse and blocks. More important, Mary began to imagine a permanent place in the theater.

Somehow she got herself onstage at Shea's, a Toronto vaudeville house, in a playlet called *The Littlest Girl*. In those days, some great names slummed in vaudeville; this kept their names before the public until they found a better vehicle. (Even Sarah Bernhardt trod the vaudeville boards.) *The Littlest Girl* starred a then-famous actor named Robert Hilliard; he had his own cast, but "the littlest girl" herself – a bit part, really – was cast with a child from each town on the tour. The show, which opened in Toronto on April 9, 1900, involved a wife who left her husband for the stage, taking their beloved infant daughter. Years later, after the mother's death, a friend tries to reunite father and daughter. He refuses to accept her – until, that is, he sees "the littlest girl" in a frilly dance costume and is overwhelmed. Mary, who had turned eight the day before, was billed as "Baby Gladys Smith" (all actors were babies till they reached adolescence). Feigning sleep, she was carried onstage, and one actor placed her in another's lap. Because it embodied the scene's central conflict, the role gave Mary a moment in the spotlight and a sigh from over a thousand people. And it paid her fifteen dollars for a week of "sleep."

The Littlest Girl was at the top of the bill, and Mary slid into a seat beside Charlotte after the curtains swept shut on her playlet. Third on the bill was the young Maude Nugent, who was only eleven but already a favorite on the vaudeville circuit. (She would later be known as Elsie Janis, and she remained a stage star throughout the jazz age.) The core of her act was her knack with impressions, and in 1900 she specialized in Anna Held, the Ziegfeld girl whose voluptuous figure and milk-bathed skin embodied Paris when it sizzled. The sight of an eleven-year-old imitating this creature must have been arresting, though Maude was aided by the fact that the tantalizing Held was only five feet tall. Maude appeared in a knee-length dress, with jewels that glittered onstage like diamonds and a white staff set with shining stones. But the Smiths were more dazzled by Maude's staggering salary, seventy-five dollars a week, and they soon beat a path to her dressing room door.

"Take her to see the finest plays and artists," advised Maude's mother. "But she must never imitate anyone, other than to be a mimic. In anything else, first and above all, let her be herself." As the women chatted, Mary surveyed Maude's wardrobe — a different dress for each performance, hung round the walls of the dressing room — and added fine clothes to her list of career goals.

Next she turned up — or intended to — in *The Bohemian Girl*, which the Strakosch Grand Opera presented at the Princess on May 9. Her instructions were easy: simply stand on a bridge. But despite her exposure to melodrama, Mary found opera's spectacle overwhelming. In dress rehearsal a clash of music, light, and some pistol shots rooted her to the spot; then, out of the gloom, a red-faced man with "ferocious whiskers" came looming toward her. Her heart in her mouth, Mary ran offstage, and her sister, who had better nerves, replaced her. This was probably the only time that second-best Lottie stole the show from Mary — for though Charlotte loved the children, she was practical, too, and she knew which one was the powerhouse of talent. In the fall, when another stock troupe called the Valentine Company moved into the Princess, it was Mary who sat on Charlotte's lap, taking in their repertoire of plays and dreaming she would someday join the cast onstage.

The child showed other theatrical leanings, including small vanities. From an early age she claimed her middle name was Marie — so much more romantic, she thought, than the despised Louise. (She may even have been baptized this way.) Mary also ate roses from the local florist, hoping to digest their beauty somehow. A neighbor once reported that she found Mary pinching her cheeks with a hairpin till they glowed; she hoped to look like the Valentines' adventuress, Nettie Marshall. Mary also learned to engage a camera, showing up for photos of *The Littlest Girl* with a staff in her hand, Maude Nugent–style, and in a dress that resembled a wedding cake. In other photos Mary crosses and clasps her knees, her expression strangely grown-up and dreamlike, or lounges coquettishly on a chair. Her face is now a perfect oval, dominated by her eyes, which seem almost painfully perceptive. The curls are gentle, not yet teeming.

In November 1900 the Valentines advertised *The Silver King*, as trusty at the box office as Old Faithful. Charlotte dressed Mary in her Sunday best and took her down to the Princess Theatre to apply for the parts of Big Girl and silent Ned. But Mary had a bigger role in mind. In attending the Valentine matinées, she had developed a crush on an actor named Jack

Webster, whose appearance and manner in his many sympathetic roles touched her yearning for a father. She wanted to be near him, and she had the ambition to make it happen. When she met Anna Blancke, the Valentine manager, Mary stated flatly that she wanted to play the daughter of the heroine, Cissy.

"I don't see any reason why you shouldn't," answered Blancke.

Charlotte's first reaction was apology. She doubted that Mary could memorize a long role: because of lack of schooling, she couldn't read.

Blancke was small, with a sweet expression. Mary looked searchingly into her face, then walked up and gave Anna Blancke her hand. "Please, lady, let me try," she said simply. It helped that Mary looked picturesque. Pickford later told a version in which she turned her appeal – as well as a burst of tears – on Charlotte. Either synopsis shows her canniness. Even at this age, Mary possessed a knowledgeable little face. Her gaze was unnervingly direct, and she was assertive with those who could help her. "Where I was born and brought up," she remembered, "the principal duty of a woman [was] to properly cook a chop." So Pickford, both as a child and as a woman, tempered her candor with feminine appeal. When she became a major actress, she confounded men with the contradiction between her flowerlike appearance and her businesslike brain. Even women were disoriented. In 1914 Frances Marion, later an influential Hollywood screenwriter, asked her for a job and expressed amazement that Pickford's voice had a "deeper tone" than she had expected. She, the job applicant, could only think that Pickford was "such a little girl that I felt more like putting my arms around her than shaking hands formally."

Now Mary gazed from her mother to Anna Blancke and back again. "Well, there can't be any harm in trying," Charlotte decided. "We'll begin working on it tonight, but I know she can't remember such a long role." Mary was determined to prove her wrong. She and Charlotte set to work as they waited for the streetcar, with Charlotte reading Cissy's lines and Mary repeating them. The part is attractive; while adults agonize around her, Cissy behaves in a no-nonsense fashion, hugging, chatting, and sitting on knees. In a strange echo of Pickford's life, the poverty-stricken Cissy receives precious cash from her father's hand, which she immediately gives to her mother. And the play shows a charming, alcoholic father who means well but finally leaves the family. Nevertheless, his daughter adores him, just as she adores her heroic mother.

As Cissy, Mary looked morose but striking: a plaid scarf wound around her face showed the mournful eyes to advantage. By the close of *The Silver King* on November 24, Pickford had become the Valentines' official child actress. Late in the season, the Princess distributed "souvenirs of Gladys Smith." Souvenirs were blotters, bookmarks, or other ephemera marked with the actor's name and troupe. Mary's were, somewhat mysteriously, "buttons" – possibly these were cardboard disks. The Valentines honored each member this way, as part of their publicity; even the box office man was immortalized on a souvenir. Still, a little girl must have been overwhelmed. Her salary was thrilling: fourteen dollars a week. And she took the stage to heart, as she did everything in life.

Years later she recalled a walk through the flowers and trees of University Avenue in which she had passed an old man in rags. She pitied him, wondering how he had met misfortune and why there should be grief in the world. Next her eyes fastened on a patch of frowsy dandelions, gone to seed. It seemed to the child that this was a turning point in her life: she could sit and blow dandelion fluff, or ruminate on the old man's condition as she imagined an actress would, in order to develop her empathic powers. Mary's decision was in tune with the melancholy streak that sometimes seized her – a streak that told her that angst for a stranger's broken life is more worthy than pleasure with a flower. And so she ordered herself to contemplate the old man, a fumbling attempt at artistic growth and dedication.

On January 21, 1901, the Valentines presented a polite British comedy called *Bootle's Baby*. The plot revolves around a soldier (Jack Webster) who hides a dewy-eyed youngster named Mignon (Mary) in his barracks. Mary's role was large – too large, the *New York Dramatic Mirror* complained. ("Little Gladys Smith . . . had not been thoroughly drilled, and in consequence the play was uneven.") But the critic for the local *Globe* insisted that Mary had won all hearts. Whatever the truth, the audience for *Bootle* was probably sparse: the show ran the week of Queen Victoria's death and most likely played to dreary houses.

At the Little Red Schoolhouse, next on Pickford's dance card, opened at the Princess on April 1. Lottie got a role in Mary's shadow as her boyfriend, Johnny Watson. Like those of most melodramas, this script is lost, but Pickford remembered a shred of dialogue. (Lottie asked: "Do you like chicken?" She gave Mary her arm. "Well, take a wing.") One imagines the response – an indulgent laugh. But most of the play took a lurid turn, with convicts lurking in the shadows and a plot packed with devilish story twists. Its author, an American named Hal Reid, watched Toronto respond and was overjoyed. In a burst of magnanimity, he promised to cast the Smith clan, including Charlotte, in a new, improved *Schoolhouse* in the autumn. This production would tour the United States – a professional windfall, and the Smiths, like the playwright, were galvanized into action.

Charlotte, though it was only spring, sold the family furniture so the Smiths could depart at a moment's notice. And as Mary continued with the Valentine company, Charlotte became her acting coach. Some of her lessons were uncannily modern. Pickford remembered her mother saying, "'What were you thinking about tonight, darling? . . . I didn't believe you. When you spoke to your mother, you were speaking to an actress – you weren't speaking to your own mother. Now, if you don't even believe it yourself, you can't make me believe it.' She was never cross with me," Pickford added. "She was never what was known as the stage mother."

Charlotte's advice contradicted the grandiose acting style then prevalent. We will never truly recapture this turn-of-the-century style, but photos indicate gestures and expressions, reviews call up images, and early silent movies filmed stars in their stage roles. Called "histrionic" or "aesthetic" by historians, the style represented reality rather than closely reflecting it. Actors indicated feeling through a code of signals. In 1854 an actor's handbook written in Italy described the indication of fury: "Rise, put hat on, jam it down on the head, fling it on the ground, pick it up, tear it to pieces; walk in great, awkward strides, now straight, now obliquely. . . . Strike the fist hard on the furniture; overturn chairs; break vases. . . . Slam doors shut; sit down hard. Stamp the foot, wheel around, spring up again."

The style endured into the twentieth century, with agonized heroines sinking to their knees, arms stretched to heaven, or casting themselves hysterically to the floor. The greater the extension of the arm, the greater the emotion – thus, women fended off villains at arm's length, and heroes defied fate by shaking fists heavenward. Actors froze in such poses for emphasis. A fluttering back of the hand to the forehead meant weakness or distress. Hands clutching the head showed an unbearable agony, and one hand pressed to the heart signaled love or heartbreak. But Charlotte thought gilding the lily with gestures sat badly on a child, and she instructed Mary in methods several decades before their time, as well as some keep-it-simple maxims that paid off later in the movies. In this, she was remarkably prescient, telling Mary: "Don't think about your hands or feet or your ears or your eyebrows. If you feel something enough, every-thing will fall into place. . . . If [actors] think they can fool an audience, they're mistaken. A person has to live it out, *be* it, and forget about your hands and feet. If you're conscious of any little gesture, any little move, it's artificial."

Charlotte touched on another weakness: Mary's voice. At the turn of the century, voices that stage-whispered, rolled *r*s, and bellowed were part of an actor's essential equipment. Mary thought her voice was small and brittle, but Charlotte had a theory to make it carry: "Each word is like a rounded pearl, but they're all on the same string, and the string is your breath." And knowing the delicate conscience of her daughter, she pressed her with some moral blackmail: "There may be a poor little man or woman away up in the last balcony who has gone without their dinner in order to go to the theatre. Now those little people are more important than the people down in the loges. And I want you to pronounce each word clearly so they can hear you."

With this in mind, Mary played the pinnacle of innocence when she took a starring role in *Uncle Tom's Cabin*, based on the book by Harriet Beecher Stowe. *Tom* is certainly the strangest, and the most popular, piece of theater in U.S. history. The book appeared in the United States in 1851 and stormed the melodramatic stage the next year. The story was crammed with narrow escapes, pursuits, black infants torn from their mothers' arms, and a saintly, golden-haired child who dies. The plot offered ready-made victims (slaves), villains (those who owned them), and heroes (those who help them in the cause of freedom). The novelty of these homegrown types (at the time, most melodrama came to the States from France and England) and the outrage whipped up by Stowe caused the show to become a craze. By 1900 there were five hundred *Tom* troupes in North America, traveling the continent by railway, cart, and boat, to churches, opera houses, and barns. Some *Tom* companies brought their own tents and set them up to seat two thousand. Others outdid one another with parades. Some actors played *Uncle Tom* all their lives, beginning in child roles, then working their way through the adult characters. Such "mammoth" or "mastodonic" shows became folklore; audiences knew the plot and expected favorite bits of business and ever more bloated production values. Perhaps the play's strangest outgrowth other than board games, songs, and crockery was the "double" shows, which split the featured players into pairs. Topsy, a lively black girl, might dance while her alter ego played the banjo. The bloodthirsty slave driver Simon Legree turned up in a double-barreled whipping scene – two of every slave, two Legrees, two whips.

Canada took to the story with relish, even a strain of superiority; as many as thirty thousand blacks had crossed the border to safety through the Underground Railroad. The Cummings company first attempted the play in 1898 and 1900. The initial production had a cast of fifty, "donkeys and bloodhounds galore," and two mangy-looking dogs. But the troupe was overshadowed the following month when Al W. Martin's "mammoth" *Tom* rolled into town with a trainload of livestock and "real coloured people," "18 Real Georgia Plantation Shouters, Mlle. Minerva's New Orleans Creole Girls' Fife and Drum Corps, the 'Original Whangdoodle Pickaninny Band,'" an "8-foot colored boy," and "10 Cuban and Russian ferocious, man-eating hounds." Productions settled for any vicious-looking species, but the actors had to gather in the wings to simulate howls for the frequently silent onstage dogs.

Pluckily, the cash-poor Cummings troupe stripped its version in 1900 – for the sake of realism, Cummings said. Next the Valentines took up the challenge with a *Tom* that "sticks closely to the text of the book, and in which there is none of the cheap melodramatic effects which have marred recent presentations of the play." Nevertheless, the Valentines offered "a genuine negro pickanniny cake walk, a good quartette, and a cotton-picking scene, with a coloured jubilee." Anna Blancke played Topsy – for despite Stowe's message of liberation, whites wearing blackface played the slaves for decades.

The production opened on April 8, 1901: an exciting time for Mary, who turned nine that day. Her role was Evangeline St. Clare, nicknamed "Little Eva," a child to whom Uncle Tom becomes a slave. Surrounded by circuslike ritual, Eva epitomizes melodrama's cult of the saintly child. Devoid of bigotry and filled with love, Eva represents God's love for children and rejects a racist system. She appeared in *Tom* parades on a pony or was carried on a float representing heaven, dressed in white with a papier-mâché halo. In the play, her idea of putting Tom to work is to listen to him singing a hymn, or to let him sit while she hangs a wreath of flowers round his neck. This made a pretty scene: Mary wore a bonnet with a mass of daisies, a long, high-waisted dress of pale cotton, and Mary Janes. She had barely recovered from pneumonia, a predicament that encouraged her father-fantasies for Jack Webster. ("I'm so glad to see my little baby girl again," he told her.) Mary's Eva had listless arms, a worried hunch, and a faint, ironic smile. Visually, she cried out for protection.

Eva's final wish, before her death – and indeed, such a character seems too good to live – is that her father free his slaves. In her last moment she utters the phrase "Oh! love! joy! peace!" and goes straight to heaven in a blue-white light. "Oh, Evangeline!" cries her father. "Hath not heaven made thee an evangel to me?"

Eva was not the only child in melodrama to reform adults; Mary played another one in May 1901 in the Valentines' *East Lynne*. It was an old play from the 1860s, but it packed in the audience for decades. The heroine is a fallen woman, enticed by the villain to leave her husband. After repentance she gains employment in her husband's house, disguised as a governess. There she witnesses the death of her own child, William (Mary), who declares, "It is nothing to die when our Saviour loves us." But few in melodramatic literature can touch Evangeline for her hyperactive conscience. "These things *sink into my heart*," says Eva in the novel. Indeed, the plays sank into Mary's heart. Their moral lessons marked her for a lifetime. Melodramas also confirmed Mary's intuitions about duty in the family. They maintained that life, with its sudden reversals, is ultimately hopeful; the heroes gain dignity through suffering and attain their goals. Mary, too, though she sensed life's uncertainty, saw its flip side. If you work, implied the plays, you can make your life work. Nothing can stand in the way of a man (or a good girl) with his shoulder at the wheel. So Mary worked, and the following years strained her moral and physical strength to the utmost.

Strangely, Eva's description in the novel also depicts how Mary

Pickford's audience responded to the actress when she scored her gigantic success as a child-woman on the screen years later: "Her face was remarkable less for its perfect beauty of feature than for a singular and dreamy earnestness of expression, which made the ideal start when they looked at her, and by which the dullest and most literal were impressed, without exactly knowing why. The shape of her head and the turn of her neck and bust was peculiarly noble, and the long golden-brown hair that floated like a cloud around it, the deep spiritual gravity of her violet blue eyes, shaded by heavy fringes of golden brown – all marked her out from other children."

For woman or child, such a standard was impossible to live up to. But Mary tried. It seemed as if she somehow yearned to move other people as Eva moved them, effortlessly bringing happiness to those who were hurt or who depended on her. She was aware that a rival *Tom* production had put Eva on a pink cloud, which wafted her magically up to God. In other shows the child sprouted wings, riding to heaven in a skyborne chariot or levitating upward on a hidden footrest. Mary loved to do a death scene, and naturally she was crushed when Blancke asked her to die on an ordinary sofa with a minimum of fuss. Nevertheless, little Mary seemed ready, for the sake of the Smiths, and later for the sake of her admirers, to step into *Uncle Tom*'s final image:

Gorgeous clouds, tinted with sunlight. Eva, robed in white, is discovered on the back of a milk-white dove, with expanded wings, as if just soaring upward. Her hands are extended in benediction over St. Clare and Uncle Tom who are kneeling and gazing up at her. Expressive music. Slow curtain.

3

—

THERE MUST BE
MORE MONEY

Mary had hoped, by joining Hal Reid's tour of *At the Little Red Schoolhouse*, to escape her poverty – and to work. She wished to enter a larger dramatic world, one of exciting plays and roles, exposure to influential people, and doors labeled "Opportunity." She wanted the Smiths to be rich and happy. Instead, they joined a treadmill of demoralized actors, lugged by train across the continent, underfed and underpaid. Tours were planned in New York and Chicago with a single purpose: to crisscross the United States and sometimes Canada, sparing no economic shortcuts, wringing out actors like a sponge. In 1905 – a flush year for touring – more than three hundred troupes fanned out across North America. Even the smallest towns (Deadwood, South Dakota, was one) played host to more than two hundred one-night stands. And though a performer might act for forty weeks, his anonymity was certain, for no professionals saw his work except others in the company. Broadway was theater's genteel flagship. Tours were something else: the trenches.

The Little Red Schoolhouse (its title now shortened by one word) began its tour in Hamilton, an industrial town near Toronto, on November 26, 1901. The local critic, who had seen many Hal Reid melodramas, showed little patience with the production and saved his highest praise for the scenery. The tour trundled on through the American Midwest and ended in Chicago, where the curtains mercifully swept shut.

Mary never mentioned this tour, if she was in it. Instead, she recalled how the Smith family waited, with dwindling hopes, to receive a call from Hal Reid and begin their new life as traveling actors. But Reid sold the *Schoolhouse* rights to another producer, who launched it on another tour – again, without the Smiths. Then a fair-haired girl named Lillian Gish, who was playing Mary's former role in upstate New York, left the show when her chaperone took sick. Someone in the cast, probably a member from the Valentine production, told the manager about the Smiths, and they received a wire seeking "Gladys – only Gladys." But Charlotte played hardball, demanding that all the Smiths be given jobs. Somewhat remarkably, this worked, and in the fall of 1901 the Smiths were in Buffalo, relearning lines.

Picking up parts in other plays, they began five years of cross-country touring. Mary was only nine and a half years old when this sprawling but limited life began. By age fifteen, she was a miniature adult, tough but with pockets of painful immaturity – for though the road made rough-and-ready children, it robbed them of any continuous experience beyond train windows and a circuit of stages.

The turn-of-the-century touring system was shaped by "the Syndicate," a combine begun in 1896 by six New York producers. The Syndicate regimented tours by signing exclusive deals with more than seven hundred theaters inside and outside New York City. Syndicate producers were low on scruples and ran their Broadway shows at a loss in order to bill the plays as "long-running." They compromised critics by paying them to rewrite scripts or giving them bribes (called "consulting fees"). The Syndicate made sure its productions would be praised by pulling advertisements from papers that failed to rave about its shows and to pan non-Syndicate productions. Such independents did exist. Their troupes were impoverished and lacked the combine's access to comfortable hotels and theaters. Usually, well-known actors signed Syndicate contracts rather than endure the cruel conditions of the fringe. Only obscure actors suffered them – like the Smiths.

Few memoirs and scripts have survived the era of "barnstorming" melodrama through the heartland. But the *New York Clipper* (an early incarnation of *Variety*), the *New York Dramatic Mirror*, and local papers suggest vague dates for Mary's early career. On May 18, 1903, Pickford opened for a week's work in *The Soudan*, playing a consumptive boy. This – her last appearance in a stock presentation – occurred in Rochester, New York, supporting Jessie Bonstelle (who was a star in the Midwest) and two hundred soldiers in full military glory. But the balance of her vitae was made up of degrading tours. In 1904, for instance, Pickford ventured out in *Wedded But No Wife*; in 1905 she toured *The Gypsy Girl*, playing a boy named Freckles. A year later Pickford took another boy's role in the Hal Reid show *For a Human Life*. Other titles included *The Child Wife*, *In Convict Stripes* (a potboiler by the ubiquitous Reid), and nineteen weeks of one-night stands in a warhorse called *The Fatal Wedding*. These tours, with Mary on board, rode the rails between 1902 and 1906.

The stress of touring was accentuated by the dulling sameness of the plays. Theodore Kraemer, who wrote *The Fatal Wedding*, used to think up titles and then fit stereotypes around them. No wonder Pickford could remember almost nothing of the scripts she played, or where and when she played them. But she did recall the horrors of touring – lucidly.

Casting is a painful process, as there are always many more actors than there are parts. By 1905 there were twenty-one thousand actors in the U.S., all with theater their principal outlet. "No one can have an idea of what this means who has not personally looked for work on the stage," wrote Mary. New York producers opened their doors each Monday, ostensibly to meet performers. But eager actors, once through the door, were quickly dismissed by office boys. There was no reason why these employees should have had brusque or peremptory manners, but somehow such traits were deemed essential. When playwright and director Moss Hart was an office boy, he flung the doors open and chatted with the unemployed, changing his manner only when his boss said he would fire him unless he kept the office empty.

On other days, actors sat side by side, bright and alert as waiting dogs, hoping the producer – or his assistant, son, *anyone* – might take a shine to them. Hart remembered their expression: "The too eager, too bright smile, the glint in the eye serving notice to the steely office boy of the implacable desire to wait, if need be, all afternoon; the knowing air of being conscious of some secret casting going on that the others in the already crowded office did not share." Pickford felt frightened and demeaned by the process, though Hart praised "the way actors talk among themselves. . . . Part of an actor's equipment is a gallantry he must carry along daily like a shield; whatever despair he may feel as he faces himself in the mirror in the morning before he sets out on the daily round, he must learn to dissemble completely as he stands waiting in the outer office." Mary, on the other hand, could not forget the "rudeness of the receptionists; the sight of starving actors with their celluloid collars and brave faces; the overly bleached blondes with their inevitable turquoise jewelry and one lingering piece of soiled finery, like a blouse or jabot, and the lip rouge that would begin to wear off as the heat grew and the day lengthened. The picture of Mother, Lottie, Johnny and me trudging along to these offices will stay with me to my dying day."

Most casting offices were in New York, and the Smiths often lived there between engagements. Broadway, of course, was the actor's mecca. Electrified in 1901, the Great White Way – a star-laden stretch from 13th to 46th Streets – became a carnival of shining marquees and billboards. It was also the home of desperate souls. Out-of-work actors, con men, and tramps milled about at the lower end. So did Manhattan's younger criminals, children adept at prostitution, gambling, extortion, racketeering, drug-running, violence, and fraud.

The Smiths feared the shadow of New York's gutter life as much as they lusted for the splendor of Broadway. But they were desperate to find a home, any home. Hotels refused to receive "theatricals," unless they had achieved the fame of a Langtry, a Bernhardt, or a Modjeska. Stage stars, trailed by an entourage, were welcomed as an entire – and probably spendthrift – household.

To meet the profession's lack of housing (some actors finally sought the flophouse), theatrical boardinghouses sprang up. They might supply soup once a day and a dormitory or a private room, as well as a curfew to benefit females. Actors and actresses packed these houses and, despite the down-at-heel surroundings (stained walls, threadbare chairs and carpets), found a kind of happiness "between engagements." But Mary was shamed by boardinghouses. Her dislike was triggered when Mom Barrow, who ran one, burst into her room at nine in the morning, snarling, "You'll be down in five minutes or no breakfast!" "People of the theatre," wrote Pickford primly, "do not rise early. . . . I said nothing, but the expression on my face must have given more than a hint of my feelings. I learned later from Mother that Mom Barrow had come up to her quivering with rage and said, 'Mrs. Smith, I like little Lottie and Johnny, but as for Gladys, she's a fresh kid.'" The fresh kid felt as though Barrow had stabbed her, and the memory of this incident damned boardinghouse life in her mind forever.

Sometimes performers could afford a flat, and from time to time the Smiths resided in a fifth-floor walk-up with two seamstress friends, "aunts" Kate and Minnie Whelan. They also crossed paths with Mary Gish, who traveled the rails with Dorothy and Lillian, her acting children. Once the clans shared a flat at 39th and 8th – a dicey area – combining budgets. Actors truly down on their luck appeared in flickers. Long lines formed on casting days, because silent films paid cash, and quickly. The only alternative to such slumming was touring a melodrama – any play, at any pay, for many months.

Here the Smiths proved moderately castable. Mary made a dazzling child at ten. She had grown a bit chubby, but this was much admired. And her eyes, hair, and humor epitomized melodrama's ideal waif. Such a child, central to any company, was often loathed by older actors. Charles Dickens recorded the tendency as far back as *Nicholas Nickleby* (1839), in which the title character joins a troupe called the Crummles. Their best-known star is the Infant Phenomenon, a thoroughly irritating golden-haired "child." Indeed, her age is a matter of debate. Her parents, who have stunted her growth by feeding her gin-and-water since birth, insist the phenomenon is ten years old. But Dickens notes the phenomenon's "aged countenance" and that she has claimed the age of ten for "five good years." Her acting is a travesty of innocence; rehearsing "the Indian Savage and the Maiden," she leaps onstage with "a pirouette, then, looking off at the opposite wing, shrieked, bounded forward to within six inches of the footlights, and fell into a beautiful attitude of terror."

The phenomenon, like many child stars, is spoiled. Pickford recalled that in one touring troupe, she attracted the label of "a typical theatrical brat, blond curls and all." And Mary's head apparently began to swell while she played "the Little Mother" in *The Fatal Wedding*. As the heroine's daughter, she had a heart-stopping scene in which she tried to nurse her ragged, ailing mother. "While the child's back is turned," remembered writer Edward Wagenknecht, "the villainess uncorks a small bottle of poison and pours its contents into the medicine glass. The child, unaware of what has happened, picks up the glass and starts to carry it across the room to her mother, while the audience holds its breath. When she has nearly reached our heroine, she stumbles and drops the glass, spilling its contents upon the floor. How the villainess cursed! How we cheered! How our hearts revived within us!" The playbill for *The Fatal Wedding* screamed, in orange and magenta, "Baby Gladys is a Wonder."

One day Mary entered her dressing room, looked around, and issued an ultimatum. "The idea of expecting me, the star, to dress in a filthy place like this. I simply won't go on tonight."

Charlotte, who had tucked a towel around her waist and begun to scrub, caught sight of Baby Gladys in the mirror. Slowly she said, "I want that speech repeated." The little wonder did so, rather feebly. "I'm grateful for one thing," Charlotte told her. "That no one in the company heard you. You're not the star of the company! You're nothing but a naughty, spoiled, swell-headed little upstart. . . . That I should have lived to hear such a revolting speech from my own daughter." As punishment, she threatened to let Lottie play the role that evening. "You are not going on," Charlotte lectured Mary, "until you can learn humility." This cut Mary "more than a thousand whips" and soon she was elbow-deep in suds. And though she persuaded Charlotte to allow her to act that night, Mary never repeated her offstage performance. "From that moment to this," she wrote in her sixties, "I have been in such terror of having it said that I had a swelled head that I'm afraid I have often gone to the other extreme."

Beside this model older sister, Lottie seemed a bit shortchanged. She was not what the stage, or film, called beautiful. Instead, she possessed a normal-kid face, with eyes a bit widely spaced, snub nose, and dark hair. But she could (and did) understudy Mary, or play a tinier part than her sister. Lottie made up for the casting slight by becoming a tomboy and mischief-maker.

In 1915 Pickford claimed in a newspaper story that Lottie, at seven, was "a mischievous, fun-loving youngster whom the terrors of travel did not always subdue." As Mary's understudy, Lottie helped her button her dress and keep her shoes polished and her costume clean. It is difficult to imagine a circumstance, other than in a fairy tale, in which a child waits on a sister only one year older than herself. But Mary presented Lottie doing these things, and apparently not liking it. According to the column, Lottie stuffed a beetle down the stocking of Mary's costume, hoping to make Mary scream, hop about, and miss her entrance. It worked: soon Mary was hopping, self-control gone with the wind and screaming, "You bad girl!" "You wicked little thing!" Lottie watched and waited, unperturbed. It is almost a relief to picture the ever-so-proper Mary transformed into a furious, screaming child. But the bitterly silent Lottie makes an even more compelling picture.

Lottie idolized Jack, who was small and fine-boned, with regular features and an often irregular sense of humor. He usually played bit parts, and once – under protest – a little girl. The straw that broke the young boy's back was the wearing of pantalets, a trouserlike garment that hung a bit longer than a little girl's skirts. Mary had to lecture, beg, and sweet-talk her brother into donning these dainties before an entrance.

As Charlotte grew round, then barrel-shaped, she too became castable. A director might look at her, hear her brogue, and think "Irish cook" or "Irish maid." Melodrama overflowed with kind domestics, and Charlotte soon found herself decked out with rolling pins and frilly caps.

But the Smiths were not always cast together. Charlotte and Mary once appeared in *Wedded But No Wife* for eleven weeks while Jack and Lottie waited in Toronto. Jack once toured alone with Charlotte, a separation that left the girls bawling with grief in New York. Sometimes Mary, with or without Lottie, toured with an actress-chaperone. Possibly the chaperones felt the children's censure for not being Charlotte; for some reason, Mary claimed that most ignored them. In fact, she and Lottie once slipped through their chaperone's fingers and booked themselves a room above a tavern. And though Mary loyally explained that "Mother was a very beautiful woman and could easily have married again," the three young Smiths were worried that Charlotte might let them down and give them a new father. This would not do; the children wanted no one to steal the thunder from John Charles, let alone share Charlotte's love. They behaved like brats when suitors called, and Charlotte failed to scold them. Mary remembered a Mr. Jones who could not endure Mary, Lottie, and Jack. They chose his visit to march around the room and recite a Cockney jingle ad nauseam. (It began with the phrase "Little Papsy Wapsy" and proceeded downhill.) After the nerve-racked suitor left, Charlotte's only comment to Mary was that her Cockney accent needed training.

Even on precious all-family tours, Charlotte's reassuring touch was dulled by a pattern of upheaval and fatigue. Every autumn multiple melodramas lurched along the railroad and gave performances wherever the train stopped. In a large city, the actors reveled in staying three to five days in one location. But usually they left for the station as soon as the curtain call was over or boarded the milk train before the sun rose. They often reached their next engagement just in time to throw on their costumes. As for sleep, a week might pass before an actor could stretch his legs. "In our fondest dreams," remembered Pickford, "we never knew the luxury of a Pullman berth."

In 1934 Pickford wrote a story called "Little Liar." In it she imagined a child actress, wearing a dress handsewn by her mother, who folds her hands together "so tightly that every finger ached from the effort. She snuggled her head into the corner of the red plush seat and wished that it weren't scratchy. She tried to make words out of the sound of the train as it labored through the night, but somehow the train sounds wouldn't make words. They were sobs, instead." The child remembers sobs in theatrical boardinghouses, her own sobs and those of her mother. But somehow one doubts that the real Mary Pickford or her mother cried.

Mary once used a newspaper for a blanket. Newspaper also lined her dresses, while cardboard did the job in tattered shoes. Sometimes she slept sitting up, or standing. On other nights the child lay across a seat, with her head on a newspaper-pillow or the armrest, feet on the burning radiator. By morning she was coated by the drifting coal dust.

Hotels offered little refreshment; most were close to the railroad track, and these were the dreariest rooms in town. Better hotels, like those in the cities, did not admit theatricals; second-class rooms were snapped up by the Syndicate. Broken mattress springs and windows often greeted the exhausted troupe, and the usually filthy bathroom was down a dark and narrow hall. Meals were scheduled not for human needs but around the show and train departures. Breakfast for the Smiths consisted of stale ham sandwiches and water, eaten as they huddled for warmth on a train seat.

Matinées over, they dashed to their hotel, where Charlotte, before taking off her hat, turned on the gas ring, washed her hands, tied a clean towel around her waist, and started peeling vegetables. Beating cheap steak with a rolling pin, she produced a dish called "heavenly hash," which the children loved. She also saved the water from tinned vegetables as a base for soup and other dishes. Mary's starry-eyed admiration reflects her unwavering love for Charlotte – or the fact that she knew nothing whatever of cooking.

At night the family washed their clothes. Keeping clean and neat was a challenge, as actors outside the Syndicate worked at what Mary called "small, hopeless theatres" – in other words, lacking heat and water. They did offer drafts, flooded basements, and vermin. Managers apologized with signs backstage: "We know the theatre is rotten! How's your show?" It was rotten, too. Most tours lacked the scenic wonders that resident companies might provide. Instead, they used the faded backdrops – city street, open plain – that were standard installations on local stages. And histrionic acting often creaked. Jaded and hollow-eyed, touring actors seldom bore the charisma of a big-name star. And though small-town audiences snapped up tickets, they were loath to rub shoulders with the troupe. One actor recalled his group's departure from South Dakota, where behind him the baggageman remarked, "Well, now we'll get the fairies out of town." Another actor overheard him. "And to all you sodomists staying here in Gomorrah, we wish you continued success!" he waved. Children raised in such surroundings learned a certain cynicism.

Sometimes – many times – the audience hated the show for its own sake. Child actress Isadora Bennett told of one stop on a tour of *The Squaw Man* in western Canada when two patrons who disliked the actor playing a British fop began to shoot at him from the audience. Bennett, standing at the back of the house, stamped her foot and screamed at the offenders, "Now you *stop* that. That's my *brother*!" – and in fact, he was. Sheepishly, the gunmen put away their weapons.

Mary endured her share of "hooting, jeering galleries. I loathed it all." Many of the jeers were in the "ten-twent'-thirt's," a term used for bottom-of-the-barrel tours, with cheap production values indicated by admission price (ten, twenty, thirty cents). Pickford pointedly turned her back on audience misbehavior – this is a common response from performers –

and glared over her shoulder at the viewers. But the need for more money obsessed her; touring salaries were small, and actors paid their own living expenses. (The Smiths, of course, pooled salaries. When the children toured alone, they stuffed their payments in chamois "boodle bags," which they hung round their necks. Then they converted the cash to money orders, which they mailed to Charlotte.) And Mary knew touring was professionally futile. Its profits reached the coffers of a few producers, who enjoyed the added perk of sending actors as far away from their doors as possible.

Realizations such as these encouraged a streak of temper in Pickford that lasted a lifetime. Previous moodiness now took the form of sudden, almost willful depression, marked by helplessness and resentment, followed by almost crushing guilt. As if to neutralize these feelings, Mary's concern for others deepened. And toward her mother she grew wildly empathic, using Charlotte as a beacon amid the rootlessness of touring. When Lottie and Mary were alone on the road in *The Child Wife*, the children received a package from their mother containing handsewn lambskin coats, hats, and muffs. The children proudly wore the coats but, rather than muss their mother's handiwork, refused to sit down in them. And Mary, who had been so impressed with the blisters on her father's hands, imagined Charlotte's martyrdom, her tortured, unprotected fingers, "pricked and bleeding from working with the stiff hide." Similarly, Mary's love for Charlotte was almost as painful as it was tender, open as a wound, and unprotected.

The summer of 1903, spent in Toronto before the Smiths began rehearsals for *The Fatal Wedding*, was one of Charlotte's most difficult times. Funds were scarce, and the children were highly upset when she killed the backyard rooster for a meal, though this was common practice at the time. Charlotte's woes continued when she underwent surgery at home; the Smiths lacked money for the hospital. During the operation, Mary became convinced that she would lose her mother, and she rocked in despair against the sewing machine pedal. Twenty-four hours later Charlotte boarded a train to New York, slept sitting up, and reported for rehearsal first thing in the morning, three children in tow. She had not had breakfast.

It was *The Fatal Wedding* that provided Charlotte with her first role (she had previously understudied), but in order to appear as the Irish cook, she had lied and claimed to be a veteran. This lie is regularly told by actors – as by job seekers of all kinds – and Charlotte had an irreproachable motive: to keep the family together. Once onstage, she probably hoped to make up with good will what she lacked in talent (though Mary called her, as she did Grandma Hennessey, a natural mimic). But Charlotte had also taught her children, "You can lock from a thief, but never from a liar," and the fib about her résumé shocked her offspring.

Unfortunately, Charlotte had the play's first line. Immediately the director snapped, "You'll have to do better than that or I'll replace you." "Those words lashed me," Mary wrote. She froze with fear when a director sneered at anyone in rehearsal, but Charlotte was so much her alter ego that Mary felt paralyzed with hurt. When her mother entered with a prop bowl of flowers, the director asked, "And what would you have us suppose you are carrying there, Mrs. Smith, a piece of Limburger cheese?" "He felt very inferior and tried to cover it up with crucifying everybody," Mary concluded. "He was a man of little talent, or no talent. . . . He wanted to, in the vernacular, strut his stuff." He even spoke nastily to Mary, who panicked: "I just freeze up if a director treats me like that, I can't do anything." She later recalled her sense that she was "the only one of the children to realize fully what Mother was going through at that moment. I knew that she was in pain, weak, tired, and frightened, that the whole uncertain future of the Smith family hung on the outcome of this cruel day." In what seems a much-embroidered coda, Pickford reported that on opening night in Pottsville, Pennsylvania, the children fell to their knees in the wings and prayed that Charlotte would remember her lines – and also be forgiven her falsehood.

Indeed, Charlotte's life was no happier than Mary's. Even this powerful mother must have experienced doubts when raising her children in trains, strange cities, and hotel rooms. Pickford remembered one morning when Charlotte woke the children at three to catch the milk train. Jack, then about seven years old, slept on, and when Charlotte tried to move him, he cried out for more rest. Charlotte suddenly sat down and wept. This unfamiliar sight so alarmed the girls that they dragged Jack out of bed – and finally out the door – themselves. But as they crossed toward the railroad tracks, Jack stopped in the snow near a low iron railing. Charlotte marched on, till her youngest, alone and terrified, mewled like a kitten. This time Charlotte returned, but rather than gathering Jack in her arms, she tossed him over the railing. Even Mary was shocked: "That was the only moment in my life that I actually disliked my mother." When Jack called to Charlotte, she kept on walking; neither did she turn around when Lottie and Mary ran back to Jack and the anxious trio dragged themselves toward their leader.

Absolute loyalty or expulsion. Yet even a mother so intent on preservation of the family must have recognized the price. Her children lacked rest, recreation, and nutrition. They lacked education, although they read books and found a few tutors among their chaperones. Pickford claimed she attended school for only three months and learned to read off billboards on the road. Perhaps most damaging, the Smiths had few chances to form relationships beyond the family. Actors fall into friendships on a tour, but these usually dissolve when the play disbands. As for rebellion, there was none. In the face of Charlotte's implacable rule, it seemed inconceivable. As well, trouping children were expected to behave. "Nonsense is not tolerated round the stage," explained Pickford, and the hotels "would soon discourage any use of their halls as playgrounds."

The weary Charlotte found comfort in alcohol. It is hard to pinpoint when her habit began; she may have been a drinker long before she started acting. But life on the road seems a likely setting for developing a dependence that eventually ruled her, especially since the theater, in those days, was full of alcoholics.

Probably the family as a whole found solace in the theater's motto, "The show must go on," a point of honor that attested to personal courage and commitment, the public proof that one was heart and soul an actor. By enduring tour after hopeless tour, actors proved they were stage aristocrats. Only a few gave way to illness. "If you complained," explained an actor who survived the system, "if you couldn't keep up, you got a reputation, and what manager was going to send you out to complicate things on the tour? That's why they were a very select group of people. My boy," he told a journalist, "we were *troupers!*"

When the tours petered out at the end of spring, a casting drought prevailed till the autumn season. Sometimes the Smiths spent their breaks in Toronto; they were there in the summer of 1904, the year of Grandma

Hennessey's death. Jack and Lottie spent part of 1906 with Aunt Lizzie until Mary and Charlotte joined them, after touring in *Wedded But No Wife*. At least one student remembers Jack playing in the yard of Grace Street School that year while a golden-haired sister stood nearby, watching. Thus Toronto remained the children's touchstone: the Princess Theatre, leafy streets, their father's grave – and now Grandma Hennessey's.

One summer found the family living in Manhattan with the Gishes. Mary and Lillian grew close – so close that, late in life, each made the sentimental statement that she couldn't remember a time they hadn't known each other. Indeed, the Gishes and Mary appeared in different productions of the same plays: *In Convict Stripes*, *The Child Wife*, *The Little Red Schoolhouse*, and *East Lynne*. Both Lillian and Mary had a much-adored mother who acted and sewed. Each had been left by an erratic father. Both, though ethereal, had nerve. And their temperaments were ideally suited: Lillian, the thinker who liked to listen, and Mary, the leader who liked to lecture.

Now Mary lectured the other children in the art of obtaining free theater tickets. The secret: flatter the box office manager. "Do you recognize professionals?" Mary would present her card. "We hear you have a very fine play with good actors. Perhaps we could learn from them." The children filed in. "There was never any question when she told us to do something," remembered Lillian. "We did it." Another summer Mary Gish opened a candy stand in the Fort George, New York, amusement grounds. The two families took the streetcar to the site, then popped and bagged corn before the crowds arrived. The children wrapped candy in paraffin paper, drinking in the cool morning air. At lunch they wandered over to the fried-potatoes stand, where five cents bought them a sizzling lunch. Awnings flapped lazily in the wind. There was a merry-go-round, and ponies. Back in Manhattan on summer nights, the children bought cold turkey, pickles, and ice cream, or sat on the stoop and looked out at nothing. Years later, Dorothy Gish let slip the loneliness of touring children when she called these easy, tranquil evenings her first interaction with children her own age.

But Mary, while earning her stripes, was also totaling up her losses. She must have felt, from time to time, that she was living in a tin can. Her life on the trains continued into her fifteenth year, a time of considerable change for girls and (to adults) unpredictable attitudes. What did Mary do with these energies? Smothering rebellion required a marvelous devotion, one that honored "the unbelievable courage of Charlotte Pickford Hennessey Smith." And she "didn't mind" the memory of water and stale bread; the family "had a wonderful time together. There's nothing wrong with being poor if it's accompanied by a loving parent. That to me is about the ultimate in life."

In 1905 the Smith children were huddled in the office of an agent on Broadway. "[We] scrunched down in our clothes to appear as small as possible," remembered Mary, "the idea being that if they wanted us taller we could always straighten up." Still, there was a problem: the agent was looking for two boys and a girl, not two girls and a boy. But Charlotte, stepping in, assured him that her children could cross-dress convincingly. The roles were theirs.

Edmund Burke opened at Brooklyn's Majestic Theatre on November 2, 1905, as part of a turn-of-the-century vogue for coy Irish musicals. Chauncey Olcott, whose silver tenor brought him a hundred thousand dollars a year, was its star. The show, decked in shamrocks, buckles, and brogues, resembled an Irish sing-along. The real Edmund Burke was an eighteenth-century Irish parliamentarian who sympathized with the revolt in the American colonies and drafted Britain's East India bill. Edmund Burke of the musical finds himself "in the old days of dueling and fine sword play, of satin knickers and silk polonaise, when men spent their days in rose gardens, their nights in ballad-making." Here Burke defends the Prince of Wales against his would-be kidnappers; in return the prince promises to produce a comedy by Oliver Goldsmith (well, Edmund Burke *did* know Oliver Goldsmith) and to give Burke a seat in the House of Commons. Mary, Lottie, and Jack played young lords and ladies. Jack's costume included a wig, a satin skirt, and a brocaded dress. To add insult to injury, the program dubbed him "Edith Milbourne Smith." (In keeping with the high tone of Olcott shows, the Smiths had conjured up a stately middle name.) But the children were well received – "charming and lovable," according to the *New York Dramatic Mirror*, though the paper also noted that they couldn't sing or dance.

"We were playing better theatres in better towns and before better audiences," wrote Pickford. "The more harmonious colors and the whole atmosphere of the better hotels appealed to me. I wanted nice things." But although the Smiths stepped up into a higher rank of tours when they played with Olcott, their combined talents in *Edmund Burke* paid only twenty dollars a week. Pickford, who hoped to step up in income, compared her clothing and sparse belongings with those of other children across the country. "When I saw things that other girls had, I determined to have them. I'd work for them."

But in 1907 Mary was back on the road, alone, in a ragtag tour of *For a Human Life*. It stopped for an engagement in New York's Bowery. An established slum and brawling place, the Bowery expected corpses, vulgarity, and buckets of stage blood. *For a Human Life*, which featured a large exotic idol with multiple, knife-throwing arms, delivered. Mary, in a wig, played Patsy Poore, a red-haired boy who dies in his effort to save the hero. "Dear God," he asks, with his dying breath, "don't open the gates wide; it's only Patsy."

The Thalia theater, where Mary played, was, as she remembered, at "its cheap tinsel worst." It was hung with lurid lithographs of "violence and crime." Inside, everything "spoke of decaying grandeur: cracked marble, dulled gilt, creaking seats, raggedness, and dilapidation." Fistfights broke out among the viewers. Policemen with billy clubs passed among them, cracking heads and throwing out hoodlums. At Mary's rooming house, "the furniture was chipped and rickety. Dust hung in the air. The windows in my room probably hadn't been washed for years. I washed them and then wished I hadn't. The view was not inviting."

The lives of the older actresses in *Convict* had alarmed her: "My heart was filled with pity for them and dread for myself. They were fading so fast. Life had trampled them. . . . Day by day their eyes became more dulled and hopeless. Yesterday they had been leading women. To-day they were abject suppliants of the theater. Tomorrow," thought the realistic child, was "oblivion."

Mary was fed up but didn't know where to turn. She would work, without question – but at what? She was only fifteen, and the only other job she could imagine was sewing. Charlotte and Mary Gish did fancy work, and Aunt Minnie Whelan was a fitter on Fifth Avenue. After the

Thalia, as middle America rolled past her window, Mary mapped out an alternative existence. She would live with the Whelans in New York, tearing out basting threads by day (this paid five dollars) and taking a dress-design class at night. She would also pick up extra cash by selling subscriptions to the *Ladies Home Journal*. She would one day open a dressmaking parlor – that is, if exhaustion didn't kill her first.

Who knows – Mary might have made it work. Those who knew her as an adult declared she could have run General Motors had she wished to. Still, "Dresses by Gladys" would have to wait while Mary laid a last-ditch siege of Broadway.

As Lottie and Jack summered in Toronto with Charlotte, Mary stayed with the Whelans in New York. She had only twenty dollars to her name and kept house in exchange for living free of rent. At night she slept on a Morris chair with the back let down and an overstuffed chair beneath her feet. The arrangement forced her to sleep with her arms folded on her chest, a habit that lingered for years. A good night's rest must have been elusive, as Mary also flung her arms up above her head after sleeping for years on narrow train seats.

New York's gentleman producer was Charles S. Frohman, a shy man with somewhat British tastes. He emphasized charming, ephemeral plays, notably those of James M. Barrie. (When Frohman drowned in 1915 aboard the *Lusitania*, he reportedly went down quoting *Peter Pan*: "Death will be an awfully big adventure!") Mary might have met success at Frohman's office, given her youth and his inclinations. In fact, Frohman bankrolled several plays for an elfin actress named Maude Adams. One was *Peter Pan* – and if the tomboyish Adams embodied Peter, Mary was the perfect, responsible Wendy. But Frohman had helped create the Syndicate, and perhaps Mary held this against him. She also claimed she had read Barrie's *Sentimental Tommy* while trouping, and hated it. Instead, she targeted David Belasco – in those days, a name of charismatic powers.

Belasco left his mark on plays by producing, directing, co-writing, and designing them. His pride and joy was verisimilitude: the scrupulous pursuit of pictorial realism, won with fanatic devotion to detail. One writer, viewing original photos of the props for *Du Barry* (1901), decided the effect "defies description. Nothing was artificial, everything was reproduced as if from a plaster cast of the original." Indeed, Belasco boasted that some of the props had been owned by Madame Du Barry herself. Later *The Governor's Lady* presented a Childs restaurant, down to real restaurant chairs and tables, dirty napkins, and the slap of wheatcakes. In *The Girl of the Golden West*, a snowstorm swirled about a log cabin. "The audience heard the wild moaning and shrill whistle of the gale, and at moments, as the tempest rose to a climax of fury, could see the fine-powdered snow driven in tiny sprays and eddies through every crevice of the walls and the very fabric of the cabin quiver and rock beneath the impact of terrific blasts of wind.... Operation of the necessary mechanical contrivances required a force of thirty-two trained artisans – a sort of mechanical orchestra." Soon this veracity of detail became a spectacle in itself, and guessing what Belasco might come up with next turned into a game for both audience and critics – one that lasted well into the 1920s.

In 1912 critic Robert Grau made a list of the world's great music and theater artists, placing Belasco alongside Beethoven, Shakespeare, and Offenbach. But others believed Belasco's stage effects diverted attention from the plays themselves. And they thought this a mercy (*Du Barry* was "a plenitude of needless talk"). As early as 1908, critic Walter Prichard Eaton was searching for "the glow of intellectual excitement, the thousand zests of daily existence," in *Zaza*, a Belasco play.

Meanwhile Isadora Duncan danced without her shoes and England had a new word: suffragette. Theodore Dreiser and Edith Wharton graced the bookshelves, and *The Jungle*, Upton Sinclair's exposé of corruption in the meatpacking industry, caused an uproar. Stubbornly, Broadway remained insensate. Let Europe embrace the likes of Ibsen, Gorki, Chekhov, Strindberg, Tolstoy, Synge, and all the others. New York preferred *Ben-Hur* (real horses).

The result, wrote Eaton, was "a stale conventionality that none but the most childish can possibly believe in, can possibly be aroused by." Belasco "could buy the materials of reality," added critic Brooks Atkinson. "It was paradoxical, nevertheless, that the truth of reality escaped him.... He believed in stage buncombe, in the shabby materials of the artless dramas of his youth – heroism, sacrifice, villainy, purity, immorality, voluptuousness: also retribution, sweet tears, kindly laughs, noble sorrow. Life never got inside Belasco's head or heart. All he knew was theatre."

Belasco's best show – and his longest-running – was his own mystique, and though his techniques were transparently theatrical, he mesmerized the public with an aura of genius. He wore a costume – abandoning, with some nerve, any reference to his Jewish roots and donning a clerical collar and black suit. This gave him the air of someone humble, holy yet exalted. Thus his nickname, "the Bishop of Broadway," a phrase that drove his critics crazy. "The only vow he's ever taken," snarled one, "is a vow of cheap theatrics."

The public shrugged off the war of words. Belasco dazzled them. He dazzled Mary, who equated theatrical class with the use of upscale props and flats. And he evidently dazzled Mrs. Leslie Carter, Blanche Bates, Lenore Ulric, Ina Claire, and Frances Starr. The fame of these actresses has faded, but under Belasco, their names burned bright. In exchange, they endured the Belasco treatment – rounds of magisterial kindness offset by moments of shocking temper. Some of these displays were planned. A common ploy was to lose his temper, rip off his watch, and smash it to the floor (the watch was phony). He once dragged Mrs. Carter across the stage and kicked her in the backbone: he was trying to instill in her the meaning of pain. Mixing such moments with others of humility, Belasco bred in his actors a cultlike need for his approval. Indeed, a Belasco performer belonged to him, in part of her own mind and the public's, as surely as if he had stamped his initials on her forehead.

Mary had decided to belong to him. In New York she had once seen Mrs. Leslie Carter, whose salacious private life, titian hair, and overwrought acting had made her a notorious Belasco star. She was gliding by in her "big, imported yellow automobile, with its imposing liveried footman and chauffeur! To have a car like Mrs. Carter's became the height of my ambition, and although I admired her as an actress and never dreamed of being as magnetic as she, that yellow car always stood out foremost in my mind." Mary's fixation with cars was sealed when a limousine splashed her skirts with slush at the corner of 42nd and 7th. "Never mind, Mabel," she told Aunt Lizzie's daughter, who was with her. "We're going to have a car even nicer than that – and very soon, too."

Lying on her Morris chair, Mary fantasized a face-to-face encounter with Belasco: how she would be made to wait for hours outside his office, how pale and interesting she would look when she finally crumpled to the floor. The swoon would be timed to the second Belasco emerged from his sanctum. He, of course, would look darkly glorious – "a sensitive, poetic face," Mary dreamed. And indeed, the producer had flashing eyes, black brows, and thickets of curling hair (pure white).

Belasco would lift Mary in his arms and bring her to his office. There she would give an affecting death scene – starting up, falling back, reaching toward visions with fluttering gestures. When she had melted Belasco's heart, she would bounce up, laugh, and announce he had witnessed a performance. In lieu of applause, the stunned producer would whip out a contract and sign her on the spot.

Same dream, with a twist: Mary stands outside a theater, swaying after long hours rooted to the pavement. When Belasco emerges and approaches his limousine, she faints at the Bishop of Broadway's feet. "Then I saw myself lifted up by the great Mr. Belasco himself, and heard him say: 'Take this poor little girl to her home in my machine. I am afraid she is ill.' At which I would open my eyes and say, 'Pardon me, Mr. Belasco, but I am really not ill at all. This is just such acting as I would do for you if you would give me a chance to work in one of your companies.'" Belasco then turns to the office boy. "Take this young lady in and sign her up for a five-year engagement."

At first Mary followed the conventional path of sending Belasco photos and letters and appearing Mondays at his casting office. Gradually she realized she "might as well try to see St. Peter." "Week after week I went up there to meet my fate. Week after week I was sent away without even a peek into that office where sat the genius whom I longed to meet. Like all deferred hope, it began to magnify until it seemed almost as if my very life depended upon this interview."

She decided to announce herself to someone else: Blanche Bates, who had taken Belasco's *The Girl of the Golden West* on tour and was playing it at Brooklyn's Majestic Theatre. Mary, who had acted there in *Edmund Burke*, hoped that the doorman would remember her and slip her backstage. Then she would find Blanche Bates and persuade her to recommend her to Belasco.

Luckily, Mary's melting appearance reduced the shock waves born of her tenacity. She certainly seems to have charmed Bates's maid, who met her backstage and swung into action. The maid pleaded with Bates in her dressing room: "I've never asked you to do me a favor in all the years I have worked for you. But I ask you now. Please, Miss Bates, send that little girl with the curls to see Mr. Belasco. I know you'd feel the way I do, if you saw her." "All right," snapped Bates, "tell her to say to Mr. Belasco that I sent her, but don't bother me any more about it."

Mary strode back to Belasco's office. She delivered the message from Bates, but the office boy knew his job, and though Mary was imperious she couldn't move him. Naturally she began to argue, and as she grew strident William Dean, Belasco's associate, opened his office door and asked what the trouble was.

Mary immediately entered Dean's office. Summoning every brash nerve in her body she uttered one sentence for posterity: "My life depends on seeing Mr. Belasco!"

Dean found her hugely entertaining.

Several weeks later a message from Belasco's office invited Mary to meet the producer following a performance of *Rose of the Rancho*, his current Broadway entry; Belasco usually opened one play per season. On the big night, Mary, unbearably keyed up, stood in the lobby of Belasco's Republic theater, properly chaperoned by Aunt Min or Aunt Kate (she often changed the story). When Belasco appeared, Mary lowered her eyes – not a strange reaction, as even grown-ups found him daunting. But then she raised them.

"What's your name?" the producer asked her.

"I saw him then as only two eyes – two enormous eyes," remembered Mary. "Two deep pools of light looking down at me."

"At home in Toronto, I'm Gladys Smith; but on the road I'm Gladys Milbourne Smith."

Belasco had a touch with children, and Mary cannily saw that he enjoyed her. Indeed, he was trying to hide his laughter. The name seemed ridiculously self-important.

"We'll have to find another name for you. What are some of the other names in your family?"

"Key, Bolton, De Beaumont, Kirby, Pickford . . ."

"Pickford it is. Is Gladys your only name? Haven't you another?"

"I was baptized Gladys Marie," said Gladys.

"Well, my little friend, from now on your name will be Mary Pickford, and will you come back, please, with your aunt, tomorrow night and see our play?" After a pause Belasco dropped a bombshell. "Be prepared to give me a sample of your acting."

Mary stopped in mingled fear and rapture. After a pause Belasco asked her casually, "By the way, what made you say your life depended on seeing me?"

Mary drew a breath. "Well, you see, Mr. Belasco, I'm thirteen [actually fifteen] years old, and I think I'm at the crossroads of my life. I've got to make good between now and the time I'm twenty, and I have only seven [no, five] years to do it in. Besides, I'm the father of my family." She was looking "straight up into his face now." He asked why she had chosen to approach him. "Mother always says I should aim high," replied Mary, gazing up at Belasco, "or not at all."

Pickford later told several versions of the story; one scrapped the Bates angle altogether, and in another her age was only ten. Belasco's versions seem like falsehoods, especially when he describes Mary saying, "I'm getting a splendid salary [on tour], and you may not want to pay me as much, for I realize that the part you have for me is a small one. But don't tell me how much; I'll take whatever you will give me." Nevertheless, the producer revealed that he knew the real Mary Pickford when he wrote of her powers of persuasion: "She looked straight at me, her big, beautiful eyes looking straight into mine. Not for a moment did her glance waver."

The following night, Aunt Min (or Kate) accompanied her to see *The Rose of the Rancho*. *Rose*, which was co-written by Belasco, dramatized the settlement of California. The play's main attraction was Frances Starr, whose "buoyancy of youth" and "charm of dainty personal loveliness" was supported by fresh fruit hanging from the stage trees, a genuine western bar, and breathtaking sky effects. But Mary was thinking only of her audition. The road had taught her a miserable stage fright, marked by a typical actor's nightmare in which she entered from the wings to find there was no one in the audience. But she found her audition even worse. "An empty theater," she remembered, "is rather formidable in appearance, especially when you are to stand out alone on the stage, knowing that in the box will be a crucial group of the men and women who have your destiny in the palm of their hand, either to mold or to mar."

Belasco asked her if she needed any props.

"I would like a chair, sir, to represent a policeman."

Belasco settled himself in the orchestra. Mary began with an apology; she had learned the speech, she explained, under bad direction, and knew it was threadbare. She then proceeded to impersonate Patsy Poore, who, in *For a Human Life*, begs a policeman not to arrest him and invokes his poor "blind mother in the cottage over yonder hills." "My voice did not quaver," remembered Mary, "but I could hear the commonplace and almost melodramatic lines which rang out and jarred upon me. They did not belong in this theater and I was conscious of it." Belasco, nevertheless, listened politely, then joined Mary onstage, where he took her hands in his.

"So you want to be an actress, little girl?"

Pickford's reply was brilliant. "No, sir," she replied. "I have been an actress. I want to be a good actress now."

Belasco listened gravely, then led her backstage to meet Frances Starr. Mary was stunned by the grandeur of the dressing room, which looked like a boudoir, upholstered in linen. "Frances," said Belasco, "here's a young lady who wants to be a good actress like you." "Yes, Miss Starr," said Mary, with a sure nose for flattery. "You see how ambitious I am." Starr answered grandly: "That will not be difficult, my little dear. Under the Maestro's guiding hand I know that you will go far." And Mary, aiming high or not at all, swept her gaze around the dressing room, seized by a moment of pure ambition – a yearning not for family, nor for fathers, but for something she wanted for herself. She wanted Frances Starr's dressing room, top to bottom, from the pale blue trim to the star nailed glamorously to the door.

The same night she wrote a letter to Charlotte in Toronto that resembled a triumphant newspaper headline: "GLADYS SMITH NOW MARY PICKFORD ENGAGED BY DAVID BELASCO TO APPEAR ON BROADWAY THIS FALL." Indeed, on December 3, 1907 – the tail end of Broadway's fall theater season – Mary Pickford premiered at the Belasco theater as Betty Warren in William C. de Mille's play *The Warrens of Virginia*.

Warrens shared the season with a high-toned selection of Shaw and Shakespeare, though foreigners – Ellen Terry and Russia's Alla Nazimova – brought such fare to Broadway. Typical American entries were trivial: *The Hoyden*, with Elsie Janis (the former

Maude Nugent was now Broadway's "little ray of feminine sunshine"), the first Ziegfeld Follies, and the indefatigable *Uncle Tom's Cabin*.

The Warrens of Virginia is a genteel melodrama. The ingenue, Agatha Warren, falls in love with a Yankee lieutenant, but civil war turns the delight of their romance to desperation. Mary played the heroine's twelve-year-old sister, with a handful of lines and two affecting scenes. One shows Agatha's father, "the worn, ill, suffering Confederate general . . . sitting with his wife by his side and their two young children [Mary and Richard Storey] at their knees." Another involves "the little children, concocting a letter to their soldier brother." "Dear Brother Arthur," recites Mary, "We take pen in hand to tell you that Pa was toted home today safely, and is now resting and I reckon is as well as can be expected, and says he isn't as sick as he is, and looks awful sick; but he talks on 'bout the same as usual." Storey remarks that "awful sick" is too alarming, and suggests she replace it with "right pert." "That's a right down smackin' lie," says Mary – thus foreshadowing her future as the screen's most spirited ingenue.

If the script of *Warrens* was routine, the theater that housed it was deluxe. The marquee of the Belasco, at 111 West 44th Street, was made of wrought iron and hung, like an awning, from the theater to the curb. Inside, the elegance was austere. Seats, for which viewers paid two dollars, were covered with silver-green tapestry, embroidered with bumblebees ("B" was for "Belasco"). The audience trod on green velvet carpets and sat beneath a dome of gold, pink, and gray. A rose velvet curtain hung across the proscenium, and tapestries showing an autumn landscape hung round the audience on the walls. A rosewood screen lit by crystal lamps stood near the lobby to shield the play from street noise. "What a magnificent sight it was from the stage in those days!" sighed Mary. "The women wore gorgeous evening gowns and the men were always in formal attire, their white shirts and waistcoats gleaming in the dimness. And I shall never forget the wave of perfume that wafted across the footlights to us on the stage. How happily we all basked in it!" In fact, it was the middle class, splendidly turned out, who kept the Broadway scene alive. They hissed the villain and encouraged the hero, just like their small-town counterparts. "Matinée girls" – young, single women who came to admire the male ingenues, their "matinée idols" – chatted loudly and, heading for a gab session, rushed up the aisle during curtain call. But the audience was generous and easily amused – soothed, like Mary, by the atmosphere of civilized well-being.

Belasco, of course, delivered splendor. The "special charm" of *The Warrens of Virginia* was "a sweet and gentle domestic atmosphere." Mary's costume was sewn from a pale pink tablecloth. Walter Prichard Eaton praised the "outdoor scene with its trees and saplings and broken gun carriage and running brook," as well as the interior set, "which, by the simple but imaginative device of a window opening from the great room into the hall, allows the audience to see the tall clock, the stairs and the heads of people passing in that second room and begets an overpowering suggestion of the spaciousness and solidity of the mansion." These were "elegant proofs of [Belasco's] scenic power, a power that is not without its touch of poetry too, and never without the painter's taste." Every prop was, if possible, authentic – real crystal, real silver, and, as Pickford remembered, real molasses.

The child was sleepily watching rehearsal when she heard Belasco shout, "Hold everything!" He then clambered up on the stage and "elaborately stalked the molasses jar." The actors watched as he tasted the contents, flung down the spoon, and bellowed for the prop man, who confirmed that the jar contained maple syrup. "And if you please, what does the manuscript call for?" asked Belasco. "Molasses, sir." "And you dare waste my time and the time of the ladies and gentlemen of my company with maple syrup?" Belasco hurled the jar to the floor "and began to jump up and down on the sticky mess, thereby driving it deeper and deeper into the beautiful Oriental rug." Mary watched from a stage box, terror-stricken. Then Belasco joined her and asked, in a confidential tone, "What did you think of my performance?" Mary stared, and Belasco continued, "This is a great secret between you and me. I find it absolutely necessary to break something at least once before opening night in order to keep the cast on their toes." Pickford was aghast and reminded Belasco to expect a big cleaning bill for the carpet.

"I liked [him] immensely," she remembered. "Still, it was more awe than liking. You can't like a deity; you fear it; and Belasco was a deity to me. When he would look at me my very bones would almost freeze. Once, when I was five minutes late, I was 'called down' before the entire company. It was a very great disgrace."

On another occasion Mary tried the patented Smith trick of staging a pantalets rebellion. Like Jack, she had a horror of the undergarment, and in a mutinous moment she rolled the "unmentionables" under her skirts during dress rehearsal. "There's something wrong with her costume," said Belasco. Then he saw the problem: "I know, I know!" In what Pickford called "a monstrous growl," he continued ominously, "Where are her pantalets?" The wardrobe mistress rushed onstage. "Mr. Belasco, I put them on Betty myself," she said, trembling. Belasco looked at Mary, who stood rooted to the spot. "What have you done with them?" he asked her sternly. The wardrobe mistress lifted Mary's dress, which was "a thousand times worse than what I had tried to avoid. . . . I was embarrassed almost beyond endurance."

Belasco never told this story. When Mary became the world's best-known actress he made unctuous statements concerning her virtue ("loved by everyone") and talent. Under direction, she was bright-eyed and bushy-tailed, the first at rehearsal and the last to leave, and exceeding careful with her Southern accent. Pickford backed him up on this, noting proudly that the playwright's mother had thought she was Southern, born and bred. But one of his comments is suggestive: Mary Pickford was "all repose – easy and graceful at all times." He was probably alluding to her magnetism, a word that in Mrs. Leslie Carter's heyday meant hair-tearing, trembling, shrieking fireworks. Mary embodied its modern meaning: the effortless authority of simply being.

Meanwhile Mary's life hardly changed. She made only twenty-five dollars a week – not much for Broadway – and managed to live on only five. The balance, as always, was sent to Charlotte, who was touring with Lottie and Jack in a melodrama. When *Warrens* closed on Broadway in May 1908 (a healthy run), Mary joined the tour, where her salary crested at thirty dollars. She bunked with Blanche Yurka, who had also played in the Broadway run and had understudied several female roles. Yurka, like most of Mary's roommates, received constant tips on saving money. In New York, Pickford's recommended breakfast was bananas and milk for a nickel at Childs. It filled her up more than expensive meals, and who knew when hunger pangs might return?

In January 1909, when *Warrens* reached Toronto's Royal Alexandra, the critics made a fuss about their hometown girl. They stressed her connection to the local stage, to Sarah Key Smith on MacPherson Avenue, and her preternatural sangfroid. "Gladys Smith is not as young as her years.

Ten years of life behind the footlights has been a rapid system of educa-
tion and to-day she has the carriage and conversation of a grown-up." That
education had also brought her street sense. While playing the Colonial
Theatre in Cleveland, Yurka and Mary were followed down the street by
two men (probably drunks) who mistook the innocent pair for whores.
After enduring a spate of catcalls, Pickford turned to Yurka and whispered,
"Don't answer yet; wait till we get to the hotel. I'll tell them what's what."
Then the warrior let them have it. "The flood of invective that poured
from the lips of that golden-haired child would have startled a dock-
worker," Yurka reported. "For a moment the men just stood there frozen
in astonishment, then took off and scuttled up the street. Mary grinned at
me as we went indoors. I felt a little like a St. Bernard being protected by
a barking poodle."

But if Blanche saw the heir to Grandmas Hennessey and Smith, she
also saw that a fear of humiliation lay like a sliver under Mary's skin. When
Pickford and several *Warrens* actors attended a tattered melodrama, Mary
sank into remembered agony. The Belasco troupe "made a kind of Roman
Holiday of the whole afternoon," laughing at the script "and, of course,
at the actors." There was, confessed Yurka, "a note of smug superiority in
our attitudes." When the play ended, Pickford turned on Yurka, sobbing.
"You were all just awful. Those actors were working just as hard to be convincing as any of you snobbish Broadway actors. I think you all behaved
dreadfully."

It was this lurking hurt and panic that prevailed when *The Warrens of
Virginia* wound its way back to New York and closed on March 20, 1909,
at the West End Theatre in Harlem. The Smiths had two hundred and fifty
dollars. Still, they felt rudderless. Tunis F. Dean, who had managed the
Warrens tour, told a reporter that "Belasco thinks the girl has a promising
future, and he's going to give her the chance to show what she can do."
Mary, in return, assured Belasco she would always be ready to act if he
needed her. But when would he need her? She was almost seventeen —
too old to play children, but a shade young to play ingenues. In a matter of
weeks, her spirits plunged. She was jittery, anxious, and prepared, for
Charlotte's sake, to try something "loathsome," "cheap," and "despised,"
something "worse than a come-down, complete disgrace" in order to scare
up some cash: the movies.

4

—

IN THE DARK STUDIO

Charlotte first suggested it. In March 1909 she was playing at Brooklyn's Majestic Theatre in another Chauncey Olcott show, *Ragged Robin*; it provided Jack and Lottie with bit parts, too. Several members of the cast had made a few dollars in flickers at Biograph, the leading film company in New York. There were scores of such studios across the country, many of them fly-by-night operations. Gradually a handful emerged on top, including Essanay in Chicago, Lubin in Philadelphia, and Edison and Vitagraph in New York. But Biograph led them all, because of the higher technical quality of its films and because of its resident director, D.W. Griffith, whose storytelling charmed the public and the critics.

Mary, faintly humiliated, felt obliged to contribute to the family cash flow. Films paid quick money – an easy five dollars a day, some said – but, as Mary knew, their reputation was dubious. Short films had entered vaudeville as early as 1896, and the nickelodeons by 1905. By 1907 there were ten thousand nickelodeons ("nickel" to indicate the price of admission and *odeon*, meaning theater in Greek) in the U.S., selling two million tickets a day. Most were converted storefronts, filled with chairs and hung with muslin or a sheet for a screen. A projection booth with tin walls stood at the back, and the lamp within heated it like a furnace. This setup and the lack of ventilation made most nickelodeons rank and fetid. Inside the booth the operator cranked the projector. Near the screen a violinist or piano player craned his neck to accompany films with urgent music that film actors called "the Russian hurries." Many of the viewers could not speak English. But they learned it, connecting the motions of the actors with written titles. To the millions of immigrants in New York alone, the silent movies were both a lesson and a welcome mat.

In fact, film opened a social floodgate. Vaudeville and Broadway were expensive, shutting out the lower class, who nevertheless could afford a flicker. Movies became fixtures of their social lives and created a cultural common ground. Chatty slides treated them like family: "A Woman Who Left a Baby Carriage Outside Is Wanted Immediately," "Lady, There's Someone Behind You, Will You Kindly Remove Your Hat," and, to apologize for the threadbare theater as well as to hint at the thrills in store, "Please Do Not Stamp, The Floor May Cave In." The films were colloquial and rose from the street. Some elements of melodrama lingered, but ideas also sprang from the newspaper, popular songs, and jokes. Viewers saw their New World neighbors – policemen, laundrywomen, mobsters, newsboys. They adored the flickers for the same reasons the upper class despised them: movies were fast, immediate, and crude. Detractors called movies "the galloping tintypes." Nevertheless, an editorial in *The Nation* recognized silent film's importance, calling flickers "A Democratic Art" and remarking that Tolstoy, the common man's champion, would have loved them. "They [the lower class] talk about them, on street corners, in the cars, and over the hoods of baby carriages. ... The crowd discusses the technique of the moving picture theatre with as much interest as literary salons in Paris or London discuss the minutiae of the higher drama."

Unlike the audience, actors thought flickers were low-down, freakish, and abnormal. And just as the middle class once regarded acting on the stage as common, a pecking order among performers now designated movie actors vulgar. Film acting seemed a fall from grace, a desperate choice for luckless actors, forced to advertise their failure. Film acting carried no aura of art. In fact, it was often described as "posing." Most actors would just as soon join a sideshow. Movie tickets were sold from a roll – exactly, performers pointed out, the way patrons bought tickets at the circus.

Charlotte broached the idea of film with care. "Would you be very much against applying for work at the Biograph Studios, Gladdie?"

"Oh no, not that, Mama!" cried Mary in panic.

"Well, now, it's not what I would want for you, either, dear," answered Charlotte. Then she played her trump card. "I thought if you could make enough money we could keep the family together. . . ."

Mary thought of tiny hands, waving goodbye.

"I'm sure," her mother continued smoothly, "it would make up for the lowering of our standard."

Mary agreed.

"It's only to tide us over," said Charlotte. "They say the pay is good . . . and besides," she added, sweetening the deal, "I'll let you wear your first silk stockings and high-heeled shoes."

The next day Mary emerged from the Smiths' flat on West 17th Street. She was wearing the grown-up shoes and stockings, as well as her best blue Easter suit and a $3.50 straw hat, finished off by Charlotte with a navy bow. Still, she felt snappish with resentment.

"How could Mama ask me to do this," thought Mary, as she made her way carefully in her new heels toward the Biograph office. "How could she ask me, a Belasco actress!"

Besides, she had humbled herself already. In 1907, when times were hard, she had ventured into the office of New York's Kalem. In those days exhibitors bought films by the foot, as if they were purchasing rolls of barbed wire. The typical one-reeler, a thousand feet, was about twelve minutes long and was marked frame by frame with the company trademark. Kalem stamped its films with the image of a rising sun, but its offices were decidedly down-at-heel. (Pickford, much to her disgust, stepped into a freight elevator, then scrambled up a ladder to the top of a warehouse.) Later that year Kalem stumbled on fame with its one-reel version of *Ben-Hur* – length: twelve minutes, chariot race included. But the firm let Mary Pickford slip through its net. The actress arrived, saw no one, and departed.

In Chicago Mary had called on Essanay ("S. and A.," for Spoor and Anderson, its founders). Essanay later hired Chaplin, who directed and starred in fourteen one-reel shorts. But in 1908 its low-rent image was reflected by its trademark: the head of the Indian chief that appeared on the one-cent coin. When *The Warrens of Virginia* visited the city, Mary and another child actress paid Essanay a visit. They found the entrance and dark stairs ominous – but perhaps they wanted an excuse to leave anyway. Clutching each other, the explorers fled, then stopped for breath at a nearby lunchroom. There, Mary saw several Essanay actors, still in their pallid movie makeup. She thought them ghoulish and, shuddering, turned away.

In 1908 she had even paid a call at the Biograph office, tonily located (for the raffish movies) in a brownstone on 14th Street, east of 5th Avenue. Pickford was seen by the young Gene Gauntier, one of film's earliest actresses, producers, and scenario writers. Gauntier "recorded the color of my hair, eyes, and that I could swim, but gave me no job," Mary wrote in 1923, the sting still fresh.

But nothing made movies seem more loathsome than Mary's experience at a Hale's Tour. The tour first appeared at the St. Louis Exposition in 1903, where it was a sideshow; then Hale, its inventor, put his hit on the road. When the *Fatal Wedding* company reached Chicago, the Smith children went to sample Hale's creation. They entered a long, narrow store on State Street that was made to resemble a railway car; the man who took their tickets played conductor. A jangling bell set Mary's teeth on edge, and she felt her seat shake. Soon the entire car was rocking, while footage shot from the back of a train showed quickly receding curves and landscapes. Mary felt her stomach lurch, but Jack and Lottie, who adored the experience, would run off, when money allowed, to a Hale's Tour or, better still, a nickelodeon. Mary thought this behavior degrading, as well as a waste of hard-earned cash. Hale's Tour left her feeling queasy, and she thought all films would do the same. As she "finally managed to stumble through the pitch darkness," past the Hale conductor, Mary swore she would never see another film – or anything by Hale ("that crude and truly awful thing").

If the movies were anyone's fault, they were Edison's. The American inventor made his name through the benign applications of electricity that revolutionized both industrial and domestic life in the late nineteenth and early twentieth centuries. Thomas Alva Edison patented more than a thousand inventions in his lifetime, including the phonograph, the microphone, and the incandescent electric lightbulb. But initially he showed no interest in the movies, or in efforts of previous engineers to animate photography with movement. He claimed he worked only for the dollar, and he considered the movies uncommercial. (Edison also saw no future for the airplane.)

But after an experiment by Eadweard Muybridge, Edison realized he was falling behind. In 1877 Muybridge proved by way of sequence photography that the hooves of a galloping horse would all be off the ground at once at some point in its stride. This famed strip of photos was obtained by running a horse before the Zoöpraxiscope – a machine that, in the simplest terms, resembled a series of twenty-four cameras. The cameras went off at split-second intervals, creating an image of simulated movement. A French professor, Étienne-Jules Marey, made a similar discovery; the problem now was to take a series of images with one camera.

William Kennedy Laurie Dickson, an impressively named engineer who worked for Edison, did the trick in 1892. Edison had commissioned him to make an amusement that was later dubbed the Kinetoscope – a half-ton cabinet resembling an icebox. Film ran in a continuous loop on sprockets while the viewer fixed his eye to a peephole. The film was perfected by George Eastman, best known as a founder of Eastman Kodak. Andrew Holland, an enterprising businessman from Canada, sensed the slot machine's potential and opened the world's first Kinetoscope parlor in a Broadway shoe store. There, for a span of less than twenty seconds, the viewer might glimpse trained bears, a strongman, a girl's pretty leg, or a vaudeville stunt. Edison and company made these cameos with a single camera in a tar-covered shack. Part of the roof rolled back to allow the sun to shed light on the performance, as solar illumination was essential. Actors were stubbornly unimpressed. Instead they developed contempt for those who cavorted on the Edison stage (called the "Black Maria," slang for paddy wagon) and ended up the size of a postage stamp, to be watched by strangers through a glorified keyhole.

Nevertheless, a worldwide effort began to free film from Kinetoscope's enclosure. Irascible Edison did not join; he opposed showing movies to more than one person at a time, convinced that the practice would cut into profits. But the vast potential of projected film was revealed in 1895, when Auguste and Louis Lumière unveiled their Cinématographe in Paris. The projector showed sixteen frames per second (which became the standard speed in the silents) down a beam of magical light – or so it seemed to its spellbound viewers, who watched it flow above their heads and pool into an image on a far-off screen. The Lumières showed a baby eating breakfast, workers departing from the Lumière factory, and fun with a garden hose. These were the world's first publicly projected films. The heavy camera stood in raw sunlight and recorded whatever passed before it. The result, little more than moving postcards, dazzled the Lumières' unschooled audience. Movements they took for granted in life – ripples on water, the quiver of leaves – appeared miraculous on film. The atmosphere crackled with shared emotion. Here was something Edison had missed: the communal experience of the movies. The Lumières made them a group experience, one that astonished and even frightened. During *The Arrival of a Train at a Station* (1896) viewers stirred uneasily when a train rolled toward them, preparing, so they thought, to burst through the screen.

America's first public film experience occurred in April 1896, through the Vitascope projector at Koster and Bial's, a music hall on West 34th Street in New York. (Today Macy's occupies the site.) Vitascope was "Edison's latest marvel." The inventor had finally been convinced of film's potential, and soon he built a full-scale production studio. That night the Vitascope attractions included the dancing Leigh sisters on a twenty-foot screen. These mini-documentaries were nicknamed "views." "The effect," raved the *New York Dramatic Mirror*, "was the same as if the girls were there on the stage; all of their smiles and kicks and bows were seen." Such comments underline respect for the camera as ingenious hardware; its creative potential was yet to be imagined. Later the program showed the sea at Dover, and critics behaved as though they had fallen down a rabbit hole. "Wave after wave came tumbling on the sand, and as they struck, broke into tiny floods just like the real thing," crowed the *Mirror*. "Some of the people in the front rows seemed to be afraid they were going to get wet, and looked about to see where they could run to, in case the waves came too close."

William Dickson, who had broken with Edison, was working on the

Mutoscope, inspired by his previous slot machine. It gave the Kinetoscope a run for its money with a similar peep show. Actors down on their luck appeared here; rumor has it that Jack and Lottie showed their talents on the Mutoscope. Dickson then made a rival to the Vitascope, a superior camera that produced larger, sharper images. He dubbed it the Biograph and used it to shoot views. In 1896 the American Mutoscope and Biograph Company – usually called "Biograph" – was born.

Biograph and other groups fed the hunger for sensation, with views of waterfalls, trains, and fires. Other views showed the passing scene – bicycles, streetcars, Ellis Island. Inevitably some favored sex and violence: an upturned lady revealing her petticoat, an elephant cruelly electrocuted. Then why did the craze for views suddenly vanish? After a year or two of wonder, they were used, ignominiously, as "chasers," shown between daily vaudeville shows as the crowd filed in and out, no longer spectacle but filler.

A filmmaker might have sensed the problem if he had spent a few moments with the audience. They were waiting, like children, for something to happen. Over the following several years, filmmakers learned, through trial and error, that film should not simply follow the world but call up a new one. Filmmakers needed to see the camera not as a technical trick but as a means toward an imaginative end. The end, they eventually found, was narrative.

D.W. Griffith did not spring fully formed into the void. A French magician named Georges Méliès popularized film narrative in five hundred mystic films, drenched in special effects and fancy. His best-known image – in *A Trip to the Moon* (1902) – shows a spaceship flying toward the lunar surface. The man in the moon looks down benignly until the spaceship plops in his eye. Méliès made his films tell stories just as one might see them on the stage, arranging his scenes as if stringing beads – each shimmeringly beautiful, yet separate and enclosed. The scenes proceeded, in stately fashion, like the illustrated pages of a fairy-tale book.

The point was not lost on Edwin S. Porter, a camera engineer and projectionist who made two little films in 1903: *The Life of an American Fireman* and *The Great Train Robbery*. Together these twenty-four minutes of celluloid changed the course of movie history.

Rather than observing action as though it were framed with a proscenium arch, Porter used different camera angles, changing distance and affecting the audience focus. *Fireman*, for instance, used a close-up of a fire alarm; *Robbery* added a pan shot, a moving camera placed atop a train, and primitive crosscutting of events. There was even a medium close-up, showing a mustachioed bandit aiming his gun and firing directly into the audience – still a spine-tingling moment. The shot exists for no other reason than to underline or symbolize the violence of this twelve-minute movie. *The Great Train Robbery* started a tradition in American films of realism, chase scenes, crime stories – even westerns, though *Robbery* was filmed in the thickets of New Jersey.

More important, Porter's rudimentary techniques ignited the imagination of an audience accustomed to the theater. "No longer are the protagonists confined within a lighted box," film scholar Iris Barry wrote in 1926. "No longer may we watch them only fixed at one point in space at a certain distance from us. On the screen the hero and heroine move freely in a vast unbounded world of what seems like fact." G.M. (Broncho Billy) Anderson, who acted in *The Great Train Robbery*, attended the movie's Manhattan premiere. "They all started to get boisterous, and yell and shouted 'Catch 'em! Catch 'em!' and different kinds of epithets, you know. And after the picture was over, they all stood up and shouted 'Run it again, run it again.' ... Finally they turned on the lights and they had to put them out." Anderson also watched the film as it played at Hammerstein's vaudeville house. "They sat there, stupefied. They didn't yell, but they were mystified by it. And after it was over, with one accord they gave it a rousing reception. I said to myself then, 'That's it. It's going to be the picture business for me.'" And it was: he went on to co-found Essanay. "The future has no end," exulted Anderson.

Sadly, Porter's influence waned. When he accomplished an innovation, he failed to explore its artistic potential. All the more reason to lament that in his following work (and Porter directed for twelve more years) innovations ceased and the daring mind behind *The Great Train Robbery* retreated.

Enter David Wark Griffith. He did not retreat. He had been groping for years toward a way to express his creative gifts, and when he married them to film, he gripped the medium with the power of a birthright.

Griffith was born in Kentucky in 1875. His early years instilled a craving to succeed along with a need for self-expression. In place of Charlotte, Griffith had "Roaring Jake," Jacob Wark, his soldier father. At age twenty-seven Jake had abandoned his medical practice to volunteer for the war in Mexico. In 1850 he left his wife of less than twenty months to join a wagon train and stake a claim for gold in California. He returned to the homestead two years later. And though Kentucky was not secessionist, Jake volunteered for the Confederacy in the Civil War and became the colonel of the state contingent. By all accounts he was a talented soldier – brave, even joyful in the field. But Jake found peacetime emasculating. In his own mind, he shone when cast in some grandiose adventure. He could not exorcise his bravado, nor his restless energy, back on the farm with wife and children. In midlife, crippled in one arm, Jake reflected bitterly on his losses, giving David a sense of destiny cut short. Meanwhile the family fortune crumbled. The Griffith homestead, Lofty Green, survived the war but burned to the ground a few weeks later. It left behind a carriage road, edged by double poplars. The road led nowhere.

Griffith was touched by the beauties of his childhood. He recalled a moment as a tiny boy, gathering dewberries in a pail. He found larks "soaring up and down ... singing ecstatically in the clear spring morning. In memory, I always seem to see around this entire scene a luminous glow of joy. As I walked, it seemed that my bare feet hardly touched the ground." Or, in the winter: "There is snow on the ground. Vision [sic] an old schoolhouse, a very small one. On the eaves of its windows icicles glitter in the light of lanterns held by groups of farmers." Jake and David entered the building to view another kind of lantern – a magic one, the harbinger of movies. Magic lanterns began in the seventeenth century as primitive slide shows, and through the centuries they developed many forms, filled with shifting images and light. For Griffith, the lantern may have displayed a few painted scenes, rendered in delicate, opaque colors. Perhaps a moon rose over a seascape. Whatever the picture, it spoke in images – not words – and formed a beckoning light in darkness. Presciently, the future director imagined a creative form that recalled experience through intangibles. "What a grand invention it would be if someone could make a magic box in which we could store the precious moments of our lives and keep them with us ... and later on, in dark hours could open this box and receive for at least a few moments a breath of its stored memory."

Jake passed many traits to his eager son, who remained in the soldier's thrall for a lifetime. When Griffith was young, his father recited romantic poems and passages of Shakespeare to the older children. David, supposedly in bed, once sat hidden beneath a table, spellbound. Later, as a lonely teen, David found solace in Tolstoy, Browning, Hardy, and Dickens. At age twenty-one he became an actor, though he also nursed literary ambitions. His dramatic talent was apparently hambone, but Griffith found roles in the usual chestnuts and finally hit bottom in the ten-twent'-thirt's. He had ugly memories of the flophouse. At other times, Griffith scraped rust from the subway, picked hops, and shoveled iron ore – miserable work that, he claimed, built his character.

In 1904 Griffith met an actress named Linda Arvidson while appearing in a play in San Francisco. They met again the next year in Los Angeles. She listened while Griffith read her poems. "No one else among his associates seemed interested," remembered actress Florence Auer. But Linda made up for that, eyes aglow. She and Griffith were married in 1906. The groom's ambition and Linda's belief in him kept the marriage going through humiliating times. And Griffith's memoirs of this period indicate an almost jazzy resilience. His sense of destiny was ironclad, and he wore poverty in style. When an important contact, an editor, visited Griffith's New York apartment, the couple had labeled the flat for his safety (and also, perhaps, in the hope of a handout): "Don't lean [on this table]; the legs are loose." "Do not sit here; the springs are weak."

Griffith was inventive; there was joy in battle. He took up arms and wrote by the hour. The tide seemed to turn when, in 1907, his poem "The Wild Duck" appeared in the magazine *Leslie's Weekly*. ("Ah me! but the wind soon changes in these parts. / Ah me! Ah me!") Griffith was overwhelmed. "The world was full of words" and each had a price tag. "The Wild Duck" paid him a grand six dollars. *A Fool and a Girl*, a play by Griffith, opened that year at Ford's Theatre in Washington; most of the play's reviews were scathing.

Finally Griffith's friends advised him to apply for acting work in the movies. In December 1907 he performed as an extra in Biograph's *Professional Jealousy* – easy money, so Griffith cast his net a bit wider: he wrote an outline of *La Tosca* and took it to the Edison studio in the Bronx. In those days not all films used scenarios. Some were purely off-the-cuff. Others might be *on* a cuff, a napkin, or a playing card – a casual graph meant to indicate structure. But when the director required a breakdown, scene by scene, the author received from five to thirty dollars for his efforts.

Edison passed on *Tosca*. But the studio didn't entirely pass on Griffith and cast him in a film called *Rescued from an Eagle's Nest* (1908), a one-reel adventure in which a bird of prey makes off with an infant. Griffith played a mountaineer who climbs to the eagle's nest and fights the predator for the child. Griffith's work is jerky and stiff. He and the eagle perform at par, and the eagle was simulated by a stuffed bird. But the Edison studio seemed pleased and chose him again for *Cupid's Pranks* (1908). Meanwhile Griffith made more inroads at Biograph and moved up to become a director in June 1908, when an unexpected gap occurred in the staff. Then everything changed, as the young man's previously misapplied talents were aligned in the right way with the art he would instinctively transform.

"What happened within the next few years," wrote critic Arthur Knight, "is probably without parallel in the emergence of any art form." Critic James Agee was equally fervent: "To watch [Griffith's] work is like being witness to the beginning of melody, or the first conscious use of the lever or the wheel; the emergence, coordination, and first eloquence of language; the birth of an art." In fact, the techniques once attributed to Griffith, such as close-ups, fade-outs, and many others, were in use already. Then why did it seem, to many scholars, as if Griffith had invented them?

Because he had mastered them so completely. Griffith synthesized all that had gone before him and showed film's breathtaking possibilities. In Griffith's hands, silent film perfected a new way of signaling narrative thought, a code called film "grammar" or "syntax." In a similar metaphor, one may imagine that Griffith was the first director to make film's half-realized techniques – the letters of the alphabet – into words. Before Griffith made this celluloid language, most films followed life through the eye, rather than as understood by the mind. Scenes, in imitation of those onstage, had a beginning and an end. But Griffith made scenes that were incomplete. The edited shots fused into meaning, as well as action, in the viewers' minds. In this way the audience followed the narrative of images not as they appeared in nature but as the camera and mind arranged them.

At first some audiences resisted. The *New York Dramatic Mirror* complained of Griffith's *The Seventh Day* (1909): "Changes in scenes from one location to another are effected too suddenly. The characters leave the mother's parlor and immediately appear in the judge's chamber and vice versa, giving the impression that they are adjoining rooms, or at least in the same house." About an intuitive jump in *After Many Years* (1908), a Biograph executive objected: "How can you tell a story jumping about like that? The people won't know what it's about." Griffith, unperturbed, replied, "Doesn't Dickens write that way?" "Yes, but that's Dickens; that's novel writing; that's different." "Oh, not so much," replied the rebel director. "These are picture stories; not so different."

Long, panned, and tilted shots created context and a point of view, while close-ups of faces, trembling hands, or a frayed garment generated sympathy, fear, or tension. With each technique – be it changing the shape of the screen through an iris, deepening focus with foreground, middle ground, and background, or rhythmically cutting the film between plot-lines – Griffith gave the movies the tension of drama, the complexity of fiction, and the beauty of painting. Film came to resemble, like no other art form, the flow of life.

If someone had told Mary Pickford that she was approaching the greatest filmmaker of her age – or perhaps of any age – she would not have cared. She intended to make short work of Biograph and spend the balance of the day in Broadway's theatrical offices. There, she believed, lay fame and fortune. And perhaps she had seen, reflected in the window of the Biograph premises, the sign of the company across the street. It read "Singer Sewing Center," a ghastly reminder of her plan to be a seamstress.

The Biograph brownstone had once been the home of a fashionable bachelor. But little survived of its former glory, though the floor was marble and a circular staircase wound lazily upward. Biograph had moved there in 1903 and constructed a studio in the ballroom. The Biograph bean counters crammed the lobby, and film editors, engineers, actors, and cameramen jostled elsewhere. The basement, for instance, once featured dressing rooms, film developing facilities, the wardrobe, and what Griffith "laughingly called the prop department." As for Griffith, who had become the operation's raison d'être, he didn't have an office he could call his own; sometimes his desk could be found in the hallway, at other times it was cluttered with props in the studio.

He was at this desk (location unknown) considering a film of "Pippa Passes" when Pickford came calling. In the preceding year, Griffith had filmed *The Taming of the Shrew* as well as two Jack London stories, hoping a bit of cultural cachet would improve film's image with the critics. "Pippa," a poem by Robert Browning, was then widely read. The title character, ragged and ethereal, walks with her mandolin till dusk through a pastoral scene: "God's in his heaven – / All's right with the world!" With this, Pippa passes. She has no idea of her effect on others. In fact, her elusive, spiritual beauty is such that she transforms the life of every character who hears her.

Spiritual beauty was a passion with Griffith. About the time of Mary's arrival, he was starting to introduce a new strain of female grace to the screen – fragile, delicate women, filmed on the cusp between adolescence and womanhood. His ideal sprang from the willowy women whose image competed in the nineteenth century with the rounder Lillian Russell genre. Griffith favored the ethereal woman – or, in his hands, the child-woman. She had flowing hair and a doelike expression. Her predecessors haunt Botticelli's *Primavera*, the art of Burne-Jones, and Tennyson's poetry. Oscar Wilde described her image when he wrote of actress Ellen Terry: "She stands with eyes marred by the mists of pain, / Like some wan lily overdrenched with rain."

Griffith's attraction to such women would complicate his personal life, but for casting it was practical. In 1909, sixteen or seventeen was the right age to enter movies and do well. The primitive light of film production was cruel to skin, and layers of makeup failed to shield it. "Deep lines on the face of a girl are almost fatal to good screening," wrote Griffith, "for on the screen her face is magnified twenty times, and every wrinkle assumes the proportions of the Panama Canal." At one time Biograph sent to an orphanage for a three-week-old infant for use in a close-up. Griffith took one look and returned the infant, with a note: "Please send us a young-looking baby. This one photographs like an old man."

Griffith's ingenues, though petal-fresh, had wills of steel. They lived by simple, eccentric logic. The result could be touching or oddly humorous, whichever the director wished. Griffith saw Pippa as one of these nymphs – bypassing the humor, in this case – and when he met Pickford he had not yet decided who should play the role.

Mary, who had hoped to make her visit short, was waiting impatiently in the lobby. This is when Robert Harron saw her. Harron, the prop boy, was turning fifteen – just the age to notice women. He hurried up to Griffith and told the director, through a mouth full of chewing gum, that "a good-looker" was in the lobby.

"All my life," wrote Griffith later, "I have been accused of being a devoted admirer of the opposite sex and somewhat of a connoisseur of feminine pulchritude." Now, to amuse himself, he trimmed his sawtooth collar and sauntered offhandedly into the lobby, making his appearance through a swinging door.

"Too jaunty and familiar for my taste," thought Pickford.

Indeed, he dispensed with all formalities. "Are you an actress?"

"I most certainly am," answered Pickford, offended by Griffith's bald beginning. He towered over her, but Mary was used to looking up and did so now, unintimidated. She saw a tall man with a hawklike nose, balanced by fine eyes and a wide mouth. His voice was a Southern baritone. Griffith, like David Belasco before him, seemed to find her confidence funny.

"What, if any, experience have you had, may I ask?"

"Only ten years in the theater, sir, and two of them with David Belasco."

"Small, cute figure," Griffith thought. "Golden curls . . . creamy complexion . . . sparkling Irish eyes – eyes with languorous capabilities. . . ."

But what he actually said, according to Mary, was, "You're too little and too fat."

Griffith, like Harron, was taken with Pickford, whose face seemed to move from round good humor to unsettling beauty. Her hazel eyes held a melancholy sweetness. Her bones were fine, her build small. Her back fairly dripped with springing curls. She stood up proudly on size-five shoes; the longest finger on her hand was two and a half inches. Yet she spoke with the aim of a torpedo.

"Well, Miss – "

"Miss Pickford is the name – Mary Pickford."

"Well, Miss Pickford, I think you'll do," said Griffith, in an exception-ally quick decision. "We'll take you on trial and guarantee three days' work each week at $5 a day, and if we should need you more often, we'll pay $5 for each extra day."

"Well, Mr. Griffit – "

"The name is Griffith."

"Well, Mr. Griffith, you must realize that I'm an actress. I have had important parts with Mr. Belasco on the *real* stage."

Mary made no headway with this one; Griffith heard this refrain every day from actors. "I'm an actress and an artist," Pickford continued, "and I must have a guarantee of $25 a week and extra when I work extra."

"Boy!" remembered Griffith. "When that little girl talked up that twenty-five bucks, her eyes fairly gleamed." He told her he would men-tion her proposal to the board.

"Pompous and insufferable," thought Pickford. Still, she could not turn her back on cash. Besides, she had worked herself into a tizzy and wished to show this inferior creature the brilliance of a Belasco actress. But after Griffith whisked her to the women's dressing room, told her to wait, and disappeared, Pickford's anger turned to mounting panic. She looked round the dangerously empty room; a shelf, some porcelain bowls, a heater. For the first time in years she felt afraid. Mary was a private person who used stage decorum to determine her behavior. She knew what to do in the theater world, where she could control other people, or at least practice self-control. At Biograph she saw chattering actors brush past Griffith and call him "D.W." behind his back. She thought this shockingly disrespectful (though Mary herself had shown disrespect) and almost slovenly personal relations.

Worse, she felt sexually vulnerable. A woman who engaged in films, even more than an actress on the stage, was thought to be "easy," and sev-eral studios fought the image. "Mr." and "Miss" were the order of the day; presumably such salutations raised the social tone of the labor. The Vitagraph company went so far as to eliminate couches from the premises so virgins need not fear seduction. In contrast, Griffith addressed his prin-cipals by surnames; he rarely used "Mr." or "Miss" unless he was making a joke, or angry. And Pickford would have cringed to know that a shadowy

Biograph accountant once cozied up to the female extras by letting them keep silk stockings from the wardrobe. (The sinister Mr. Waite was fired.) Now, as she waited alone for Griffith, Pickford's imagination ran wild, as if she had already been seduced – if not by a man, then by film itself, and by the mere act of walking to the heart of a studio.

Suddenly Griffith reappeared and announced he would prepare her for a screen test. Without further comment, he applied her makeup. Pickford, seeing her white face and pitch-black brows in the mirror, was horrified – she looked like the actors she had seen at Essanay. Next she explored the "wardrobe," a trunk and steel rack in the cellar. Actors often wore their own clothes in film, but Biograph also supplied some dresses – found in secondhand stores and pawnshops, fumigated, pinned, and altered. These, in due time, soaked up the fumes of developing chemicals. All of these aromatic outfits were too long for Mary, who hastily yanked a hem up. Thus prepared, she joined the others who were gathered in the studio.

A few years earlier, it might have been a rooftop. Before moving to the brownstone, Biograph filmed on top of its building on lower Broadway. The practice ensured hard, even light. Actors – those who didn't fear heights – worked on this precarious stage in front of painted canvas flats, sometimes rented from a vaudeville house, that shuddered dangerously in the wind. They stared over chimneys as they acted and ignored the breeze that played havoc with curtains and tablecloths. Sometimes a bird flew through the shot. The Biograph camera was better protected than the performers; it stood in a shed of corrugated iron that dwarfed the creative team before it.

Instead, Mary entered what was probably the movies' first "dark" studio – a room that firmly shut out sunlight and called up a Hallowe'en all its own. Mary saw figures in semi-darkness, stepping through jumbles of rolled-up carpets, furniture, and flats. Banks of mercury-vapor lamps provided illumination for the camera. Their glass tubes stood on the floor in stands or hung from the ceiling on wires, leaning dangerously near the actors. Arc lights with metal hoods clustered at the ceiling, emptying blue-white tunnels on heads. Beneath this narrow color spectrum, the chatting actors resembled zombies. And the heat was volcanic – menacing, searing, like a hot plate.

For Pickford's screen test, Griffith instructed the group to improvise

"Pippa." He failed to introduce Pickford to the actors, which she chalked up as another insult. The group knew the plot; if not, Griffith told them. Indeed, no one cared if they knew the text; reproducing dialogue hardly mattered. An average viewer saw actors speak phrases: "Yes!" "Okay!!" "I love you!" "God!" Lip-readers sometimes caught obscenities, and flat-footed prose replaced blank verse. Extras, for instance, winged their way through a silent *Macbeth* with: "To arms, men! We'll slaughter the lousy buzzards!"

Now Griffith outlined Pickford's role. Mary absorbed it, despite the camera aimed in her direction. The machine stood about five feet tall on its platform and weighed three hundred pounds. Its lens bore a startling resemblance to an eye — a lurid, strangely protruding eye, which reminded the uneasy actress of a Cyclops.

Suddenly there was a hush from the actors — at last a custom Mary recognized — followed by a deafening jolt from the camera, which spit out sprocket holes as it filmed. The noise, which was constant, resembled a blend of spitting cat, machine gun, and thresher. Pickford, startled, felt as though she'd met a firing squad — and realized that the test was on.

She struggled gamely with her instructions — unfortunately, she never described them, only her humiliation trying to perform them. Presumably Pippa would pass by several groups of actors — graceful, dancelike, a spring in her step — qualities difficult to capture when one feels embarrassed and displaced. To make matters worse, Pickford had to play guitar — which she didn't — and sing, which she did, but not unless asked to by Chauncey Olcott. As Mary awkwardly passed a group — trying not to bash into a rack of lights while strumming, singing, and looking happy, "the floor kept going up and down in waves." Finally an actor muttered, "Who's the dame?"

Not only was Pippa not a "dame," Mary Pickford (who understood the word to mean "loose woman") was not a dame. She lashed out furiously at the actor with the pent-up frustration of the day: "How dare you, sir, insult me? I'll have you understand I'm a perfectly respectable young girl, and don't you dare call me a bad name!"

"With that," reported Mary, "Mr. Griffith let out a roar that would have done the M.G.M. lion credit. 'Miss . . . Miss . . . what the devil is your name? But no matter . . . Never, do you hear, never stop in the middle of a scene. Do you know how much film costs per foot? [Two cents, at the time.] You've ruined it! Start from the beginning!'"

Armed with the knowledge that "dame" meant different things to different people (the actor protested he had meant no harm), Mary tried the scene again. Later in the day she performed a walk-on in *What Drink Did*, suggested by the stage play *Ten Nights in a Barroom*. Apparently Pickford's scene was later cut. It was eight in the evening when she finished, retreated to the dressing room, and scrubbed off her makeup as though she could wash the whole experience away. Then a thunderstorm, showing fine dramatic instincts, entered the Manhattan area. The drama continued when Mary emerged from the dressing room and found her director lurking in the hallway, armed with a smile and an umbrella. "Will you dine with me?" he asked.

Nothing made sense to Pickford now. "I'm sorry, Mr. Griffith, I've never dined with any boy, let alone a man, and besides I have to leave immediately for Brooklyn. My mother and sister are playing there with Mr. Olcott."

Griffith pressed her. "Will you come back tomorrow?" Mary was again nonplussed. She judged herself according to her work, and she believed her work had been ignominious. "I knew it in my heart," she wrote later. "I knew whether a performance was good or bad. Mine that day ... was distinctly bad." Still, out of sheer nerve, she told him she required ten dollars a day. Griffith laughed and, this time, relented. He agreed that she would receive five dollars for the day's work and ten for the next day – extraordinary lenience from a director who opposed special salaries and vigilantly watched his group for growth of star plumage. (In fact, the next week, he bartered Mary down from ten dollars a day to a guarantee of forty dollars weekly.)

"Keep it to yourself," he advised her. "There will be a riot if it leaks out." Pickford took a voucher for her day's work to the studio cashier. Then, with Griffith striding beside her with his umbrella, she set off toward the subway. There he abruptly bid her farewell – "Till tomorrow at nine sharp" – and disappeared.

A few minutes later Pickford emerged at her Brooklyn subway stop without a coat. Soon the proud blue bow was dripping, and even the five-dollar bill was drenched.

D.W. Griffith had hurt her that day – questioned her talent, damaged her pride, and mocked her hard-won Broadway credentials – and Mary was angry and demoralized. She also believed he had harassed her. He had not touched her sexually but he had intruded himself in another personal place: her art, or the pretty performances she called art. Pickford had sensed throughout her screen test that translating stage acting onto celluloid demanded a sea change in technique. Few shared this insight as lucidly, in 1909 or for many years after. And the insight raised a glimmer, a new direction for ambition. Pickford liked to be excellent – first, not second, not third, and not last, as she feared she must have seemed to the Biograph actors. Bewildered, she lost her footing and landed in a puddle on her rear. She got up and sloshed on, lost in thought.

At the Majestic, she found the family dressing room and waited for Charlotte – still wet, still thinking. When Charlotte entered the room, she shrieked, stripped off her daughter's clothes, and laid them – and the precious bill – out to dry.

"They're going to pay me ten dollars a day from tomorrow on," Mary told her, shivering.

"You see," said her mother, "I was right after all, dear."

Mary didn't answer. But if she returned – and return she must – she would tussle screen acting to the ground.

5

—

THE BIOGRAPH GIRL

The next day, April 20, 1909, when Pickford rolled out of bed, she was "never so reluctant to rise in my life." She showed her contempt for the movies by refusing to waste a nickel on the streetcar. Then she marched off to change the course of an art form.

She spent the day at Biograph in the background, appearing as an extra in *Her First Biscuits* (1909), a comedy starring Florence Lawrence. A year before, Lawrence had emerged from the blur of screen performers through her work at Vitagraph. This was an accomplishment as, at most companies, film actors' names were not released to the press or displayed onscreen until 1910. (Biograph waited until 1913.) Producers believed that stressing actors, rather than the studio seal of quality, would lead to escalating salaries and give performers the whip hand in the industry. But Lawrence had a vivid, buoyant presence, and viewers began to fixate on her. "That girl was simply out of sight," wrote P.C. Lever to the *Moving Picture World*. "She simply took the rag right off." In 1908 Griffith staged a raid, offering Lawrence a ten-dollar raise; she was making fifteen dollars a week at Vitagraph. She gratefully jumped ship and made an even greater splash at Biograph. Fans, with no other name at their disposal but yearning to lay claim to their favorite, began to call her "the Biograph Girl" — an honor that would later pass to Pickford.

Lawrence, a Canadian from Hamilton, Ontario, came from the gesticulating stage; she was once "Baby Flo, the Child Wonder Whistler." But she partially shook its effects in movies. Stage acting strikes a false note on film, and the turn-of-the-century manner sometimes surfaces in early silents. Until 1907 many films were still made without directors. In the meantime cameramen reigned supreme, and they put film's emphasis on mechanics. When directors appeared, they guided body traffic, not performance. "There was no coaching for the acting," remembered Linda Arvidson. "Only one thing mattered, and that was, not to appear as though hunting frantically for the lines on the floor that marked your stage while the scenes were being taken."

Some odd traditions were de rigueur. "Will you gentlemen never learn," producer Charles Pathé once lectured his directors, "that in the cinema an actor must be photographed so that his feet touch the bottom of the screen and his head the top." Conventional wisdom ruled that the viewer, who paid a nickel for the privilege, deserved to see every inch of the actor. A close-up would have been thought a cheat, as well as gross dismemberment. Dutifully, directors told their cameramen to film performers full-length and full-front — and the phrase "full-front" became the actor's byword. An actress fleeing a gunman might move from the front of a table to the back by dashing sideways, running backward, then swooping her body sideways again. Other actors seemed to be moving under water, as filmmakers thought that viewers could register only so much action at a blink. Obligingly, actors in the background made their movements large and lugubrious, and, as on the stage, they held poses for emphasis.

Erratic projection speeds and shutters made film images jump and twitch. An actor — such as the struggling D.W. Griffith — might assume such frenzy was intentional. He diligently copied what he saw, and the results amazed even his contemporaries. "One day," wrote Biograph cameraman Billy Bitzer, "I was called on the carpet for having allowed [Griffith] to be photographed in such a manner that he seemed to have three or four arms instead of the usual two.... The second time I encountered him, he overacted the part of a bartender ... I asked him if he was trying to get me fired, or wasn't he aware his mugging was taking the action away from the lead?" Griffith told Bitzer that a friend had advised him to act this way. He also sought advice about becoming a director. "I advised him against it," wrote Bitzer flatly, "for I couldn't see how a man who wasn't a passable actor could direct a flock of geese."

Only one stage tradition proved a model for silent-film acting. Eleonora Duse, born in 1858, was an actress of singular approach and spirit. Many reviews of the Italian diva describe a technique that finally surfaced in the silents. They also read like slaps at Bernhardt, whose histrionic self-display seemed suddenly dated. Duse did not admire herself along with the audience, nor introduce flourishes for their own sake. Her gestures were all the more rich for their simplicity. In 1892 an Austrian critic compared Duse's work in *A Doll's House* with the generalized signals of the histrionic style: "[Duse] plays only what is individual; we experience what is universal." Her effect was still felt in the 1920s, when Charlie Chaplin took a turn as a critic and reviewed Duse in *La porta chiusa*, a play in which Duse's character reacts when her son reveals that he knows he is illegitimate. "An actress of lesser genius would have torn this emotion absolutely to tatters. Duse sank into a chair and curled up her body almost like a little child in pain. You did not see her face; there was no heaving of the shoulders. She lay quietly almost without moving. Only once through her body ran a sort of shudder of pain like a paroxysm. That and the instinctive shrinking of her body from her son's outstretched hand were almost the only visible movement."

Simple, acutely observed behavior became the standard for silent-screen acting, and Griffith, whose perspective changed when he moved from the front to the back of the camera, was one of its earliest proponents. In 1910 the *New York Dramatic Mirror* declared, "People in the pictures now move about somewhat after the style of human beings, instead of jumping jacks." After crediting Biograph with the innovation, the *Mirror* remarked that at first the practice seemed "nothing short of sacrilege." Apparently producers feared that "attempts to introduce real acting into the films would be met with derisive laughter. Possibly to their astonishment the change at once met with the approval of the public." With the words "real acting" the *Mirror* critic referred to the subtler Broadway style as opposed to the wretched excess of the road. By praising this, critics hoped to give movies snob appeal and lure the middle class into the cinema. But film was not groping toward theatrical standards where, even on Broadway, actors did not imitate reality but produced an imaginative parallel to it. Film found its own creative imperatives, requiring that the actor hold a mirror up to nature.

Yet gesture was needed to clarify action, as film disallowed the luxury of speech. This was a conundrum. After all, the maxim "less is more" works at cross-purposes with narrative signals such as "murder" (drawing a finger across the throat) or "hanging" (simulating a noose). In this language, women announced pregnancy by knitting booties. Indeed, the silent actor's hands were second in importance only to his face. Covered with chalk so they would catch the light, hands fluttered, pointed, outlined objects, struck the forehead in resignation, or settled, trembling, on a beating heart. But as the medium developed, mime was done more subtly, with conviction. And the element of music helped the fusion. Silent films were never shown in silence. The interplay between live performance (the pianist, the organist, perhaps an orchestra) and the movie itself was uniquely kinetic. The result was acting that combined realistic and symbolic styles with as much con-viction as a narrative ballet.

Unfortunately, Griffith – who championed acting-through-the-eyes – preferred extreme behavior in hayseed and villain roles, a leaning shared by other silent-film directors. As well, he insisted that a "Gaga-baby" – a phrase thought up by Lillian Gish to describe his ideal ingenue – perform what Gish called the "St. Vitus dance," a kind of hopping about and squealing designed to illustrate naive youth. "How else," he asked her, "can I get the contrast between you and older people, if you don't jump around like a frisky puppy?" To show what he wanted, "he would get up and hop about, shaking his balding head as if it had a wig of curls. A stranger would have thought him mad."

Consequently, Griffith's early Biographs show some actors working with economy, others who gallivant and gape, and some who flit between approaches. Comic material – particularly farce – poses special problems. Not every actor can master comedy, just as not all are at home in tragedy. Both forms demand stylization and are aided by distance from the audi-ence. Film eliminates the distance, leaving the actor with (for some) an insoluble problem: how to work both broadly and minutely.

Her First Biscuits was a farcical anecdote and showed the troupe succumbing to their broadest instincts. Florence Lawrence plays a newlywed fussing about the stove. Brimming with pride, she brings a tray of home-baked biscuits to her husband (John R. Cumpson). Aware that the eyes of his bride are upon him, Cumpson chews approvingly. Lawrence runs rapturously from the room and Cumpson, who has found the biscuits disgusting, gags and leaves hurriedly for work. But Lawrence sneaks a bag of her treats into the lounge of Cumpson's place of business, a theatrical booking office. There the Biograph troupe, playing unemployed (therefore ravenous) actors, sample them as they exchange career notes. Each does a usually overwrought turn in which he delineates his character and nibbles. Each, of course, becomes violently ill. Pickford slips in as a child actress. She lacks a scene in which she reaches for a biscuit, but stumbles into the connecting sickroom, clutching alternately her stomach and her hat. She is usually hidden by the others, who are writhing, staggering, and showing off for dear life. Indeed, her role is minuscule, one that any tiny actress might have played. But Pickford had been singled out, and every actor working in the movie knew it.

No one was too good for the stitched-over, secondhand clothes of the company wardrobe. But before the cameras rolled, Griffith had told his wife, "Buy this child a linen and lace dress, size ten, and shoes, socks, and hat to match for the role she's going to play." No doubt Arvidson raised an eyebrow, for there was more to this than even the actors knew.

When Griffith became a film director, he and Linda decided to conceal their marriage. This was useful: his image as a bachelor enhanced his aura of artist and maverick, and his hidden connection to Arvidson sidestepped charges of nepotism. There were other advantages, in Griffith's view, for he was often attracted to his ingenues; "it is not one, but many," he would later tell his wife of his liaisons. And his attraction to Pickford had been strong and instant; his indulgent surrender to her first demand for money, his invitation to dinner and the walk to the subway, her resemblance to his ideal child-woman — all reveal not only a director's instincts but more personal interests (which would fade with time).

It must have been an interesting shopping trip, with Linda befriending the apple of her husband's eye, and Pickford sensing a certain reserve in Linda. Eventually the two women found a dress that, Mary wrote, "cost all of $10.50. If I had had any doubt before, I had absolutely none now that the picture industry was mad." Yet the madness infected her. She found *Her First Biscuits* "less irksome" than her screen test – so much less that she planned to leave her mark at Biograph. Watching others perform had probably fired her up with such thoughts as "I can do that" or more likely, "I can do that better than you can." Always covetous of dressing rooms, Mary quickly checked out the Biograph facilities. Twenty-five actresses shared one room with a narrow dressing table down the middle. Those with seniority and who were, by inference, better actresses, applied their makeup on one side. On the other side were new recruits or, as Mary called them, the "lesser persons." Despite her lifelong sympathy for under-dogs, Pickford had decided she would not be among them in the movies. "From the first day," she artlessly remarked, "[it was] my ambition to get on the other side."

She had hit the ground running. As she left the brownstone that day, Griffith stopped her. "Will you play the lead tomorrow?" Pickford, no doubt waiting for the question, almost turned a somersault: "Why, yes, sir!" The relationship would be filled with moments like this one, and others of a more loaded kind – taunting, even hostile. Now Griffith floored her with a question so personal, so invasive, that it took her breath away. He asked her what she knew about making love.

In 1909 the term "making love" meant ardent but modest expressions of courtship – holding hands, compliments, flirtation. In Mary's day these were daring actions. "I was fifteen years old," she remembered tensely (in reality, seventeen), but she still had not dated nor kissed a boy. After "several inaudible gulps" she assured her director that she knew all the ways of making love.

Griffith, perversely, flagged down a prop man who was carrying a papier-mâché pillar down the hallway. "All right, Pickford, make love to that pillar." Mary was incredulous: she would have to put her arms around the pole, brush it with her cheek, and adoringly caress it. She scrambled toward a dignified exit. How, she pleaded, could she make love to an unre-sponsive pillar? Griffith immediately raised the stakes. Owen Moore, the actor who had insulted Pickford by calling her a "dame," appeared in the hallway from the men's dressing room. Griffith called him over and directed him to stand a few feet from Mary. "Miss Pickford doesn't like to make love to a lifeless pillar," he told the puzzled actor. "See if she can do any better with you."

Mary, who blushed to the roots of her hair, called the moment "sickening" but tried to make the best of a demeaning job. "I made up my mind right then and there that there would be no kissing," she wrote primly. Kissing in public was "vulgar in the extreme and completely unnecessary in the theater, where one could pretend." Griffith told Moore drily, "Miss Pickford has had a great deal of experience." In terms of love and acting, "there is little we can tell her."

The actress took a deep breath, sidled up to Moore, and clung to him, murmuring "I love you" with her head bowed. Griffith rearranged the embrace and pressed Mary's nose into the wilds of Moore's suit. Pickford, who was much shorter than Moore, looked tenderly compliant, and Griffith liked her maidenly embarrassment. He assured her, "After ten years of life and rehearsal you should be able to do a love scene very well," and Pickford, thoroughly mortified, flew home. But she turned up next day, wound a peasant shawl round her curls, and successfully carried off a love scene in her second film, *The Violin Maker of Cremona* (1909).

In this Italian costume piece, two eligible bachelors, Filippo and Sandro, compete to make the superior instrument. The prize: a gold chain – and Giannina (Pickford). Taking her cue from her director, Mary referred to her role as the lead. In fact, she plays a supporting part; the moral center of the piece belongs to David Miles as Filippo. He is the best violin maker in Cremona and loves Giannina, according to the Biograph *Bulletin*, a publicity sheet for exhibitors, with a love "more spiritual than material." In keeping with his elevated feelings, Filippo, who knows that Giannina loves Sandro, places his instrument in Sandro's box to ensure that his rival will win the contest.

When Pickford is told about the competition that threatens to divide her from her true love, she brings the back of her hand to her forehead and falls to her knees. In another scene, she executes a "freeze" when David Miles declares his love, holding him at arm's length for several seconds. This movement grows from stage tradition: the physically extended gesture sweeping the air with great emotion. Pickford would later reject such signals. But their presence in *The Violin Maker of Cremona* suggests how she may have worked on stage – Giannina, after all, was her first role of any size since Broadway. And she does it well, holding back just enough for the viewer to tolerate the melodrama. One can imagine the alarm that turns the girl's blood to ice, and the panic that shocks her into fleeting paralysis.

Just as intriguing is watching Pickford begin the transformation from stage to movie actress. At moments in *The Violin Maker* she seems to inhabit, not perform, her character. The process of such immersion is mysterious. Emotion springs from inner stillness rather than flamboyant, overwrought displays. Audiences found the stage equivalent in Duse: "A sobriety of speech and movement. . . . A glance, a gesture, a silence – and the state of her soul appears to the public in its true light." Griffith tried to describe the same effect on film: "It isn't what you do with your face or hands," he explained to *Photoplay* in 1918. "*It's the light within.*"

Such phrases are ephemeral, but in this era (decades before Method brought self-analysis – some would say self-indulgent analysis – to acting) actors lacked a vocabulary to express their inner process. "The art of [film] acting is at once very simple – and altogether impossible," said Griffith, and indeed, as crystallized by Pickford, acting for the camera removed every weapon of the stage actor's arsenal while adding an unprecedented intimacy.

She could lapse, on occasion, into stagy gestures, particularly during her first year with Griffith. But she gradually peeled them all away, and in time outpaced the other Biograph actors in the new, quiet style of observation. As an actress, she approached the camera simply and directly. Her effect was immediate. Watching her, viewers felt exposed, as if by sunburn, to unguarded emotion. Pickford could look through the lens with utter candor, reflecting the view, again attributed to Griffith, that the movie camera photographs an actor thinking. Pickford's thoughts passed across her face like shadows, and she let them speak for her, forcing nothing. It was this riveting self-revelation, combined with a palpable charisma, that, according to actor Owen Moore, foreshadowed "what moving picture acting might eventually become. We all saw it as well as Griffith."

Of course, some admirable acting was done before Mary's arrival in the silents. And because of the loss of so many films (about nine-tenths of the silent canon has been lost), the work of many actors can no longer be screened for comparison. But Pickford, like Griffith, intuitively grasped all that went before her, then focused and refined it. The camera drew from her a kind of radar that made her behavior uncannily natural, filled with inherent psychological insight. Indeed, Mary quickly changed her description of the lens from a monster to "something sacred." The jump-start that she gave the movies, and that the movies gave Pickford, moved them both into a new creative era.

In 1909 Mary Pickford played forty-five roles for Griffith, and in 1910 she played thirty-five. Some of these were bits and walk-ons. The director liked to keep the troupe off balance, and a performer who played the lead in one story might serve as background interest in the next. But the prominence of Jack and Lottie on the payroll hints that Mary had become a major presence in the studio. In only two years, Jack made twenty-eight Biographs for Griffith – quite a number, considering that the director had promoted Robert Harron, a superior small-boy type, to acting. Lottie, whose talents were even weaker, made twenty-five. According to Arvidson, Pickford had sized up her sister's chances, decided she wasn't pretty enough for film, and tried to avoid bringing her to the Biograph brownstone. On the other hand, Pickford family values decreed that each member of the family work. Apparently Lottie found a reason to hang around the ballroom, snatched the odd role, and worked as a stand-in, probably for her sister. Lottie even made the Biograph softball team.

The group worked fast, for the studio sent two reels a week to exhibitors. These might represent two or three movies, as one could be a "split-reel" containing two films, each running five hundred feet. And they had competition, especially from the Vitagraph and Edison companies, who staked out far-flung Flatbush and the Bronx. There the actors worked in sun-catching factories – long glass lodges that funneled sun, enriched it with studio light, and sheltered equipment from the rain. Such factories might increase production by lining up platforms side by side and shooting films simultaneously. They had plenty of actors, but getting there involved long subway rides. Biograph's studio was at the theater district's southern tip. Actors could drop by while making their daily theatrical rounds. Or if Griffith needed a certain type, he could walk down Broadway and find a suitable performer on the sidewalk. Thus the possibility of replacement kept Griffith's in-group on their toes.

These favorites formed a repertory company and worked on a handshake for a weekly guarantee. Studios needed a pool of actors they could count on, and whom the audience could anticipate. Viewers grew used to the crowd at Vitagraph, Biograph, and others, and though actors' names were not usually released, familiar faces warmed a studio's identity. And the Biograph actors looked better than others – thanks, in part, to Griffith's presentation. His instinct with actresses was brilliant: Kate Bruce, Claire McDowell, Marion Leonard, Dorothy Bernard, and a phalanx of ingenues. But with few exceptions Biograph's male juveniles were bloodless. Its most interesting actor – at least in hindsight – was the burly, unpredictable Mack Sennett. He and Biograph's Arthur Johnson (a physical mismatch: Johnson was tall and romantic-looking) used to set out on pub crawls, claiming they were brothers. Sennett would pretend to be mentally handicapped. Johnson revolted other customers by telling callous stories about him and refusing to order Sennett any food.

These were happy days, buoyed by what Griffith's wife called his "happy way of working": shadowboxing, reciting poetry, snatching up an actress and twirling her in a dance, and singing – not well, though he thought he did. "Let the notes fall where they may," observed cameraman Karl Brown, who joined the Griffith team in 1913. Brown also remembered Griffith's "two distinct manners – one for normal conversation, another for direction." While he was directing, "the a's broadened, the voice deepened, the rhythm rolled, and the manner became intensely theatrical. He would often recite scraps of verse ... with an exaggerated manner hard to pin down. Nobody who ever worked with him can forget: 'See this garment that I wear? / It was knitted by the fingers of the dead! / The long and yellow fingers of the dead!'" Sometimes Griffith roared for "me thermos flawsk!" "We all fairly ached to imitate this call," wrote Brown, "but nobody quite dared." For Griffith was essentially isolated. He correctly sensed that film was on the verge of becoming art, and that he was the man to shepherd the transition. His energy and drive were catching – but there remained a loneliness about him.

He could play any prank to get results, as the silents did not require silence in the studio. When Dorothy and Lillian Gish auditioned for

Biograph in 1912, Griffith fired a gun several times at the ceiling. "You have expressive bodies," he told the cowering sisters. "I can use you." When an actor seemed lost, he would shout his thoughts. "Go to hell!" he thundered when a timorous actor tried to face the villain. "He'd cry, laugh – he'd simply draw it out of you," said Claire McDowell. Sometimes Griffith would cheer from the sidelines: "That's fine, that's dandy – do it some more." Once, in a somber scene, he told her: "You're standing amid the ruins of everything you tried to do. Ashes all about you." The words sank in, and McDowell wilted. Most scenes were completed in a single take. These high-adrenaline conditions produced a raw energy that transferred onto celluloid.

So did film's spur-of-the-moment nature. Movies were outlined and rehearsed Monday morning. Filming began that afternoon and continued Tuesday – hot, noisy work, with a set crammed into the back of the ballroom. An electric fan tried to beat the heat, and sometimes a lighting tube went crashing to the floor. (Fascinated, Mary used to gather the mercury and roll it into balls between her fingers.) Actors acted, painters painted, and carpenters pounded nails off camera, while Griffith directed from a kitchen chair. Actors who had completed their work were reluctant to go home and hung around the ballroom. At the end of the day, they lined up for vouchers, which they redeemed with the cashier on the main floor. Many then gathered in the former master bedroom, where they sat with their director, watching rushes.

Location shots were filmed on Wednesday. This was bitter work in winter, when fingers froze and makeup hardened. Actors huddled around a bonfire while Bitzer used a lamp to warm the camera. In summer the troupe rushed around New England. Film companies often left New York, most notably Kalem, which sent a unit to Palestine and Egypt. Other troupes simply crossed the Hudson to Fort Lee, New Jersey, which offered attractively low rent and sunlight. By 1908 the town, now studded with revolving stages that followed the movement of the sun, was the film-making capital of the world.

Biograph kept its New York roots but organized day trips to the country. The actors rose in the still-cool dawn, caught the subway to 125th Street, then, holding their hats, caught the Hudson River ferry at 8:45. Later they gathered at a hillside, a gully, or some point of interest in New

Jersey. *What the Daisy Said* (1910), which features Pickford, a boathouse, dazzling rapids, a field of gauzy flowers, and an almost tangible joie de vivre, resulted from just such an outing.

Long shoots spanning several days involved a train trip through the Orange (or Whechung) Mountains, where a carpet of sweet corn and blossoming buckwheat took them to Cuddebackville, New York, and a small hotel called the Caudebec Inn. The actors were mad for it – doubling or tripling up in beds, taking their turns in the single bathroom, and raiding the hotel kitchen at midnight. They adored the parlor, the homey rag rug, the shade of the fragrant apple orchard. They lingered by the stone wall and old graveyard or splashed and canoed in the Delaware River. Often these shallows were filled by men washing off bolamenia – red-brown, clammy makeup used while performing as native Americans. Mary, whose hazel eyes photographed dark, was often pressed into service for the Indian movies. They required her to rise at five-thirty in the morning, don a heavy horsehair wig, then sweat through the day weighted down with beads, leather, and old animal teeth. After this work, cooling off was delicious – strolling to the general store to buy postcards or rocking in a string hammock on the porch. There were evening auto trips through the mountains, using the hotelier's car. Hijinks intensified with the moonlight. One actor showed off declaiming Shakespeare. There might be a songfest around the piano, magic tricks, or ghost stories told around a tombstone. Genteel card games proceeded in the parlor, while craps, their "one little touch of sin," took place under wraps in a building near the icehouse. Griffith, who seldom joined in the capers, was once awakened by a noisy séance, but his disapproval failed to dampen any spirits.

Mary was suited to this life. It blended the Edwardian with the raffish; she could kick up her heels but insist on propriety. For a while, for instance, she insisted on the sleight-of-hand love play of the stage (hence her Biograph nickname, "the Great Unkissed"). But she reveled in the actors' esprit de corps, and the day-to-day changes in technique intrigued her. "Everything's fun when you're young," remembered Mary, "and we were pioneers in a brand new medium of art." But fun, in Pickford's mind, meant work. She soon became a student of editing, lighting, and camera-work, always asking questions and observing. This made her Bitzer's favorite; he recalled her trying different makeups. "Do you think I should put in a little more yellow? More pink?" Like many actresses, she realized the value of a sympathetic cameraman.

In 1915 *Photoplay* remembered Pickford's conduct. "Made up for her part, she would enter the studio and sit unobtrusively on one side until called. Occasionally her very real sense of humor would prompt her to speech. Once in a great while the resounding temper that lurks unsuspected under her serenity would smash forth in an abrupt, natural, flashing explosion." Mary directed her anger at Griffith. "I think in his way he loved me, and I loved him," she said, after years of consideration. This was a sanguine evaluation, for the love was complex, full of snags.

Griffith would never find another actress who so embodied the naive, comic adolescence he loved both on and off the screen. His biographer Richard Schickel notes that he later used two Gishes – the ethereal Lillian and the mischievous Dorothy – to attain the traits he had found in one Pickford. Griffith traced his fixation to a memory of childhood. A game was in progress amidst golden leaves and silver beech trees. Running through the landscape was "one who was not exactly a star, but she was the first.... A slim nut-brown maid with curling chestnut tresses. Her name I have, of course, forgotten. But I do remember that she often wore a red cap and my vision of her running tauntingly from her 'camp' over to mine, and then flashing away from us all through the autumn woods, is still clear and dear. Of course, I loved her."

Griffith no longer dreamed of such women: he paid them. And, almost to a girl, they became his acolytes – a retinue of starry-eyed maids, each holding a torch for the resident genius. But Mary put the torch down, and Griffith knew it.

According to Biograph actor James Kirkwood, Mary handled Griffith with "keen perception." When he turned on the charm, she stopped him cold like "a little old lady" – cutting him dead with a glare, one imagines, or sudden primness. As well as playing the romantic hero, Griffith sometimes liked to play indulgent father, asking after his actresses' health and hiding little gifts for them in his pockets. But Mary refused to be Griffith's little girl. Instead, she was headstrong, insolent, rebellious: the teenage daughter Griffith never wanted.

Sometimes she adored him – as an artist. "Griffith said that I was so crazy that if he set the house on fire and put me on the roof and he said to me, 'jump' I would. I'm very obedient in some respects." But a sense of entitlement often accompanies great talent, and Pickford would occasionally stage a rebellion. She couldn't bear it when Griffith, whose direction was usually verbal, leapt up to show an actress how to play an ingenue. "He'd exaggerate," Dorothy Gish remembered, "looking awful and [doing] things you couldn't do. But out of them you'd get something." Mary was less tactful. "I will not exaggerate, Mr. Griffith. I think it's an insult to the audience."

The St. Vitus Dance was a sticking point. Mary described it as running around "like a goose with its head cut off crying 'Oooooh . . . the little birds! Oooooh . . . look! A little bunny!'" She usually refused to do this rigmarole, protesting, "I'm a young girl, and I don't go into ecstasies." "You'll do it or you'll go home," replied Griffith. "I'll go home, then," retorted Mary, who often made it as far as the doorstep before "His Majesty" caught up with her.

Sometimes he chose her smallest movements: "Turn your head, see the letter." These details – a way of moving, a certain coy manner with head and fingers, and an O-shaped pout – embodied her propriety, sweetness, and rage. Mary recognized their value, repeating the trademarks throughout her career. But at its inception, she was seething. Griffith, she swore, made her feel "like an automatic doll. If he told me to move my left foot, I moved it."

In 1978 journalist Adela Rogers St. Johns called Griffith and Pickford "two dominant rulers" who "just never got along." Sparks flew – both bitter and inspired. Both artists, for instance, were attuned to what critic James Agee called the "middle range of feeling" – the fleeting but concise details that inflect experience. Histrionic acting, tuned toward the poles of agony and ecstasy, bypassed this emotional field. But Pickford was born to it. In later years, she would come to a decision: she "was not and never would be a great tragedienne. . . . In stature, temperament and general appearance, I was not fitted for great emotional roles." "Emotional roles," in those days, meant stage parts in which an actor staggered or collapsed. In movies, Pickford captured the same range, using small, well-chosen movements – biting her lip, perhaps, or fiddling with a shawl.

Her costume for an unnamed film comprised "the most miserable-looking hat, with a moth-eaten feather on it and a terrible little coat that was too small for me." With the camera rolling, Mary entered a room and threw the items on the bed. Griffith stopped filming – "a great reprimand," remembered Mary, "in front of the whole company." He told her the moment was out of character for a poor but proud heroine, then set up the retake with a warning: "I'm not going to tell you what to do, but don't waste any more film." Entering again, Pickford blew on the feather, straightened it lovingly, shook out the coat, stroked the velvet collar, and hung the coat carefully on the back of a chair. "Now you're a heroine again," said Griffith.

But, sadly, the pair were often ruled by tensions they barely understood. Griffith, confronted by an actress who defined his feminine ideal, was often testy and inflexible. And Pickford, feeling her creative oats, released the rebellion she had never yet aimed at Charlotte. In November 1909 all hell broke loose.

They were making a film called *To Save Her Soul* (1909) in which Pickford played a choirgirl. Her suitor (Arthur Johnson) is a curate. When Pickford starts singing on the wicked stage, Johnson drops in on a theatrical party and finds his love in a revealing dress, behaving loosely – or so he thinks: she is standing on a chair, flourishing a champagne glass. "Crazed by jealous love," reads a title, "he would kill her that her soul remain pure." Johnson pulls a gun – which Mary, in rehearsal, found unbelievable. "For one thing," she wrote defensively, "Arthur had enjoyed a short nip at lunch and was waving the gun at me as if it were a piece of hose." She also felt awkward in her dress, a low-necked velvet gown with a train that was trussed up the back with pins. When Mary could not hit emotional pitch, Griffith grabbed her by the shoulders and shook her, shouting, "I'll show you how to do this thing! Get some feeling into you, damn it! You're like a piece of wood!"

Pickford's response was, to say the least, original. "I reached down and bit him – the first and last time I have bitten anyone." Lottie, watching on the sidelines, screamed, "How dare you do that to my sister?" and sprang on Griffith's back, holding on by his ears. "Sir," declaimed Mary, in full dramatic stride, "if I am not an actress you cannot beat it into me. What gave you the right to lay your hands on me? I'm finished with you and motion pictures and the whole thing." Griffith shook Lottie off and stared at them, bewildered. "And I'm finished with you two wildcats!"

The young women retreated to the dressing room, where Mary freed herself of the costume; then she set off down the street with Lottie. Soon Griffith caught up with them, running hatless. "I'm sorry," he panted. "I didn't behave very nicely. You must forgive me. I know you can do that scene. Let's try once more." Mary returned, still stunned and angry, and Griffith turned her loose without rehearsal. "Come on, now," he shouted, "let me see the real Pickford! I know you can do it!"

An electrifying scene unfolded. Johnson, hysterical, aims the gun, then suddenly smashes a vase of flowers off the table. Mary, frightened, drops to the floor and crawls like a dog that expects a beating. Her need to keep her back from the camera pays off, as she also keeps her back from Johnson. In a desperate moment, Mary tries to placate her angry beau by pulling down her gown and exposing a shoulder; in other words, she shows him her sexual wares. This was shocking in 1909; today an actress would have to appear nude to get the same effect, and might not achieve it even then. Finally Pickford kisses Johnson's hand, which makes him hide his eyes in shame. Encouraged, she takes both his hands in hers; Johnson drops the gun, and the pair embrace.

Through Griffith's casting, Pickford found the roles that would define her career for years to come. From time to time she played a child – in fact, *Examination Day at School* (1910) shows the whole troupe as children, with Pickford rejecting showy business and emerging, in the process, the most convincing. In *The Call to Arms* (1910), Mary even gives a nod to the boys she had often played on tour, cramming her hair beneath a Patsy Poore wig. Pickford also appeared as a series of slaveys, and timid, oddly fearful daughters; these women carry grief like beasts of burden. The guilt-ridden Mary played such roles with a masochistic lack of vanity, wearing flat makeup, hair scraped across her skull. The result, as in *An Arcadian Maid* (1910), is astonishing – a tragedy in twelve minutes, featuring Mary's slavey Priscilla, who walks as though someone had her on a leash and curtsies with gratitude when Sennett, as her suitor, bestows a kiss.

But she captured most hearts with her ingenues. She is charismatic in these movies: sweet and fiery, proper but furious, humorous and somehow sexually expectant. She releases the fury in attractive ways – slamming doors, kicking chairs, and tossing curls. In 1910's *Wilful Peggy* she fends off suitors with her fists. Variations on this moment surfaced endlessly throughout her career. Five years later, for instance, as the title character in *Rags*, she would clear a bar by brandishing a chair. Seven years after that, she refuses a kiss from a villain by smacking him in the mouth with a dead fish. Such signature moments defined her to the public as a passionately strong-willed comedienne.

The key to comic acting is elusive. Technique, timing, and a sense of humor mean little without the simple belief in one's actions that makes outrageous behavior seem natural. This point escaped many of the actors in *Her First Biscuits*, whose comic behavior seems more assumed than genuine. And it seems to have eluded William A. Quirk, a frenetic actor often paired with Mary. In 1909's *They Would Elope*, he and Mary, as his ladylove, attempt a marriage. Quirk takes her hand and they run through the garden of her parents' house; Mary, reveling in the drama of her great escape, waves kisses to the flowers as they run. From then on, everything falls apart. The couple set out in a horse and cart, which loses a wheel, then hail a passing car and hitch a ride – until the car goes up in smoke. Soon they're running again, Quirk gesturing madly, and Mary growing oh so very tired. Finally Quirk plops her into a wheelbarrow and carts her to a lake, where the couple climb into a canoe and capsize. Throughout *They Would Elope*, Mary really does nothing but blend her bewildered fatigue with a slow, long-suffering inner burn – and, in the end, she is much funnier than Quirk, with his attention-getting gestures.

She was even sensual. *The Violin Maker of Cremona* shows her leaning through a window to chat with Filippo, throwing him a flower, then tossing a farewell over her shoulder as though she were flinging peanuts to a squirrel. She throws Sandro, played by Owen Moore, a glance that is beseechingly sexual. When she offers him her cheek to kiss, she draws back to feel her own shiver of excitement. This was bristling provocation, but Mary had a catalyst at hand. For as soon as she had met him, she'd fallen head over heels in love with Moore – her notorious "dame" man.

She called it love. Certainly it hit her with whirlwind velocity. Only to look in Owen's direction made Pickford feel she had climbed aboard a Hale's Tour: shaky, alert, almost sick with excitement. Perhaps it was the nature of their first meeting (Mary in a blaze of temper, Owen defensive) that broke the ice so completely between them. Somehow it left Pickford sensitive to Moore, and she probably followed her tirade with lacerating guilt. By the time Griffith threw the pair together for their love scene, Mary had lost her grip. "I shall never forget that moment when Owen Moore put his arms around me. My heart was pounding so fast from embarrassment that I was sure he could hear it." Performing the moment on film was excruciating, "not because I was afraid of him, especially, but because the camera confused and frightened me, the empty studio and the mechanically silent camera man embarrassed me, and I held back, and trembled, until the director shouted: 'For heaven's sake, do you love this man, or hate him? Put your arms around him, and let him put his arms around you!'" When the scene was finished, remembered Bitzer, Mary and Owen "stood apart, just looking at each other, sort of puzzled at the suddenness of the impact."

All this sounds like an immature crush on a man five years her senior, and the reasons Mary gave for loving Owen – his looks, his manner – suggest infatuation. She listed his attributes: "Five-feet eleven inches tall, extremely handsome," with dark blue eyes, ruddy Irish complexion, a "musical voice" – and, not to be overlooked in these early days of dentistry, "perfect teeth." Moore's regular features and slicked-back hair made his face a marvel of well-bred innocence. And his clothes lacked the frayed look of anxious actors. Such vanity was practical. Studio wardrobes were usually tattered, and those who sought work at Biograph put both their talents and their clothing up for hire. (One young man made a healthy living by regularly leasing out his spring overcoat – the only such overcoat to grace the premises.) It was in Moore's interest to be beautifully turned out, down to his ten-dollar Brooks Brothers shoes. And he wore his clothes well – another asset.

Despite the veneer, Moore's origins were humble. He was born in Ireland's County Meath on December 12, 1886. His family emigrated in 1898 and eventually settled in Toledo, Ohio. In the theater, Moore endured the usual indignities. He and his brothers, Tom, Matt, and Joseph, shared a physical resemblance and worked in the movies with some success. Owen, who penetrated Griffith's inner circle, had forty-one Biographs under his belt at the time of Mary's screen test. Her lack of experience made her feel like a kid beside him, and the age gap, combined with Pickford's appearance, probably made her seem like a kid to Owen. This would have pleased him, for the actor was riddled with insecurities. And Mary was affected by his volatile moods, for she was volatile herself: "We're the Black Irish, you know," she once explained of the Smith clan, adding laconically, "the dangerous kind."

The danger in Owen Moore was alcohol. He often nipped out to a bar with Arthur Johnson. Johnson was perhaps the best-loved member of the troupe; fifty years later Pickford still spoke of "darling Arthur Johnson," who, with his whimsical Irish wit, had become "the great hero of the Biograph company." "To my mind," Linda Arvidson added, "no personality has since flickered upon the screen with quite the charm, lovableness, and magnetic humor that were his. He never acquired affectations, which made him a rare person." Rarer still, Johnson once refused a raise.

In contrast, valentines to Owen Moore are conspicuously few among Biograph memoirs. Even Mary, in later years, couldn't find much to say about him – this from a woman who loved to tell funny or affectionate anecdotes. (She allowed that Moore didn't swear in front of ladies.) In Cuddebackville, they often slipped off to canoe by moonlight. Bitzer remembered them standing apart from the others on location while the sun bounced off a gravel path and cast their faces in radiant focus. Griffith described the same moment with the two leaning over a white tablecloth at lunch; either way, the result inspired the invention of reflectors. Bitzer also remembered Moore running for shelter through the rain with Mary laughing in his arms.

Linda Arvidson had no use for Owen Moore. In 1909 the troupe filmed Tolstoy's novel *Resurrection*, sweltering in fur and woolen costumes. The heat made Moore so touchy that he played his role as a brutish officer by throwing chairs and tables at the other actors. "He nearly killed us," remembered Linda. "I objected to the realism." Moore "had an unfriendly way of disappearing. None of the herd instinct in him." Frequently she discovered Owen hiding among the rolled-up carpets and flats. Perhaps he was recovering from a binge. "I hate to tell you this," the studio carpenter told Pickford, "but I've seen him in the wardrobe sleeping off the effects of a 'beer too many' at Lüchow's." This, admitted Mary, "wasn't altogether a revelation."

In the circumstances, Owen's charm is hard to fathom. His Biograph work was at best conventional, though early audiences found him pleasing. He was so pleasing to Mary Pickford that she overlooked his love of alcohol. After all, Charlotte indulged, many of the Biograph actors drank, and she worshipped her father, though drink had ruined him. When Pickford and Moore worked together in her fourth film, *The Lonely Villa* (1909), the couple were well along the primrose path. Owen, when not before the camera, watched Mary perform, his face wreathed in smiles. "How little we know when our troubles are going to begin!" wrote Arvidson in hindsight.

Charlotte, too, disapproved of Owen and, in a stunning turn of events, now found it difficult to discipline her daughter. Mary called her mother "not only mid-Victorian" but "antediluvian" regarding courtship. Actors occasionally dropped by the Pickford apartment to socialize, and Charlotte humiliated Mary by refusing to let Owen through the door. This, remembered Mary, was a fatal step. Adult disapproval gave the courtship the frisson of forbidden fruit, and the lovers simply met in secret (Pickford never explained exactly how). Griffith once surprised the couple necking: "Not on company time!" Then he drew Owen aside for a lecture. "Don't you *dare* do anything to hurt that girl!" And he seemed to take pleasure in insulting the actor while directing Pickford. "Why waste time with that wastrel, Owen Moore? If he thought anything at all about you, he wouldn't be drinking at a bar, he'd be right here." Mary glared, and Bitzer rolled the camera. Griffith used the tactic with other actors, but in Mary's case, his thwarted attraction gave these incidents an edge. "I'm not certain that he was the greatest director in films," said Pickford later, in an ornery mood, "but what he did have was the confidence that he was right."

In January 1910 the Biograph troupe decamped for a winter shoot in California. Later Mary groused that the move was both sudden and inconvenient. But with other movie companies, the trip west was already common practice.

In the autumn of 1907 the Selig Polyscope Company had been trying to shoot *The Count of Monte Cristo* in Chicago. But miserable weather made the shoot impossible, and the following spring director Francis

Boggs shot the rest of the movie in California. Not only were the broad skies reliably sunny, but the buildings of Los Angeles were enchanting, and the troupe set up shop in an empty Chinese laundry. Soon California's rolling landscape, cheap labor, and exotic architecture brought Kalem, Essanay, the American Film Manufacturing Company, Pathé, and Bison to experience its Yankee-Spanish charm. In 1911 the Nestor company of Bayonne, New Jersey, would nestle in a failing roadhouse near Los Angeles, creating the first permanent studio in the state, and the first in a tranquil tract called Hollywood.

But the desert had charms beyond the sun. It was easy to hide in, and many of these pioneering troupes were outlaws.

At the turn of the century, anyone with a minimum of dollars, a camera, and the know-how to crank it could make a movie. This maddened Edison, who zealously pursued enforcement of his patent on the Kinetoscope, from which, he claimed, all other cameras were devised. In the fall of 1907 a federal court agreed that Selig had violated Edison's patent. Selig and Biograph, Vitagraph, Essanay, Lubin, Kalem, Méliès, Pathé, and a distributing company, George Kleine, decided they couldn't beat Edison, so they joined him. In 1909 they pooled their patent claims to become a trust called the Motion Picture Patents Company. Each received a license to use the trust's hardware and paid the inventor a fee for each movie shown. The trust then set up a distribution agency to put its members' films into American theaters.

But film was too picaresque to be controlled. Independent companies made movies, with movie equipment from Europe, where Edison's patents did not apply. And because George Eastman, the major manufacturer of film stock, made a deal to sell only to the trust, independents used inferior stock or stole cans of film from his delivery trucks. The MPPC slapped them all with lawsuits. But it also took the low road, employing gangsters to attack their rivals. The hoods shot up the cameras, not the actors. This stopped production in its tracks. In response, the independents also hired thugs and used them as extras when the subject was a crime film. Often their studios burned to the ground. Nitrate film was exceptionally flammable, and some of the fires were spontaneous. An equal number were undoubtedly set. (In 1913, when the Thanhouser studio burst into flames, the troupe, undaunted, turned the cameras on themselves and produced

When the Studio Burned.) Filming in the remote Southwest – from which one could quickly flee to Mexico – became essential to the independents' game plan.

Biograph, safely within the trust, joined the migration for more artistic reasons. Griffith selected thirty-odd actors and technicians, and at first Owen Moore was to be among them. But Griffith was strict on the salary issue. When Moore asked for a ten-dollar raise, Griffith dropped him. Even Charlotte, who demanded a raise for Pickford, retreated when Griffith answered mildly that actress Gertrude Robinson would do as well. Meanwhile Jack (who appeared at the station to wave goodbye) began whining about wanting to go to California. "Don't be silly, Johnny!" Mary remembered saying. "You haven't any luggage!" "Oh, take the poor little fellow!" said Charlotte. "The train was already in motion," wrote Pickford, "as Mother, undaunted by my protests, picked my brother up bodily, and with the cry 'Look after your sister, Johnny!' deposited him on the steps of the moving train." There is more here than meets the eye. Neither Lottie nor Jack – a "little fellow" of about fifteen – was among the chosen, and the scene was probably planned to get another Pickford on the payroll.

The Black Diamond Express pulled out of Jersey City with the actors piled breathlessly on board. In Chicago they switched to the California Limited. Their cars were marked "the Biograph Special," and for four days and five nights, they sang, played cards and dice, and danced. Others, like Mary and Dorothy Bernard, sat with their noses to the window, and kept up a continual "Ooh!" and "Aaah!"

Griffith had toured the West Coast as a stage actor. Now he fell fully beneath its spell. The California films show an almost tangible lift of spirit, as Griffith and Bitzer pulled back the camera to capture the sagebrush and undulating palms. Life acquired a sense of leisure and release unknown to the nature-starved New Yorkers. Even Los Angeles, though something of a boomtown, retained a bracing, natural exuberance. "The grass there is so strong," recalled choreographer Agnes de Mille (William's daughter, niece of Cecil; she arrived in California in 1914), "with a virility somehow that is just exciting. And in the grass would be tangled the lupins, the poppies, the brodiaea, all of them exquisite, and all of them just blooming wild and in the gutter." Even the air, perfumed by sea foam, eucalyptus, and citrus, seemed voluptuous. And in Los Angeles, remembered de Mille, the streets ran into "the wild, wild hills. [There were] sage brush, and rattlesnakes, and coyotes and the little wild deer that came down every night."

A gloriously named dirt road, Sunset Boulevard, connected Los Angeles to Hollywood. Holly was not a crop there, though the tiny suburb was once a ranch and its chatelaine, Mrs. Wilcox, had tried to grow it. Instead, the town was thick with lemon and orange groves, interspersed with market gardens. Pepper trees lined the unpaved streets and occasionally showered the road with berries. "There was hardly a store," remembered Pickford. "There were gardens everywhere, and they ran down to the very curbs, and flowers spilled into the roadway." Bylaws kept the atmosphere sweet and tranquil. It was a crime to drive more than two hundred horses, cows, or mules through the streets, or more than two thousand sheep, goats, or hogs. But who could have anticipated film? Actors and crews arrived almost daily, grinding cameras, staging fistfights, and gazing at each other, moonstruck. When evening fell, they returned to Los Angeles. Griffith had a car, and actors in favor piled in. Pickford, a self-described "outlaw," caught the streetcar.

It was unusual for Mary to spend when she could have scrimped. She was watching her money. A few actors chose to live in style at the Alexandria Hotel, the beginning of its fame as a hotel for film folk. Others, more raffish and more hard up, took humbler rooms and managed to shoplift their coffee and vegetables. It is safe to assume Mary didn't steal, though Jack may have done so.

And she worked with a will, from bucolic Pasadena to the ruins of the mission at San Juan Capistrano. Pickford waded through oil-rich muck in Edendale; she rode a burro up a mountain for *The Twisted Trail* (1910); she nearly sat on a rattlesnake while filming in 120-degree heat. Perhaps the most stunning footage of the summer was taken in Ventura County for *Ramona* (1910). The story is set against sweeping palisades, with Pickford appearing at a dizzying height on a mountainside, holding an infant girl. She did some dizzying acting, too, falling back into breast-beating histrionics. Perhaps the style was triggered by the grueling shoot: "I had to take care of the baby ... all day long," said Mary later, "and try to keep her in the shade and worry about her bottle and still play the leading part and be the nursemaid at the same time. Of course," she added hastily, "I was delighted."

In her spare time Mary wrote scenarios, because Griffith, who often found himself without a story, asked for story ideas from actors. In 1909 she had sold him three. Now she approached him with three more. Griffith took only a split-reel for fifteen dollars; undaunted, Mary headed for Essanay's Los Angeles location and sold the other two for forty. Never one to waste an hour or a dollar, she was generous with free advice to those actors she considered spendthrift. One day Dorothy Bernard bought a feathered hat – a criminal extravagance, in Pickford's view. Bernard watched, amused, as "the sweet little Irish-American kid" put her hands on her hips and gave a lecture. "You'll regret anything so silly. You'll have that worn-out bird of paradise hat. And I'll have property."

By April, when Biograph trained back east, the Pickfords had twelve hundred dollars between them – an astonishing sum for four months' work, with Jack making only five dollars a day and their rooms costing more than ten a week. In New York Mary changed the money into twenty-four fifty-dollar bills. When Charlotte and Lottie returned from a road tour, Pickford handed her mother the cash in triumph, with a brand-new purse as wrapping paper.

"Stage money," said Charlotte. She had never seen a fifty-dollar bill. Told that the money was real, she counted it with "mounting excitement. ... That," concluded Mary with a hint of pride, "was the beginning of affluence for the Pickford family." And the start of even more ambition.

The same month the Biograph group left for California, Florence Lawrence became the leading lady of the Independent Motion Picture Company, where producer Carl Laemmle not only met her price but revealed, and exploited, a previously unknown asset: her identity.

Laemmle, though physically unassuming (he was called "Uncle Carl" by his employees), had built his business on daring and defiance. The name of his company – "Independent" – underlined its anti-trust standing. Its nickname, "IMP," defined its attitude. When Laemmle identified Florence Lawrence, he broke the unspoken pact among most producers. He knew the star system might lead to star salaries. But he also knew it might lead to marketing gold mines. Besides, the practice of withholding names was causing resentment among the fans. "How do you feel," wrote a Biograph viewer to the *Moving Picture World*, "when, attending a play ... the stupid usher forgets to give you a programme?" Biograph, he raged, was a stupid usher.

On March 12, 1910, IMP announced: "WE NAIL A LIE." The trust, IMP fumed in the *Moving Picture World*, had planted a story in the St. Louis papers that Lawrence had died in a streetcar accident. "Miss Lawrence," raged IMP, "is in the best of health, will continue to appear in 'Imp' films, and very shortly some of the best work in her career is to be released. We now announce our next films: *The Broken Path. . . . The Time-Lock Safe . . .*" A follow-up announced that, to reassure the public, Lawrence would show herself in St. Louis. Needless to say, both the story and the denial were IMP creations. But the hoax went off without a hitch: Lawrence was met in St. Louis by fans who were not only glad to know her name but glad she was alive. They tore "the buttons from her coat, the trimmings from her hat, and the hat from her head." The reaction, too, was an IMP creation. The publicity stunt had another spin-off: Lawrence is believed to be the first film performer to be asked for an in-depth interview, which ran on March 20 in the *St. Louis Post-Dispatch*.

Meanwhile, after only a year in film, Pickford was gaining fast as the actress of choice at nickelodeons. Her presence was hawked on sandwich boards as "the Girl with the Curls" or "Goldilocks." When Lawrence went to IMP, Mary slipped on the mantle of "the Biograph Girl." But she bore such honors with mixed emotions. After all, as a Belasco actress, she still considered film a guilty pleasure. When Jack sidled up to her on the subway, whispering, "If you don't promise to give me a dime I'm going to tell everybody in the car that you're The Biograph Girl," Mary quickly paid him off. Later she tried to use her shame to wrangle a pay raise out of Griffith.

"Are you any better as an actress this week than you were last week?" he asked her drily.

"No, sir, but two people recognized me in the subway today. And if I'm going to be embarrassed that way in public, I'll have to have more money."

Griffith burst out laughing. "I'll give you just five minutes, Pickford, to think up a better reason than that. I'd give my whole salary if just one person recognized me in the subway."

Perhaps Griffith guessed that in her heart of hearts, Mary loved the recognition.

Before the year was out, Florence Lawrence left the IMP troupe and became the Lubin company's leading lady; there she teamed up with Arthur Johnson, who had joined the growing ranks of Griffith refugees. Unruffled, Carl Laemmle went after Pickford, who no doubt reported his terms to Charlotte: $175 a week (she was earning $100 a week at Biograph), the employment of Charlotte, Jack, and Lottie in bit parts, and reams of star publicity. But IMP's most spectacular attraction was the promise of Owen Moore as Mary's leading man. He had never recovered from Griffith's decision to leave him, jobless, in New York while the rest set off merrily for the West. Embittered, Owen never worked for Griffith again. Instead, he signed with Laemmle – and when IMP approached Pickford with an offer, Owen had been working for the troupe for months. It is likely Mary failed to tell this most relevant news to Charlotte.

The affair had resumed furtively that spring, and once again Mary was swept away, whirling through the fall of 1910 in the thrall of calf love and mesmerizing guilt. She had always known one loyalty: to Charlotte. It tore her apart to deceive her mother. But the thought of confession agonized her. So did the prospect of losing Owen, who told her he would leave her unless she not only told her mother everything but married him. Arvidson noticed her depression as they sat by a canal near Cuddebackville. "I used to think this canal was the most beautiful place I'd ever seen," Mary told her one day. She looked for a moment in the lazy water. "Now it just seems to me like a dirty, muddy stream."

In December 1910 she signed with Laemmle. And on January 7, 1911, Mary Pickford married Owen Moore in Jersey City. The mother of the bride was not informed, though Mary wore Charlotte's sealskin coat together with a dress with a train and uncomfortably high heels. As she wobbled toward the magistrate, she experienced a series of revelations: "I scarcely know him . . . I don't love him at all . . . What am I doing here?

... I'm disobeying Mother ... I don't want to leave my family ... If I get up and run very fast I may get to the subway before he catches me." Then she saw herself rushing like Cinderella down the stairs, tripping on her train and perhaps her shoes, to a waiting taxi. She was pondering the fact that she had no cab fare when she heard herself consent to marry Owen. Then she walked from the courthouse in a daze, her mind reeling – not with joy but with panic.

The bride, who was not yet nineteen, did not spend the night with the bridegroom. She bid him goodnight on the Pickford doorstep, then crept into the bed she shared with Lottie. "I looked at my sister's peaceful face on the pillow and at that moment I almost hated her – hated her because she didn't have the terrible burden of guilt that was in my heart." Perhaps Mary hated Owen, too. "I lived in the dreadful and growing conviction that I was going to lose Mother and Jack and Lottie, all because I had married Owen Moore." She could not tell Charlotte she was married. She waited, in agony, to be discovered.

Somehow she continued making movies. Soon after joining IMP, Pickford and Moore filmed *Their First Misunderstanding* (1911) – Mary's introduction to life outside the trust. The ambience was colorful; some thugs appeared to stone both the actors and the cameras. Anticipating more East Coast disturbances, IMP's director, Thomas Ince, and the actors set off to visit scenic Cuba. This was Mary's worst nightmare – her husband and her mother living cheek by jowl – and at last she confessed to the sin of marriage. Her punishment was watching Charlotte sob, and a mute cold shoulder from Jack and Lottie, who stared at her, wet-faced, in silent reproach. Pickford absorbed every nuance of their pain. For years, she was tortured by a memory of Jack, "standing at the rail, his cap pulled over his eyes, his arm around his little dog, and tears streaming down his face. I felt like the greatest sinner who had ever lived." She never mentioned Owen's misery. When the company docked in Cuba, he coped in the only way he knew and embarked on a three-day drinking spree.

IMP set up shop outside Havana. The studio was built in an abandoned jail, a choice that would later seem appropriate. The humidity was stifling, the hours long, and the spirit of the enterprise expired in the heat. The actors were badly fed and paranoid; they even thought a trust goon was trying to poison them. (A property boy put a five-pound tin of cold cream in the icebox; a Cuban cook, thinking it was lard, served it up in pies, and the actors who ate them were taken ill.) In a company photo, the actors look miserable, even mean.

Pickford missed Biograph's esprit de corps. She even missed Griffith. In her mature years she realized that "no one during my entire career ever reached me, mentally or emotionally, as he did." Ince failed to reach her on any level. He was later a powerful Hollywood mogul who profoundly improved production standards and was key to establishing the western. But the few remaining Cuban IMPs (most have been lost) are both thoughtless and undistinguished. Scenes go on forever, the camerawork is tedious, and shots sometimes lop an actor off the frame. And the light, which was blinding, often plunged the actors' faces into shadow (in these scenes, Mary looks like a laughing ink blot). Luckily for Ince, viewers loved the Cuban scenery. And despite the fact that they also loved Mary, whose talent survives these films by a hair's breadth, the actress felt publicly disgraced. The IMPs were a comedown; in artistic terms, they were roughly the equivalent of the ten-twent'-thirt's. But Laemmle, as promised, played them up. An ad in the *Motion Picture News* showed a heart-framed still from *Their First Misunderstanding* with Mary in an intimate moment, fixing Owen's tie while he watches adoringly. In private, there were probably no such moments.

When Mary looked back on this wretched marriage, she blamed Owen's misbehavior on the fact that her salary in those first months had eclipsed his by seventy-five dollars a week. But the problem encompassed more than money. Owen could never match Mary's talent. Nor was he accepted in the family cell. Soured by drink and insecure, the actor grew moody and abusive. One hot afternoon Owen bickered with Ince's assistant and attacked him. The cause was an imagined insult to Mary, whom Owen felt free to insult in private. The assistant charged Owen with assault. According to Pickford's memoirs, Charlotte saved the day. "Go to one of the actors you can trust and ask him if he can hide Owen till the police have gone. There's a boat sailing for home tomorrow morning, and we'll put him aboard secretly tonight. And you, Mary, must go with him."

Later Mary gave a more likely explanation for her sudden departure. She was ill and had lost eighteen pounds in Cuba. "I felt that if I had to work three more days with that company that I'd die." Sympathetic Uncle

Carl wrote her a "beautiful letter," releasing her from all obligations. In spring Pickford sailed away, at peace.

Eventually the demoralized actors followed, and Pickford made a few more IMPs in New York, though her patience was rapidly wearing thin. One of the final straws was *In the Sultan's Garden* (1911), in which Pickford played an East Indian girl who breaks the law by taking an American beau. Her punishment – being sewn into a bag and tossed into the Bosporus – was filmed in the dirty Hudson River. According to the plot, Pickford smuggles a knife into the bag and slashes her way out underwater. As she bobs to the surface, she discovers her admirer roaring to the rescue at the helm of a speedboat.

For the shoot, Mary dog-paddled in the water while the IMP troupe, the cameraman, and Charlotte watched, safe on a floating dock. Unfortunately, the man at the helm of the boat was a movie novice. Excited by the presence of the camera, he came roaring toward Pickford at tremendous speed. It looked as though he might slice her head off, and a man assigned to watch for the actress's safety swam wildly toward her, grabbed her heels, and dragged her violently underwater. Mary assumed he had gone mad and was attempting to drown her. The boat streaked by and smashed into the dock, toppling Charlotte and the actors off their feet. When Pickford was dragged from the water, she was ice-cold, terrified, and semiconscious.

By late summer Mary had had enough. She advised Carl Laemmle that she was leaving IMP. This was followed, in September, by the news that she and Owen had signed with Majestic, a new concern tailor-made for her talents. Then Uncle Carl finally lost his temper and obtained an injunction that forbade Mary from "posing" for his rival. In October the actress fought her case. In court she earnestly described the "affront to her art" that IMP had forced her to endure. But first she had to prove such art existed. She read aloud a review of her work from the *New York Dramatic Mirror* that compared film acting to the pedigreed stage and raved about her in the process: "Her spontaneity and depth of resource recall the long gone days when Ada Rehan reigned, and Ellen Terry charmed London with her finesse and gentle delivery, and all was young and beautiful." Now the affront: Pickford was compelled to play opposite the general manager's brother-in-law, who had once been a mechanic and was now a bad actor.

She also claimed that Ince had fired both Lottie and Owen, whose contracts he had guaranteed. But the court sidestepped the question of artistic merit: its decision in her favor hinged on the claim that "Moving Picture Mary" had been a minor when she signed with Laemmle. On December 6, 1911, the *New York Dramatic Mirror* ran Pickford's photo on the cover – a gesture previously reserved for stage stars – and Majestic trumpeted its acquisition.

Her price was $225 weekly. For the same amount, Owen both acted and directed. Wisely, Pickford never told him that she had made his employment a condition of her contract. She was trying, furtively, to mend his ego, which had shriveled in the glare of her escalating fame. But apparently Moore showed no directing talent. When Mary asked a question about direction, Owen lashed out at her in front of the company: "Don't put on any of your Mrs. Owen Moore airs around here! Remember you're only Mary Pickford!" The moment, for all its bluster, was pathetic, for in virtually everyone's mind Owen was Mr. Mary Pickford. And the public nature of these quarrels was painful for a woman who set store by appearances. "It was," she remembered, in a generous mood, "an inadmissible position for any man. I was the leader, and I was so much younger. Those blond curls hanging down my back didn't help matters either. They must have been a grotesque and daily reminder to Owen that a child headed the family."

But she did not see – could never see – that the central problem of the marriage was her refusal to break away from Charlotte. It seems that after leaving Cuba, Owen and Mary spent a few quiet days in the Hotel Flanders in New York. But any hope Owen may have nursed of establishing a married life was stymied when Charlotte returned and moved directly into Mary's room. Owen spent the next week in his cups. At another hotel, when Charlotte joined them in the lobby, Moore blurted rudely, "Where is *she* staying?" "With me," answered Mary, who remembered, with painful clarity, that the scene occurred before the night clerk, an elevator operator, and five bellboys. Upstairs Owen told his wife, "I will get my things and go, and the two of you can go to hell." He returned at daybreak, locked himself in a separate bedroom, and fell into a deep sleep.

And so it went – an endless round of quarrels, tears, and professional panic. Majestic's publicity struck an odd counterpoint. Ads for the couple's debut appearance (*The Courting of Mary*, 1911) featured photographs of "mischievous Mary," bearing flowers, and "woman-hating Owen," glowering darkly. There would be few such photos. The couple's ghastly private life made work at Majestic so intolerable that they bolted after only five films. How this was accomplished remains a mystery; pertinent records and films are lost, and to Pickford the memories were unspeakable.

They tried once again to take control of their careers. In the spring of 1912 Owen signed with Victor films, who snapped him up to partner Florence Lawrence, recently departed from Lubin. The professional separation would be followed, in due course, by an unpublicized domestic one. And Mary threw dignity to the winds. In January 1912 she had returned to Griffith like a prodigal daughter, waiving her new, exalted rates for the privilege. Griffith offered her $175 a week. Legend has it she was so relieved that she fell into her old director's arms and wept.

6

—

THE GUTTER ANGEL

Pickford traveled with the troupe to California, where Biograph was due to spend the winter season. She quickly noted that during her absence some once-minor actresses not only had been promoted but were acting superbly in her stead. Later she praised them extravagantly; Mabel Normand, in her spotted veil, was "one of the loveliest things I'd ever seen." And the silver-blond Blanche Sweet "made me think of some rare plant, like one of those pale yellow orchids we sometimes see in the flower shops." Still, her return was the cause of heightened rivalry among the women. After all, the public knew Mary's name; protectively, they called her "Little Mary." (The Biograph players still worked in anonymity.) And, at $150 a week, she probably made much more than they did. But nothing, at first, marred Pickford's joy. "Oh, was I happy!" she remembered later. "When I stood in front of that camera . . . it was just like heaven."

She could live with the tensions within the troupe. She was less successful at de-escalating tensions with D.W. Griffith. In a typical spat, Pickford criticized stage actress Billie Burke.

"You – criticizing Billie Burke! You can't hold a candle to her!"

"Well . . . I can have my likes and dislikes – "

"No," said Griffith. "You're not privileged."

"And you're not privileged to criticize me."

Mary also complained that Griffith gave her only roles that other actresses rejected. In fact, in 1912 he increased her expressive range to a degree she would never again achieve.

In *Friends* she plays a prostitute. ("I'm sure my mother never saw that picture.") In *Fate's Interception*, Pickford plays a wronged woman who asks an admirer to kill her lover. *The Female of the Species*, a film so atmospheric it is almost surreal, shows a trio of women on a brooding desert landscape. The women have survived a massacre, and Claire McDowell, who has lost her husband, thinks Dorothy Bernard was his mistress. Pickford, who plays McDowell's sister, twiddles an ax suggestively and spends her time glaring at Bernard. She twiddles her face, too, twisting her mouth in a perpetual smirk in an effort to suggest the sister's mental deformity.

But her most arresting moments, as before, were as teenage girls and newlyweds. *A Beast at Bay* shows her now sublime sense of comic timing, as well as her assertiveness: waiting in vain for her beau to trounce the villain, Pickford enters the fray and administers the coup de grâce herself. On the other hand, *The One She Loved*, in which she plays a young wife who leaves her husband, and *Just Like a Woman* show a spellbinding vulnerability. In the latter Mary plays the role of Doris Vane, described on the screen as "a school-girl still playing at life" who decides to marry a much older man – for money, not love, as her mother has recently lost her fortune. In a long moment, Pickford considers his proposal. She is absolutely still. Her face seems transparent as anguish, desolation, and acceptance move across it. Griffith once claimed that every aspect of performance was trivial in comparison with the eyes. Mary's eyes were exceptional, and she knew it. She used them in everyday life to scorn, plead, shame, and manipulate. In moments like these she turned them, like searchlights, toward the camera, which absorbed the effect like blotting paper.

Pickford had now regained her footing. She had superb direction, a following, and genius. Still she fell prey to attacks of melancholia. This was the legacy of touring: anguished moments in which it seemed her work was wretched, her pay an outrage, the future hopeless. Then Mary found herself longing for the stage. She was not alone. Most movie actors felt similar nostalgia, and at times even Griffith doubted his vocation. He preached that film was an art form – and in so doing reassured himself, over and over again, that it was. But theater people were not convinced. Playwright William C. de Mille had this to say in a letter to Belasco:

> Do you remember that little girl, Mary Pickford, who played Betty in *The Warrens of Virginia*? I met her again a few weeks ago and the poor kid is actually thinking of taking up moving pictures seriously. ... That appealing personality of hers would go a long way in the theater, and now she's throwing her whole career in the ash-can and burying herself in a cheap form of amusement which hasn't a single point that I can see to recommend it. There will never be any real money in those galloping tintypes and certainly no one can expect them to develop into anything which could, by the wildest stretch of imagination, be called art.

Mary was beginning to agree. In May 1912 Griffith gave the lead in his film *The Sands of Dee* to Mae Marsh, a former salesgirl with no acting experience. Griffith, Claire McDowell recalled, "wanted Mae to work in place of Mary to deflate her self-importance, to show her she couldn't run things." Though Mary and the ingenues made dire predictions, Marsh gave a sensitive performance. This left Pickford shaken, wondering how "a little girl fresh from a department store could give a performance as good or better than any of us who had spent years mastering our technique." Did film acting really require a gift? She imagined Marsh's inevitable progress up the dressing table, where Pickford now held the star position. "Cold reason" told her to "go back where you cannot be unseated" – back to the theater.

She began to fling her Broadway past in Griffith's face. "Do you suppose for one moment," he responded, "that any self-respecting theatrical producer will take you now after spending three years in motion pictures?"

Griffith may have been right about producers, but Mary's old friends from touring days were easily won over. Dorothy and Lillian Gish, taking in a flicker in St. Louis, were amazed to find Gladys Smith, whom they hadn't seen for several years, in *Lena and the Geese* (1912). They ran to the candy shop next door where their mother had a job and related the news. Mary Gish slowly shook her head and sighed. "Gladys Smith has fallen from grace. The poor girl must be very poor indeed to have so degraded herself." (In fact, the poor girl had not only acted in the movie but written it.) When they returned to New York, the sisters, in decorous leghorn hats, inquired after Gladys at the Biograph brownstone. There Mary spoke of her Belasco connection, conceded that movies were "great between stage jobs," and introduced Lillian and Dorothy to Griffith. "You have courage to introduce me to two such pretty girls," he teased her. "Aren't you afraid of losing your job?" "If they can take it from me," Pickford answered, "it is obviously not my job."

It didn't take long for Mary Gish to see things as Charlotte did; the Gish girls joined Biograph the next day. After all, reasoned Mary Gish, if Lionel Barrymore of Broadway's royal family had signed up (and he had), the movies must have something to recommend them. And the three young women fell together again as friends, even though they competed for the same roles. Griffith seemed to like setting members of the troupe against one another. He often rehearsed two or three for a role and then assigned the part, no reasons given. The practice caused jealousy – especially among the actresses – but kept Griffith's leadership unquestioned. Fortunately Mary and Lillian saw through him. In California he once told Pickford, "Look at your friend. She looks better than you do. Maybe I should let her play your part." The pair went off to fetch better costumes. "He wants to get me worked up for the coming scene," said Mary. "Lillian, promise me you'll never let him, or anybody else, interfere with our friendship." But she couldn't let the matter rest. "It's too bad," she taunted Griffith later, "that you can't get a good performance without trying to come between two friends."

"I'll have none of your lip," the director answered. "I'll run my company as I see fit without the insolent criticism of a baby!"

"I won't be treated like a baby!"

"Well, that's all you are, and you know it!" said Griffith.

"Mr. Griffith," said Pickford, furious, "I don't care for the way you direct. I never have. If you were a real director you wouldn't have to try to turn me against Lillian to get a good scene. Why don't you think of a more honest way of directing me?"

Now Griffith shoved her, and she fell to the ground. Mary played this for all it was worth, declaiming from the floor, "You call yourself a

Southern gentleman! You're not only a disgrace to the South, but to the North as well! Never speak to me again, sir!"

Both became conscious that the quarrel was ludicrous. But Mary announced her resignation and brushed Griffith off when he tried to help her up. "Don't you dare touch me, sir, or even speak to me again as long as you live!" In the dressing room she began to pack, with the wild idea of catching the earliest eastbound train. Luckily the actors, at Griffith's suggestion, began to serenade her through the door. ("So long, Mary, how we hate to see you go!") Pickford could now relent without losing face, and she sat down with Griffith for a glass of sarsaparilla.

But she did leave him, in the end.

By December 1912, recalled David Belasco, "Mary Pickford was famous, and had become known throughout the land as 'The Queen of the Movies.'" Biograph had returned to New York and Belasco was planning his coming season. "No sooner had I read the manuscript of 'A Good Little Devil' than I thought of her for the part of the little blind girl, *Juliette*. I sent for her. She came to me that very day." Belasco remembered telling her, "I have a beautiful part, one that is just suited to you. You will make a great success in it, and it will help in your artistic development." But in Pickford's less lofty account, she made the call. Belasco's associate, William Dean, suggested that she hide behind some flats at the theater and surprise the Broadway Bishop. At the sight of her, Belasco was overcome, and Mary Pickford, who had once bitten D. W. Griffith, began to skip about the stage like an adoring spaniel.

Belasco handed her the script of *A Good Little Devil* and Pickford, thrilled, took the subway to Biograph. Although she worked there without a written contract, she wished to give Griffith formal notice and render him speechless in the process. She burst into the ballroom and discovered the actors in rehearsal. She tried several times to get Griffith's attention, and he finally cut her off, enraged: "Why do you bedevil me like this?" "It can't wait," said Mary, "because I start rehearsals Monday for a play and I want to know if it's all right with you. May I go?"

"You're an incorrigible tease," said Griffith. But then, wrote Pickford, "he turned and scrutinized my face with such a concerned look that all my triumph vanished in a flash. I suddenly realized how much I would miss my beloved Biograph and the guiding hand of this brilliant man."

"Well, Pickford, bless you," said Griffith finally. The actors were looking on, openmouthed. "Be good," he continued. "Be a good actress."

He cast her in a final film, *The New York Hat* (1912), the first screenplay by satirist Anita Loos. *The New York Hat* shows Pickford as a motherless ugly duckling. On her deathbed, the mother had asked the local priest to use her savings to buy her daughter an occasional trifle. Town gossips see him buy a hat, and when Pickford gads about in it, they assume the good father has designs on her virtue. Every element of the film is delightfully realized, and Mary's work as a lonely adolescent is unsentimentally observed.

Still, there was sentiment offscreen, as Mary's Biograph friends made a fuss, and Mary fussed back, with a party at her Riverside Drive apartment. Then Griffith and a few of the Biograph actors attended one – perhaps both – of *Devil's* out-of-town premieres; there were runs in Philadelphia and Baltimore. By the time Pickford finally arrived on Broadway (*A Good Little Devil* was unveiled at Belasco's Republic Theatre on January 9, 1913), her ascension had an air of finality, akin to Little Eva's flight to heaven on a pink cloud. And there, among the stars, Pickford rested in contentment – for a while, at least.

A Good Little Devil was a fairy tale, adapted from a script by Rosamund Gerard and Maurice Rostand. Pickford played a blind child whose sight is restored through the spiritual assistance of Queen Mab, Titania, Viviane, and Dewbright, with Lillian Gish (who had left Biograph after an eight-month stay) appearing as a fifth fairy, Morganie. In those days, grown-ups flocked to such productions. They recognized their mythic themes, their ability to call up images and feelings that, as adults, they had buried or forgotten. After all, such recent writers as Dickens, Thackeray, and Wilde had all turned their talents to the fairy tale, while James M. Barrie was a great and contemporary literary force. *The New York Times* admiringly noted that *A Good Little Devil's* scenic beauty could be grasped by anyone; still, "something of life's experience" was required to grasp the poignancy of the play. In 1913 the play's

Broadway rivals were *Snow White*, starring Marguerite Clark, and *The Poor Little Rich Girl*, with Viola Dana. Both Clark and Dana also entered the silents, and all three plays became silent movies.

Reviews for *A Good Little Devil* were excellent – for Pickford, Ernest Truex, her co-star, and the production's starlit skies and gardens. According to a critic, Mary "lived the part. Such an utter absence of apparent playing for effect . . . is not often witnessed." Credit for this must go, at least in part, to Griffith. Ironically, Pickford spent most of rehearsal worried that the silents had defiled her talent, especially her voice. Belasco favored a precious, ornamental way of speaking, and the dialogue coach told Mary she pronounced the letter *r* too harshly. She endlessly rehearsed the word "garden" and the dreaded phrase "my little gold scissors." (Lillian Gish spent pointless hours trying to pronounce both *p*s in "apple.") But critics made a point of praising Mary's diction; one even suggested that if this was how film actors spoke, a few Broadway stars might dip a toe in flickers. "I had every reason to be gratified with my stage work," Pickford later sighed, "and yet . . ."

She tried telling Belasco how much happier she would feel with a twenty-five-dollar weekly increase in her salary. Unlike Griffith, he answered promptly, "From now on your salary will be two hundred a week."

But a malaise began to nag her. She decided that she didn't like *Devil's* set, although Belasco's eye for detail had once impressed her; next to film, the effects were stiff and artificial. Pickford also decided that her role, which was painful to perform (to appear blind, she had to focus on nothing, which – eight times a week – left her tense and nerve-racked), was a badly written bore.

Pickford finally faced the music, with a sinking heart: just as she had once sought salvation from the movies on the Broadway stage, she now yearned to act before the camera. "I had been so determined never to go back to motion pictures; I had reviewed, almost daily, all the superior attractions of my old home the theater; I had thought of its greater dignity and prouder heritage." Part of Mary's prouder heritage was Frances Starr's dressing room, trimmed to her taste in blue brocade, with a five-cent silver star on the door. This was a marvelous wish fulfillment. But Pickford had changed since the years of trundling across the country on trains, dreaming of Broadway's airs and graces. Film had become her creative home. After only a few days on Broadway she found herself missing "the exciting jigsaw puzzle of a motion picture in progress – the novelty, the adventure, from day to day, into unknown areas of pantomime and photography."

She had also read a newspaper story about a producer named Adolph Zukor, who was defining the cutting edge of the movie business.

Years later, when he had made a fabulous success in America, Zukor turned his mind back to his Hungarian childhood: "A new pair of shoes was an event." When he arrived in the New World in 1897, he had forty dollars sewn for safekeeping in his vest, and he immediately declared himself, at age twenty-four, "a newborn person."

Zukor had been in the United States only a few months when he saw a popular flicker called *The Kiss*. Six years later, he was fully assimilated, a sleek Manhattan burgher with a thriving fur business and a wife and son. But the enchantment of *The Kiss* still lingered. Zukor spent more and more time at arcades: cheap amusement halls, full of phonographs, Kinetoscopes, Mutoscopes, and patrons plugging them all with pennies. Soon he built his own (with a cousin), called it "Automatic Vaudeville," and filled it with mechanical fortune-tellers, strength-testing gizmos, and plenty of peep shows. Automatic Vaudeville's second floor became the glamorous "Crystal Hall," devoted exclusively to flickers and reached by a staircase made of glass. Admission to the Crystal Hall was a nickel, though Zukor at first believed that people paid not to see the films but to climb those stairs. He soon learned otherwise and, never a man to miss an opportunity, opened a nickelodeon next door.

Zukor even ventured into Hale's Tours, purchasing a franchise in 1906 with vaudeville producer William Brady. Unfortunately, the cost of the railway car accoutrements and the Tours' sudden drop in popularity put Zukor $160,000 in debt. But the threat of bankruptcy gave him nerve. Perhaps he connected the fate of the movies with his own acceptance in America. Zukor began to imagine how film – and, by inference, he himself – might gain approval from the middle class.

Perhaps, Zukor reasoned, the brevity of movies made them seem inconsequential. Even the double- or triple-reel films that emerged, on rare occasions, from American studios had an air of the ephemeral. Meanwhile spectacles from Europe – Italy's *Quo Vadis?* (1913) had eight reels – were finding their way onto screens across America. A new word was coined for these longer movies: "features" usually had at least five reels, running for an hour or more. The profits of feature films were grand, but so were their production costs. Studios, with an audience and distribution system geared toward one-reelers already in place, were loath to make changes. And the MPPC required one-reelers, arguing that movies were industrial products that would benefit from standardization. Zukor observed that the trust mentality "belonged entirely to technicians. What I was talking about – that was show business."

As he pondered the problem on the subway, Zukor scribbled a phrase on the back of an envelope: "Famous Players in Famous Plays." Film, he theorized, might make inroads with the middle class by becoming a celluloid archive of the stage. The idea had already blossomed in France through a snob-appeal project called Film d'Art. Participants – usually stage actors and directors, poets and classical musicians – used film as a handmaiden to their own, more august cultures. A typical product was 1912's dreary *Queen Elizabeth*, which filmed Sarah Bernhardt with twelve camera setups in four reels (as opposed to, say, sixty-eight angles in Griffith's one-reel *The Sands of Dee*). And the actors mouthed every line of dialogue. But despite such absurdities, Film d'Art broadened the appeal of movies by targeting an audience of theatrical diehards.

Zukor bought the rights to show *Queen Elizabeth* in America. But the great Sarah's acting was sadly dated. "If you run Queen Elizabeth," advised an exhibitor, "stop with the scene before the last, cutting out that absurd death flop into the pile of cushions placed before the throne for no other reason than to save the Bernhardt bones. It gives a comedy finish that is hurtful." But Zukor showed the film in a high-minded venue – the Lyceum theater in the Broadway district – and counted *Queen Elizabeth* a succès d'estime.

Now he embarked on a Film d'Art scenario for his own Famous Players in Famous Plays. First Zukor took on a partner of theatrical distinction – Daniel Frohman (brother of Charles), a producer in his own right and a

Broadway aristocrat. Zukor believed that first-rank, long-standing Broadway stars, filmed in their international triumphs, would attract a new audience to film. And the stars he needed were drawn to Frohman. The first to succumb was *The Prisoner of Zenda*'s James K. Hackett, who repeated his performance in 1913 for Zukor's cameras. Minnie Maddern Fiske, Lillie Langtry, James O'Neill, and other luminaries followed.

Mary was a mongrel in this context. She was a new, not a venerable, star, and most of her audience came from film. But her devotees proved to be fanatic. Fans at the stage door cried out more often for film's Little Mary than for Belasco's Juliet. This intrigued Zukor, who filmed *A Good Little Devil* (1914) with its Broadway cast in May 1913. Naturally, Mary was overjoyed – with one reservation. The actors would film on days without matinées. For this, they received one-ninth of their stage fee. Pickford thought the fee should be at least one-eighth. But at the last moment she looked at her priorities, came to her senses, and concluded that "the most important thing, and I think it is at least 33 1/3 per cent important, is to get with the right associates." Now she "felt instinctively that a new pathway would open for me, and it did." This despite the fact that the film of *A Good Little Devil* was "one of the worst [features] I ever made. . . . It was deadly."

The finished movie featured Belasco, sitting before a fireplace, visualizing the story. And the actors recited every line of dialogue, which Pickford, understandably, found inane ("the eyes must speak rather than the lips"). Apparently Zukor, who kept *Devil* from release for eleven months, agreed. But Mary's performance was impressive. When the stage *Devil* closed shortly after filming, Zukor set up a business luncheon. There Mary sat beside her mother and affected a reluctance to spoil her newly celebrated image with a long-term commitment to the movies. Besides, she had promised Belasco she would star in the Broadway tour. But, cannily, Zukor sensed a lingering doubt in both Mary and Charlotte about her voice. He boldly advised them that film would play solely to Mary's strengths. "What salary," asked Charlotte, "would you consider paying Mary?" Zukor was vague – a few hundred dollars a week, he said – and the Pickfords retired with a promise to get back to him.

Now Charlotte contacted D.W. Griffith. Pickford was receiving two hundred a week from Belasco. What salary, asked Charlotte, would Griffith give her? "Three hundred," said Griffith, who must have smiled a bit at Mary's change of heart. "That's the best I can do." Charlotte warned Griffith he'd regret it, and that Mary could get five hundred dollars elsewhere. In fact, this was the fee she exacted from Zukor – and a teacher, a factory worker, or a farmer would have laughed in disbelief. Such income-earners (and many of them were among the movies' first fans) made five hundred or less in a *year*.

Mary didn't laugh; instead, when she heard of Zukor's offer, she fell mysteriously ill and confessed to Belasco that she feared the strain of touring would endanger her health. Belasco, who was something of a trickster himself, must have seen this transparent ploy for what it was. But for unknown reasons he acquiesced. Mary promptly put her name to a contract with Zukor, and a partnership began that changed the history of film.

Zukor hoped to alter public taste by flooding the market with features. He had plenty of help. By 1913 an assortment of production companies, large and small, with charming names such as All-Star, Eagle, Colonial, and Venus, were churning out multi-reel attractions. Their films were distributed at first by regional organizations, who were able to operate outside the MPPC because the trust's monopoly covered only one-reel flickers, now declining in popularity. An industry giant was born when a firm called Paramount consolidated eleven regional distribution agencies. Exhibitors responded by forming theater chains that increased their bargaining power with the big distributors and studios. By 1914 Paramount would handle not only Zukor's features but those of Bosworth, Morosco, and the Jesse L. Lasky troupe. Zukor and other producers bought shares in Paramount in order to protect their interests.

But the public knew nothing of such machinations. Audiences around the world were spellbound by multi-reel films; those made in America, like those made in Europe, were quickly marketed internationally. Lavish features filled the eye in a way no human had ever known. And smaller, character-driven features made the actors seem intimately near. Features gave viewers the luxury of time – time to gaze at the adored one, to read his mind, imagine his dialogue and thoughts. Patrons internalized the actor, engulfed him in private, irrational fantasy. All the while, the star's reflected light bathed their faces, his image larger than life and therefore, seemingly, more true. Moreover, the nature of silent movies demanded fixed attention from the viewer. At a talking movie, the viewer may look away, tie his shoe, close his eyes. But each defining moment in a silent is visual. Faces, hands, eyes – all are signals. The audience had to give more, and in return they got more – a kind of rapture.

Rapture for Pickford began with her first three Famous Players features – *In the Bishop's Carriage* (1913), *Caprice* (1913), and *Hearts Adrift* (1914). The roles stressed the usual Pickford traits: humor, fire, and independence. They also fixed Mary in her feature-film image, that of a picturesque urban guttersnipe, half savage, half angel, dressed in tatters, living from hand to mouth, untamable. Or she played mining-town Annie Halls, Gold Rush urchins decked out in flannel and feathers – all of them dead shots – or illegal immigrants and small-town women encountering, then mastering, city life. By playing these roles Mary cast her lot with the class that had created her – and with film. Whatever her wealth in private life, she was theirs onscreen: pugnacious, street-smart, humorous, and hungry. And just as Chaplin's tramp was a gentleman, Mary played angels with dirty faces. She was also rewarded for her virtue, usually discovering she had wealthy relatives, or attracting the love of a rich but decent-hearted beau. In any case, inheriting a silver spoon and appearing in shy gowns failed to spoil her. Instead, her new setting simply augmented what had always been Pickford's innate refinement.

In the Bishop's Carriage, released in September 1913, has vanished; it is known, though, that Pickford appeared as a teenage girl, Nance Olden, who escapes from an orphanage, lives by stealing, and after some futile attempts to go straight, triumphs on the stage. *Caprice*, which followed in November, is another lost feature. Mary played a mountain girl who falls in love with a man who mistakenly shoots her on a hunting trip. Apparently the girl spends much of the movie struggling to acquire the society ways that will please her heartthrob's family. Initially she fails and, in desperation, aims a gun at her head, crosses her eyes in expectation – and discovers the gun has no bullets in it. Slapstick, it seems, was central to her features from the start. And it seems that, at least for the first few months, she wished to make Owen Moore central, too.

In *Caprice*, he played her city beau – the casting was probably a favor to Mary from Zukor – while the couple attempted to reconcile. Their marriage saw several such futile efforts. Mary later claimed that she was still a girl, unable to grasp the severity of Owen's drinking problem. And because she was still a girl, she could not yet separate from Charlotte, who remained her first loyalty and love. Owen, in response, drank even more; he attacked her with silence and stinging looks. Still the marriage staggered on, though when and where the couple were together is impossible to know. Often Mary left him to live with Charlotte. But it seems she took him back again, when Owen, sober and sick with remorse, besieged her with flowers and regrets. She even took him back in the wake of a nightmare appendectomy – if it was, indeed, an appendectomy. In those days, the term was often a code word for abortion.

It is rumored that Pickford had an abortion early in her career. Certainly a pregnancy would have been a public-relations catastrophe – interrupting her work, and soiling Little Mary's girlish charms. One can imagine, too, that Charlotte might have feared a rival for her daughter's love, just as she resented and feared Mary's husband. A close friend of Mary in later years believes that Charlotte virtually forbade her to have any children, and that Pickford, in some deeply buried part of her heart, could not forgive her. Perhaps Mary was unwilling to bring a child into the world with her horror of Owen Moore as the father. And of course, she may have undergone no abortion.

But the drama of the appendectomy has a strange ring. The crisis occurred shortly after the filming of *Caprice*. Supposedly Mary had suffered a fall while carrying an actress down a flight of stairs. Surgery was arranged without Owen's knowledge, and Charlotte took her daughter to the hospital. Suddenly Owen burst in. "What right have you," he snarled, "to operate on my wife without my consent?" In those days, a husband's consent was necessary for any operation on his wife. But why would a husband so covet his wife's appendix, and why would a wife keep its removal secret? Moore was drunk and the staff had to forcibly sedate him. Mary, on the table, was praying: "God, I want to be obedient; but if it is your wish that I return to Owen I would rather die." When she emerged from the anesthetic, she endured four more visits from her husband. He shouted abuse, she wept, and the staff finally barred him from her room.

In the 1910s and 1920s, Pickford often told her friends she hoped to have children. Finally she concluded she was sterile, feebly suggesting that a fall from a horse was the cause of her condition. But if she had indeed had an abortion, the methods applied in 1913 might well have made bearing other children impossible.

Fresh air and sunshine were what she needed, and after completing *Caprice* with Owen, Mary left him and boarded a train for Los Angeles. Her mother came along, as well as Edwin S. Porter, of *The Great Train Robbery*; he was now director general of Famous Players. Together they established a West Coast office in a pleasantly unpretentious farmhouse.

Other feature troupes had done the same, and the town was soon dotted with wooden stages, their muslin awnings rustling like palm leaves. At noon the parks filled up with actors. "You were apt to see Bluebeard and all his wives cozily eating ham sandwiches and hard-boiled eggs, while the Apostle John sat under a pepper tree with his arm around a bathing beauty," wrote a city dweller. Meanwhile, L.A.'s sunny streets were displayed on celluloid around the world. Films showed off the Spanish homes, the Mission bungalows and banks, the booming construction and splendid weather. The only dark note, for actors, was housing. Mary and her mother moved into a spacious craftsman-style bungalow on Western Avenue. But lesser lights found, to their dismay, that certain landlords forbade Jews, dogs, or movies. "Movie" was then a pejorative term for anyone who worked in film. Like stage actors, "movies" were often empty-handed on rent day, and they attracted thieves by jamming what money they had into dresser drawers or slipping it under mattresses – hardly their fault, as film folk could seldom open bank accounts.

At Famous Players everyone wore several hats. Porter, for instance, was not only the director general but vice president, cameraman, and electrician. Mary's way with a scenario came in handy when, while chatting in the farmhouse kitchen, she remembered a story she had read in a magazine. Zukor paid her a hundred dollars to transform it into *Hearts Adrift*. In February 1914 the movie was released – or unleashed upon the public like a helium blast.

It featured Pickford as twelve-year-old Nina, the sole survivor of a shipwreck. For five years Nina lives on a desert island and, while taming a wolf, becomes both a woman and a "wild child." Eventually John, another victim of a wreck, is swept ashore. A production still shows Mary creeping up with a whittled spear, but soon he tames her. Their feelings deepen; John and Nina fall in love and improvise a wedding, and Nina has a baby. Now the plot turns toward *Madame Butterfly* – John's wife, who survived the shipwreck, arrives on the island with a rescue party. Nina, devastated, takes the infant and, clutching it, leaps into a bubbling volcano.

The disappearance of *Hearts Adrift* is calamitous, for Nina, the child-woman, was the very heart of Mary's image. According to *Photoplay*'s Julian Johnson, Pickford "revealed unsuspected suggestions of physical voluptuousness" in the role. Indeed, Pickford's work was far from prudish, though her sexuality was not announced in the manner of a silent-movie vamp. Sex did not define her; it was noted as a passing, often funny, fact of life. The discovery of sex is also key to growing up, and Pickford, for the most part, played teenage girls, as well as children on the cusp of adolescence.

It seems that the older Nina, though a woman with a baby, was childlike. "Her tragedy," wrote *Photoplay*, "was convincing, logical, soul-wrenching in its quaint piteousness." "Quaint" in those days implied something vulnerable and unworldly. However tough or comic the character, "quaint" lay at the heart of all Pickford performances. The audience responded the way the first viewers of film had reacted to a train or the quivering of a leaf. They watched in "waves of perfect understanding" and, en masse, fell in love with her.

Reviews of Mary's work in this period glow with elation, even a tendency to fall to pieces. "Here was feminine fascination, luminous tenderness," wrote Julian Johnson, "in a steel band of gutter ferocity. Here were flame-spurts of primitive wit, inexorable determination, that sort of dewy sweetness which, beheld, often makes women weep and men curse."

Otis Barnum wrote a poem for the *New York Dramatic Mirror*:

Silent enchantress! Are any as blind to you
As not to feel the glad charm of your art?
Time spare the youth of you, fortune be kind to you,
Queen of the Movies and queen of my heart!

The *New York Review* ran a photograph of Pickford with ethereal pronouncements below it as though she were a deity:

"I move, like a Fairy of Childhood's Wonderland, across the white screen of the Universe. The very azure skies are not too far reaching for my silent drama."

"I bring to the darkness of side streets and the melancholy of desolate hearts, and the bitter byways of Less Fortunate, a sudden majesty of peace that passes all understanding."

"I am the delicate Femininism of Picturedom. The art seems to have culminated in me – in my diffidence and in my unassuming, reposeful manner ... Have you not choked back the impulsive sob and brushed away the persistent tear drop as you watched my curly head bob downward, and you knew that I, too, was suffering; that I lived the part for that moment and your sympathy for me was born of a quaint but quite real love. I am the wistful, butterfly-like, elusive quality of supreme Innocence as I peer out at you, night following night, with my big, round, tender eyes."

This dreadful passage (and there was more) tells much about the culture that cherished Pickford. "It has come, this new weapon of men," wrote poet Vachel Lindsay, "and by faith and a study of the signs we proclaim that it will go on and on in immemorial wonder." Features were an art without a history. The audience had no frame of reference with which to temper their experience. Their love of movies approached the ecstatic. Small wonder they assigned to Mary Pickford – the first film actor to capture their hearts and minds in features – the outline and essence of religion.

A poem to Pickford, written by a fan, described her "weird magnetic grip." Indeed, the public's obsession with Pickford was not simply with her film characters. It was a passion for the existence of "Little Mary," a creature of exquisite sensitivities. She seemed to possess an inner sadness; they read this in her eyes. "[Mary] has the saddest eyes in the world," observed *Photoplay*. "Even while she laughs, her eyes stay wistful, and seem ready to brim over with tears. I asked Mary Pickford about it – and she laughed."

"She gives one the impression of being absolutely honest, incapable of saying anything she does not feel, or of any affectation." This illusion sprang from Mary's unassuming public conduct. She had never recovered from being cut down to size by Charlotte in the "I simply won't go on tonight" episode; an unadorned manner was ingrained. The contrast to grander-than-thou stage stars was a stimulus to further adoration. Critic Alan Dale, who received the Pickford treatment in 1914, emerged from his interview declaring: "A simpler and more diffident maiden I had never met in the rose-garden of maidens that I have traversed." She was infinitely touching – "quaint," if you like – and this inner beauty was reflected in her little white face, her small hands and feet, and, most important, her hair.

Pickford's hair waved across her head, then streamed down her back in ringlets, perfectly arranged and spun. Today the fashion seems cloying, but in Mary's time ringlets conveyed a complex message. Abundant hair was a woman's glory. In Edwardian times she patiently sat before her mirror, combing her hair with a hundred strokes. But luxurious hair was frankly sensual. Modesty insisted it be harnessed. And, once an adult, a woman always, *always* wore her hair up. In public, Mary obeyed the custom. But onscreen, the tresses inevitably came loose, forming a rampant Pre-Raphaelite mass or the modest, miraculously curling ringlets, arranged like a bouquet around her face. This made her both childlike and erotic.

The color of her hair was important, too. Blondness, in those days, suggested a woman's angelic nature. In the teens, Mary freely told her fans that her hair was light brown (it had grown darker since the days of Baby Gladys). Yet critics and journalists insisted that her hair was blond, yellow, or the glimmering "golden" – hues suggested by the halo effect when she was lit from the back, but which also matched the way viewers felt about her. Years later Pickford bought into the myth when she resorted to peroxide – and, sustaining the fiction, claimed she had been golden-haired throughout her life.

Touching Mary's hair onscreen was verboten; any man who dared received a wallop from Pickford. Films in which her hair was cut brought moans of protest from the crowd. When Mary thrust her curls in a bucket of suds, the audience gasped as though the shock were physical. At times, Pickford worried that her curls were growing more important than she was; "I think shorn of them I should become almost as Samson after his unfortunate meeting with Delilah."

The public, of course, believed her curls were real. And they were – for the most part. But Mary had eighteen false ones ready for use when her fine hair drooped under lights or in humidity. They were also pinned into her hair when a movie required that her curls look especially bountiful. The ringlets were made by a Los Angeles hairdresser, who obtained the strands from Big Suzy's French Whorehouse. (Mary paid a startling fifty dollars apiece.) Thus, with a little professional help, the crown jewels were trotted out in mint condition. And it seemed only natural, to the public, that Mary's hair was supernaturally perfect. After all, it symbolized her inner self: grown-up and childlike, wild and proper, sensual and pure – the perfect halo.

Mary's mystical attraction had a precedent: in the late 1880s, the American public had felt a special fondness for a now forgotten actress named Mary Anderson. Most critics thought her talent mediocre, but she may have been simply ahead of her time. William Winter recalled that Anderson "appeared to have grasped each character by intuition, to have entered bodily into it at once, and to be living it without conscious volition." Somehow the public responded by wishing to protect the actress. She seemed so refined, so pure, so unaffected. When Anderson, who lived abroad for several years, returned to the United States in 1899, the headlines announced, in high excitement, "Our Mary Is Coming," "Our Mary Has Arrived," "America Greets Its Favorite Daughter," and finally, "Our Mary Is in Our Midst." This feeling of possession now surrounded Pickford, who received her predecessor's sobriquet – "Our Mary" – and was asked if she and Anderson were related.

In the 1890s a similarly luminous aura surrounded the unassuming figure of Maude Adams, whose fame began to thrive through her appearances in plays by James M. Barrie. She was not considered beautiful; instead, she was homespun, virginal, unpretentious. *Photoplay* attributed Adams's fame to "a rare and wholly individual charm [that] swept the land from sea to sea." Her flock wanted not only to see the actress but to enter the penumbra that surrounded her. But at the request of her producer, Charles Frohman, Adams rarely let herself be seen offstage. She lived an entirely secluded life – endorsed no products, supported no causes, never gave an interview. The public thought this adorably unglamorous. They proclaimed her a force for good in the world simply because she was – Maude Adams. And Pickford, film journalists decreed, was their own reluctant angel; she was baptized the "Maude Adams of the Movies."

But unlike Adams, Anderson, or anyone on the stage, Pickford's image was ubiquitous. A theatergoer might wait a lifetime to see Duse or Bernhardt. Then the great night would come and go. But more people saw Pickford in a night than saw Duse or Bernhardt throughout their stage careers. And, of course, they could see Mary Pickford on any night they chose; several times a night, perhaps. Rather than making her common coin, familiarity made her appeal even more hypnotic. A new, commanding chemistry was at work. In the theater, collaboration, however subtle, occurs between the audience and the actor. But a filmed performance is finished and immutable. "Instead of becoming companions or even combatants," writes Walter Kerr, "we become faithful dogs and follow adoringly at heel."

Other silent-film actors, of course, had followings. In popularity polls Pickford ranked sometimes above, sometimes below such passing fancies as Clara Kimball Young, Earl Williams, Mary Fuller, and J. Warren Kerrigan. But only Pickford was loved throughout the entire course of silent film. Only Pickford inspired a peculiar intensity that made her "the intimate possession of all the people." And Mary was forever set apart from other actors as the first pop icon who took shape through moving images. The romantic shock with which she entered viewers' hearts hung about her for decades.

Tess of the Storm Country (1914) brought this delirium to fever pitch. This, the fifth Pickford feature and the earliest to survive, was also the first in a year-long contract with Famous Players. Fittingly, it showered her with laurels right from the opening credits: "Daniel Frohman Presents America's Foremost Film Actress, Mary Pickford, in the famous tale of a woman's heroism, 'Tess of the Storm Country' by Grace Miller White. Miss Mary Pickford as Tessibel Skinner." At which point the Foremost Film Actress, wearing a delicate, frothy dress, steps through a curtain with an armload of roses. She carries them to a nearby vase, arranges them, and breathes in their fragrance. Now she looks into the lens – the equivalent, in this context, of a stage bow – and buries her face in the bouquet again.

Enter Tess, an "expressive-eyed tatterdemalion" living in a shantytown of squatters who fish illegally. She spends her time striding round the beach, tossing a fabulous head of curls, and getting into fistfights with a lecherous neighbor. In the course of a fairly complex plot, she takes a baby from a suicidal unwed mother named Teola and cares for it as her own. This is at some personal cost, as Tess's suitor, Frederick, is Teola's brother. Unaware that Tess did not bear the child, he drops her after ripping up her Bible. Tess must steal to feed the baby – in fact, she must steal from Teola's rich family. When Teola's father catches her, he whips Tess savagely, with Frederick and Teola looking on. Then Pickford asks, with considerable dignity: "I has been beaten – now air I to have the milk?" (In a nice irony, she spills it.) Later, when the baby grows ill, Tess observes: "That brat air dyin'." She attends a church service with the baby, asking that it be baptized, but the priest refuses. Tess is astonished: "Be ye agoin' to let him go to a place where God can't find him?" She baptizes the child herself while the congregation murmurs. Finally Teola, who is watching from a pew, cries out, "He is my baby!" Tess, with mixed relief and scorn, gives the baby to Teola, and walks out, back straight, head held high.

The movie cannot live up to its star's performance. There are some stirring storm effects. The village of squatters is picturesque. But Edwin S. Porter, in Pickford's view, was less a born director than a born mechanic. She complained that he failed to show "the slightest interest in acting or the dramatic aspects of motion pictures." Indeed, Porter violates the simplest film grammar. The actors rush stagily through their scenes, while the camera watches, static, from a distance. One can only wonder if Porter was similarly careless with *Hearts Adrift*. (J. Searle Dawley, younger and more flexible, directed *Caprice*.) Yet Pickford's bossy, witty Tess survives through sheer force of temperament and talent.

Riding the wave of this triumph, the actress's profile rose higher still. She was commonly believed to be "the best known woman who has ever lived, the woman who was known to more people and loved by more people than any other woman that has been in all history." The statement, made in the 1980s by Pickford's contemporary, journalist Adela Rogers St. Johns, is impossible to prove. But in Pickford's day it was accepted as gospel, and even today it is seldom challenged. And if silent film, as Hollywood claimed, was the universal language, a medium that would teach love among nations, bring cultures together, and eradicate war, then Mary, as its supreme representative, embodied a new world understanding. Or so wrote her apostles in the press.

Movie magazines grew up with features and re-created the film experience by publishing plots in short story form and writing, rhapsodically, about the stars. *Photoplay* moved to the front of the choir with especially softheaded prose about Pickford. "If everybody were as pure minded as she, there would be no sin in this world," wrote its astrologer. Pickford fever reached a rarefied height when the magazine had a nun sing her praises. Regarding Mary's charitable activities with the Los Angeles Orphan Asylum, the Mother Superior commented: "Do you remember Lowell's poem, 'The Vision of Sir Launial,' in which Christ appears to the impoverished knight who has shared his last crust with a leper, and says, 'Who gives himself with his alms, feeds three / Himself, his hungering neighbor / and Me.' It is because Mary gives herself with her alms that she means so much to us. . . . The children simply cannot get enough pictures of her."

Publicity pictures were a stage tradition that became a kind of movie madness. Photos of Mary circa 1914 show her swathed, like a bride, in tulle or modestly turned out in cuffs and collar. Such photos appeared in movie magazines, were reproduced as postcards, and were slipped into cigarette and chocolate boxes. Fans who wrote letters were rewarded with eight-by-ten photos of Pickford, stamped with her signature, and a note. She asked that they send her their photos in return, and many of them did so. They also sent poetry, drawings, and music. She received shell necklaces from Bermuda, boxes of candied fruit from Hawaii, and rafts of ivory ornaments, painted fans, and sandalwood boxes from the Orient and India. Supposedly a Chinese prince wrote a letter of praise, and the city of Sydney, Australia, sent her an official loving cup. And much was made of the deerskin boots and moccasins that arrived from a Princess Red Feather in Saskatchewan. "Dear Miss Pickford," read her letter. "I am a little Indian girl, 13 years old, and I have your picture cut from a magazine our teacher had. I like the way your face looks, and so I am sending you boots and moccasins. I wear the same kind. Will you send me the kind you wear, please?" Mary sent her pink satin mules and high-laced brown suede street shoes.

In public, Mary's clothing was demure. She would have enjoyed wearing elegant clothes; in fact, at first she refused to play Tess because she couldn't bear to play another waif in rags. And she felt like a "drab little wren" when she boarded a train with the glamorous Pearl White (cliffhanging heroine of 1914's *The Perils of Pauline*; a vogue for movie serials had seized the nation). White was decked out in a black velvet Russian coat, a red fox muff, and a huge black velvet picture hat. But Mary was restricted not only in dress but in behavior. She never drank alcohol in public. Nor did she handle any object – lipstick, a pencil, a piece of paper – that might be mistaken, at a distance, for a cigarette. Now Zukor forbade her to join Pearl White in the club car, where the actress sat smoking and drinking highballs. Instead, Mary buried her face in a magazine.

She was pestered, of course, to endorse some products. Later Mary said she refused them all. But in 1916 a page in *Variety* extolled the work of Mme. Kahn, who ran a dress emporium in New York: "The mere fact that Miss Mary Pickford, THE GREATEST MOVIE IDOL IN THE WORLD, has selected our establishment for her gowns should be proof positive that WE CAN PLEASE YOU." Presumably, Mary chose such ads with care and drove a hard bargain for each endorsement. She also gave her name to Pompeian Beauty Products and a household soap. But allowing herself to become a trademark for anything shoddy or second-class would be conduct unbecoming for America's newly christened sweetheart.

"Calling Mary 'America's Sweetheart' was not exactly a stroke of genius. I was simply putting down in two words what everybody in America seemed to be feeling about her." B.P. Schulberg wrote both publicity and scenarios for Famous Players; in fact, he had written *Tess* and *In the Bishop's Carriage*. "I was standing in front of a theater one day watching people buy tickets to see Mary in one of the early movies I wrote for her when a middle-aged couple stopped in front of a display of stills from the picture. 'There she is,' the husband said. 'My little sweetheart.'. . . 'She's not just your little sweetheart, she's everybody's sweetheart,' his wife said. It rang a bell." Thus the phrase "America's Sweetheart" was put into the ad copy pushing Mary's pictures.

Pickford insisted that the phrase was given to her by the San Francisco exhibitor D.J. "Pop" Grauman. But Schulberg's point – that Pickford's image was created by the public, and augmented by publicity – is crucial.

The cult of America's Sweetheart was unique in its innocence, intensity, and fervor. And though Pickford helped create Little Mary ("The press," she once said, "is as much a part of me as my make-up"), the intensity of movie fame surprised her. "People ... consider me their personal friend," she observed to a journalist. "They follow my every step, and they get to the point where they not only want me to be, but expect me to be, in real life exactly what I am in the pictures." One true believer was William Bartels, a homeless fan who attracted a crowd as he built a shrine to Pickford in a New York park. Who was his sweetheart? Mary Pickford, he told the arresting officer – though, he admitted, he "was not yet on speaking terms with her."

Today this phenomenon – in which a fan fancies a relationship with an actor, or tries to forge one through harassment or even murder – is a danger performers tacitly accept. But no one in early features could have known that movies would so shape the psyche. Mary felt anxious (how could anyone live up to such worship?) and guilty (how could anyone deserve it?).

Many who wrote to her asked for money. Others sued her. One such litigant charged that Mary and Charlotte, while renting her apartment, splattered the floor and furniture with liquor, allowed their dog to sit on fine upholstery, dented the floor, and steamed the walls by doing laundry. "We did a little washing," conceded Charlotte. Then, with middle-class pride, she added, "It was our own washing – we don't take in washing, Judge." "How about spilling liquor on the floor?" he asked her. "That's not so," answered Charlotte, scandalized. "Liquor costs too much to spill."

Indeed, they lived simply, made sensible investments, and managed to bank almost all Mary's salary. Nothing had changed, Pickford told the papers, and she seemed a bit muted, even low. "I've worked since I was five years old." And as she was still working – all the time – she didn't "really seem to be anything different to what I once was." Her fame and her paycheck seemed abstractions; she was grateful, of course, but didn't feel "one bit rich." To provide the lift she needed, Pickford went to Adolph Zukor and proposed a raise.

She could bolster her argument two ways. Pickford's unprecedented fame had vastly increased her talent's value. She also served Zukor as a trusted adviser, for no one else on Famous Players' staff had her all-round acumen in film.

In New York, where at this point Pickford was still making most of her films, she sat down once a week for a meeting with Frohman and Zukor in the Lyceum theater (Frohman's office). There they determined by committee what roles she should play, how her films would be produced, and who would write them. Zukor kept an unblinking eye on business. Frohman, with his encyclopedic knowledge of Broadway, was a fountainhead of possible Famous Plays. But for knowledge of the movies they relied on Mary. "I was only an apprentice then," remembered Zukor. "She was an expert workman."

To discuss her salary, Mary made an appointment to meet her employer in his New York office. Her opening gambit was a testimonial to her love and respect for him as a person. Then she dropped a bombshell, explaining she had been offered two thousand dollars a week to appear in *The Diamond from the Sky*, a serial in the spirit of *The Perils of Pauline*. With twenty-three installments planned, Mary stood to make a fortune. The two then proceeded to a restaurant, where maneuvers continued around the teacups. "Mary," said Zukor, "I want you to know that your happiness means everything, not only to me personally, but to my pictures and to my company as a whole. . . . How would you like to have your salary doubled?" Pickford, who had never seriously entertained a move to serials, was happy. But she wondered, as the minutes passed, why Zukor seemed reluctant to leave the restaurant. Finally dusk fell. Zukor led her to the mezzanine and posed her at the window. There Mary saw the marquee across the street light up. She later remembered it as advertising *Hearts Adrift*, although it was probably another film. More important, for the first time in her life, Mary Pickford saw her name in lights. "That dear, sweet man," she later wrote, "had planned his surprise with such loving care, and I had repaid him by asking him for a raise!"

Of all the adjectives ever used to describe Adolph Zukor, "sweet" and "dear" occurred to no one but Pickford. Others called him a shark, a killer, or his nickname, "Creepy." Zukor's outward veneer was gracious – his voice soft and slow, his manners impeccable. But his eyes were flinty. Behind them lay a tension, an almost predatory watchfulness, a will to control. This, combined with a skull-like head, made him seem like an elegantly tailored bull terrier. Businessmen approached with caution, for Zukor's ruthlessness was chilling. "Zukor kills," wrote a journalist, "and then buys the corpse from the family of the deceased."

But to Pickford he was nothing less than "Papa Zukor." In return she was his "sweetheart-honey." Mary even referred to Zukor's son and daughter as her siblings, a relationship that developed while Mary was a weekend guest at Zukor's farm near Nyack, New York. Guests on these weekends numbered ten to forty, and only two silent-film actors were among them: Pickford and leading man Thomas Meighan. But only Mary bypassed Zukor's reserve and saw his sympathetic heart. She knew him as well as she knew herself: his deprivation as a child, the scramble from obscurity toward security, the gnawing sensation that there must be more money. She knew why he needed to rule, to dominate. Together they intended to dominate features, and the lever they would use was Little Mary. It was in Zukor's interest to provide the public honors Mary craved, promote her image, and administer positive reinforcement. And perhaps, as Pickford believed, he loved her.

At any rate, the finished contract paid Mary a flush thousand dollars a week, and she slept a bit more sweetly with her fattened purse.

At first glance, Pickford and *Cinderella* (1914) would seem to be ideally matched; the heroine is outrageously oppressed and rises from picturesque rags to riches. But the film, for the most part, is inert. There are a few revealing moments, as when Pickford, incredulous that a rat has become a footman, tickles him to see if he is real. And the numerals on the all-important clock shrivel and curl like the legs of dying insects as the hands reach twelve. But the tale's passive heroine fails to tap Mary's greatest asset: spunk. Watching it, the viewer longs to see Cinderella appear at the ball dressed defiantly in rags – or, if nothing else, kick the prince's door down.

Owen Moore, improbably, played Prince Charming. "A seizure of pity and weakness" had affected his wife, who, a few weeks later, also had him cast in *Mistress Nell* (1915), the tale of Charles II (played by Owen) and his mistress, Nell Gwyn. Pickford has a grand, scampish time in the unaccustomed role of a sexually amoral woman – such a grand time that she blots out her husband. Indeed, though Owen appeared in almost thirty features throughout his marriage, Pickford's fame rendered him almost invisible. In 1916 she told the story of an actor friend (she called him Frank). "No longer was he the happy-go-lucky, carefree boy who had courted the obscure little actress.... He was really as negative in his own home as the furniture, and it was not often he could see his wife, so surrounded was she by the admiring public, clamoring managers and the press. One never hears of Frank these days. No one asks what he is doing. 'I am just the shadow,' he said to me the other day, 'the shadow thrown by a great, scintillating light.'"

They were apparently trying to live together, in New York, where *Mistress Nell* and *Cinderella* were shot, and also in California. That spring the Moores symbolically remarried at the Mission San Juan in Capistrano. At first the pair were asked to be attendants at the wedding of director Allan Dwan and actress Pauline Bush, but it became a double ritual, with Catholic vows. "A wedding," said Mary, "should be something pretty and dainty, to look back upon with pride." But despite the mission setting, which was redolent of order, fragrant nature, and serenity, Pickford's marriage did not renew itself. Soon Charlotte had moved into their Los Angeles quarters, where, as Mary pointed out in martyred tones, she rose every day at five to cook Owen breakfast. "Real, unselfish devotion ... is rarely appreciated in its true worth," Pickford later lamented. "Over and over in our profession I have seen it utterly wasted on some man absolutely unworthy of it." But Owen, a man of his time, thought his wife should be making breakfast. Instead, he received his scrambled eggs from – in his opinion – a large, smiling hypocrite. "He called my mother terrible names," remembered Mary, "names I do not care to repeat, and I said he would have to apologize. He said he would not." Owen also complained that his marriage to Pickford cost him money. Mary, who was careful to pay her share of the bills and supported her mother with her own funds, was mortified to tears.

Some believe she found a handsome shoulder to cry on. It belonged to James Kirkwood, the former Biograph actor. In 1914 he directed a few films for a small film company called Colonial. Later that year Zukor hired him to direct nine Pickford features.

Their rapport was instant. Kirkwood was just the sort of man Mary liked: flamboyant, irreverent, and raffish – somewhat like her brother, Jack, who was one of Kirkwood's drinking buddies. Kirkwood was tall, more distinguished than gorgeous in appearance, and equipped with an arrestingly clear-eyed gaze. He was charming when drunk (and he often drank). He was also a notorious ladies' man.

He had seen at Biograph how Mary threw tantrums when Griffith gave orders. He had also seen her blossom under easy banter. Accordingly, Kirkwood threw the creative ball among the cast and kept the atmosphere light and bright. When Pickford needed tears, he sat down with her and chatted about some heartache in her past. He would keep musicians or a phonograph on hand to play melancholy tunes (this was a silent-film tradition). For happy scenes, Kirkwood would kid her or ask her to talk about Toronto. He was not above taunting her into rages – a practice Mary deeply resented from Griffith, but which she accepted at Kirkwood's hands.

Years later, Kirkwood told his son that at one point he and Mary were lovers, so happily in love that they dreamed of getting married. Indeed, it was later claimed by one of Charlotte's employees that she asked him to raid a film director's apartment. There, at three in the morning, he found Mary and removed her. The director in question, ran the gossip, was Kirkwood – and everyone in silent movies seemed to believe it. But Kirkwood directed Owen as well as Mary in *Mistress Nell* and *Cinderella*, and despite a certain looseness in film society, it is hard to imagine a blasé Owen winking at his wife's affair and slapping his director on the back. The actor, when furious or insecure, took direct action – against his wife. Actress Madge Bellamy, for instance, claimed Owen Moore sometimes took a whip to Pickford, a tidbit she received straight from Charlotte's lips.

Five of Kirkwood's films with Mary have survived. Before *Cinderella* and *Mistress Nell*, he directed *The Eagle's Mate* (1914), surrounding Mary's hillbilly antics with some attractive, deep-focus photography. He found a role for Jack (as a pipsqueak member of the Ku Klux Klan) and one for himself, as a man who kidnaps – then tries to control – Mary as a kicking hellcat. ("If ever you strike me again," he tells her, "I'll either beat you or kiss you to death.") Of the five, it was the smashingly successful *Rags* (1915) that best distilled Mary Pickford's fire.

In the title role of an urchin in a mining town, the actress makes a rousing entrance on a goat, then, in quick succession, scatters some children who are torturing a dog, breaks up a bar brawl, and slaps several men who touch her hair. But Rags allows Marshall Neilan to touch it; as Keith, her beau, he helps her disentangle her curls from a bush. The scene, as Neilan slowly unsnags and snips her hair, is a delicate cameo of sexual suggestion. Later Rags invites Keith to lunch and creates the most elaborate feast her poverty allows. Unfortunately her father, the town drunk, devours the meal before Keith arrives. Rags is left with a table of scraps, which she offers with the statement, "I was so hungry I jes' couldn't wait for you." She then watches Neilan eat with the ardor of a lover and a famished dog. This scene has been compared by film scholar James Card to the dinner gone wrong staged by Chaplin's Tramp in *The Gold Rush* (1925).

An even stronger resemblance to Chaplin appears in *The Foundling* (1916). As the orphan Molly-O, Pickford fashions a doghouse in the park by turning a wheelbarrow upside down and sleeps there with some homeless dogs. In the movie's best moment, the dogcatcher chases one of Molly-O's "family." Pickford runs desperately toward the dog and crouches over it; the butterfly net ensnares them both. The image of Pickford enveloped in the net defines her, literally, as the underdog. The parallel to Chaplin's *A Dog's Life* (1918) is striking. In fact, nearly all of Mary's features are filled with touches that today one might call "Chaplinesque." But in 1915 Chaplin was only beginning to investigate pathos. In the early teens the art of poignant comedy was "Pickfordish."

Pickford first saw Chaplin in the mid-1910s while dining with Charlotte at a restaurant. The actor was writing – perhaps, Mary fancied, an idea for a poem (Chaplin's offscreen appearance was aesthetic). Then she overheard Chaplin tell Mack Sennett he had figured out his next year's earnings, to the tune of $350,000. The figure, if true, was far removed from the first film salary he ever received – $150 a week from Sennett, who put Chaplin in his comedy shorts at Keystone. There the most anarchic slapstick of the silents took shape through the antics of the Keystone Cops. The Cops were *too* antic, Mary thought – when she read an early outline by Sennett, she told him, "You'll have to change all those policemen into private detectives. Their behavior is scandalous!"

But Sennett's films thrived on disrespect. He set up authority figures only to knock them down, blow them up, or cover them with custard. He introduced the Keystone Cops specifically to suggest that police were idiots. And those who denounced the movies as vulgar used the Keystone Cops to prove their point.

The nascent film community, scorned by Broadway's self-appointed nobility, was sorting out its own top and bottom drawers. Keystone comics – and in 1913, Chaplin was among them – were considered coarse and second-rate. When Pickford officially met Chaplin at a ball, she was appalled to find him, shoeless, doing his impression of silent-film actor J. Warren Kerrigan. Mary considered this undignified. (Chaplin imitated everyone, including Pickford. Perhaps she was aware of this.) Mary was also repelled by his handshake – "what my mother used to call a cold-fish hand" – limp, she thought, and uninterested.

Possibly she was growing jealous, for a Chaplin craze was picking up steam. His walk was widely imitated. In 1915 a fan could buy a Charlie Chaplin outfit, including a gold tooth, a mustache, and a roll of stage money. Using these, and perhaps a Charlie Chaplin squirt-ring, he could enter one of the Chaplin look-alike contests taking place around the country. In July over thirty theaters in Manhattan held Chaplin amateur nights.

Chaplin moved that year to Essanay, where he began to introduce a pathetic, chivalrous tone to his performances. This only deepened his appeal. When he moved to Mutual in February 1916, his salary was spectacular. In exchange for twelve movies, to be produced in a year, he would collect $10,000 a week, plus a $150,000 bonus for signing. These figures were a thorn in Mary's side. It rankled that Chaplin, "a cheap, hamfat comedian," made more money than she did although she far outpaced him in production. Chaplin had terrifying mental blocks; it took him two years, not one, to deliver his dozen movies, and these were two-reelers. Mary, in contrast, made six features in 1914 and nine in 1915 – and all but one were five reels long. "Pickford was a fancy staple," observed their contemporary Terry Ramsaye. Chaplin, on the other hand, became "rare spice."

Chaplin's salary also fanned a spark of resentment toward Zukor that was sheltering in Mary's heart. In 1914 he put Broadway's Marguerite Clark under contract. Four foot ten and ninety pounds, Clark, "a fascinating thing of thistledown," had huge, dark eyes, a childlike face, and the smallest feet Mary had ever seen. And though silent film soon overflowed with Mary types, Pickford was shocked that Zukor was developing one within his own ranks. In fact, in some minds, Mary Pickford was a Clark type.

"Her mannerisms were enchanting," raved a fan who fell hard for "the use of the delicate hands, the throw of the head." Mary later admitted that Clark "had me down for the count in the South," and she found she could no longer claim every urchin in a Zukor script. She pined, for instance, for 1915's *The Prince and the Pauper*, but Zukor gave the dual roles to Clark. Things grew messier still when Charlotte, who resented Clark hugely, began a feud with Cora, Clark's sister and manager. Jack, not to be outdone, joined the fray by developing a raging crush on Clark. Later Pickford made light of Clark ("an amusing, charming little person") though she also allowed that she reacted badly when her brother appeared in two Clark productions. Clark's presence on the payroll seemed a hint from Zukor that she, Mary Pickford, was dispensable.

In fact, Mary Pickford was indispensable, which she proved in January 1915 by raising the stakes with Famous Players, requesting – and receiving – twice her previous wage. More important, she began to receive half the profits of her films. Rather than raid Famous Players' coffers, Zukor raised the new sum by driving a harder bargain with Paramount, which in turn hiked its fees to the exhibitors of Mary's films. They grumbled but paid the new, inflated rates. Then Pickford discovered in another way just how significant she was in the scheme of things.

With the advent of features, nickelodeons had folded in favor of large, clean theaters, often with an edifice of columns, flags, and eagles to insist on the movies' upright nature. These, in turn, became more opulent as films became big-business fantasy. Movie palaces – "Temples of the Silent Drama" or, as New York's legendary Strand was called, "the Temple of Thespia" – sprang up everywhere. Viewers were swept away by tapestries, statues, mirrors, rugs, gilt paint on everything, chandeliers, and domes. An army of uniformed ushers, trained in bowing, saluting, and clicking heels, took tickets and showed patrons to their seats. And what seats – thousands of them, curving in balconies and loges. Throughout the feature, an orchestra or gargantuan organ sighed and thundered with the images. The powder room at the Strand was so resplendent it was opened with a formal tea, attended by film stars.

Pickford's chauffeur usually drove her past the Strand, at Broadway and 47th, on the way from the Famous Players Studio to Broadway and 91st, where she lived with Charlotte. In the summer of 1915 Pickford had seen and enjoyed the overflow crowds, filing in and out, for *Rags*. But after it closed, she saw the crowds for another Famous Players film – or rather, the lack of them. The sidewalk was deserted.

In those days Paramount rented the Famous Players movies through a process called block-booking. Rather than offer exhibitors their choice of films, Paramount offered packages – sometimes an entire season of movies, of which perhaps a half dozen were Pickfords. Theaters, eager for Mary's product, bought the package sight unseen. But Pickford was not aware of how heavily her films were subsidizing others. By the time she reached 72nd Street she had decided to find out. She returned to the Strand and marched into the theater. The orchestra was half full. "As for the balcony," she remembered wryly, "a cannon could have been fired into it without harming anyone." Mary, whose contract was due to expire in January, "went home very thoughtful that night."

The next day Mary asked Zukor, politely, how much the Strand had paid to exhibit *Rags*. Warily, he told her: $3,000. And what, asked Mary, had Paramount charged for the following feature? Zukor sighed, examined the books, then told her: $2,800. Mary thanked him. No one voiced the obvious – that Pickford's name had been used to obtain a healthy fee for a movie which could not make money on its own.

She was also beginning to brood about less-than-perfect films. Zukor had come up with the superfluous idea of augmenting Mary's worldwide appeal by casting her as women from different nations. The experiment began with *Little Pal*, directed by Kirkwood in 1915. Pickford played an Inuit girl in the drooping, dispirited style she had brought to her Biograph slaveys. She punctuated the gloom with some comic kicks, but the film was still greeted with dismay. "Square-souled, square-bodied, square-headed," wrote a critic who rather liked the film. But others were shocked by Mary's costumes and her long black wig.

Later that year, she was drastically miscast as Madame Butterfly. Pickford's director, Sidney Olcott, insisted she play the role with Japanese reserve; Pickford wished to make the role more Yankee. Inevitably, tension broke in a "furious quarrel which resulted in Olcott stalking off the set. I was shaking with anger," remembered Mary. Then she called the company together and proposed they continue under her direction, with the crew and her co-star Marshall Neilan assisting. At this point Olcott, who was hiding in the scenery, emerged. "He assured me that no one but Sidney Olcott would ever direct any scenes for *Madame Butterfly*. Then it was my turn to walk off the set." The shoot ran long and over budget – in part, because of Mary's behavior. She began to play the spoiled star, always finding something wrong with her costume, at one point refusing to wear her shoes, and dubbing the movie "Madame Snail." In the end, she poured mascara on her curls, pulled back the corners of her eyes, and played the role as Olcott wished it. Fans were appalled: where was Little Mary? And Pickford decided she must try to avoid men of Olcott's rigid temperament. She wondered how she might gain a little influence.

In May 1916 she and Zukor got around to negotiating another contract. "Personal feelings," observed Will Irwin, a Zukor associate, "did not in the least cramp their style when it came to bargaining and trafficking, any more than it would have hampered them in a friendly game of cards. Otherwise they would have esteemed each other less." Meanwhile the industry was watching, eager to tempt the actress with blandishments and money. Among the most interesting (rumored) offers was that of the American Tobacco Company, which was contemplating entering the movie business. Also laid at Mary's feet were proposals from the year-old Triangle company, from Carl Laemmle, who was running a concern called Universal, and from Albert E. Smith of the redoubtable Vitagraph. The latter offer was a near thing: Mary was about to sign, goes the story, when she suddenly asked if she might see Albert Smith's new baby. "Let's get the business off our minds first," he told her. Mary, who was looking for the same family feeling she knew with Zukor, told Smith tartly, "Then I'll never see it."

Finally Mutual, home to Chaplin, upped the ante to a million dollars. It was a figure Adolph Zukor refused to meet. "I'm going to give you half of the profits of your films and a voice in selecting them," said Zukor. "And a guarantee of ten thousand dollars a week. And, Mary, that's my limit."

She accepted.

Personal feelings, it seems, had tipped the balance. "We have the same ideas," Pickford once said of Zukor. "We've been down in the world and up in the world together, and I'm sure of him." In fact, her devotion had been sealed when Famous Players' New York studio, neighbor to a junk shop and a Chinese laundry, burned to the ground in 1915. The facilities were crammed into the top three floors of a former armory on West 26th Street. On September 11 a fire began in a braid and rope factory on the second floor. While fire trucks tried to get down the narrow street (which was jammed with horse-drawn wagons), flames licked, then swallowed up the building. Pickford stood crying in the street beside Zukor, who was staring, expressionless, at the rubble. "Thank you," he said, as a sympathizer murmured his regrets. He looked back at the flames. "We'll build a better one." Mary believed she had seen, while Zukor watched the fire, a flicker of anguish behind the mask. The moment of empathy fused her to him.

Nevertheless, her new contract, which she signed on June 24, 1916, was not softhearted. Through it, Mary ceased to be an actress only. Instead, she became the first film actress to produce her own work. She was given her own production unit – the Pickford Film Corporation – within the frame of the Famous Players organization, and Zukor, as its president, became Mary's partner, not her boss, in film production. Charlotte, as treasurer, was also on board, to keep an eagle eye on Mary's interests. If Pickford didn't like the roles selected for her, she could appeal to her board of directors. Mary also had a voice in the final cut, a decision she shared with the film's director and an officer of her corporation (a two-thirds vote settled all disputes). But her word was law in the choice of film directors – and these, one assumes, would wisely be amenable not only to Mary's input on the set but also to her vision of the final film. In addition, the actress held final approval of the supporting cast and the advertising.

The contract slowed Mary's pace of production, requiring that the actress make a maximum of six films a year (the year in which she had made nine had been a brutal treadmill). The new quota ensured that her films would be made with care. In addition, fewer films might increase demand and, in the end, bring greater returns for all.

As for Mary's specific returns, Zukor agreed to pay her half a million dollars a year, or half the net profits of her films, whichever sum was greater. Because the term of the contract was two years, the actress would be guaranteed at least a million dollars, a sum that was reported to wide amazement. Zukor also agreed to distribute her movies through a special division of Paramount called Artcraft, which did not block-book. Thus Pickford freed herself of the arrangement that she believed oversold other movies and undersold her own. All this, a bonus of three hundred thousand dollars, and various perks – a press agent, a secretary, a private studio in New York, and travel in a parlor coach to the West for winter shoots. But the contract's pièce de résistance was a clause in which Zukor agreed to pay Mary ten thousand dollars a week for the period of May 29 to June 24 – in other words, the four weeks she and Charlotte had spent hammering out the contract.

Decades later Chaplin wrote: "I was astonished at the legal and business acumen of Mary. She knew all its nomenclature; the amortizations and the deferred stocks, etc. She understood all the articles of incorporation, the legal discrepancy on page 7, paragraph A, article 27, and coolly referred to the overlap and contradiction in paragraph D, article 24." But, reflecting the prejudice of the era, he found these gifts unseemly in a woman – particularly in a woman so blond, so little and physically childlike. Brilliance in art – so said the men in charge – was feminine. A gift for business, with its implied ambition and aggression, was manly. Some women shared the prejudice: "That pretty little thing with yellow curls thinking of money like that!" remembered Linda Arvidson.

Even remarks in Mary's favor ("In appearance so typically feminine, Mary Pickford gives to the romance of business all of a man's response") reflected the sexism of the time. "Mary is the most practical woman I know," said director Ernst Lubitsch. "She talks money, discusses contracts and makes important decisions with disconcerting speed." Then he noted with amazement that "nothing of this prevents her from playing scenes filled with sweetness and passion." The implication – that a woman who could both think and emote was freakish – made Pickford seem like a two-headed monster. Either that, or her "feminine side" was a fraud, a swindle created by a grasping, mendacious brain.

"I don't think the brain has any sex," said Mary. And as her image as a sharpie thrived, her self-defence became slightly frantic. "I'm not the money-lover that I sound. I always thought that the public would catch up with me one day and find out that I wasn't really a good actress and that I was too little or too fat." As for her pre-eminence in film: "I never enjoyed it, to tell you the truth. I don't like business. . . . There's something about a typewriter that upsets me. It looks as if it's going to bite me. I really detest it." She pleaded insecurity: "It may sound rather harsh, my dealings with Mr. Zukor and maybe other business associates. But it must be borne in mind that an actor's life, at best, is very short-lived. Any one of many things can happen to him – loss of health – but the greatest menace, of course, is the loss of popularity. And so he must make hay while the sun shines." As for all those "dry, dead meetings," she was forced to endure them: "I had to assume the business role in order to protect the thing I loved, my work."

But many within the industry insisted that Pickford's business acumen lent a fraudulent touch to Little Mary. Chaplin summed up the ambivalence when he called her "Bank of America's Sweetheart." Mary hated the nickname, which pursued her to the grave.

Charlotte Hennessey, Pickford's mother, c. 1892. Mary called her a woman of "unbelievable courage."

Pickford's father, John Charles Smith, c. 1892 — charming, impractical, and alcoholic.

Mary Pickford's birthplace (center) at 211 University Avenue, Toronto.

Mary Pickford (right) and
her neglected, less talented
sister, Lottie, c. 1902.

Jack, Pickford's
brother (c. 1902), was
indulged as a child and
ran wild as an adult.

In 1900 Pickford played her first major stage role as the fatherless Cissy in *The Silver King*.

On her ninth birthday, in 1901, Mary played the saintly Little Eva in *Uncle Tom's Cabin*.

A glum-looking
Pickford, c. 1907,
in *The Warrens of Virginia*.
Soon afterward, the
actress was reduced to the
"disgrace" of movie acting.

David Belasco (c. 1910), who
put Pickford on Broadway.
The actress approached him
with "more awe than liking.
You can't like a deity; you fear it."

The Biograph "dark studio" — a former
ballroom, banked with ultraviolet lights.

The Biograph brownstone
at 11 West 14th Street,
New York City, c. 1909.

Legendary director
D.W. Griffith
(c. 1909) told
Pickford she was
"too little and too
fat" — then cast
her in Biograph
films for years.

Mack Sennett, who later created the Keystone Cops, with Mary Pickford in *Won by a Fish* (1912).

Actor Owen Moore (c. 1916) wed Pickford in 1911. The disastrous marriage was a misery for both.

Pickford in her last Biograph, *The New York Hat* (1912).

Biograph promotional postcard showing Mary Pickford in native costume, c. 1913.

Harold Lockwood with Pickford
in *Tess of the Storm Country* (1914).
The movie distilled Pickford's image
as a comic guttersnipe.

Producer Adolph Zukor (c. 1914),
who launched Pickford in features.
"Zukor kills," wrote a journalist,
"and then buys the corpse from
the family of the deceased."

Pickford as the brawling title character in *Rags* (1915).

Frances Marion (left, 1917) became Pickford's screenwriter and trusted friend.

Mary Pickford, c. 1914. "The best known woman who has ever lived, the woman who was known to more people and loved by more people than any other woman that has been in all history."

A poem to Pickford, written by a fan, described her "weird magnetic grip."

Pickford (left) cuts loose as the rambunctious *Rebecca of Sunnybrook Farm* (1917).

Mary Pickford in *The Poor Little Rich Girl* (1917). Her childhood had been "walled up inside me.... I needed to express it."

Pickford and her favorite director, Marshall Neilan — "delightful, aggravating, gifted and charming" — on the set of *M'Liss* (1918).

Fans and critics were stunned by Pickford's grim appearance in the tragic *Stella Maris* (1918).

Pickford, who wrote an advice column from 1915 to 1917, poses to advocate women's rights.

Douglas Fairbanks, Mary Pickford,
and Charlie Chaplin map out their
appearances to sell war bonds, c. 1917.

Court-martialed, sentenced,
and almost shot: Pickford in the
anti-Hun propaganda picture
The Little American (1918).

An honorary colonel in the U.S. army
(c. 1918), Pickford sent soldiers off to battle
and kissed the American flag for cameras.

Mary Pickford, propagandist, c. 1917. Her fundraising efforts were
so effective that the U.S. army named two cannons after her.

The founders of United Artists at the Chaplin studios: Douglas Fairbanks, D.W. Griffith, Mary Pickford, and Charlie Chaplin, 1919.

Douglas Fairbanks and Mary Pickford with Charlotte, Jack, Gwynne, and Lottie Pickford, c. 1920.

7

THE LITTLE AMERICAN

Pickford's new contract was a land-
mark — not only for her but also for Zukor, who, in order to be able to
afford his star actress, had worked out a deal with one of his biggest com-
petitors. On June 17, 1916, Famous Players merged with the Jesse L. Lasky
Feature Play Company, creating between them the largest motion picture
enterprise in the world.

The creation of Lasky's company had been as slapdash as the founding
of Famous Players was deliberate. Lasky, once a cornet player, had become
a Broadway entrepreneur. His brother-in-law, Sam Goldfish (he later
changed his name to Goldwyn), was a glove salesman with a crush on film.
Cecil B. DeMille was the youngest brother of an eminent Broadway family, and the way Lasky told it, he and Sam formed the company to save
Cecil's neck.

Cecil's father, Henry C., co-wrote *The Main Line* with David Belasco,
who directed the play in 1886. It became Belasco's first success. Several
close collaborations followed, and Cecil and his older brother, William,
grew up more or less on Belasco's knee. And although their father
requested on his deathbed that his sons choose careers outside the theater,
they disobeyed him, aided by none other than the Master. William became

a Broadway playwright, while Cecil, a jack of all stage trades, worked in his shadow. A small role in *Warrens* (Cecil played Arthur, Pickford's older brother) offered some security, but then it was back to catch-as-catch-can while William steadily grew more famous.

Cecil hit bottom in 1910 when he wrote *The Return of Peter Grimm*. He showed the play – a meditation on the spirit world – to Belasco, who never got back to him. The next year, Cecil was astonished when *The Return of Peter Grimm* opened on Broadway. Belasco had rewritten it, though the program billed him as sole author, an impression bolstered by his curtain speech, in which he explained that he had written the play after a ghostly visitation from his mother. "Probably he believed in all sincerity that *The Return of Peter Grimm* owed more to his work and less to mine than was actually the case," DeMille wrote halfheartedly. Then, with thinly disguised resentment: "Perhaps it was like the pony he promised me when I was seven or eight years old. Perhaps he just forgot." Cecil's niece Agnes believed that DeMille went on to spend his life "proving, first, that he was as smart as his older brother, second, that he was as smart as Belasco, and third, that he was smarter than anyone else."

Lasky put several of Cecil's plays on the boards in his Broadway venue. The pair lunched regularly in New York, but in 1913 Cecil declared, "I'm pulling out. Broadway's all right for you – you're doing well. But I can't live on the royalties I'm getting, my debts are piling up, and I want to chuck the whole thing. Besides," he added, "there's a revolution going on in Mexico." Lasky listened with alarm while DeMille described war as a stimulating change of scene. He quickly laid out a counter-proposal: a movie company, with Lasky producing, DeMille directing, and Goldwyn selling. In fact, it was Goldwyn who had first sold Lasky on the concept, insisting that features would prove more lucrative than his other dream: selling hot tamales. Now Lasky sold Cecil on the movies, and the partners signed the deal on the back of a menu.

Lasky, who had always hoped to move from vaudeville to something distinguished, was set on making distinguished movies. The first was *The Squaw Man* (1914), chosen in part for its western theme (cowboys could be filmed outdoors, where light and scenery were free) and because Dustin Farnum, a popular stage star, was willing to slum a bit in film. Naively, Lasky sent Cecil and the cast to "real Indian country" (Arizona), but Cecil discovered neither Indians nor suitable topography in Flagstaff. "Want authority to rent barn in place called Hollywood for $75 a month," he wired from California. After Goldwyn "hit the ceiling," he and Lasky wrote a cautious wire, insisting that Cecil rent only month-to-month: "Don't make any long commitment." Cecil immediately turned the stalls into an office, a projection room, and dressing rooms. By 1917 the partners would be millionaires.

Lasky's biggest coup was a deal with Belasco. Prestigious Belasco titles – including *The Girl of the Golden West*, *The Rose of the Rancho*, and *The Warrens of Virginia*, which starred Blanche Sweet in 1915 – reached the screen through the barn at the corner of Selma and Vine in Hollywood. Meanwhile Zukor watched Lasky's progress like a cat at a mouse-hole. Lasky was gentle and easygoing. Far from considering him a threat, Zukor cultivated Lasky's friendship and proposed a merger in 1916.

Both Lasky and Zukor released their films through Paramount; together they provided more than three-quarters of Paramount's business. And both loathed Paramount's terms – an advance of thirty-five thousand dollars per film, against 65 percent of the profits. Zukor, who had anticipated most of Mary's contract demands, knew he would have to gouge exhibitors further to find the funds to pay her. But he also knew that Paramount would probably balk at the increase in fees. Through their alliance, sealed five days before Mary signed her contract, Famous Players and Lasky not only pooled bank accounts and talent but – through Lasky's and Zukor's shares – took control of Paramount itself. (One result was, eventually, a tripling of the rental fees for Mary's films.) Now Famous Players–Lasky – with Zukor as president, Lasky as vice president in charge of production, Cecil as director general, and Goldwyn as chairman of the board – became the most formidable power in the industry. And Zukor, who had warned DeMille, "I can break you like that" (he thrust two fists together and slowly drew them apart to illustrate), became film's undisputed czar.

But Mary, who hated the new arrangement, would not accept the interlopers. She refused to believe that Zukor was the architect of the merger. Instead, Lasky's group was "high-hat and snooty." In Mary's view, Zukor was "completely bewildered. . . . Friends, associates, and kin had been talking to him, and he had become a house divided within himself." In the place of "an intimate little family group, threshing out its problems in a warm, personal spirit of teamwork, there was now a huge machine – cold, critical, automatic, and impersonal." Mary particularly hated Goldwyn, who later complained of "adhesive relatives … standing around back of the screen to see that justice is administered."

He was thinking, principally, of Charlotte. Single mothers who had once put their children on the stage now hovered over their movie progeny, monitoring their virtue and their bank accounts. Charlotte pioneered the new cliché: at Biograph, she had lurked in the background, curling Mary's hair and applying her elbow grease to scrubbing the toilet. Now she was present on Mary's sets, putting her foot down on dangerous stunts and sometimes objecting to direction. Mary often teased her out of these suggestions, but wisely trusted her in business. Pickford detested its day-to-day minutiae, although she had a talent for it. Charlotte, on the other hand, once spent a day clipping coupons in the bank vault until her hands blistered from the scissors. "I am not going to sympathize with you," laughed Mary. "You had a wonderful time cutting and if your whole hand had been blistered you would have been very pleasured."

Goldwyn was further annoyed by Mary's power; he complained that "it often took longer to make one of Mary's contracts than it did to make one of Mary's pictures." "My God," he joked, as he watched her make her way across a lot. "Ten thousand dollars a week and she's walking to the set yet. She should be running!" Push came to shove when Mary tried to see Zukor about her contract (there was money owing). Mid-conversation, Zukor reached beneath his desk and pressed a button. An office boy materialized and stated that Mary should report to Goldwyn. Outraged, Pickford bit her lip. "What's all this nonsense?" asked Goldwyn as she strode into his office. "It's not nonsense at all, Mr. Goldfish," said Mary. "I made an agreement with Mr. Zukor that I scarcely think concerns you. . . . Mr. Zukor and I will decide it, if you don't mind – "

"Now, you listen to me – " said Goldwyn.

"And the next time," continued Mary coolly, "please don't send the office boy for me. If you wish to see me, come yourself. Good afternoon."

She began to express dislike for her movies. She was always hard on herself in this respect; she would damn one for a bad review, a stray remark, or a box office slip. A gradual slide in her audience receipts had made her fret through the better part of 1916. She hated *Hulda from Holland* (1916, now lost): "You can talk about your old days," she wrote in a newspaper column, "when you tripped the light fantastic through a Virginia reel or turkey-trotted fifteen miles around the ballroom, but I will have it that dancing in wooden shoes, hop-clickity-click, hop-clickity-click, is about the most violent form of pleasure you ever indulged in." Later she added: "I just begged the company to suppress it."

Pickford's films, produced at a rate of six or so a year, were often less luminous than the star. And at first critics wanted little more. But at the time of the merger even the effusive Julian Johnson took note of Pickford's "eerie feat: she has remained the photoplay queen, the regal personage of black-and-white" − without a decent screenplay. He predicted that Famous Players–Lasky would improve her product. The actress, however, had convinced herself that the Lasky contingent was waiting for her to use her new right of approval of story and director − and fail.

In fact, she did fail her first time out, when she approved John Emerson to direct her in *Less Than the Dust* (1916), a rags-to-riches tale of India. Emerson was relatively new to the business, eager to make his mark, and genial − an excellent collaborator, one would think. Ironically, he proved so malleable that Mary despised him as a sycophant. And perhaps she disliked the movie for its own sake; it comes to life only in the final scenes, and today critics rate it among her worst. ("Oh, Miss Pickford," a fan once told her, "I loved you in the picture, *Cheaper Than the Dirt*.") But Pickford was probably most affected by *Less Than the Dust*'s box office performance. Its profits were modest − a slap in the face, she thought, from the public. Later she blamed the movie's failure on Famous Players–Lasky.

Mary's "new masters," as she called them, were watching closely as, late in 1916, she set to work on *The Pride of the Clan* (1917). The movie describes her standard odyssey: a penniless waif, this time in plaid, is claimed by faraway, wealthy parents. Unfortunately, none of this happens to Mary − it happens to her sweetheart, played by Matt Moore, Owen's brother. (Mary plays the woman who loves him and heroically lets him go.) Pickford, as producer, should have caught this flaw. It seems she noticed it during production; the movie jolts from magnificent atmospheric segments, the creation of director Maurice Tourneur, to others that bear Mary's comic stamp. The results never meshed, and Pickford feared rumblings from the Lasky camp. All the more reason to be overjoyed when she went to work on *The Poor Little Rich Girl* (1917) and sensed she was finally working on a jewel.

It was written, from the stage play, by Frances Marion, who had rapidly become Mary's closest friend. In the spring of 1914 she had arrived, disheveled by a gale-force wind, at the Famous Players plant in California, hoping to show Mary her poster work. In the editing room she met a young woman without pretensions and with a towel wound, turbanlike, around her hair. Pickford let Marion catch her breath while she kept up a stream of professional chitchat. The artist noticed that "a strange watchfulness lay behind her steadfast gaze, a penetrating analysis which enabled her to see past the outward shell and read your character as clearly as if it were etched upon a stone tablet." And Mary made oddly personal comments: "When I was a child I used to retreat into a dream world and hide from reality. Unfortunately, as we grow older we learn that there is no escape." She spoke affectionately of the Gishes: "I've found out that friendship sometimes sustains us, where love sometimes fails us." Instantly Marion sensed the problem. She had already met Owen Moore at a party and listened as he held forth on Pickford's "expressive little talent. Hardly what one would call cerebral." Owen's condescension, and Mary's tone, made Marion realize that "in all the articles I had read about [Pickford] she was never referred to as Mrs. Moore. In fact, I couldn't recall even in interviews where she or the interviewer had ever alluded to her love affair with Owen Moore or her marriage. Was it because there was little congeniality in their relationship?"

By 1915 Marion had found her vocation writing – particularly films for Mary Pickford (she began right away with *Mistress Nell*). And though she was quickly in demand throughout Hollywood, Marion had a special knack for Pickford films. Indeed, she was so in tune with Mary's image that in 1916 and 1917 she wrote a newspaper column for her: "Daily Talks," which appeared under Mary's name coast to coast. In it Pickford talks about life, movies, and morals, and responds to queries from her readers.

The tone is wholesome, the content a mishmash of truths, half-truths, and outright lies.

"Brush those cobwebs off your brain, Lazy Girl, and take a lesson from Mr. Ant," ran a sanctimonious item on cleaning house. Much of "Daily Talks" reads like a cross between Louisa May Alcott (as presented in the column, Little Mary bore a striking resemblance to Alcott's Polly in *An Old-Fashioned Girl*) and a fan magazine. Still, some anecdotes from Mary's own life ring true and, especially in answers to readers' queries, a bit of Pickford's tartness sparks off the page. Actresses, Pickford scolds, "do not think much of Mr. Sentimentalist who writes: 'You are my ideal and I am madly in love with you.'" Another letter queried Mary's age. Was she not just a tiny bit older than she claimed? In a fit of guilt, Pickford tore a strip off the writer: "Would you have me send you the family Bible to prove it, Miss Inquisitive Maid? And don't you think you could have made your letter a little less caustic?" "Yes, I am married," she tells another reader. Nothing more, for Pickford's image demanded she downplay Owen's presence.

In *The Poor Little Rich Girl*, Pickford and Marion created a new note for Mary's image. Instead of appearing as a childlike woman, she appeared as a child, pure and simple. And yet this is not a children's movie. *The Poor Little Rich Girl* is a film about a child that speaks to anyone. And in Mary's day, everybody watched such movies. The Victorians and Edwardians treasured childhood. They painted sentimental pictures of children with pink skin and glossy curls, surrounded by puppies, birds, and kittens. They plastered valentines with cherubs. Their adoration explains, in part, the lingering taste of silent viewers for actresses who were physically childlike (a long list: Pickford, the Gishes, Marguerite Clark, Mary Miles Minter, Mae Marsh, and others). It also explains why Mary often posed with kittens, puppies, or a birdcage.

Like Broadway, silent movies often turned to children's classics for their themes. Scores of films featured odd, spunky orphans like those in the pages of L.M. Montgomery and Frances Hodgson Burnett. Viewers recognized and indeed loved the hypocrites who surround this child – the grim old aunt who refuses to smile, perhaps, or the snobbish society matron – knowing that they would eventually melt in the face of the heroine's humor and virtue. And the charming child becomes a beauty, finds a good man's love, and rests secure.

"In the Home of Everything except the love she cared for, dwelt Gwendolyn, the Poor Little Rich Girl." Gwendolyn is a rare role for Pickford: she is wealthy. She is also a prisoner in her own house, living an overprivileged life, surrounded by sneering servants ("Everything her heart could wish, and she still isn't grateful") and parents who do little more than pass her in the hallway. Gwendolyn asks no more than the pleasures any child enjoys – going for walks (forbidden: she might be kidnapped), the company of other children, and occasional contact with her parents ("Mother is very busy today, dear"). When two servants, hoping to make Gwendolyn sleep, accidentally give her too big a dose from a bottle labeled "Poison," Gwen nearly dies. Her parents, stricken, now provide the love for which Gwendolyn yearns. They also follow her doctor's prescription: a trip to the country, gingham dresses, going barefoot, and making mud pies. "Oh!" cries Gwen blissfully. "I love mud."

Most of us retain hazy memories of childhood. A feeling or a mood may remain, but we cannot re-experience the world as children. But sometimes an artist remembers acutely and creates a portrait that is startlingly fresh. In film, Steven Spielberg has sometimes done it. François Truffaut succeeded always. In silent film, Richard Barthelmess, a grown man in 1921, seemed convincingly thirteen in Tol'able David. And in 1988 Tom Hanks became thirteen again for Big. But few performers accomplished the physical transformation that, to Pickford, was second nature. She was physically suited – short, with a head a shade too large for her body. She added technique to this advantage, a process that she described to Vogue: relax the brow and corners of the mouth, point toes inward, loosen legs. Indeed, Gwen is wonderfully observed – as in the difficult business, for instance, of going downstairs hand in hand with an adult, hanging back, attempting to use the feet as brakes, then giving up and hanging like a dead weight. When Pickford rises from the floor, she lets Gwen place her weight on her hands, then pull herself up from the rear to meet them. She carries a stuffed bear by the leg, ends her skips with flat-footed jumps, throws a kiss as though she could taste it, and plays unselfconsciously with her mouth. She is also seen dancing with manic concentration, a star in her own dream and utterly absorbed.

But this would have been mere puppetry if Mary had not been able to call up a child's inner world, untouched by the filter of adulthood. "That phase of my life," she recalled, "was unlived." While she was playing the father to other children, her own childhood had been "walled up inside of me.... I needed to express it." To do so, she used a technique of turning on a dime emotionally – flashing, for instance, from tears to anger, anger to boredom, tedium to joy. The practice, when applied at Biograph, made her ingenues funny, capricious, and adolescent. And it proved exactly right for children, who can swing from rage, pain, or skinned elbows to joy – and back again – in an instant. In a short schoolroom scene in *The Poor Little Rich Girl*, Gwen looks intimidated by the teacher, yawns, nearly falls asleep, shakes with laughter, affects concentration, refuses to do lessons, earnestly follows the dancing master, then collapses inconsolably into tears. The cumulative effect is uncanny. The child seems vulnerable, open to experience, unable to dissemble, yet resilient. She also seems even shorter than five feet, as art director Ben Carré used furniture two-thirds larger than scale. Maurice Tourneur's stylized direction polished off Gwen's gloomy world. The servants, for instance, enter in a surreal march, as though they were flying monkeys guarding the castle of the wicked witch. And the nightmare sequence (Gwen, on the verge of death, becomes delirious) includes a vision of the "two-faced" maid, her head bulging out of the end of a snake, her two faces spinning like a top.

This might have been too much of a good thing had not Frances Marion – who wrote the scenario – and Pickford insisted on adding humor. They took credit for some simple gags: a child sitting in a pie, for instance. But they threw in the slapstick unannounced. Tourneur, who liked to work with small women (they made him feel powerful), was bewildered. "Mlle. Pickford," he protested, "show me where in the script it says you are to do that." Indeed, the book by Eleanor Gates and the Broadway production in 1913 were unrelievedly melancholy. "It is not in the play," explained Tourneur, "and I do not find it in the script. *Mais non; c'est une horreur!*" Mary thought Tourneur had no sense of humor. "I am a dignified man," he agreed, "and my pictures should be dignified." He would complain at length, years later, about curly-haired, interfering actresses, and Pickford chose other directors for her projects. But they finished *The Poor Little Rich Girl* with a smile, though perhaps a strained one. Maxine Elliot Hicks, present on the set to play the girl in the pie, saw only civilized differences and courtesy.

The picture was shown first to studio executives. Pickford and Marion joined them, nervous but anticipating triumph. On the contrary, Pickford's "masterpiece of comedy," filled with Marion's "spontaneous combustions," played to the silence of a tomb. When the lights came up, the word most frequently voiced was "putrid." But the viewers realized, with sinking hearts, that Artcraft was obliged to release it: nationwide bookings had been made, and exhibitors were counting on a Pickford feature.

To the Lasky contingent, Mary appeared to be nothing but a power-hungry, spoiled prima donna. The impression was all the more distinct because, in an ill-starred moment, she had barred Lasky's people from the set. Now *The Poor Little Rich Girl's* reception struck her Achilles' heel of guilt. She had failed Papa Zukor and failed herself, and she drove home and cried herself to sleep. Frances Marion drove home, too, crawled under the bed, and sobbed that she had ruined Mary Pickford's career and hoped she would die soon. All very well, remembered Pickford. "But I had to live and face the music."

As expected, Zukor called her, and Mary, cringing, appeared in his office. She listened in shame as he announced that Cecil B. DeMille would direct her in two films. The message, though unspoken, was clear. Cecil made financial gold mines. He had also insisted, at the time of the merger, that he keep his own production unit and exercise absolute power in it. DeMille's word, not Pickford's, would be law.

Cecil was a potentate, "stocky and straight," recalled his niece, "with his legs planted like a wall, a barricade, a mounted gun." He had triumphed over William, who had left New York in 1914 to visit Los Angeles, liked what he saw, and was now writing screenplays – a lesser position than Cecil, who, always on show, strode about the lot in boots and riding breeches. He had also beaten Belasco at his own game, not only directing the Master's plays (*The Rose of the Rancho* and *The Girl of the Golden West*) but building a copy of Belasco's office: churchlike, cramped, selfconsciously dramatic, with a beamed, vaulted ceiling and a stained-glass window. Gradually his themes onscreen took on heavy dollops of sex and scandal; and his taste for grandiosity finally coalesced in biblical epics, which far outdid Belasco for realism, cost, and crowd-pleasing spectacle.

On the lot, he was trailed by a fawning retinue, ready at a word to provide a chair or take a note. On one occasion they followed him, waist-deep, into the Pacific. An underling reported that Cecil "was a man who could swagger while seated behind a desk." A Hollywood joke – which would have pleased Cecil had he heard it – ran that a psychiatrist was needed in heaven because God had delusions that he was Cecil B. DeMille. Pickford and Marion used to whisper, "Here comes the Celestial Host. Shall we prostrate ourselves before him or merely bend the knee?" But they, too, were intimidated.

Cecil had consented to work with Mary but would not give up his autonomy. "A commanding general," he maintained, "does not allow the supply corps to decide all by itself when and where to deliver the needed material." Ordinarily Mary would revolt at such a statement. But the woman in Zukor's office was not Mary Pickford, the powerful actress. It was Baby Gladys, ready to kneel and scrub.

"Now, Mary," said Zukor with a voice like syrup, "be a darling and go back to your hotel and write Mr. DeMille a nice telegram saying that you were a naughty little girl and that you promise never to [issue orders] again." "Yes, Mr. Zukor," said Baby Gladys. "I'm so sorry for everything, Mr. Zukor." "Now, let me see how fast you can do it, and read it to me on the telephone before you send it." Tongue-tied, Mary turned to leave. "Make it plenty humble," added Papa.

"I have no desire," Pickford wired to DeMille, "to interfere in the choice of stories, in the casting of the different actors, including myself, and in the final editing. I am placing myself unreservedly in your most capable hands." She signed the telegram, "Obediently yours."

Later Mary wrote of the "unending marathon of work, a blessing in many ways, but a deadening weight on my spirit when anything, however small, went wrong." Exhausted, she declared to the press that she wished she were "a shop girl working ten hours a day for $8 a week." She had made twenty-four films since starting features. Of course, she was intent on making money. And the public expected her to work, to prove she was indeed their servant. (*Photoplay* was shocked, a year later, when Mary spent two months without making a single film.) But there was little outside this fishbowl to sustain her – certainly not Owen, who seldom surfaced. Somehow the public had discerned that all was not well at the Pickford residence, and when he emerged, a charade took place. "Oh, my dear," says Mary to Owen as transcribed by a writer who witnessed the act. "What *will* they say about us next?" "That I've been arrested for beating my wife, or that you've eloped with the organ-grinder," laughs Owen. "But what do *we* care?" "We *don't*," says Mary.

They also clowned for *Photoplay*. Mary is seen as she steps from a car, looking mortified. "She is telling Friend Husband that he missed one bump on the way home, and he can't drive her any more." Another caption unknowingly comments on their sexless marriage: "Mary and Owen are more like friends than married folks." Finally Mary, on her knees, tries to rescue a golf ball as Owen, club high, starts to swing. "Mary is so tender hearted, she just can't bear to see Owen hit the poor little inoffensive ball with that nasty big club. Who wouldn't be a golf ball, in such circumstances?" It was during this period that Mary once leaned out from her New York hotel room and reflected that the sidewalk looked inviting.

Yet there was an avenue of hope, which had opened up two years before. In 1915, Elsie Janis began something of a salon for millionaires, chorus girls, and artists at her mansion in Tarrytown, on the Hudson just north of New York City. In mid-November she invited Pickford, who was filming in New York; Mary and Owen settled glumly into a limousine for the trip. Elsie also asked Douglas Fairbanks, once a Broadway leading man and now a new face on movie screens, who set off with his wife in a jazzy Stutz Bearcat. This was a suitable car for an actor renowned for gallant, athletic dash. In the Broadway play *The Cub*, for instance, Fairbanks had met the heroine by vaulting, not running, to the top of a staircase. The moment — catlike, seemingly effortless — thrilled the audience. Offstage, Fairbanks used to bypass the door of open-topped automobiles and simply leap to his seat.

At a crossroads Owen got out to check directions, and the Bearcat pulled up beside the limousine. Fairbanks and Owen exchanged hellos. Mary, peering from the back seat, was pleasant, while inwardly questioning Fairbanks's propriety — that flashy car! She had also glimpsed the soft and blond Beth Fairbanks, cuddling under an attention-getting leopard-skin lap rug.

At the party, depression overwhelmed her. She put in an ace performance, though, of laughing and making up for Owen's bad behavior.

"Poor Owen is worried about his new contract," she smiled as her husband glowered. Frances Marion, also a guest, remembered Fairbanks telling Mary, "You and Charlie Chaplin are the two geniuses who have emerged from this movie business." The color rose in Mary's cheeks – not because Fairbanks had flattered her, but because she'd seen Owen's reaction: a bitter smile, bordering on a sneer. As for Fairbanks, she was not a fan. She had seen him onstage in *A Gentleman from Mississippi*, and years later she delivered a rave in "Daily Talks." But in fact, she had found him too frenetic. "I thought he was too exuberant," she explained. "I was intolerant, maybe, and not in a happy mood that day. It was cold. It was November."

By 1914 Fairbanks also had misgivings about his work. He was incurably restless, and his Broadway career in a series of trivial plays confined him. (On the other hand, he thought that the movies were second-class employment.) Then, later in the year, the Triangle company, where D.W. Griffith, Thomas Ince, and Mack Sennett were producers, came courting. Fairbanks thought he'd take the risk and signed a contract – though a previous commitment to a play meant he couldn't make a movie till the following summer. In the meantime, film's reputation turned a corner with *The Birth of a Nation*, D.W. Griffith's account of the Civil War and Reconstruction. When the movie opened in February 1915, its technical sophistication, length (thirteen reels), and imaginative power left (wrote a critic) "tongues stilled, minds stunned." To those caught up by its filmic brilliance, *Birth* made the movies a noble calling. To others, the movie was pernicious. Griffith, with stunning naiveté, had glorified the Ku Klux Klan (the movie's original title was *The Clansman*) and patronized blacks as a childlike race. The result was hotly debated in parlors and beer halls, endorsed by president Woodrow Wilson, and greeted by rapturous praise and riots. Never before had a movie *mattered*. And it mattered to Fairbanks that *The Birth of a Nation* made film, to many new eyes, respectable.

On November 7, Fairbanks's movie *The Lamb* inspired an overwrought critic to compare its battle scenes to *Birth*. Others, more sensibly, found it an agreeable showcase for Fairbanks, who, as an effete New York City geek who follows his sweetheart to the West, "holds the eye so strongly, and without apparent effort." When the couple are caught by bandits in a Mexican rebellion, Fairbanks suddenly discovers his manhood, escapes from prison, jumps on a stallion, mans a cannon, and holds the "deuced uncomfortable" criminals at bay. For the next five years, Fairbanks's movies rang the same thematic bell. They kidded the urban East as mechanized, cramped, and faddish, a place that strangled the body and the mind. But the West is strong, unspoiled, and clean – a lot like "Doug," a strapping, can-do sort of guy who encouraged viewers to seize the day. It didn't hurt that Fairbanks was born and bred in the pioneer mining town of Denver.

"Keep Your Hero Smiling!" wrote Elinor Glyn in a book about scenarios in 1922. "A laughing, active man [is] full of the spirit of modern life. . . . [But] there should be a reason for his smiles. They should radiate cheer and optimism and determination to forge ahead!" She might have been describing Fairbanks. He was husky but graceful, and his face, though beefy, was boyishly hopeful. Watching him, viewers thought they, too, could conquer life. Indeed, Fairbanks wrote that health and joy "are the greatest assets one can have. . . . They did more for me on the stage than any other quality, for I never pretended to be a great actor."

"Dammit," he reminded Anita Loos, who often wrote for him, "I can't play a love scene." Her solution: "Cancel the sex activities and have Doug jump off an airplane." Fairbanks was a natural, insouciant athlete, the kind who would fearlessly take a broad jump toward the edge of the Grand Canyon. (Apparently he did this. He also threw a handstand on its rim.) On camera, Fairbanks amused himself by jumping over a park bench while reading the paper, leaping from roof to roof, and tossing off handsprings (on one arm). Most actors would play such scenes for comedy – crashing through ceilings, perhaps, or slipping on banana peels. But the universe moved in sympathy with Fairbanks. No boughs sagged beneath his weight. Roofs gave traction. Vines offered handholds. The actor's body, marveled writer Booth Tarkington, "yields instantly to any heathen or gypsy impulse – such as an impulse to balance a chair on its nose while hanging from the club chandelier by one of its knees."

"A sort of Ariel," wrote journalist Alistair Cooke. "It is comforting to recall Hazlitt who, after a life-time's appreciation of actors and acting, was moved to tears only once, by the exquisite and, as it seemed to him, philosophical skill of a juggler." Fairbanks played with the physical world as nimbly as Fred Astaire danced with a hat stand. He was endlessly resourceful and consummately free. And unlike most silent-movie icons, he rejected the values of Victorian pathos. A Fairbanks movie was fast and breezy, like the electric world he lived in – much, in fact, like film itself, with its rush of frames and clicking shutters. And his films always kidded the newest crazes: who's in, who's out, vegetarians, newshounds. This, and his contagious optimism, made the actor seem a man of both the moment and the future. "To me," remembered Mary fondly, "he was the personification of the new world."

Elsie, in the hubbub, was flirting madly. She and Fairbanks were longtime rivals in the business of being bright and beautiful. On one occasion, Fairbanks decided to walk the lounge of the Algonquin Hotel – then more of a hangout for actors than for writers – on his hands. Janis tied her skirts around her knees and followed him, cheerfully upside down. Now she proposed that she, Fairbanks, and Moore link arms on a hike across the property. Mary, watching from behind a magazine, grabbed Beth: "We're not going to let her get away with that." When the party reached a wide brook, Janis and Fairbanks skipped across on stones. Somehow Owen got across, and prudent, retiring Beth turned back. But Mary was determined to show her stuff. She was exquisitely dressed in a long black velvet gown and white kid Russian boots. But the heels were high and she stood, precariously, on a log. When Owen made no move to help, Fairbanks suddenly appeared beside her. "Do you mind?" he asked. "Please do," she answered. Fairbanks picked her up and placed her lightly on the opposite bank. This was a lovely but practical action, and no one present gave it much weight. But in hindsight, the gesture – literally sweeping her off her feet – proved too suggestive for Mary to resist. It was only later, she maintained, "that I saw that that was the beginning."

As for Fairbanks, the attraction took hold as he spent the next hour or so with Mary. Fresh from *The Lamb*'s unexpected raves, he sensed his career was undergoing a sea change. While Pickford lectured him on the movies, he became more impressed with their creative challenge, as well as with her beauty and authority. And his chivalrous nature was offended by Owen's open rudeness toward her. "When the party quieted down," wrote Marion, "I saw Doug gazing at Mary; it was a long inquisitorial look and for a moment there seemed to be a strange stillness within him."

She met him again, a month or so after Elsie's party, when Frank Case, who owned the Algonquin Hotel, gave a dance for New York's glitterati. Fairbanks saw her, gave a start, and bounded over. Mary, conveniently, was alone, and he immediately engaged her in movie talk: "You do less apparent acting than anyone else I know," he told her, "and because of that you express more." Mary assumed he was joking; Owen never spoke to her that way, and those who did were currying favor. But Fairbanks's ego was in top shape. He spoke to her artlessly, as an equal. Pickford was overwhelmed and touched. Fairbanks, she wrote, was "a breath of new life.... I hugged the echo of his words for days, repeating them over and over again to myself.... I had been living in half shadows, and now a brilliant light was suddenly cast upon me, the sunlight of Douglas' approval and admiration."

Their mutual attraction now was palpable. But as Fairbanks twirled her through a few dances, their conversation was outwardly professional. And Beth Fairbanks watched from a distance, smiling; she welcomed her husband's actress friends, and especially liked Pickford, who became "dear Mary." She was happy, too, in her domestic life, though Fairbanks gave six-year-old Douglas Fairbanks Jr. only off-and-on attention. And Beth thought, mistakenly, that Fairbanks was faithful. In fact, his indiscretions were legion, though Fairbanks did not consider them betrayals. They were, after all, only passing fancies and no one, until that night, had replaced Beth in his heart.

"He was a little boy, always," remembered Mary. "He was just in life as he was on the screen." She found it hard, in the face of Fairbanks's gregarious spirit, to sink into the doldrums. His company kept her off balance and buoyant. In return, Mary anchored his mercurial nature. Like Beth, she found herself mothering, scolding, and schooling Fairbanks, all the while watching and applauding. Beth resembled Mary, too, in her mix of gentleness and temper. Fairbanks Jr. recalled Beth's kindness, as well as his terror at her "sound and fury." But unlike Mary, Beth was born with money. Her childhood was spent on her father's Rhode Island estates and in his Manhattan townhouse; a debutante ball launched her into society, followed by the requisite tour of Europe. All this was catnip to Fairbanks, an unabashed social climber who adjusted, chameleonlike, to the gentry.

Now he took stock of film's social landscape. Obviously, his interest in

Mary coincided with an excellent career move. Mary could provide, as Beth could not, the sympathy one artist gives another. She could also advise and open doors. And she empathized, as Beth did not, with a central tenet of Fairbanks's nature: his vulnerability to his mother.

Ella Fairbanks, known to her sons as Tu-Tu, had fussed over Douglas, her youngest, since birth. His skin was swarthy (this before tans were thought to be attractive) and his manner grim. He was physically active, determinedly scaling walls and pipes. One day he jumped from a rooftop, thinking he could fly. When Ella, panicking, found him on the ground, Douglas looked into her face and laughed. From that day his childhood was marked with the humorous antics that later appeared in his movies — or so the story goes. As well as swinging, Tarzan-like, through trees and walking on his hands, he tossed off Shakespeare and Byron with brio. This tickled his father, H. Charles Ulman, a prominent New York lawyer who was stagestruck and had often rubbed shoulders with Broadway actors in the early years of his marriage to Ella.

Ella's first husband, John Fairbanks, was a rich young planter from New Orleans. This, her sweetest marriage, ended in calamity. Fairbanks died of tuberculosis after losing his entire fortune, leaving Ella with a son, named John (after his father). Judge Edward Wilcox, Ella's second husband, was an alcoholic. She stood by the marriage long enough to give birth to another son, named Norris, then won a divorce with the help of Ulman. Ulman had tried, before the Wilcox marriage, to retrieve the Fairbanks fortune for her. Now, in a second gallant gesture, he became her third husband, abandoned his law practice, moved his wife and her eldest son to Denver, and invested all he had in a silver mine. Norris, for reasons unknown, was abandoned (he was raised by one of Ella's aunts, Lottie Barker). And the move to Colorado proved disastrous.

Ulman, though a brilliant lawyer, handled speculation badly. As the family grew — Robert was born in 1881, Douglas in 1883 — their fortunes dwindled, Ulman drank, then drank himself into an alcoholic shambles. He deserted the family in 1889. Ella, who thought herself better off without him, changed the family name to Fairbanks and took in boarders. Douglas watched with increasing empathy. Six years later he heard that Ulman had resurfaced in Denver, and he took him home to Mother. But first Ulman stopped for some earnest tippling. Ella's reaction was ferocious.

She threw Ulman out of the house, then marched her son down to the temperance union. There she placed Douglas's hand on the Bible and made him swear never to take a drink. And he never did, till the end of his life, when he sometimes sipped cautiously from a wineglass.

Ella, like Charlotte, could not let go. After Fairbanks married Beth, she competed for attention so relentlessly that Fairbanks, who hated confrontations, finally said that, though he loved her, she must step aside for the new Mrs. Fairbanks. Ella retreated, head high, though she glowered in Beth's direction. It was not surprising, then, that when Fairbanks confided his love for Pickford, Ella's actions were ambiguous. She seemed to bless his new interest by drinking tea not only with Mary but with her mother. And she consoled her son that a man "couldn't help falling in love, nor be blamed for it, still – " Here the abused and abandoned Ella remembered her own romantic history. "Everyone must be held responsible for his actions. . . . Only you and Mary can decide . . . but be careful! Sometimes we pay dearly for the unhappiness of others."

The would-be lovers had no idea of where to turn or what to do. And Fairbanks liked to postpone decisions. In 1916 he moved his family to Los Angeles. "Room to expand, to be free," he exulted, then turned out a film almost every month. He exulted, too, in instant fame, which he wore as casually as a sweater. Soon he had established a home on La Brea Avenue, enlisted his brothers John and Robert as advisers, and sent his son to a school filled with children of film celebrities. Meanwhile Beth's father was losing money. Fortunately, Fairbanks, who received a share of his movies' profits, grew wealthy in his own right. As 1916 drew to a close, he joined the new Famous Players–Lasky venture, established his own production company, and released his films through the prestigious Artcraft.

No one knows when the affair began, but fear of scandal probably delayed it. Early film stars were believed to live wholesome lives off camera. Fairbanks, in particular, was thought to embody the Boy Scout values of his films. (In fact, in every matter but fidelity, he did.) And fame encircled Pickford like a chastity belt. Little Mary was a national symbol, "a myth and a surety, a legend and a pledge." Her name, wrote critic C.A. Lejeune, "is one of the modern cinema's foundations; her credit has become the credit of the industry." An affair, if detected, would shatter her career – perhaps, some believed, silent film itself.

Late in 1916 Tu-Tu was stricken with pneumonia. Beth, with whom she had recently reconciled, traveled from Los Angeles to nurse her. Just before Christmas, Ella died in Beth's arms, and a telegram brought Fairbanks racing east. "It was the first real sorrow that Douglas had known," recalled Letitia, daughter of John Fairbanks, "and he was quite unprepared to meet it." Indeed, he sat dry-eyed throughout the funeral and attended a Broadway show that evening. "Tu-Tu," said Fairbanks, "would have understood." At his hotel, he discovered a sympathetic note from Pickford and, still on automatic pilot, phoned her. That night, for privacy, they met in his car.

Slowly they wound their way through Central Park. Mary was murmuring her condolences, prompting Fairbanks to tell a few anecdotes, when suddenly he stopped the car, leaned on the steering wheel, and sobbed. This was a rare display for a man whose flash masked a deep capacity for sadness. The moment gained symbolic weight when Mary observed that the dashboard clock had stopped at the moment Fairbanks broke down. Little was said, but much was understood. Ella, the lovers believed, had been watching in spirit and had sanctioned the relationship. A few months later Mary moved her household to California (she made all her movies there from then on). She claimed she was having a nervous breakdown; at any rate, Fairbanks was waiting with open arms to welcome her.

Unfortunately, so was Cecil B. DeMille, with the script of her new film, *A Romance of the Redwoods* (1917), a contract, and Mary's abject telegram.

DeMille, like Belasco, played cat and mouse with actors. "If [Cecil] lost his temper," remembered Agnes, "it was in the grand manner, building up from a simple statement of displeasure, through long developments of sarcasm to a fulminating climax of operatic splendor." And, like Belasco, he was cruel to actresses. "He'd get her shaking and crying. Then he felt he'd reached the depths. Of course," added Agnes, "he'd reached hysteria."

But Mary, with a fountain of feeling for the camera, needed only a word to act superbly. And though she was teeming with ideas, she lived up to her telegram and suppressed them. Neither, in other words, got satisfaction. Cecil was robbed of his role as abuser, and an unnaturally docile

Pickford imagined she was wearing an iron girdle. Later she haltingly praised DeMille. "DeMille was a great producer, but I don't think he had any heart. He was a very commanding person, but he wasn't a great director. However," she added, befuddled, "I loved him."

Her feelings for the movie were equally tentative. By casting Pickford as a girl who loves an outlaw, played by the threatening Elliott Dexter, DeMille stressed the adult in Mary's image; this alone makes the movie interesting. The film is often sensational – preposterously so – but it also mines a marvelous comic vein as Mary, who must share Dexter's slovenly cabin, insists on setting pretty tables, saying grace, and clearing out his closets to make room for frilly dresses. Another scene portrays a cynical view of marriage as the outlaw, saved from death by hanging, is married to Pickford with the noose still (literally) around his neck. On at least one occasion, she called *Redwoods* an excellent film – but more often, the tension DeMille inspired made the film a dark memory.

Fortune finally smiled when, in March 1917, at New York's Strand, Pickford and Frances Marion attended the premiere performance of *The Poor Little Rich Girl*, now recut. According to Marion, Pickford entered with dark glasses and her hat pulled low on her face. Then she listened, stunned, as the audience laughed, wept audibly, and cheered. Mary wept, too, and removed her glasses – probably a conscious decision, as an usher soon recognized the famous face. Instantly she was mobbed by fans who begged for snippets of her hair, ripped fur from her coat, tore her hat to shreds, and called "Mary, darling!" With the help of a column of mounted policemen, Mary rose from a sea of bodies and escaped with her screenwriter into a taxi.

Pickford told a quietly different story of waking up one morning in California to twenty-five telegrams praising the movie. The most enthusiastic was from Zukor, and her spirits rose effortlessly, like a feather.

That year she shot three lovely films that reflect the good spirits that prevailed offscreen. The first was *Rebecca of Sunnybrook Farm* (1917), a title that, sadly, has dated badly. Neither the book by Kate Douglas Wiggin nor the silent film deserves it. The story is a charming entry in the strong-willed-child, dreadful-relatives tradition in which Rebecca, a bundle of reckless energy, is raised by disapproving, straitlaced aunts. "Smart enough," says one in the Wiggin book, adding, "but she's consid'able heedless."

Now back in control, Pickford asked Frances Marion to adapt it. To direct, she chose "one of the most delightful, aggravating, gifted and charming human beings I have ever known" – a former co-star, Marshall (Mickey) Neilan. In 1905 he had acted onstage with D.W. Griffith. Six years later he was working as the director's chauffeur, and in 1915 he played supporting roles in four Pickford films: *Little Pal* (for which he wrote the story), *A Girl of Yesterday* (the script for this lost film was written by Pickford), James Kirkwood's *Rags*, and Sidney Olcott's *Madame Butterfly*. Like Mary, Neilan found *Butterfly* a miserable experience, and together they visualized their own production. Neilan, for instance, thought that Pinkerton should teach Cho-Cho-San to play baseball, an idea Mary loved but Sidney Olcott squelched. "Do you know you ought to make Mickey Neilan a director?" Mary said to Goldwyn. Then she suggested a bargain fee: "He'd be worth at least a hundred and twenty-five dollars a week to you."

Neilan had a nonchalant rapport with Pickford. Like Kirkwood, he was Irish, a charming drunk, and his style on the set was lighthearted and collegial. His particular genius, in tune with Mary's, was to find the building blocks of drama through illuminating, usually humorous incidents. To create them, "he would dream up running gags long in advance," said Mary, "and then at the psychological moment unexpectedly blast them at me." He once persuaded Jack Pickford and Chaplin to dress in drag and dance off camera while he whistled "Spring Song"; he was looking for a sudden laugh from Mary, and got it. On another day, he tossed up a shower of coins, hoping to catch Pickford's face mid-rapture. He did – she was laughing at Neilan's nerve.

"To my way of thinking," she remembered, "he was the best director ever, better than the great D.W. Griffith." Though sometimes, she admitted, she could have killed him. Neilan thought nothing of turning up for work well after lunch, three sheets to the wind. But Mary was often disarmed by his excuses – "such as being called for jury duty!" She would then remind him that time was money. Neilan responded that Mary's ambition was to be the richest woman in her cemetery. A man of his type could get away with such a statement, and before Mary knew it, she was smiling. You are nothing but a bogtrotter, Mickey, she told him. You're far-down shanty Irish, and a dirty scut! Tad, he told her (she adored the nickname) – if the public knew you used such language! Then, remembered Pickford, he made up for lost time: "Before the afternoon was over his genius would have brought forth an inspired scene."

The Neilan touch can be seen throughout *Rebecca*, as can Mary's insight into children. Rebecca is stronger, more impudent than Gwen, yet her emotions are swayed by the same unpredictable eddies. She moves through small-town Americana, a world of one-room schoolhouses, horse-drawn carts, and door-to-door sales of Superba Soap, "of such pure engredients [*sic*] that a baby can eat it with relish and profit." This world was on the wane when *Rebecca* was filming, but Neilan made it live again through slapstick cameos. In fact, this unpretentious movie lingers in the mind with surprising freshness; its anecdotes attain the depth of life remembered.

Frances Hodgson Burnett's *A Little Princess* was published, to great acclaim, in 1900. In 1917 Pickford's film repeated its saga of Sara Crewe, a rich girl whose boarding school treats her like a princess until her father reportedly dies – insolvent. Then she is forced to crawl and scrub, sleep in the attic, and wait on other students. It's a magical story, and the film is almost a match for *Rebecca* in its uncanny feeling for childish detail. Neilan and Marion were again on board, and the movie presented ZaSu Pitts, a somewhat gawky, long-necked actress, in her first major role. When Pitts auditioned, remembered Marion, she entered, trembling, like "a trapped little animal. Her eyes were enormous in a small pinched face." A stagehand then reduced her to tears by referring sarcastically to her beauty. Pickford, hearing the story, was furious and immediately offered Pitts a contract.

In her Griffith days, Mary often played homely, fearful adolescents, scouring each performance clean of personal vanity and easy tears. But her feature career, with few exceptions, was studded with beautiful child-women. For her third film with Neilan, *Stella Maris* (1918), Pickford went back to the wellspring of abnegation and guilt – zealously darkening her teeth, rimming her eyes with white to make them smaller, combing down her eyebrows, smacking down her hair with Vaseline, and widening her nostrils with black paint – all to achieve a "mutt expression." Zukor asked, appalled, "What *is* this, sweetheart-honey?"

Stella Maris was a fable, involving two opposites. Mary played the title role, a ravishing invalid, as well as the misshapen Unity Blake. Their worlds, inevitably, collide. Stella, locked in an ivory tower, has been taught to believe the world is beautiful. Unity, who was raised in an orphanage and savagely beaten, knows only cruelty and despair. Both love the same man, John Risca, who is married to Unity's drunk employer. Knowing that her ugliness will never win affection, Unity, who is "pitied but unloved," shoots John's wife and then herself. Stella is horrified; her make-believe, privileged world is shattered. But with the knowledge of Unity's sacrifice (and with Risca for a husband), Stella becomes happier, wiser, and more beautiful.

Critics were justifiably ecstatic. There was a gracelessness to Unity, a scuttling, almost beetlelike quality. But it was Unity's inner life – straight from the shoulder, devoid of self-pity – that made Mary's work a grimy triumph. With Neilan on hand to find telling anecdotes, Frances Marion to write the screenplay, and a sensitive cameraman in Walter Stradling, *Stella Maris* attains a tragic stature. Today many rate it as Pickford's finest.

As a grace note, she appeared in two more Marion/Neilan works. *Amarilly of Clothes-Line Alley* (1918) is a bit long in minutes, but it is also, luckily, long on charm. Amarilly, who scrubs floors and sells cigarettes in a nightclub, becomes the center of an upper-class Pygmalion experiment. "What an interesting specimen!" crows her female Henry Higgins when she meets Amarilly. Pickford, as usual, shoots straight from the hip and turns to the woman's sympathetic son. "Another crack like that," she confides, "and I'll crown her."

Next came the rustic *M'Liss* (1918), whose heroine lives in a California gold-rush town. It was based on a story by Bret Harte, whose stock-in-trade was sentimental tales of what had been, in fact, an avaricious, violent era. Harte describes M'Liss as "nearly eleven, and, in a few years, by the rules of Red Mountain, [she] would be a woman." Mary had first played a seventeenish, subdued M'Liss under Griffith's direction in *The School Teacher and the Waif* (1912). She is far more flamboyant in Neilan's film, with an unlikely wardrobe of oversized men's shirts and big hats adorned with chicken feathers. She raises hell effectively – handily fending off a bear, picking up a five-foot snake, and meeting the man she will one day marry when she dings him with a slingshot – all charming, all rickety and undeveloped. Still, *M'Liss* exploited Mary's teenage spirit as no movie had managed to do since *Rags*.

For the space of five films, she seemed completely happy.

The affair with Fairbanks was now radiantly physical. And with it, Mary was transformed. She, who seldom misbehaved, now found herself running out of meetings to take her lover's phone calls. Mary, who, as Jack observed, never learned to play, now went on joyrides with Fairbanks through Los Angeles, wrapped in big hats, scarves, and goggles. When they found a secret place – Robert Fairbanks's cottage, perhaps, or a wood – they threw off their disguises and jumped into each other's arms. And Mary, so prone to self-reproach, expressed no guilt at stealing someone else's husband. Once, when Beth was in hospital, Mary paid her a get-well visit, then left and made a bee-line straight to Fairbanks. ("Mary's so sneaky she gives me a pain in the ass," complained Lottie, who, though far less conservative than her sister, found the hospital caper beyond the pale.) And, if one believes Anita Loos, Mary stole Fairbanks in the middle of the night. In this scenario Fairbanks, who slept on an upper veranda of his California home, would wait until Beth was sleeping soundly, slip down a column to the ground, push his car silently down a hillside, then start the engine and drive off to Mary's.

News of the affair quickly spread through Hollywood. Everyone seemed to know but Beth – who sensed, however, that her husband was straying, and pinned her suspicions on Anita Loos. Charlotte, of course, was incensed with Fairbanks, who threatened to ruin her raison d'être. Her response to Mary was more guarded. As a Catholic, she opposed divorce; she would never consent to Mary's ending her marriage. But after the debacle with Owen Moore, she knew that outright opposition would make Douglas Fairbanks more attractive. For his part Fairbanks, though infinitely more relaxed, had his own reservations about what he gingerly called "that family."

Dignified mothers, thought Fairbanks, did not drink – or at least, they didn't drink like fish. And even when swathed in fur, Mary's mother seemed lower-class, like a washerwoman, face flushed with steam and fingers dripping.

Jack ran in the fast lane – fast and loose. He had always been shiftless; silent-film veteran Harry Lewis, who played on the Brooklyn streets with Jack when the boys were seven or eight years old, remembers him taking great delight in passing off pennies as dimes to an immigrant. His unsentimental education continued when the Biograph actors encouraged him to drink, gamble, and lose his virginity at a whorehouse. When he was fifteen, theatrical gossip put Jack in bed with one of Ziegfeld's mistresses, a curvaceous showgirl named Lillian Lorraine. It was said that she once burned down a boardinghouse by dropping a cigarette; at any rate, like Jack, she was erratic, unpredictable, and puzzled by discipline and duty.

Jack appeared in small roles in two Pickford productions: a George Sand fantasy, *Fanchon the Cricket*, in 1915, and in 1916, *Poor Little Peppina*, an immigrant comedy. He worked and sometimes starred in almost thirty other movies throughout the teens. But he still found time in those years to burn the candle at both ends, get thrown off a Ferris wheel for standing on his head, and fascinate females. "No male," wrote Loos, who admired Jack, "is quite so provocative as one who lives off some adoring woman." Jack, added Adela Rogers St. Johns, was charming, and a bottle of scotch made him even more so. But Fairbanks detected an aimlessness in Jack's life, a lack of moral compass beneath the boozing. In return, Jack hated "that faker Douglas Fairbanks. . . . If just once I could feel he was – was *natural. . . .* He's always *on*, to use a theater expression."

Lottie was a greater potential embarrassment. Her Hollywood career got a curious start in 1914's *The House of Bondage*, a crusading vice film in which she played a prostitute. It was not a ladylike role, and if Charlotte approved it, she showed imagination – perhaps envisioning a career for Lottie as gritty as Mary's was sentimental. Or perhaps her neglected daughter took the role in a bid to get her mother's attention. And she did make a splash, though not the happiest kind. *The House of Bondage* was greeted as "vile and revolting stuff. . . . How any human being can have the base effrontery to offer such a digest of dirt for public exhibition is utterly beyond [this critic's] comprehension."

In 1915 a chastened Lottie turned up in *Fanchon the Cricket* with her brother and sister. In this, her presence was barely noted – the film, after all, starred America's Sweetheart. More humiliation: in 1915 Lottie appeared in *The Diamond from the Sky* – but only after Mary had turned the serial down. "Pickford the Second," blared an article in *Photoplay*. "Delightful younger sister of the famous Mary," continued her producers in a full-page ad. "Pretty, dainty, sweet, capricious . . . a delightful, piquant personality." Not a word about Lottie's marriage, which had occurred on

171

an unknown date and was kept well hidden by the Pickford family. The groom, Alfred Rupp, was a New York broker. Otherwise, nothing much is known — how Lottie met him, how they married, where they lived, whether Charlotte liked him.

There are many such gaps in Lottie's story. Did she realize, for instance, that she was pregnant when she signed away thirty-five weeks of her life to do an acrobatic serial? Lottie's director watched, appalled, as her body swelled throughout production. In the last installments, Lottie was obliged to act while peering over furniture and fences. When the series ended, she was placed on the industry's unofficial blacklist — which probably made Mary cringe. But Lottie shrugged. After giving birth to Mary Pickford Rupp (one wonders who suggested the baby's name), the actress returned to her first love: parties. These were all-nighters, with plenty of drinks and drugs on hand, and semi-nudity by morning. Lottie's maid reported that when the revelers heard Mary's car coming up the drive, "Oh, boy! did they jump into their knickers!"

If Fairbanks was less than fond of Mary's family, Mary had her cross to bear in Chaplin. He and Fairbanks were inseparable. A story of their meeting — handed down from Fairbanks, who often stretched the truth a bit — hints at the spirit of the relationship. In the mid-1910s, in California, a man is lingering outside a theater that is playing a Fairbanks feature. Along comes a small man who asks him, "Any good?" "He's the best in the business," the first man answers. "He's a scream!" The smaller man asks, "Is he as good as Chaplin?" "This Fairbanks person," replies the first, "has got that Chaplin person looking like a gloom. They're not in the same class." Choosing his moment, the small man finally says: "I'm Chaplin." "I know you are," the other says. "I'm Fairbanks."

Chaplin was moody; Fairbanks, on the other hand, papered over dark thoughts with hyperactive cheer. Chaplin loathed fame, while Fairbanks loved it. Chaplin was an introvert; Fairbanks was interested in everything outside himself. In these ways they filled each other's needs. They often made up skits at parties, thrashing through absurd duels, spouting gibberish. They set up elaborate jokes and pranks. The most famous occurred in 1921, when Fairbanks was shooting his spectacular *Robin Hood*. He and Mary were summoned to the lavish set at dawn. Slowly the drawbridge lowered over the moat; a sleepy king-figure (Chaplin) toddled out, placed two empty milk bottles on the ground, then retreated, the drawbridge closing up behind him.

"Whatever the stunt, whatever the prank or practical joke," sighed Mary, "so long as Charlie was responsible for it, Douglas thought it was great." Pickford, presumably, did not. And in quiet moments, Mary found Fairbanks's best friend "tiresome. He was forever launching into long lectures on dry subjects." One of his obsessions was the shame of the British monetary system and how he might reform it. Pickford, for all her good sense, was no intellect. Chaplin bored her when he lectured. And her innately conservative nature was annoyed by Chaplin's left-wing thinking. For his part, Chaplin found Pickford ridiculously formal, at least in the business relationship they would begin in a few years' time. At a meeting, Mary no sooner said, "It behoves us. . ." than Chaplin cracked up ("It behoves us! It behoves us!"). But she accepted Chaplin's genius and seldom passed up a chance to praise it. Mary was also moved by Chaplin's childhood (he grew up poor, with an absent father; his mother, whose psyche was frail, was committed.) But Chaplin and Pickford drew vastly different lessons from their misery. "That's nothing but spooks, Mary – loving one's family that way," he told her. Pickford brooded over this remark for decades.

They put up with each other, if for no other reason than their love for Fairbanks. Each needed his attention and competed for it. And Fairbanks wanted them to love each other – as did the public and, in fact, the world. When foreign artists arrived in the U.S. they visited the trio as they would a public monument. Chaplin, for instance, played host to Paderewski, Nijinsky, Jascha Heifetz, and Pavlova. Fairbanks bounced about with Olympic athletes, sports heroes, and a host of minor royalty. He also had the foresight to film Pavlova dancing, creating one of only two visual records. Duse wished to meet "the little angel Mary Pickford," as did Sir Arthur Conan Doyle, Tolstoy, Pavlova (again – Mary posed with her for photographs), and H.G. Wells.

For the next ten years, Pickford found herself pressured, by the love of her public and her love for Fairbanks, to take part in shenanigans that were meant to make a legend of their three-way bond. In one such episode Chaplin jumped, fully clothed, into a swimming pool, shouting, "I am an atheist. If there is a God, let Him save me." He put on a show of bobbing, gasping, and going down till Fairbanks, true to his movie image, dove to the rescue. But Mary's blackly humorous punch line hints at her ambivalence toward the comic – she ran around shrieking, "Let the heathen drown." There were also photos of the comrades standing pigeon-toed or horsing around on one another's sets. Still, none of the obviously staged frivolity deflated their magic as symbols of beauty, youth, and hope. Instead it heightened it, setting them firmly at the apex of America – a perch that made them interesting to politicians.

In 1914 a new theme had entered film: the conflict in Europe (which no one at the time called World War I) – and the moral dilemma that Americans, pleasantly far from the action, might safely contemplate in the dark.

At first the American government was neutral, and a stream of films mined the theme of peace. Typical was 1914's *Be Neutral*, whipped up in forty-eight hours to support President Wilson's formal declaration of neutrality. There were pro-war films, too, of course. *The Battle Cry of Peace* (1915) showed America invaded by the Germans, who proceed to rape their women, bayonet babies, and shatter the dome of the Capitol Building. But the cutting edge of public feeling was expressed by *War Brides* in 1916. In this the heroine (Nazimova) kills herself rather than bear a child she knows must one day go to war. The movie was a solemn validation of the ditty "I Didn't Raise My Boy to Be a Soldier."

Pickford (through Marion), in "Daily Talks," took the pacifist high road: "There is but one place where boundaries between nations really exist – in our minds." Pacifist sentiments informed the Declaration of Independence; neutrality, in other words, was all-American. "Daily Talks" echoed the theme of *War Brides*: "Can you imagine women – mothers of girls and boys – going out to kill one another with the strange deadly fatalism that seems to seize our soldiers?" But by 1916 a readiness to fight was growing in the nation. The change of heart had begun a year before, in May 1915, when the liner *Lusitania* was torpedoed by a German submarine; over a hundred of the bodies that drifted ashore were Americans. This fighting philosophy was called "preparedness." "America wages no wars of self-interest," wrote Mary earnestly, "but were an enemy to threaten her, scarcely a soul within her borders would listen silently or unresponsive."

The U.S. entered the war in the spring of 1917, though Woodrow Wilson had won a slim victory in the presidential election of 1916 by stressing that he had kept the country *out* of battle. In May an act of Congress formed the Committee on Public Information, a propaganda organ charged with creating pro-war fever. The CPI, headed by a journalist, published a hundred million leaflets, articles, and books as well as posters, slides, and photos, extolling the virtue of the Allies and the barbarous evil of the Germans. It was slow to see that it needed the movies. The army sent cameramen to Europe, but its newsreels, aimed at encouraging recruits (and stripped, of course, of all carnage), were tedious. "Viewed as drama," said Griffith, "the war is a disappointment. The dash and thrill of wars of other days is missing."

Finally the CPI turned to Hollywood, which had shown its public-relations prowess with 1916's *Civilization*. The feature, a reply to *The Battle Cry of Peace*, showed Christ grieving on a mythical battlefield. Wilson thought the movie had helped his re-election, and he publicly thanked its producer, Thomas Ince. Now the CPI asked Hollywood to turn its full talents to pro-war fever. The response was predictably ecstatic. Here was a chance, producers thought, to scotch the impression that movies were second-class. Instead, with CPI approval, movies would seem a sacred vessel, the patriotic bearer of all things American. Besides, Los Angeles, the industry's production center, was caught up in pro-war paranoia. The city was near the Mexican border and thus, some believed, a nest of spies. Any moment the Germans might invade from Mexico; silent submarines might rise from the Pacific. Erich von Stroheim, an actor who specialized in playing Germans, could not eat out; he was spat upon in restaurants.

Film actresses answered the call by putting on Red Cross outfits and running around Hollywood as though it were a battlefield. Less preposterous – but only slightly – was the Lasky Home Guard, a regiment got up of studio employees. Naturally, Cecil B. DeMille was captain. His brother, William, was now a film director who made quiet, thoughtful pictures; consequently, in the Lasky Guard, he played the quiet, thoughtful role of sergeant while his brother strode about at his blustering best. Film idol Wallace Reid (son of theatrical road-show producer Hal Reid) was the Lasky Guard's photogenic corporal. On Thursday nights the guard marched in lockstep down Hollywood Boulevard. Drills were slightly less than rigorous – they met for two hours every other Sunday, using prop rifles and uniforms. Even worse, they drew their knowledge of the European conflict from a studio production, *The Little American* (1917), of which they were given a special preview. Captain DeMille was the film's director, and Pickford, the star, offered words to live by: "I used to be neutral till I saw your soldiers destroying women and shooting old men! Then I stopped being 'neutral' and became a human being!"

The Espionage Act of 1917 squelched the making of peace films by banning, rather loosely, any disloyal acts. By 1918 such movies were outlawed by government decree. Instead, such producers as Adolph Zukor, Lewis J. Selznick, and William Fox sat on a government committee to monitor production of the "right" kind of movie. These featured crude caricatures of "Huns," whose Hunnish "Kultur" included torture, murder, rape, and a fondness for monocles and firing squads. *The Little American* delivered superbly. En route to France, where an aunt is ailing, Pickford's ship, the thinly disguised *Lusitania*, is torpedoed. "Today," Mary chats on the "*Veritania*," "ocean travel has no thrills." A few moments later, she is treading water: "You've fired on American women and children!" Cold and bedraggled, she reaches her aunt's château in Vanguy, only to find the German savage at the gate. In quick succession, Mary is manhandled, leered at, almost raped, forced to clean a Hun's filthy boots, courtmartialed, sentenced to execution, put before a firing squad, and saved. "Somewhere in this house," she tells a flank of Germans, "there must be a man who is something more than a splendidly drilled beast!" Hurling chairs at her would-be rapist: "You contemptible cur!"

Mary plays these crudities as though they were Shakespeare. A moment in which she salutes a wounded soldier achieved, in the words of the *New Republic*, "a conflict of emotion that mirrored the most subtle aspects of reality as only a great imagination could conceive them. There was nothing theatrical about it. . . . But you might go a long way and see a great deal of famous acting without meeting the expression of an emotion so true, so poignant, and so beautiful."

She need not have acted at all, of course. Coupling Little Mary with the flag – the movie starts with a dazzling close-up in which she salutes before the Stars and Stripes – set the audience's red-white-and-blue blood racing. In fact, Pickford's blood was racing, too. Mary's first performance had been for soldiers – the Boer War contingent whose farewell amusement was *The Silver King*. There had been glamour that night in Toronto, and sentiment. As a child, Pickford had thrilled to the sight of soldiers at Queen's Park. Now, doing war work, she could not resist the rows of young men, many of humble origin, "heads erect and shoulders thrown back, swept on by a mutual love of this, their country." Canadians or Americans – they blurred into one in Pickford's conscience. Soldiers moved her.

Other performers in New York and Hollywood did war work. In 1917 some of them appeared in a propaganda short called *War Relief*, with Pickford leading off the cast. She seemed to be everywhere at once – speaking through megaphones, posing for posters, collecting cigarettes to send to the doughboys, leading a marine band through San Francisco, and sending her photograph to decorate trenches. She was christened the navy's "Little Sister" and kissed the American flag for cameras. She became the patron of a Red Cross unit (if you gave, your receipt was signed by Pickford). The 143rd California Field Artillery wore her photograph in lockets; they had made her their honorary colonel. Such titles were given to a handful of actresses, but none had Pickford's symbolic power. Mary played her assigned role, heart and soul – for instance, using the artillery as extras in a film. *Johanna Enlists* (1918) describes the adventures of a farm girl who becomes an unlikely muse when a regiment of soldiers sets up camp next door. Pickford does a pratfall version of Unity – smirking, wailing, sleeping in a dog basket. Then, in an effort to be beautiful, Johanna flits across the screen – her gown vaguely Grecian, arms imploring – a comic prance that nipped, with deadly aim, at Isadora Duncan. Switching tone, a patriotic coda shows newsreel footage of Pickford's troop ("God bless them and send them safely back to us") and "Colonel Mary Pickford," dressed in a soldier's uniform and hat with chin strap. "Don't you come back," she tells them, "til you've taken the germ out of Germany!"

In 1918 the governor reviewed the Lasky Guard, and Cecil was officially promoted to major. On this occasion, Mary made a doll-like figure in "a special couturier's outfit of patriot gray with a little veil down the back," remembered Agnes. "She looked splendid." Mary presented the Guard with its colors – "she'd had [the flag] all made of silk," said Agnes, "the finest silk, and all the stars were hand-embroidered." As Cecil made his farewell address, he was overcome – aghast, perhaps, that his toy brigade was about to march into real carnage. So Mary stood up, remembered Agnes, "like a little soldier ... and sent them to death, very valiantly. The grisly part is that some *did* go to death."

Many stars huckstered for the Liberty Loan drives. America's Sweetheart, as usual, outdid them. Pickford could appeal, at the drop of a hat, to duty and guilt as well as to vicious stereotypes. Americans were fighting to "make the world a clean, decent place to live in." After all, "we are at war with beasts." German-Americans should behave: "This is not a time for '50-50' citizenship.... Why," said Mary, wide-eyed, "I saw a big bludgeon a Canadian boy in New York brought back with him. It was a terrible thing. It was long and heavy and one end was full of spikes. The Germans used that kind of weapon to kill the wounded prisoners. They won't waste their bullets, so they beat the boys to death." This speech raised thirty-five thousand dollars. No wonder the army named not one but two of its cannons for the actress.

Chaplin and Fairbanks also did their duty. In 1917 Pickford played referee as the two friends clowned their way through a prizefight; the event, at the Mason Opera House in Los Angeles, raised thousands. Fairbanks was a happy propagandist. He often wrote articles and booklets (*Whistle and Ho, Sing As We Go* was one) on physical and mental health. Now he found sunshine in World War I, especially the training camps: "The clean life in the open air, the health building exercises, the clean wholesome food and the nights of unbroken sleep have made new men of thousands." He advised one and all to write to the soldiers – "For the girls, this goes double" – and ventured into such perilous topics as closing vice districts (to keep men pure) and purging the country of enemy aliens.

Chaplin, on the other hand, was enigmatic. In 1964 he called the war "an avalanche of mad destruction." But in 1914 he kept his counsel. Viewers expected he would register for military service in Britain, but Chaplin, who was then at Keystone, kept making movies. By 1917 hawk-ish circles thought the actor, who was healthy, red-blooded, and twenty-eight, should enlist for *someone*. (Fairbanks, at thirty-four, was legally too old.) Just in time the Third Liberty Loan Drive, with Pickford, Fairbanks, and Chaplin as figureheads, returned Chaplin's name to public favor.

The drive kicked off on April 6, 1918, one year after the U.S. entered the war. Airplanes bombed cities with pro-war literature, thousands of citizens paraded in city streets, and patriotic holidays were declared. In Washington, sidewalks overflowed as Chaplin, Pickford, Fairbanks, and actress Marie Dressler (representing Broadway) were paraded like rajahs down Pennsylvania Avenue. Each made a speech in a football field, surrounded by government officials. Chaplin, who had not slept much while editing *A Dog's Life*, was still edgy and excited. He leapt like a cannonball onto the platform: "Each bond you buy will save a soldier's life – a mother's son!" At the end of the speech, he slipped accidentally from his perch, grabbed Marie Dressler on his way down, and landed on Franklin Delano Roosevelt, then assistant secretary of the navy. When everyone was dusted off, the caravan proceeded to the White House Ellipse, where a crowd of thirty thousand waited. Each actor had a booth, and as Fairbanks and Chaplin made a dash to their stations, Pickford, caught in the crowd, was mobbed. It took her almost an hour to reach her post. Meanwhile Fairbanks and Chaplin kept order by standing on their hands on top of trucks. They sold three million dollars worth of war bonds that day, and squeezed in a tête-à-tête with Wilson.

On April 8 Fairbanks and Chaplin preceded Mary to speak on Wall Street. Fifty thousand people leaned from windows, peered from rooftops, and jammed the streets. Fairbanks lifted Chaplin above his head, Chaplin waved his derby, and the crowd went wild.

Pickford did a follow-up three days later. She stood in front of George Washington's statue; the crowd filled Wall, Broad, and Nassau Streets and Broadway. Anticipating spring, she had worn a blue coat and purple orchids. Instead, she spoke in a vicious hailstorm – conditions that did little to calm the audience. "Every bond you buy is a nail in the Kaiser's coffin!" she shouted. The crowd surged forward; she pleaded for order, threw kisses, then threw the crowd a glove. The wind snatched her curls from beneath her hat. Finally she removed it and stood bareheaded as snow whipped around her. There were roars of approval, and despite the storm a landslide of Liberty Bonds were sold.

Mary then set off toward the Midwest; Chaplin and Fairbanks took other routes. Pickford handily outsold them; a single speech in Pittsburgh, for instance, was reported to have raised five million dollars. She raised two million in Chicago; it took only an hour, and the count included the price of a curl, which she auctioned for fifteen thousand dollars.

The fourth drive, later in 1918, found Pickford so deep in the war effort it was rumored she was going overseas to do relief work. She made her own propaganda short, *100% American*, in which she played Mayme, a poor girl who forgoes the streetcar and walks two miles to save a nickel; she is saving, of course, to buy a bond. In the war's final months, Mary played on pathos. She appeared onstage, according to *Photoplay*, "her small figure ... outlined against a dark drop.... Mary began to speak. She told them she'd come on business; she meant to forget she was Mary Pickford and make them forget it. They sat forward as she told them of the wounded American boys – the first – whom she had visited in Washington; of one boy with both legs gone; of another, blind – it seemed fitting somehow that Mary Pickford should tell it; and she told it all so quietly."

By November, when the armistice was reached, Little Mary had also reached apotheosis. "If all the world were gathered in one huge, darkened auditorium," wrote a journalist, "and a portrait were to be flashed upon the screen which would be recognized by the greatest number, whose would it be? Would it be the picture of Woodrow Wilson, of Lloyd George, or even of the late Kaiser? No, indeed. It would be wee Mary Pickford.... For world popularity, she is the greatest American, the greatest world citizen.... Rightly used, the moving picture might be made the greatest factor in securing world peace through its destruction of ignorance and its removal of prejudice of race against race." It followed, then, that the movies' most powerful representative, "quaint, artistic, sprightly Mary Pickford," had become "the world evangel."

Heady stuff. Too heady – at times, she resented the burden, the yoke of duty, worthiness, and guilt. "I have always felt the bitterness of life," she once said, "and I suffer occasionally from 'mal de vie.'" During the third loan drive, a startled journalist found himself on a train with Pickford and Fairbanks. Mary was fretful. She sat with her face buried in the paper, then flung it aside. "I'm tired of make-up; I'm tired of the studio; I'm tired of pictures." Gently, Fairbanks tried to cheer her; such words, if printed, might do damage. But Pickford, disconsolate, would not respond. What, asked the journalist, would she do instead of acting? She was going to live on a farm, said Pickford. She already owned one. End of interview.

8

—

OLYMPUS

Little by little, Beth heard the gossip. In public she shook her head and smiled. In private she doubted, then accused her husband. And despite Fairbanks's protests and denials, she came to believe he was unfaithful. It must have been numbing to learn that her rival was none other than the universal evangel. Nevertheless, Beth believed, with some justice, that Fairbanks still cherished his marriage – or at least lacked the courage of his new convictions. "Terribly hot trip," he once wired her from Utah. (He was probably shooting on location; many of his films featured scenes in the Southwest.) "Sorry I did not tell you more that I love you before I left. Cheer up and give my best to the boy – Douglas." He was trying his best to be husband and father – and the latter, it seems, took special effort. The young Douglas, who was seven at the time, was a bashful, slightly dumpy boy; perhaps, the child reasoned, this repulsed his father. At any rate, Douglas Sr. would later confess, with appalling candor, to "no more paternal feeling than a lion has for his cubs."

Two months later Fairbanks sent Beth, who was now at a New York hotel, another telegram: "Wired you affair was off because you thought it was on. You have misjudged me terribly. There never was anything wrong. Will finish picture and leave Friday for east. Can you join me in Chicago?

Want to see you alone. Am worried about your condition. Wire me how you are. Love – Douglas."

Owen, too, had questions for his wife. "Owen came to me one day," remembered Mary, "stating he had the right to know since he was still my husband – although we had ceased to be man and wife. I told him the truth, and he asked me what I was going to do about it. I replied, frankly, that I wasn't planning to do anything." At the time – about 1916 – divorce made the actress sick with fright. Influenced, perhaps, by Charlotte's Catholic views, Mary called it "a form of amputation, to be avoided even at the cost of my own happiness and that of the man who loved me." But by 1917 her mood had changed. For by that time, the grapevine was alive with rumors, and her private life was quickly becoming public – mostly because of Owen Moore's displays.

It began in a maudlin moment, when Owen sat down to make peace with his wife. He was ready to make the ultimate sacrifice: in other words, he promised to be nice to Charlotte. Mary listened coldly.

"You're several years too late for that speech, Owen." As she spoke, she cruelly observed "the tears that were streaming down his face, meeting in a rivulet under his chin, and dropping down on his immaculate tie."

Mary finally said the dreaded word: divorce.

"I won't have it, Mary! Mark my words, I'm going to kill that climbing monkey!"

Mary called Fairbanks, who burst out laughing and said he couldn't wait to get his hands on Owen. Besides, he doubted if a drunk could shoot straight. But he may have found it prudent to leave the city. Director Allan Dwan, who often worked with Fairbanks, was bound for Los Angeles by train when the actor reached him by dramatic telegram. "Imperative. Meet me in Salina, Kansas and we will return to New York." In Kansas the actor pulled Dwan into the drawing-room car of the train and whispered, "Your friend Owen Moore says he's going to shoot me." Obligingly the director helped Fairbanks plan *A Modern Musketeer* (1917), which they shot out of Owen's reach in Utah. Meanwhile Mary's husband lurched around Los Angeles, brandishing a gun and calling out for Fairbanks. It was whispered (wrongly) that he tracked him to a hotel, aimed to kill, and shot Fairbanks in the hand. In another version, he succeeded, leaving Fairbanks in a pool of blood.

By April 1918 Beth had had enough. She and her son were in a suite at the Algonquin Hotel. Fairbanks had arrived in town, sold war bonds, then taken a room at the Sherry-Netherland — a cowardly abandonment that broke Beth's patience. "I have come to realize," she told the press, "that the only way to stop this gossip along the rialtos of both the Atlantic and Pacific Coasts is to plainly state that this time gossip has foundation in fact." She behaved with dignity: "For 12 years I have put my husband's happiness first. Now his happiness lies in paths away from mine. He has always been the kindest and most considerate man in his home life. I can only wish him happiness in the future." After all, Fairbanks and the mystery woman felt "that theirs was the one big love of their lives and that nothing mattered in comparison with it. I am big enough," said Beth, "to stand aside." If she mentioned Mary's name, the papers didn't print it. Hinting that the mystery woman was an actress, Beth let slip that the culprit "is associated with my husband in business." Fairbanks, selling war bonds in Detroit, was stunned at the news of Beth's announcement. "My wife and I have no differences whatever and the story is untrue from beginning to end." It was only, he suggested, German propaganda aimed at stopping his work with the Liberty Loan drive. ("Not quite playing the game," sighed Beth.) Mary, asked for her reaction while dining with Charlotte in a New York hotel, replied that Fairbanks's marital problems had nothing to do with her. Hoping to clear her name, she added, "We are simply associated together in business."

Somehow Owen got a word in edgewise. In the guise of standing up for Mary, he fingered her publicly as Fairbanks's lover: "The other woman is now ill and under great nervous strain. So I feel it obligatory upon myself to make a statement to save her from humiliation." Pickford, her husband improbably continued, was "little more than a child, with a child's winsomeness, appealingness and trust." Indeed, their marriage had been "one of mutual sympathy and affection" — that is, before the stealth of Fairbanks, who "combined a strong fascination for women with an instinct for possession." And, though he found the act "repugnant and distasteful," Owen was prepared to sue Fairbanks for destroying his marriage; it was in the best interest of the fragile little wife he loved.

Mary tried to downplay the messy business, airily explaining that she and Charlotte were "too busy working, too busy assisting in war work, too busy in income taxes, to read the papers." But even in taxation she was linked with Fairbanks. Income tax was then a fairly new phenomenon. Who paid what had curiosity value. According to the *New York Times*, the size of Pickford's check "startled the cashier." Both Fairbanks and Pickford received extensions; when they produced their checks they "were so greatly in excess of any other professional income taxes received to date that no comparison was possible. It was asserted that both checks were written in six figures and almost touched the seventh." In 1966 Pickford claimed she had paid $277,000. "And I want you to know that I was a brave woman, and I smiled as I gave it to the collector."

Charlotte had remained in the background through most of the drama. She had chaperoned Mary on the Liberty Loan tours, watched as she carried on with Fairbanks, and simmered but haughtily taken the high road as Owen impugned Mary's reputation. On April 13, 1918, she was standing near the platform as Pickford sold war bonds in the Bronx. Amidst the cheers she heard Dennie Joseph, a Hungarian immigrant, shout what she considered an insulting name. Perhaps it alluded to infidelity. Charlotte at last reached the end of her tether. She tackled the young man, called a nearby policeman, and ordered the immigrant arrested. The patrolman, cowed by Charlotte's fury, did so. Charlotte, still outraged, told the press that Joseph's words were so degrading she could not repeat them – though she would force herself to do so in a courtroom. The outcome of this incident is unrecorded.

A few weeks later, mother and daughter set off for Los Angeles – Fairbanks allegedly was on the train – and retired to Mary's home on Western Avenue. "At dinner," a journalist reported, Pickford was "tired and much distraught." This he probably learned from Lottie, who was dining with Charlotte and Mary and fended off the press at Mary's door by declaring her sister was having that old standby, a nervous breakdown.

"I was really slipping," remembered Mary – not only in private life, but in her art. She had not made a movie since *Stella Maris* that lived up to the standard she set herself. Now she wanted to use subjects that were already tested, and she got them when Charlotte bought the rights to the novels *Pollyanna* and *Daddy-Long-Legs*.

The fame of these children's books was spectacular; Pickford was determined that her films would match them. It was also time to renegotiate her contract – a regular event that, as usual, all Hollywood was watching. The price of Mary Pickford was the price of domination of the industry. And the actress had grown dangerously restive.

She knew she could virtually name her price, to almost any studio that pursued her. She was also growing insecure about her relationship with Adolph Zukor. As Famous Players–Lasky had grown (and its growth was prodigious), Artcraft – which once distributed Pickford exclusively – had swelled to include the films of Marguerite Clark, the wholesome Wallace Reid, William S. Hart (austere king of the western), and Douglas Fairbanks. Meanwhile, Zukor had become distant from Mary, working from the sprawling New York studio while Pickford made movies at the California plant. Inevitably they saw each other less, and Mary grew nostalgic, then depressed. She missed Papa Zukor's "sheltering arm" – the way, for instance, he used to hover at her shoulder, fretting she would catch cold without a shawl. He had once known her movies inch by inch; in 1917 he had stopped by the set of *Stella Maris* and asked her what the plot was. Gradually, wrote a friend of Zukor's, "the silver cord of personal understanding frayed and snapped."

Late in 1917 two exhibitors, Thomas L. Tally and J.D. Williams, had led a revolt against block-booking. They were sick of Paramount, sick of its sky-high rental fees. "I answered," wrote Zukor, "that the price of the stars was very high." Stars, more than any other factor, sold movies. And Paramount, which handled not only Famous Players–Lasky but a flock of other studios, distributed virtually every star that counted. Tally and Williams decided to eliminate the middleman by making and exhibiting their own productions. But their firm, called First National, needed stars, too, and to get them it drove their fees even higher. First National snapped up Chaplin, who promised to direct and star in eight two-reelers for a breathtaking million and some dollars.

As Mary neared the end of her two-year deal with Zukor, First National approached her, bearing gifts: $675,000 for three pictures. This, combined with 50 percent of the profits, would probably give Mary a million dollars – some thought as much as two million – a year. In addition, fifty thousand dollars would be paid to Charlotte, for performing unspecified services. One clause expressly forbade block-booking. Equally precious, Mary would win total creative freedom; from choice of role to final cut, her word was law.

"Let her go to First National," a friend told Zukor. "I guarantee you it will deflate her swelled head, destroy First National, and bring her back to you on her knees." ("A charming individual," Mary sniffed.)

In fact, the proposed break was traumatic. Zukor and Pickford had created a springboard for American features. In the process they had created each other – he as the czar of the feature industry, she as its foremost financial asset.

A story has it that Zukor, rather than pay Mary what she wanted but hoping to keep her from First National, offered her $750,000 a year for a period of five years. The idea, surely unique in film history, required that Pickford appear in no films for *anyone*. But Mary, more than ever, needed work; rather than deal with her domestic problems, she "had carved out my future in my career. It was my solace, my high fortress, where no one and nothing could molest or harm me." Her response to Zukor was that she would stay with him – provided he matched First National's offer.

"I'll tell you what, Mary," he replied. "Think it over while you're having lunch, and then let me know if you still feel the same way." Yet, when she returned, it was Zukor who spoke first.

"Mary, it is too big this time. It wouldn't be sound business to pay you what you want to stay with us."

"I'm sorry," said Pickford. "I'm very sorry."

"Well," said Zukor, "we have nothing to complain about, you and I."

She smiled weakly. "No. We've done the best we could for each other." Despite the smile, she could hardly bear it. Her grief, she recalled, was as if she were "saying good-by forever to a member of my own family."

"Call me after you talk to First National, won't you, Mary honey?"

Pickford shook hands with J.D. Williams, returned to her New York hotel, and telephoned.

"Yes," came a voice that seemed frail and distant.

"I have given my word to First National," she told him. After an agonizing silence she asked, unsteadily, if Zukor could forgive her. The reply: "God bless you, sweetheart-honey." Now she was sure they were both in tears. "I can't talk any more," he told her. "I can't either," said Mary. And that, she remembered, was the end.

For days she felt not triumph but shock. She had never been torn between personal relationships, art, and business; instead, they had dovetailed into common cause. Mary noted that her break with Zukor had occurred on November 6, 1918, the day before World War I's false armistice. She tortured herself with the fear that First National might prove to be a similar false victory.

Zukor, who was notably less masochistic, declared he would embark on a buying spree: "I'm going to turn my back on the whole star system and build up a chain of theaters across the country." Still, he saw the wisdom in replacing Little Mary with another of the same name – Mary Miles Minter, born Juliet Reilly. She had entered films at the age of ten, and in 1918 she bore an astonishing resemblance to Pickford. Zukor put the sixteen-year-old girl into roles Mary should have played (most notably *Anne of Green Gables* in 1919) and often gave her sets and plots that shamelessly reprised Mary's key successes. Minter knew what she was up against and tried to "not only come up to [Zukor's] expectations [but] exceed them." "She is working night and day to do this," *Photoplay* promised, but in her few surviving films, Minter seems merely competent, milk-fed, and vapid. And Pickford didn't turn a hair when told of Papa Zukor's action; in later years, when a film fan mistook her for Mary Miles, Pickford sweetly signed the autograph in Minter's name.

Meanwhile Beth Fairbanks was unraveling her marriage. At first she had tried to force Pickford out of hiding. "If no statement is made within the next few days either by the woman ... or by my husband, I shall verify my own statements by proofs." Mary responded by circling the wagons around her new home on Fremont Place – a street that, conveniently, had a locked gate. But Little Mary's aura subtly altered. An unusually acid journalist observed that though Charlotte and Lottie lived with Pickford, "nothing has been said of Lottie's husband." Presumably Lottie and Alfred Rupp had parted. Mary Pickford Rupp, though still an infant, had her own suite of rooms, and "apartments are held for Jack whenever that now jolly tar can drop in for a visit." (Jack had joined the navy's aviation unit.)

"Again," wrote the journalist, studying his press release, "nothing is said of Jack's wife." He had one: Olive Thomas, a Ziegfeld showgirl turned movie actress whom Jack had married in 1917. Such items show an element of doubt, if not malice, tainting Mary's press.

Fairbanks fared better, but his conscience nagged him. The actor saw echoes of his father's desertion of Ella in his own near abandonment of Beth. Rather than confront his guilt, he tried not to think or feel about it. When Beth filed suit on October 22, 1918, on the only possible legal ground in New York – infidelity – her husband absurdly denied the charge. Then, in an about-face, he bowed to the inevitable. On November 30 two of his close friends, actor William Clifton Crawford and director John Emerson, appeared in court in New Rochelle, New York. Rather than sully Pickford's name, they manufactured a string of seamy anecdotes. Crawford, for instance, told how Fairbanks once enticed him to a party of "beautiful girls" in a house on 33rd Street. There Fairbanks sat in a bedroom with a woman who was wearing a negligée and smoking. Emerson added a mysterious "confession" that Fairbanks had made to him in Hollywood, concerning "a certain escapade of his in New York with a certain woman." "Not a soul – not even Mother – believed these stories," wrote Fairbanks Jr. later. But the judge believed them and granted a provisional decree. The event drew an agitated press, which reported that Beth received four hundred thousand dollars in securities and a one-hundred-thousand-dollar trust for young Douglas, who remained in his mother's care.

Then something wonderful happened: nothing. Beth got on with her life (she remarried in 1920). And Pickford and Fairbanks made some movies. For a time, it seemed they had escaped scot-free.

With leftover money she had raised for the soldiers overseas, Pickford plunged into another project: a relief fund for film actors who were down on their luck. Pickford hadn't forgotten the degradation of her days living hand to mouth on tour. "Pride means a lot to people in our business. It's not so much the cold and the hunger," she continued. "It's the shame that gets you." In 1921, thanks to Mary's campaigning, the Motion Picture Relief Fund would officially take shape, and for decades Mary held important posts within the ranks.

There was a reassuring day of Mary-madness when the actress made a farewell appearance as a war bride. On January 3, 1919, she marched down the streets of San Francisco, her artillery behind her, in a welcome-home parade. She "looked very 'nifty' in her officer's uniform," observed a journalist, who gently kidded, "One could tell she hasn't been in service long.... She had her spurs on upside down." "Oh folks," said Pickford, eyes dimming with tears, "this is the saddest day of my life. I don't like to be mustered out." The actress told the soldiers they were part of her family. To prove it, "I've brought Mother Pickford and Sister Lottie with me." Luckily no one mentioned Jack, who spent his days in the service drinking. He also ran errands between a lieutenant and certain wealthy doughboys who wrote checks to earn danger-free assignments. The scam, which occurred in New York State, was detected, and Jack turned state's evidence to save his skin. Still, he was slapped with a dishonorable discharge. But the judge had reckoned without Charlotte Pickford. Soon the president's personal secretary deleted "dishonorable" from Jack's record, ostensibly so the actor could appear in a propaganda picture (it was never made). When questioned, the secretary, Joseph Tumulty, insisted he knew nothing of the bribery charges – but admitted that, yes, he had heard from Charlotte.

More woe: First National was in peril. A few weeks after Mary packed her uniform, a rumored merger of First National and Famous Players–Lasky shook the industry. From Zukor's point of view, this would have quashed his new rival and put him at the top of a titanic power. In Mary's view, the merger would have eliminated the venue for her self-produced films and put her once again under Famous Players–Lasky's thumb. Despite her fondness for Zukor personally, she was not prepared to compromise her contractual gains. She must have been dumbstruck, however briefly. But soon she was privy to a daring new scheme called United Artists.

The seeds of the company are obscure. Many people claimed to have inspired it. The Fairbanks family likes to credit Pickford, but she usually disowned the starring role. Some historians believe it was the brainchild of two disaffected film executives: Hiram Abrams, who left Paramount to join the new venture, and B.P. Schulberg, who had worked with Zukor since the days of Famous Players. They had watched First National form with interest. They noted that Pickford and Chaplin, despite their staggering salaries, shared the profits of their films with the parent company. But why share the bounty of their talents? Why not go into the distribution business themselves?

Quickly Schulberg drew up a manifesto – "89 Reasons for United Artists" – for presentation to the five biggest box office draws in the industry. These were Pickford, Fairbanks, Chaplin, William S. Hart, and D.W. Griffith. United Artists, the pair explained, would simply be a distributing entity, a pipeline for the stars' wholly owned productions (none of which, needless to say, would be block-booked). Schulberg and Abrams would run the company, receiving 20 percent of the profits.

An industry convention was in full swing at Hollywood's Alexandria Hotel, and the mood, reported the *Moving Picture World*, was electric: "Doug has signed up with First National." "Doug has done no such of a thing." "Charlie's going to Europe.... Mary will renew her contract with First National." "Mary will not." "Mary may, but Charlie won't."

Chaplin claimed that he, Fairbanks, and Pickford stationed Pinkerton detectives throughout the Alexandria to find out what exactly was afoot. The most successful was Operator 8, a woman with brains and sex appeal who picked up a lonely convention-goer and learned that the industry was verging on a forty-million-dollar merger, a gargantuan trust that would sew up all of the nation's exhibitors, then – by presenting a united front to distributors – drive down rental fees and therefore star salaries at its leisure. On January 14, 1919, Sydney Chaplin, the actor's brother and business adviser, called a conference at his home. Present were Chaplin, Fairbanks, Griffith, Hart, and Charlotte, sitting in for Mary, who had the flu. On January 15, the artists, known as the Big Five, signed a notice of intent:

We believe [United Artists] is necessary to protect the exhibitor and the industry itself, thus enabling the exhibitor to book only pictures that he wishes to play and not force upon him (when he is booking films to please his audience) other program films which he does not desire, believing that as servants of the people we can thus best serve the people. We also think that this step is positively and absolutely necessary to protect the great motion picture public from threatening combinations and trusts that would force upon them mediocre productions and machine-made entertainment.

Impressive. But the industry reacted with derision. "The lunatics have taken charge of the asylum," cracked Richard Rowland, president of Metro Pictures. "Actually," replied Arthur Mayer, who worked in distribution in the 1920s, "the founders of United Artists displayed the same brand of lunacy as Rockefeller, Morgan, and duPont." Still, few insiders believed that actors – childlike, insecure, flighty creatures – could run a company. The prejudice remained despite the announcement on February 5 of UA's impressively pinstriped executive. Abrams had emerged as general manager; Schulberg, who was offered a minor post, departed in a rage, sued Abrams, and settled out of court in 1922. But the loftiest names on the roster were federal.

Fairbanks, it seems, had the bright idea of extending the Washington connection. During the war bonds tour, he had sent a rare missive to his son, scribbled on Oval Office paper. "Dear boy, This is written from the executive office of the White House while all around us they are settling some of the greatest questions in the history of the world – Daddy." "He never signed himself Daddy before or since," his son remembered. "Had it been typed, I would have thought someone else had signed it." Fairbanks was inspired by the White House aura; he wore his D.C. connections like a medal. Now he asked William Gibbs McAdoo, President Wilson's son-in-law and former head of the treasury department, to serve as United Artists' president. Cautiously McAdoo refused, but he consented to become UA's general counsel. The presidential post went to Oscar Price, a former treasury official who had monitored the loan drive. These two names from the nation's capital gave United Artists much of the gravity and weight that the Liberty Loan drives had given Hollywood. But no one, no matter how well connected, could eliminate the snags in UA's start-up.

Early on, Hart withdrew, lured by a financially persuasive deal with Zukor. Each of the four remaining principals was given a thousand shares of common stock; the purchase entitled each to elect a member of the board and thus have a voice in the company management. Mary promptly put her mother in this position. If any of the founders wished to leave, the others had the option to buy his or her holdings. This way, the founders controlled who came and went within UA's inner circle. But a stickier issue was obtaining product.

Only a regular stream of movies could meet the cost of UA's overhead, and each of the partners pledged to meet a quota. This was a particular strain on Griffith. *The Birth of a Nation* had brought immense profits (though, after he had paid off all its investors, a mere million dollars went to Griffith's pocket). His 1916 follow-up, *Intolerance*, a film of unprecedented cost and ambition, was a box office failure, and Griffith lost all his *Birth of a Nation* profits. In 1917 Triangle was absorbed by Zukor. After that, Griffith was distributed by Artcraft, whom he owed two features when he joined United Artists. And after signing the United Artists papers, Griffith made an additional three-picture deal with First National (still an independent chain, despite the best efforts of Adolph Zukor). With his profits from these films in hand, he planned to make features for United Artists.

In fact, only Fairbanks had no lingering commitments. Obligingly he turned out UA's maiden feature: *His Majesty, the American*. Surprisingly, Griffith contributed 1919's second entry, *Broken Blossoms*, a tragedy so delicate yet relentless that Zukor, for whom it had been made, rejected it. (Or so the film's star, Lillian Gish, has claimed.) *Broken Blossoms*, which eschewed happy endings, was a box office triumph for UA, a triumph indirectly shared by Mary, who had suggested the material – "The Chink and the Child," an unfortunately titled short story – to Griffith. No one looked to Chaplin for product at this point. He owed First National five short movies, a daunting number when considered alongside his mental blocks. Mary, on the other hand, was accustomed to meeting relentless deadlines. She owed First National three films and went to work, brilliantly and fast.

Daddy-Long-Legs (1919), first published in 1912, was probably near completion when United Artists was incorporated. It was ideal raw material not only for Pickford but for her colleagues Frances Marion and Marshall Neilan. Its structure – a series of letters from a foundling to an unknown benefactor who removes her from an orphanage, educates her, and finally marries her – allowed for elastic interpretation. The Broadway version, which starred Ruth Chatterton, was plaintive. Pickford and Neilan, in typical style, rediscovered the material through slapstick. In contrast, its dramatic moments, including the death of a baby in Mary's arms, are all the more moving and surprising.

After a few homilies – "Baby Souls," explains a title, are the "bearers of the Earth's great secrets" – the movie attends to its own baby soul, Pickford's Judy Abbott, abandoned in a garbage can, wrapped in newspaper by the police, and delivered to the terrible Mrs. Lippett, matron of the local foundlings institution. Lippett, an efficient type, chooses Judy's first name from a gravestone and her last name from the phone book. She is also a sadist – at one point, she places Judy's finger on a hot stove. ("God will punish girls who steal; He will send them into a burning hot hell....") The movie's comedy is equally merciless. A sequence in which Judy gets drunk on hard cider is a tour de force of comic architecture. Its vignettes were created in what Mary called "creative frenzy" – Neilan's eyes "popped with excitement" as he thought up the climax: the entrance of a drunken dog, walking on its hind legs, teetering against a wall for support. But the simple bits have equal charm. In her first shot, Judy starts to sing; an arm reaches round a corner, grabs her by the throat, and yanks her, like a rag doll, from the screen.

But the film is most remarkable for its fluidity, the way its seemingly disconnected incidents transmit a deeply experienced childhood. These culminate in the closing image, a happy metaphor for sexual awakening. Here Judy finds, to her joy, that the man she loves is Daddy-Long-Legs. She sinks with him into a chair, and only her legs are visible. At first they kick in protest at some unseen activity. Then they stop; a foot curls thoughtfully. Next the legs collapse and lie still – then begin to kick again, contentedly, rhythmically, until she is bicycling high in the air.

The movie, released in May, induced euphoria. Even the *New York Times* surrendered. In general, the paper admired Pickford while deploring her material. *Daddy-Long-Legs*, sniffed its critic, was "coated and permeated with sentiment" – nevertheless, he admitted, he loved it. Pickford was elated. This was the first film on which she had acted as a totally independent producer; although it was a First National release, its success boded well for United Artists.

The Hoodlum, released in September, is a lesser but sweetly persuasive film. Pickford, as rich Amy Burke, has been living with her grandfather in New York while her father, a widower, travels on far-off lecture tours. When her father becomes a social worker, Mary joins him and confronts, for the first time, the reality of New York's underclass. Her arrival on the Lower East Side shows the worlds colliding: Pickford, beautifully dressed, peers out from the car window, shuts her eyes, and summons up her nerve. Then she steps from the car and stops as the impact – and the smell – of the neighborhood overwhelms her. A street kid, who finds Pickford just as odd as she finds him, approaches and holds up one of her salon-perfect curls in wonder.

Amy soon becomes the slum's most popular resident. Among her new skills are slang, shooting craps, and a daredevil shimmy. Pickford was expert at manic dancing, and after Amy shimmies in the street, an admiring onlooker throws her a bouquet of vegetables. Thanking him, she removes one and inhales it as though it were a rose. There is also a brilliantly funny sequence that shows Amy, drenched and desperate, in the rain. She solves her dilemma by sneaking beneath a passerby's umbrella – stopping, starting, and turning corners with split-second timing, all unbeknownst to the umbrella's owner.

In *The Heart o' the Hills*, which followed in November, Pickford turned up as Mavis, a hell-raising mountain girl bent on murder. This tough little movie is unique in Mary's canon for its casual brutality. Mavis is introduced on horseback, hair in a single braid, galloping around a tree for target practice. Her father, it seems, was killed by a sniper: "I promised pap I'd git him," she declares. When unwelcome interlopers happen by, Mavis shoots at their feet. At home, Mavis's mother attempts to beat her. Mavis breaks the hickory cane over her knees and says she expects to be treated like an adult. She then asks, with menace, "Be my dinner ready, mammy?"

The movie includes another manic shindig, in which Pickford does an industrious step dance. The usual sexual awakening follows. Mavis gives her hand to a man at the barn dance. He takes it; she cries that he is hurting her, and runs away. Attraction and repulsion are thus expertly wedded. At the end of the film, Mavis (six years older) discovers that Steve, her mother's second husband, is her father's killer. As he beats her, she pulls him off her mother, takes aim, and kills him. "Tragedies are quickly forgotten in the mountains," chirps a title.

The Heart o' the Hills is notable on two counts. First, it contains an extremely attractive appearance by John Gilbert, who in later performances was suavely known as the screen's Great Lover. But more important, *The Heart o' the Hills* distills the strength, the aggressive self-possession, that defined Mary Pickford, on and off the screen.

"Mary Pickford's threatened retirement from professional life," a reporter wrote wearily in 1919, "is becoming as chronic as Sarah Bernhardt's farewell stage appearances." It seems that, though she thrived at work, Pickford's emotional life was ruled by inertia regarding Fairbanks and outbursts of hopelessness and resentment.

She had already witnessed the fall of an actor due to adverse publicity. Francis X. Bushman was a favorite throughout the teens (his nicknames – Francis Sex Bushman and King Romeo – are revealing). But the actor's muscles and granite jaw did not protect him when female fans discovered that their allegedly single hero had been married for years, had fathered five children, and had then left his wife for actress Beverly Bayne. Pickford had never denied her marriage; neither had she stressed it. But her aura was that of the Virgin Mary; she had farther to fall than any actor, and scandal would plummet her to earth.

"My whole life is ruined," Pickford once told Marjorie Daw (who had appeared in *Rebecca of Sunnybrook Farm* and then did a series of Fairbanks films). She confessed she was near the breaking point: "Just at a time when I should be at the height of my career I am surrounded by misery and sorrow. I can't stand the worry and strain much longer."

At one point she sat down with Adela Rogers St. Johns for her opinion as a member of the press. "I can see her now," St. Johns remembered. "She was so tiny, and her feet didn't touch the floor. And all of a sudden she just leaned forward and with tears in her eyes, she said, 'Adela, if I divorce Owen and marry Douglas Fairbanks, will my people ever forgive me?'" St. Johns thought a minute – noting, in passing, the use of the royal phrase "my people." Then she said carefully, "I believe – and I can only tell you what I believe – that they will forgive you anything." But another time, when Pickford queried Frances Marion and Adela, the women conferred and decided that the outlook was fifty-fifty.

Fairbanks comforted, coaxed, and romanced her; he asked her again and again to marry him. He "wanted all of Mary," his son remembered, "herself and her talent and her fame and her exclusive devotion. And he longed to be able to display their union to the world like a double trophy." He even tried threats to shock her into action. One day Mary was with Zukor, still a close friend, when Fairbanks called. She left the phone in panic. Fairbanks, she reported, had threatened to leave her if she didn't set her own divorce in motion. "Think what you mean to millions of people," said Zukor, who opposed divorce. "You're their idol – "

"I didn't ask to be anybody's idol. I'm merely an actress playing children on the screen."

A *Photoplay* reporter paid a visit to Owen, who was making an effort to repair his reputation. "You don't know what good nature really is until you have met Owen Moore," wrote the journalist in wonder. "Instead of the glowering, sulking bulk of masculinity I expected, there was a perfectly cool, cheerful young man who beamed on me with the famous Moore smile and twinkled with the half humorous, half pensive Moore eyes.... It's hard to imagine anyone failing to 'get on' with Owen Moore." Without alluding to his ruined marriage, the reporter marveled at "the heart without rancor and the memory without bitterness." This was the sober Owen that Mary fell in love with.

It was also the man who put a price on her divorce: a hundred thousand dollars, a fraction of her fortune and much less than the half million Fairbanks had given Beth. But Pickford recoiled from his proposal. "If any spark of tenderness or compassion remained in me," she later wrote, Owen's "act of cold calculation killed it." It is possible, of course, that Pickford had offered Owen the money herself; when she felt most guilty, she would distract herself, almost hysterically, by pointing the finger elsewhere. At any rate, Charlotte felt similarly stung and at last saw that Mary must divorce her husband. She burrowed deep within the Pickford vault, emerged with a bundle of bonds for Owen, and promptly ran into his mother on the sidewalk. The women, who had once posed for a photo arm in arm with Mary, were tongue-tied. "Oh, sure, Mrs. Pickford," said Mrs. Moore lamely, "poor Owen must have something." Charlotte, who didn't believe poor Owen needed anything, was furious.

In February 1920 she accompanied her daughter to Nevada, where divorce laws were more liberal than those in California. Divorce in California would have required her to wait a year before remarrying. Owen, per agreement, was in Nevada's Douglas County, ready to be served with the necessary papers. The press were ready too, circling the ranch where Mary had retired with her mother and her lawyer. On March 2, Gladys Mary Moore slipped out and surfaced in the county seat of Minden. There she stood before Judge Frank P. Langen and requested a divorce on the grounds of desertion. She wore a black dress and was heavily veiled. "The world smiled a bit," admitted *Photoplay*, which then rushed to its evangel's defence; the garments worn "matched the black sorrow in her heart." But elsewhere Mary got the press she dreaded: "Information has it that Miss Pickford was poorly clad and wept. . . . The incident recalls many cinematic scenes wherein she participated. In this guise she has been known to do her most effective acting."

In order to receive a divorce in Nevada, one had to have lived there for half a year. Instead, Mary claimed that she *intended* to live there ... perhaps ... she hoped so. No one believed this but the judge, who must have been a Pickford fan. Had she come to the state with the purpose of launching a divorce? Mary virtuously insisted she had come for her health. Neither had she known of Owen's presence; he had come to Nevada, she explained, to scout coal-mine locations for a film. Surely, asked the judge, Mary meant to say a gold mine? Rattled, she quickly corrected herself. Then came the saga of separations in which Pickford swore that she had tried to live with Owen only two years before and that (neatly reversing the couple's roles) she had begged him to return to her and sent him gifts. What about the rumor that she had paid off her husband? Pickford indignantly denied it.

The unholy session took half an hour. When Pickford emerged, divorce in hand, she felt branded – not with the letter A, perhaps, but C for collusion, D for divorce, and H for hypocrite. "I was haunted," she recalled years later, "by having had to pay for my freedom in hard-earned money; by the growing danger that the newspapers might get wind of the unsavory transaction; by the certainty that people would be saying that I had bought off one husband to acquire another." But Pickford found it even harder to accept that she knew these things were true, and could never quite square her conscience with them.

On March 6, back in California, Mary spoke to reporters. She was just a bit defensive. "I am happy in the knowledge that I have done no wrong; that I have my own self-respect. So slander cannot touch me. My reputation is worth more to me than all my money.... I do not think Owen Moore will suffer any unhappiness over our divorce. We have been estranged virtually since our marriage." But guilt was not far below the surface. "If I have done anything to offend the public I am very sorry. My life work is to make people happy." Perhaps most startling was the statement "I have learned that I do not belong to myself" – she was mastered, in other words, by Little Mary and the public to whom she had pledged her troth. She would never remarry, she assured the press.

Fairbanks knew better and proposed. Just as predictably, Mary dragged her heels, asking not only for Charlotte's blessing but for that of Jack and Lottie. Chaplin suggested that she and Fairbanks simply live together; the plan's lack of realism maddened her. Once again Mary posed the questions to Fairbanks that the two had discussed for five years. "If the world doesn't approve, will your love be strong enough? If we both lose our careers, will our love be sufficient for our future happiness together?" But Fairbanks was fatally persuasive. "I love you for yourself," he said – the perfect prince.

On March 26, 1920, Fairbanks gave a small dinner at his home. Among the guests were Mary Pickford; R.S. Sparks, the county marriage license clerk; and the Reverend J. Whitcomb Brougher, pastor of the Temple Baptist Church. The hint was obvious, yet Mary again slipped through the net, saying she couldn't get married on a Friday, nor in the black dress that she happened to be wearing. And in fact, she had a wedding dress at hand, having seen it in the January *Vogue*, snapped it up, and (remarkably) modeled it herself for the magazine's February issue. Fairbanks finally got his bride – wearing white tulle trimmed with apple green and a great deal of gauze – to say "I do" at Brougher's home on Sunday, March 28. (Cannily, Fairbanks told her that the date was astrologically auspicious.) When the deed was done, the newlyweds left for Fairbanks's home, a former hunting lodge in Beverly Hills. In those days, the area was barely settled, and the house was on top of an untouched mountain. For three days, Pickford went to work on *Suds* (her film in production) with adhesive tape wrapped around her ring. At night she and Fairbanks enjoyed seclusion. Then they faced the inevitable, told reporters, and began to inform their next of kin.

"Charlie!" Mary cried, as the press took notes. "We haven't told him yet. He'll kill us for this." Perhaps it was post-nuptial nerves that then led her, for the first time in her career, to jabber uncontrollably in public. When the phone rang, Mary ran off, then came back with the frazzled announcement, "It was Lottie! She says she has been crying ever since somebody told her." Mary told Fairbanks her sister was so upset that "never, oh never, will she speak to you again." As Fairbanks coped with this crushing news, Pickford dithered about Jack's loneliness (this while he was married to Olive Thomas). Then she had a sudden inspiration, took a deep breath, and bolted toward the phone with the words "Let's tell him!"

When news reached Nevada, the attorney general prepared a seven-thousand-word complaint. In it he pointed out that Mary's quick marriage cast doubt on her intention to become a resident. He ridiculed her courtroom reference to "coal mines" and accused her of collusion with Moore and Fairbanks. A journalist watched the ensuing uproar; Pickford spent the day of the challenge "not at all worried, collapsed in a nervous breakdown ... finishing work on [her current film] under impenetrable guard, confined to her bed, participating in a benefit performance with her husband in Pasadena, extremely happy and seriously unhappy." Next the Baptist church reprimanded Brougher for marrying two divorcés. Most upsetting was a leering reporter's speculation that if Mary had a baby, only to discover her divorce had been annulled, she could choose among three names: Pickford, Moore, and Fairbanks. Papers were sold with images of Mary, touched up with shimmering, rolling tears.

But some of the public weren't buying. There was a rightness to Little Mary's union with the magical Fairbanks. Quickly this view became ascendant. In June, when the couple arrived in New York en route to their European honeymoon, the crowd that rushed to their hotel was jubilant. Fairbanks was obliged to turn a handstand on the hotel roof (Mary, in mock horror, put a hand to her mouth). At night, when they attended the theater, audiences routinely stood up and applauded as they walked down the aisle. At the Ziegfeld Follies, a short song and dance about the couple's marriage was topped when the actors shouted, "Ask the real ones to come up and do it!" A spotlight found "the real ones" looking blissful in the third row. Pandemonium.

Mary was looking forward to a fairy-tale journey, especially to Britain, which she hoped would resemble *A Child's History of England* by Charles Dickens. She dreamed of traveling from town to town, stopping for the night in quaint old inns – that is, if her fans and the press had forgiven her. Despite the hosannas in New York, she worried aloud as the S.S. *Lapland* approached Southampton. "There is nothing to hide about my first marriage or the undoing of it.... I want to forget all about that nightmare."

But England, like New York, had no memory of it. The nation was frayed by the aftershocks of war: exhaustion, bereavement, unemployment. The edgy, suggestible population needed to escape into some ideal and seized on the marriage as it would have greeted a second coming. It seems dramatically right that the couple's first welcome should fall from the heavens: tiny parachutes with garlands of roses and sacks of letters dropped to the deck of the *Lapland* from airplanes overhead. Meanwhile, as an overwrought reporter put it, Southampton "rose with the eager anticipation of a lover and went out into the rain-washed morning to greet Mary Pickford."

As soon as the public glimpsed the ship, they stampeded for the gangway. "[Their idols] had materialized ... they had become human," breathed the *Daily Mail*'s reporter. The appearance of film stars among the mortals – especially these two, whose marriage had caused such rapture – seemed miraculous. "Famous people glow, it is said," writes historian Leo Braudy, "and it's a glow that comes from the number of times we have seen the images of their faces, now superimposed on the living flesh before us." Thus, Pickford's face impressed the *Daily Mail*'s reporter: "Even at the distance from deck to dockside one could catch all [Mary's] thoughts in the remarkable mobility of her face." A group of her devotees, armed with a special illuminated scroll signed by four thousand fans, could not get near her. Swamped by a crowd that threw flowers at them, the couple finally met the mayor on a dais, accepted his welcoming remarks, and, with the help of thirty policemen, escaped with their skins into the waiting train. But Southampton was the tip of a colossal iceberg.

Next stop, London, which was suffering Pickford-Fairbanks fever.

Traffic around the Ritz hotel, where the couple stayed, was choked for miles in all directions. According to Alexander Woollcott, George V watched the masses watching – he was stalled in a limousine for twenty minutes. Perhaps he felt envious, or threatened, for the crowd was religious in its fervor. Their eyes were fixed on Pickford's balcony, "thousands and thousands of them," she remembered, "waiting day and night in the streets below, for a glimpse of us." Pickford and Fairbanks obliged them by appearing on the balcony and waving; Fairbanks even straddled the balustrade and hung above the crowd like a superhero. That evening they slipped out to see George Robey in the play *Johnny Jones* at the West End's Alhambra, arriving late because of the teeming streets. The play was stopped as the couple took their seats in the Royal Box, hung with both British and Yankee bunting. And only after a ten-minute ovation, followed by a speech by Fairbanks, did Robey and *Johnny Jones* continue.

Fairbanks was thriving on the attention. Mary, on the other hand, was weak and nerve-racked. Fairbanks, who also thrived on gallantry, took her to visit Lord and Lady Northcliffe (he was an influential newspaper baron), who promised them seclusion on the Isle of Thanet. In the morning Mary rose from bed, threw open the shutters, and nearly fainted. The sky was black with people, all seated on the ten-foot wall opposite. At the sight of Pickford in her nightgown, they burst into overjoyed applause.

Back in London, the pair were scheduled to appear at the Chelsea Theatrical Garden Party, which raised money for the needy by putting London's leading actors into tents. One could visit, for instance, the fortune-telling tent of Miss Betsy Chester, the hat-shop tent of Miss Viola Tree and Miss Winnifred Barnes, or the Grand Giggle tent with its hijinks theatricals, or one might buy tea and ices from Miss Ivy Featherstone.

Fairbanks and Pickford approached in an open Rolls, only to meet what the actor called "a lynch mob – except that it was smiling." Pickford, unthinking, put a hand out. Several hands clutched her in reply, then pulled her halfway from the car. Fairbanks, who was looking the other way, turned, grabbed Mary's ankles, and shouted for the car to stop. "I say," said George Grossmith, an actor who was also in the Rolls, "please unhand the little lady, won't you? Can't you see she's in danger of her life?" Once again the Rolls inched forward. Now came the problem of getting out. Pickford's door opened and the crowd besieged her – crushing her to the ground, reporters said. Six policemen fought them off while Fairbanks, inspired, put his bride on his shoulders. But the crowd had its way with them, dragging at Mary's hands and feet while Fairbanks staggered across the grounds. As hundreds of rioters crashed the turnstiles, Mary, to her horror, saw a branch approaching. She was winded by a limb and scratched before Fairbanks, on whom she was perched, swooped down. Next, in a rare ungraceful moment, he crashed into a tent serving buns and jam and the canvas came down around their ears. Fairbanks emerged again, holding his bewildered bride, plunged into a car, and yelled "Git!" to the driver. Fans threw themselves at the hood, the doors, and the dashboard as they drove away. "I've seen her," shouted one. "I touched her dress."

"You British people are so wonderful," said Mary gamely. "You don't do things by halves." But photos of the riot show her terrified expression. The actress had known of her fame at a distance, of course – in the size of her paychecks and the sheaves of photos sent to fans. She had also known crowds, but even at the Liberty Loan drives' height she had known she could control them. The Chelsea riot, with its impulse to touch and tear, had shocked her. London was shocked, too, and searched its soul. The couple were deluged with repentant letters, and editors scolded: "London professes to love Mary Pickford. It made such a performance of loving her on Tuesday that yesterday she had to be taken away to the country to get over it."

The debate continued as Mr. and Mrs. Fairbanks dropped in on Wimbledon (the calm and concentration of the tennis game were shattered), then zigzagged, like a funnel cloud, through Switzerland, Italy, and France. Photographs show the roiling crowds, which, as they surge to possess the car, might just as well be storming the Bastille. In Paris hysteria erupted when "Doug et Mary" tried to meet a delegation at the central market. Once again Mary was nearly trampled; according to some reports, she fainted. This time her rescue was finessed by butchers who locked her in a meat cage for her own protection. Pickford stood among the carcasses and listened to a shrieking sound like that of howling monkeys. "A fat woman dressed in green silk stumbled and fell into a crate of eggs," according to the New York Times. "Her dress became a streaming yellow, but her enthusiasm changed not." Pickford finally made a bravura exit by picking her way along the tops of the cages, negotiating mutton, veal cutlets, and pork chops.

Sightseeing, to her dismay, proved futile, unless they toured the sights by moonlight. Frances Marion, also on honeymoon in Europe, tried to keep pace, at Mary's invitation. But the balcony appearances, barrages of flowers, introductions to the nobility, gifts, testimonials, and the occasional riot made normal interaction impossible. Frances called her friends "prisoners of the crowds. I don't think they ever had time to eat — *or* sleep."

They sensed that some sort of revolution had occurred, one that would shape and control their future. So did the British press, which struggled to express what they had seen.

The amazing reception of Mary Pickford has been variously interpreted. Some people appear to think that it is due to a decadence of the national character, to an easy surrender to emotion alien from the assumed stoicism of our forefathers. Others seem to be indignant that so widespread a popularity should be so easily won.... The enthusiasm could have been anticipated had its cause been understood, and there is no reason why we should be astonished or alarmed or angry at so natural an event. Imagine if at the heyday of Charles Dickens's popularity, when an impatient public waited eagerly for each instalment of his stories, it had suddenly been announced that "Little Nell," "Little Dorrit," "Ruth Pinch," "Florence Dombey," and all the humble heroines of his creation had suddenly come to town. Well, that is what has happened now.

Indeed, Mary's honeymoon proved, as had no event since film began, the insidious reach of the movie dreamscape — a reach more powerful than images from literature, theater, and art. A few writers sensed this, with ominous twinges. "One must not ask who Mary Pickford is," groused a reporter for the *Aberdeen Free Press*. "[One] must shout with the crowd or be undone." And, as a writer, he felt defeated. "With 'the new world,'" he grumbled, "came new values."

The London *Times*, in "Heroine Worship," compared Mary Pickford and Mary, Queen of Scots, with whom "every 'nice boy,' it is said, falls in love." But the celebrated monarch became a legend after centuries of folklore had told her story. Now the mechanics of fame had changed. The images of film were so suggestive that because of a wink or a way of walking, an actor might find himself perched on Mount Olympus. "By the alchemy of a machine," explained the *Times*, "centuries have been shortened into days and nights." In other words, fame had reached its modern incarnation, and the culture of celebrity had taken root.

This culture relied not only on the movies but on the tabloids, a new-minted publishing phenomenon that fed on photos and tantalizing stories. Syndicated papers, too, needed filler that could run in coast-to-coast editions, splattering film images far and wide. Soon the lives of movie stars spread beyond such magazines as *Photoplay* and appeared with the exploits of politicians, athletes, and society blue bloods. Studied on the subway and perused at breakfast, they formed an almost parallel reality, a world that seemed larger, more important – an empire of immortality, of icons.

The rulers of this empire were Pickford and Fairbanks. They sensed this and sailed home to build a palace.

9

—

THE EMPIRE BUILDERS

They reigned from Pickfair, the story-book house on the hill that Fairbanks gave Mary as a wedding gift. The former hunting lodge on Summit Drive combined the grace of a cottage with a grand estate: two massive wings, a friendly tower, a green-tiled roof with a gentle slope, checkerboard trellises and awnings, and broad leaded windows with a view of both Benedict Canyon and the ocean. The sunlit pool, which was shaped like an oyster, featured a slide and its own strip of beach: on a fine day, visitors might find the manor's lord and lady paddling a canoe there. On other days, they repaired to the stables and cantered over their eighteen acres of lush grass, conical trees, and ponds. They might trot past the butler's cottage, the lodge that housed their fifteen servants, the kennels, or the tennis court. Or they might ride beyond through the vast, unsettled mountains, or down Sunset Boulevard's bridle path. For quiet times, they watched the water splash from their cupid fountains or strolled through the garden hand in hand, discussing the progress of the vegetables. Red fox and quail sometimes ventured out, and at night Mary often heard coyotes. On at least one evening, she heard a Hawaiian band, hired by her husband to stand beneath her window and serenade her.

"This is a happy house," said Mary. "This is a house that has never heard a cross word." (In part this was due to Charlotte's absence; she was safely tucked away in a house down the mountain.) Mary and her husband devised a solemn oath – "by the clock" – a reference to the moment in Fairbanks's car when he broke down and wept over Tu-Tu's death. They called each other pet names – she was Hipper or Tupper, he was Tiller or Duber – though to everyone else they were "Doug and Mary." Or perhaps Dougandmary, the inseparable couple who spent every night of the first eight years of their marriage together. Actress Colleen Moore recalled that when Fairbanks was detained on location, Mary had her trailer dragged three miles outside Los Angeles to meet him, spent the night, and returned to continue her own film at sunrise.

They saved the last dance, and every dance, for each other. It wouldn't be right, decided Mary, "to meet a man one minute and then the next to go into his arms and dance." Besides, "it is a promise I made to Douglas." With these words, she turned away the Duke of York, who would one day rule Britain as George VI.

The same romantic custom ruled at dinner. "Douglas and I have made it a rule to sit together always, both at home and elsewhere," Mary told her hosts. "I trust it won't inconvenience or upset your plans." Actress Pola Negri recalled the couple sitting at the head of Pickfair's table, sweetly holding hands as they told guests the grosses of their movies.

Their gifts were grand gestures: Mary gave Fairbanks a .45 automatic pistol, certified to have killed twenty enemy soldiers, and fifteen black-and-white paintings by Frederic Remington, the western artist, as well as an authentic western bar. It came complete with brass rail and bullet scars, and she hired two Gold Rush pioneers to find it. Fairbanks gave Pickford the first Model A sold anywhere in the world, as well as a 102-piece gold-and-porcelain tea set that had once been presented by Napoleon to Josephine. These gifts were signed in mystifying baby talk: "To Till de Pewr from Frin de Sprink," wrote Mary.

"I wanted nice things," she recalled of her childhood, and now she had them. As Little Mary, she dressed demurely but, despite her lack of sexual daring, still managed to achieve the dernier cri. Adela Rogers St. Johns was present when Mary's Alsatian maid laid out "an exquisite thing of shell-pink chiffon, the skirt made in a thousand dainty petals. Beside it lay a coat of the same color in a rich satin with a little fox collar." Pickford bought many such gowns in Paris. She also indulged a love of jewels: a ruby set, pearls, and canary diamonds.

The child who had once slept curled on a train seat now lay beneath an Italian lace bedspread, surrounded by pillows with taffeta ruching. Silk drapes hung from her bedroom windows and billowed from a coronet above her bed. Standing proud on the pale green carpet were her rococo dressing and bedside tables, her dainty commode, and her chairs with the cane seats – the best one could buy in a set from a department store. For though Pickfair's owners walked with kings, their decorating tastes remained middle-class. Luckily, this reinforced their roles as happy monarchs, cast by both Hollywood and the people, reflecting the fantasy of the movie world while keeping their bourgeois hearts intact.

Looking back, Fairbanks Jr. declared that Mary and his father "enjoyed a status in the world's imagination that is ... inconceivable and incomparable by today's standards." And, he added, they made it "their serious business" to prolong it. The key to their mystique was seven round-the-world tours throughout the decade. These were marathon excursions; a jaunt in 1921, for instance, took the couple to Italy, France, Switzerland, the Middle East, and Africa. In 1924 they whisked through London, Paris, Madrid, Aix-les-Bains, Interlaken, Berne, Lucerne, Zurich, Munich, Berlin, Oslo, Copenhagen, Amsterdam, and Brussels in the space of three months. As they were received by royalty, aristocrats, and artists, Pickford and Fairbanks were linked forever in the minds of fans with an international elite. The young Noël Coward knew their worth: in 1924 he found himself on board the *Olympic*, bound for England, with D.W. Griffith, Pablo Casals, and Doug and Mary. In those days, Coward's star was newly launched, but he took a "real pleasure in reflected glory." As the ship left the dock, he stood on deck beside Pickford and Fairbanks, "watching that vast sea of faces ... pallid discs with black smudges on them where mouths were hanging open." But even those who didn't have to work for their celebrity wished to meet California's Peter Pan and Wendy. (Awaiting them in London, for instance, was a party with the Prince of Wales.) With luck, the proof of such a meeting would be published in a photo, for proximity to Mr. and Mrs. Fairbanks was a feather in the cap for any king and queen.

All this appealed to Fairbanks's ego, as well as his chronic wanderlust. And it created new avenues for Pickford's guilt. Fame, in her mind, entailed obligations: to see and be seen, to spread joy simply by showing up. Still, she and Fairbanks kept the common touch. This was their charm for Europeans, for to meet Doug and Mary was to meet America. They were careful, too, to remind Americans that though they consorted with crowns and titles, they were still sparkling democrats at heart. Once, when the pair returned to California, Pickford breezed up to a microphone. "*We're delighted to be home,*" she said, her tremulous voice like that of a child waking up on Christmas day. "I haven't seen such a lovely sight in four months and 24,000 miles." Then, "Oh Douglas!" as she turned to Fairbanks. "I'll wager you forgot to stop the milk in Beverly Hills before we left!"

And, like democrats, they earned their living. Acting is hard work; acting and producing even more so. Fairbanks, fans were told, rose at five in his mauve and black bedroom, crossed his Tasmanian possum throw rug, and spent a half hour jogging round the house, turning handstands on a lawn chair, and high-jumping hedges. Back in his dressing room, the actor surveyed his fifty pairs of shoes, thousand shirts, seventy suits, thirty-five coats, and thirty-seven hats, then chose the day's adornment. At six he met his wife in their ivory-colored breakfast room. There, before an oval window, they sat in their floral oval-backed chairs, drank tea (perhaps from their silver service), and reviewed the day's schedule of activities.

Pickford and Fairbanks, who had once moved quickly from film to film, now drastically slowed the pace, conferring for six to nine months a year on the physical production of their "specials." Usually these were shot side by side at the ten-acre Pickford-Fairbanks Studio, at Santa Monica Boulevard and Formosa. "I would like to concentrate on acting alone," admitted Pickford, "but I realize I can't." Too much was riding on each production: fame, their self-respect as actors, and the sticky logistics of United Artists.

The Washington connection, so dazzling on paper, dazzled less in life; McAdoo and Price resigned in 1920. And the abolition of block-booking, so laudable in principle, proved costly. Selling films singly required more paperwork and more sales staff. Bookings took longer to sell, and films took much longer to recoup their investments.

There was also a chronic lack of product. Hiram Abrams, who replaced

Price as president, at first set the yearly quota at a dozen films but had to lower it several times. And where, once produced, would these movies play? Throughout the decade, the industry engaged in a series of mergers and power grabs as production, distribution, and exhibition – once separate entities – swallowed one another whole. The result was a handful of powerful, vertically integrated studios. Each owned not only a production lot but its own distribution wing and chain of theaters. Usually their theater chains included the sumptuous city palaces, where "roadshow" engagements might sell nearly half a movie's tickets. ("Two-fifths," said Mary, who was detail-minded.) But United Artists, which lacked a chain, had to rent screens from others or find the rare venue that remained independent.

And the company was seriously underfinanced. Bankers thought the more established studios – Famous Players–Lasky, for instance – were far more attractive investment prospects than the untried rebels. So Pickford and Fairbanks had to cover their own production costs – and production, in the 1920s, was expensive business.

In the 1910s, art direction had been incidental. Now the look of a film defined its meaning, and silent film blossomed with a gorgeous finish. Technical advances allowed the movies to be beautiful, gritty, spectacular, eerie, homely, or haunting as required. Light could be wintry, smoky, holy. The pace of movies also slowed, in part to capture their scenic wonders and in part to accommodate storytelling.

Always hypercritical, Pickford feared that the new, improved standards might make her early work – this included her Biographs – look foolish. "The stories were sudden, abrupt, and somewhat disconcerting," she wrote worriedly in 1923. "They attempted to cover too much, and the treatment was always sacrificed to the happenings, which were often not too closely related. If a character was wanted anyplace, he turned up. The sets alongside of the excellent work done today were crude and the furnishings were meager.... We never changed costumes in a picture. Ten years might elapse and the leading man would be wearing the same checked shirt." She was mortified that, for her role in *Friends*, she had worn Charlotte's wedding dress – its puffed sleeves utterly wrong for the period. Five years later, she was still preoccupied, writing that in her early films she appeared onscreen to be a "funny, fat little girl who expressed emotion by heaving the chest violently, by running around trees in moments of joy, and by shaking people."

Features in the teens had been made on a treadmill, but the results could be spontaneous, fresh and fast. In contrast, films of the 1920s allowed character and motive to be fully felt, and films, which used to race, *unfolded*. Slower movies also allowed for more lingering shots of the leading actors. More and more often these were women. It seemed inappropriate, after all, to linger on a man's face as though it were an object of adoration. Actresses dominated silent movies. As a group, they had stronger charisma, more sexual freedom, and better roles – though the confident Fairbanks didn't seem to notice.

In 1920 the actor donned cape and mask and left *The Mark of Zorro* on his acting future. Swashbucklers offered more escapist thrills and sheer beauty than the earlier Fairbanks satires. He could also reinvent the genre, a stodgy affair until he influenced it with physical irreverence. Zorro "takes any shape he wills – appears through key holes!" complains a victim. Indeed, when Fairbanks duels atop a mantelpiece he looks as if he might launch himself into the air – a masked Peter Pan with a nicotine habit. *The Mark of Zorro*, which Fairbanks made as an experiment, was so successful that he plunged into a decade of romantic adventures: dueling madly as D'Artagnan in *The Three Musketeers* (1921), leaping turret to turret as *Robin Hood* (1922), plunging forward on a winged horse as *The Thief of Bagdad* (1924), lashing bullwhips as *Don Q., Son of Zorro* (1925), and sliding down a sail as *The Black Pirate* (1926). The latter film was made in early Technicolor and featured Fairbanks swinging on a rope between two ships, one of the most beautiful arcs of movement in the movies.

Fairbanks, who was never a conventional actor, once confided to Chaplin that he rated himself "a small talent" at heart, which may have been the reason he excelled as a producer. His films of the 1920s were conceived on a grand scale, wrapping his persona in production values that rival any silent ever made. Indeed, *The Thief of Bagdad*, as designed by William Cameron Menzies, is an exquisite piece of exotica. ("Poetry in motion," said Mary proudly. "It cost a million seven hundred thousand.")

Pickford also gave her viewers Tiffany value, though at first her canvases were small. *Pollyanna* (1920), her first film released through United Artists, made a million dollars, despite her own jaundiced evaluation. "If reincarnation should prove to be true, and I had to come back as one of my roles, I suppose some avenging fate would return me to earth as Pollyanna – 'the glad girl.'" Indeed, some viewers would agree with Mary that the glad girl's cheer is "sickening." As usual in this type of work, Pollyanna's presence transforms the repressed adults around her. But unlike Gwen in *The Poor Little Rich Girl*, Sara in *A Little Princess*, or Rebecca, Pollyanna preaches to achieve her ends. No other child played by Pickford spends her time consciously lecturing adults. This makes the movie heavy going. It is also flat; few sequences feature the comic invention that might have put a spin on the saccharine plot. (The gifts of Marshall Neilan might have saved the film. Instead, *Pollyanna* was indifferently directed by Paul Powell.) The best scene involves Pollyanna's arrival at the station, where servants from her new home wait to greet her. She runs toward their embrace, but a rainstorm of hurricane proportions beats her back from their arms. Pickford charges forward several times, only to be sent careening back like a kite; the embrace is achieved when the orphan finally clings to a post for anchor.

Suds (1920) was an adaptation of a one-act play called *'Op o' Me Thumb*, which had starred Maude Adams. "Sudsy" – the grotesque Amanda Afflick – is the slapstick twin of Unity in *Stella Maris*; Mary adopts the same slicked-back hair, twisted smile, and hunch. Both characters are slaveys – *Suds* is full of comic scenes that detail the grimy life of a laundress. In a heartbreaking moment from *Stella Maris*, Unity caresses her idol's coat as though the man were still inside it. Pickford plays almost the same scene in *Suds* when Amanda cuddles up to a laundered shirt. Both films feature harrowing scenes in which a woman confronts her ugliness. "Who would love me? Who could?" asks Amanda. The way Mary filmed it, no one could – at least, not the man she loves. She does receive affection from a rundown horse who narrowly escapes being shot to make glue and spends a rainy night with Pickford in her tenement. The image of this creature – all eyes, ribs, and shuddering legs – is indelible. So is Amanda's loneliness.

But in *Stella Maris*, Mary hedged her bets; anyone who turned away from grim little Unity would soon be watching Stella in her girlish glory. The sole relief from ugliness in *Suds* is a fantasy sequence in which Amanda imagines she is beautiful. The slapstick also provides relief: "Why,"

212

asked a writer over sixty years later, "have the people who cherish Chaplin, Keaton, and the Sennett films overlooked *Suds*?" The movie even satirizes Pickford's curls when Amanda, to show her love, gives her beloved horse a wash and set. Audiences audibly protested at the movie's ambiguous ending, and Pickford had to change it to a happier, less convincing one. But despite the tinkering, *Suds* retained a touch of the grotesque. In the year of its release, this confused the critics, but the film's reputation has grown with time.

Meanwhile D.W. Griffith worked far from his partners on Long Island Sound. His production plant, about an hour from Manhattan, had once been the estate of Henry Flagler, the robber baron who grew rich from Standard Oil. It featured a turreted Gothic mansion, a summerhouse, a gatehouse, and a cottage, as well as stables, gardens, a strip of beach, and a spot of forest. Here the director worked in peace and, after a misadventure called *The Love Flower* (1920), turned out two superb productions. *Way Down East* (1920) was creaky melodrama, transformed by Griffith and Lillian Gish. Today the movie is best remembered for a breathless scene in which Gish lies unconscious on an ice floe, rushing down a river toward a waterfall. The next year, Lillian and Dorothy were terrorized in *Orphans of the Storm*, a spectacular story of the French Revolution in which Lillian's pretty neck is almost severed.

Artistically, Griffith thrived on isolation, and his partners were as pleased as the critics with the results. But often he riled them with his business practices – by personally booking his road shows, for instance. He handed them over to United Artists only after pocketing the big-city profits: two-fifths, thought Mary, down the drain. Griffith also exercised an option that allowed him to distribute his films abroad himself, rather than using UA's foreign office. And, in a remarkable indiscretion, he took a public stand against *Pollyanna*. He described it as "the most immoral story" ever put on a screen. "It takes a fake philosophy of gilded bunkum. Its reasoning, if applied to actual life conditions, will handicap its believers and leave them actually menaced." Probably Mary agreed – in private. But, astonishingly, Griffith made these comments to a movie magazine while Pickford's film was in release – conduct unbecoming for a business partner.

There were other problems; Chaplin had still not worked free of First National. And, creatively speaking, Mary Pickford was restless: "I am sick of Cinderella parts," she said, "of wearing rags and tatters. I want to wear smart clothes and play the lover ... I created a certain type of character and now, I think, it is practically finished."

Any artist must experiment to keep his talent fresh. And Pickford's ingenues in the 1920s, though never less than fine, seem a touch too easy. The tilt of the head, the pout, eyes snapping with fury, the hands on hips hint ever so faintly at automatic pilot. And she rankled at the trademark of her hair. "A wild impulse would seize me," she remembered, "to reach for the nearest shears and remove that blond chain around my neck." To viewers, Mary's hair was a psychic connection to her film adolescence. And the vulnerable state of United Artists demanded that she trade on its adoration.

Unfortunately, the years in which Pickford could play such roles were dwindling; the actress turned twenty-eight in 1920. And apparently Mary fell prey to an age-old prejudice: that art involving childhood, comedy, or fantasy is neither as challenging nor as deep as work in an adult – especially a *tragic* adult – vein.

Tom Geraghty, one of Fairbanks's writers, often saw Mary entertain at Pickfair. "[He] said he never knew what character would appear on the steps," said Mary proudly. "He said I was haunted. He thought I was at least twenty women in one, a whole harem." And she wished to show these women on the screen, to tap the "serious, reserved, even morbid" in her nature. Perhaps Pickford dreamed of being Norma Talmadge, whose onscreen women wore fashionable dresses as they wept becoming tears, or the tragic Nazimova, "an exquisite Russian type, the midnight hair brushed back and coiled in a simple knot at her neck, with wonderful, slender, caressing hands." Nazimova struck doomed and defiant poses. She was also canonized by critics.

In 1921 Pickford made *The Love Light*, in which she played Angela, a poor Italian who, in the course of World War I, discovers that her husband is a German spy. Not only that, she has unwittingly allowed him to help the enemy – even, indirectly, to kill her brother. Finally Angela's husband kills himself rather than be murdered by a village lynch mob. And Angela, who bears his child, goes mad.

It all seems rushed and undeveloped. Frances Marion, who not only wrote but directed, cast her husband, Fred Thomson, as the spy. She "was very ambitious for Fred," recalled Pickford, "and very much in love with him – and I think that explains everything." It doesn't.

Mary's work throughout *The Love Light* is fully felt. But she uses histrionic signals: hand to forehead, fists clenched, heaving breast – all lingering trademarks of melodrama. Most film actresses did the same; the style was the norm in tragic silents. Although Pickford uses these semaphores with restraint, with the notable exception of a mad scene, her work in this mood is less distinctive than her comedy. In the end, *The Love Light* failed to prove that her viewers would accept her as a tragic swan. Films about the war, which were all the rage when Pickford read Marion's scenario, were box office poison by the time this one was finished. Accordingly, the movie did middling business, and Pickford's fans soon seemed to forget she'd made it.

But they didn't forget *Through the Back Door* (1921), which delivered Little Mary, pure and undiluted. Today the film, which has an intimate, rambling sort of charm, is remembered chiefly for a scene in which Pickford, as a teenage housemaid, decides to scrub the floor by attaching the brushes to her feet like skates – a teetering, soapy ballet that rates among the best comic sequences in her work.

Through the Back Door and *Pollyanna*, despite homespun stories, were handsome productions. But *Little Lord Fauntleroy* (1921) was titanic. Cinematographer Charles Rosher filled this tale of an American child who inherits a title and estate in England with awe-inspiring views of his castle's ivy-covered splendors, dwarfing Pickford with battlements, turrets, and baronial furniture. The setting reinforced the book's appeal: the relationship between a young nation and its grand progenitor, where life seemed both enviable and decadent. The theme is repeated in the child, Cedric, who, as Little Lord Fauntleroy, conquers his class-conscious British relations with uncorrupted Yankee love and candor. Pickford played a double role: Fauntleroy's mother (known as Dearest) and the boy himself.

Little Lord Fauntleroy was a smash; Fairbanks Jr., among many others, considered it her best work. Today the movie plays less well. Though she stole Cedric's swagger from Jack and her husband, Pickford's work is less resonant as a boy. ("No woman should ever play a male role – *ever*," she said, looking back.) In theory, Cedric's beauty, which includes "charming love-locks on his shoulders," made the role ideal for Mary: Cedric's hair was as much an obsession with the novel's author as Little Mary's curls were to moviegoers. But Mary needs to bring a gutter touch to Cedric, and the plot doesn't offer her many chances. Bizarrely, the presence of "dirt" was one of Pickford's creative keys: "The more ragged and dirty I look, the better I can play," the actress once observed. But as Cedric, she is preciously turned out – with divine velvet clothes and sweetheart curls.

Sometimes Pickford even seems stiff as Dearest – but then, she was standing on six-inch lifts in order to tower over Cedric. Twice these extraordinary shoes sent her tumbling down a flight of stairs. The emphasis on spectacle slows the pace; so, one imagines, did the painstaking double exposures. In one scene, Pickford kisses herself, a few seconds of film that required fifteen hours before the camera. "It's hard work," said Pickford at the time. "Everything is done by count." The character Dearest, she suggested, might say a line "that has to run from [counts] 24 to 1." Then, she continued, she would wait two counts while Cedric, who would later share the frame, responds. "If somebody drops a hammer in the studio or the cameraman sneezes and loses count it all has to be done over." Small wonder that many of the *Fauntleroy* scenes seem played to the rhythm of a metronome.

Mary's remake of *Tess of the Storm Country* (1922) was "all very lovely and unlikely," according to the *New York Times*, which nevertheless conceded, "Against your better judgment, you enjoy it." Indeed, it is superbly done; Tess is the quintessential Pickford firebrand, and Mary spent lavishly on the remake. "It is a better production [than the first *Tess*]," she wrote. "And it ought to be. The first production cost ten thousand dollars to take, including my salary. The second, not counting my salary, cost over four hundred thousand dollars to film. In the first sum are included the studio rent, my mother's and my fares from New York to California, and also those of the director and his secretary." The first version, she continued, was shot in a month, using only the sun for illumination, in an actual seaside fishing village. The remake required months of preparation, a thirty-thousand-dollar generator, fifty thousand dollars to repurchase the rights from Zukor, seventeen weeks before the camera, and a picture-perfect village, on which Mary spent fifteen thousand dollars.

A promotional photo shows Pickford in costume on the set, listening to someone on a wireless headset. "Can you guess who's at the other end?" swoons the caption. On many of their films, she and Fairbanks worked virtually side by side. They might manage a private lunch in Mary's bungalow, which housed a dressing room, wardrobe, kitchen, bathroom, and maid's room, an office for her secretary, and a reception area – a far cry from tin stars and flooded floorboards. The bungalow was also the scene of working lunches, in which the crew sat down with Mary and were peppered with questions and directions. One day, with *Photoplay* in attendance, she worried aloud about the three hundred billboards she was planning to tout a movie. "Do you think that enough?" she asked Fairbanks, who was present. "I wanted five hundred." Then she asked how many her husband had reserved for his next film, *The Thief of Bagdad*.

Doug, whose mind was less on business than on the approaching food, was toying aimlessly with his knife. Mary took it from him and put it down. "You'll put out your eye," she reproved.

"I've got fifty billboards," said Doug. "The first of the year is a long time off."

"You need to reserve billboards a long time off," was Mary's pert rejoinder. "Douglas, the make-up on your chest is much darker than your face. There is too much contrast. I'm sure the camera is going to get it."

Doug's director, Raoul Walsh, said he thought it was all right.

"I'm sure it will pick up darker in some lights," insisted Mary. "You had better powder over it a little, Douglas."

Douglas, nibbling grapes, said, "All right, dear."

"No one ever worked for me," said Pickford strongly. "Nor did I ever work for anybody. We worked together." Her sets were happy, and the Pickford-Fairbanks lot became known as "Doug and Mary's." Pickford seemed especially aware of extras, giving them special thank-you speeches. Any suggestion, be it the director's or the prop boy's, was considered. Nor did she appear on the set for scenes in which she wasn't featured, knowing that her presence could intimidate.

"The look she gave me!" Pickford said of actress Gertrude Astor. "If

I had been a lion I'm sure it would not have terrified her more." Astor, who appeared in *Through the Back Door*, was having trouble in a scene, and Mary was summoned to the set by the director. "I just can't cry, Miss Pickford," said Astor. Mary drew Astor aside and sympathized, then told her that though she would hire another actress, she would personally guarantee that no one found out about Astor's failure. Suddenly the camera rolled, and Astor wept, just as Pickford had planned.

"I'll say definitely she was one of the finest characters I ever knew." The speaker, Charles Rosher, shot seventeen Pickfords and knew the actress well enough to nickname her "Monkey Face." This kiddingly alluded to Mary's right profile, which was not as attractive as the left. He remembered how she often took charge of her own scenes – in other words, almost every scene in the feature. "The director would often just direct the crowd." Still, each director *thought* he'd been in charge. "Bill," she told director William Beaudine, who seemed reluctant to give her orders, "I am the producer, I am the star – do you want me to be the director too? If I hadn't thought you could do it, I wouldn't have hired you. Now, let's get back to work." "We called her Miss Pickford," said cinematographer Hal Mohr. "She was the queen of motion pictures, and we thought of her with respect." Frequently the queen could be found standing fast asleep, or leaning against a wall, deep in slumber – a catnapping talent learned while trouping on the trains.

Usually Pickford was home at seven. She and Fairbanks were often too tired to change into street clothes, and sat down to dinner still in costume. The table was laid for fifteen nightly, for Fairbanks impulsively invited staff, hangers-on, and friends. He was always bringing "funny people" home, Mary once said cheerfully to a reporter, recalling how, early in the marriage, her guest list had been crowded with a wrestler (Bull Montana), a tramp, a dwarf, a Polish immigrant, and two homeless cats. John and Robert Fairbanks might bring their families, and Mary's relatives turned up – even Aunt Lizzie, who had moved to California at an unknown date. They dined on halibut with tartar sauce, filet of chicken, and hearts of lettuce, topped off with a dose of Fairbanks. When the actor got his second wind, he crawled beneath the table, grabbed ankles, yelped like a dog, and bit them. Guests also coped with rubber forks and dribble glasses. Sometimes a specially wired chair delivered an electric shock: this had been a gag in Fairbanks's Broadway dressing room. He laughed till he wept at such shenanigans.

The entrées were grander and the dishes solid gold when Pickfair's more celebrated guests appeared. "The Duke of Alba," remembered Chaplin, "the Duke of Sutherland, Austin Chamberlain, the Marquis of Vienna." He might have continued with the King of Spain, Prussia's crown princess, the Prince of Sweden, F. Scott Fitzgerald, Lord and Lady Mountbatten, Amelia Earhart, Albert Einstein, Sir Arthur Conan Doyle, Noël Coward, Max Reinhardt, Helen Keller, Bernard Shaw, Lord Byng of Vimy, H.G. Wells, Gene Tunney, Jack Dempsey, Fritz Kreisler.... All these and more snaked up the mountain in a weekly procession of Rolls-Royces and limos. Few bons mots from these dinners survive, and one might wonder what on earth Mary Pickford had to say to Albert Einstein. Whatever it was, it was probably accompanied with gestures, for the actress was mystified by Einstein's English. What, indeed, had these people in common? Only their celebrity; perhaps they decided that because they were already linked by glamour, they might as well socialize in life.

"Hello, Doug," Chaplin said one morning. "How's the duke?" "What duke?" asked Fairbanks. "Oh," shrugged Chaplin. "Any duke." In fact, Chaplin also ran in rarefied circles. And as he lived down the block from Pickfair, he found himself handling the social overflow, putting up lords and ladies for the night in his smaller, almost slapdash home. (The Chaplin residence was made so badly that those who dared called it Breakaway House, referring to the ready-to-ruin props in movies.) Later Chaplin recalled feeling used, brought out to entertain at Pickfair dinners like Fairbanks's dog. He was even less comfortable, though, as host. He envied Pickford and Fairbanks their aplomb; with the exalted, they assumed "a dégagé familiarity." This was most evident in Fairbanks's steambath.

The actor had to keep in shape, much like a dancer or professional athlete. Fairbanks exercised throughout the day to relieve his hyperactive energy as well as experiment with stunts. He paid such athletes as the boxer Spike Robinson to follow him, like pilot fish, ready at a word to take a punch or tumble. There were others in the entourage: Kenneth Davenport, once a New York actor, handled Fairbanks's paperwork, and writer Tom Geraghty thought up gags and screenplays. These and others kept an unspoken contract to keep the actor's workday lively.

After filming, for instance, they flocked with Fairbanks to the Basilica Linea Abdominal (Temple Dedicated to the Waistline) – in other words, his private gym, located on the Pickford-Fairbanks lot. There, with a masochistic will to please, guests endured a kind of basic training. Allegedly, the Duke of Alba fenced, Sir Arthur Conan Doyle punched the punching bag, the mechanical horse bucked the King of Siam, and the Prince of Sweden did his Swedish exercises. Lord Mountbatten got off easy by simply observing a game of basketball, and the lucky Duke of Sutherland received a rubdown, probably administered by Abdullah, a massive former wrestler, now masseur-in-residence.

After the agony, participants retired to the Turkish bath, where they enjoyed steam, dry heat, and cold-water plunges and often were introduced half-dressed. "Your Royal Highness," Fairbanks said to the King of Thailand, "may I present my friend, Mr. Case of New York?" Case was both naked and flabbergasted, and Fairbanks liked to claim he clicked his heels. But apparently Chaplin's gaze was elsewhere. "When a man is stripped of all worldly insignia, one can appraise him for what he is truly worth – the Duke of Alba went up a great deal in my estimation." Fairbanks, as host, asked much and got it. Frank Case recalled the actor forcing guests to run down a perilous slope near Pickfair. It was slippery with loose rocks, which slid underfoot and made the run an adventure. At long last Case, although out of shape, consented – possibly shamed into the act by Mary, who hitched up her skirt and ran down, hair flying.

Some weekend guests were persuaded by Fairbanks to rise before dawn, hoist themselves onto horses, and ride through the darkness to a canyon campsite. There they were greeted with steak and grapefruit. A cowboy quartet might warble as the sun rose, or Fairbanks would tell the tale of a Mexican bandit whose hideout, he claimed, had been on the same site. Chaplin recalled a touch of ancient Rome in the course of a fishing trip to Catalina when Fairbanks had a dead steer flung into the ocean. The water, he hoped, would soon swarm with carnivores, making fishing easy. It wasn't, but the rodeo that followed buoyed the party's spirits.

The most generous welcome was shown the Duke of York, who turned up at the studio gate to watch Fairbanks at work. But the guard had received garbled instructions and turned the duke's group away. When at last the duke reached the set, the day's shoot was finished. But Fairbanks didn't tell him this; instead he performed an athletic scene, the director shouting, the actors cavorting, the cameramen cranking (no film in the camera). The duke even munched on a sugar window – a stunt-prop substitute for glass.

Sometimes hosts and guests decamped to Doug and Mary's private beach, a leisurely two-hour drive to Laguna, where tents were set up as on a medieval battlefield. No one roughed it, though Pickford once tied an apron round her waist, puttered with a broom, and looked picturesque. The tents were large, with wooden floors and furniture. Exquisite meals were prepared by a Mrs. Bock, cook to the Pickford-Fairbanks Studio, and served in the dining tent by Pickfair staff.

All this, as well as a ranch near San Diego with a eucalyptus forest and an orange grove; the butler, Rocher, who walked as though his shoes pinched; a budgie that whistled "Yankee Doodle"; and all the peanut brittle a girl could eat. What more could Mary Pickford want? Companionship.

"The great have no friends," observed actress Ruth Gordon. "They merely know a lot of people." Mary played hostess to hordes of guests but developed few friendships; she hadn't time. And her marriage's most romantic hallmarks (always sitting by Fairbanks's side, for instance) had a flip side: her husband's obsessive jealousy. He was openly hostile to Rudolph Valentino when the sloe-eyed actor dropped by Pickfair. "I never saw Douglas act so fast, and with such painful rudeness, as he did in showing Valentino that he wasn't welcome," remembered Mary. Fairbanks also took offence when a man gave his wife what Mary called "a simple look of masculine approval." Pickford always told Fairbanks her destination, even for a shopping trip in Beverly Hills, providing a phone number where he could reach her, or promising to call him at a certain hour. "Since it was all as complicated as that," she wrote wearily, "I seldom went anywhere."

Frances Marion hated Fairbanks: "a man of superficial attachments, and an insatiable appetite for praise." Fairbanks was nothing if not frank. Once, when asked for a list of his hobbies, he answered simply, "Doug." "He'd kowtow to a duke and a duchess," Marion complained. "When some nice ordinary people like you and me were expected he'd say, 'Why are those people coming?' But then they'd arrive and he'd swagger up, shoulders back, and put on his act." Marion rarely felt free to criticize Fairbanks to his wife; if she did, Pickford gave her a chilly stare. But decades later the subject of Fairbanks still brought an outburst. "He was jealous of *me*. He was jealous of her *mother!*"

"Mary was always the queen up there on the hill," said Adela Rogers St. Johns. "I don't know whether it's true Douglas Fairbanks wanted to put a wall around Beverly Hills to keep the mortals out.... There was a psychological wall around her and her circle, if not a concrete one."

"She was very lonely," May McAvoy added. When the actress came to Hollywood, she assigned herself the goal of getting close to Pickford. But Mary met her graciously – that was all. McAvoy was undeterred, and after she had organized Our Club, a kind of support group for young actresses, she asked Pickford to serve as its honorary chairman. Mary responded by holding the inaugural meeting at Pickfair. The women were dazzled but slightly cowed, and later met at the Biltmore Hotel, which was cozier than Pickfair, and where they felt freer to let their hair down. But Mary was walled up like Rapunzel. "She explained that she never went out without Doug," remembered McAvoy. "She was almost a prisoner. She needed Our Club more than we needed her!"

But Mary did, in these years, form a deep and lasting bond with Lottie's daughter. After her divorce in 1920, Lottie, for reasons unknown, relinquished the baby (then a toddler) to Charlotte, who formally adopted her. The new mother raised the baby strictly, watching for the swellheadedness she had once knocked so soundly out of Baby Gladys. And the child – her name changes in press reports, but she was eventually known to the world as Gwynne – was regularly passed from Charlotte's home to her Aunt Mary's eagerly waiting arms. Lottie's sole comments to the press concerned her newly single status. She declared she would never again become a wife, "even if the man had golden wings and a diamond halo."

Clearly Mary and Charlotte considered Lottie unfit to raise the only Pickford heir. She was almost certainly an alcoholic, and may have been what writers of the day called a dope fiend. On the other hand, Lottie had her charms: a willingness to let the good times roll, a down-to-earth, unpretentious manner, and a pipeline, should she care to use it, to a fortune as solid as the U.S. Mint.

In 1922 Lottie took the plunge with actor Allan Forrest. Mary footed the bill for a lavish wedding, and the marriage proceeded in a carnival fashion, full of parties, and did little to repair Lottie's lightweight reputation. Donald Crisp, who knew Mary's sister from her Biograph days, spoke for many when he told a writer, "Lottie was a tramp." ("At least I married them all," she protested, years later. "I didn't have round heels.") Still, the comment is damning, as "live and let live" was the byword of silent-film society.

Its enormous public was less broadminded. At first the resentment of stars seemed to focus on their salaries: Pickford's and Chaplin's, to be specific. As early as 1914 a photograph in the papers showed Mary with the exclamation: "This little girl earns $100,000 a year." What, wondered some, had she done to deserve that? They went to the movies, fell in love, and forgave her.

In the teens little bad behavior surfaced. What social life there was took place at the Hollywood Hotel, a rambling structure with rocking chairs, overgrown gardens, and verandas. "The big night was Thursday night," recalled actress Viola Dana. "They used to clear the lobby and we had a dance.... There was an old gal that ran the hotel, a Mrs. Hershey, and she was a regular dowager, black ribbon and all that sort of thing. And I want to tell you, there was nothing that went on in that hotel that she didn't know about. She had an eagle eye, and there was no drinking at these dances, or anything like that.... It was a case of everybody back to their own room, too!" When Mrs. Hershey learned that actors were climbing the walls to slip through the windows of their female favorites, she filled the flower beds below with cacti.

But the growth of the industry spawned a far more sophisticated nightlife. Film, once the theater's bastard child, was the nation's fifth-largest industry by 1926. Its estimated eighty million viewers were far more film-literate than the viewers of the 1910s. Their gaze, once tender and naive, became a bit envious, even vengeful. As the number of movie celebrities mushroomed, so did the public's need to tear down the idols whose fame they created. In this way viewers asserted that they were the masters, not the slaves, in the celebrity relationship. This urge ran wild when a series of scandals made Hollywood seem like a sinkhole of depravity.

Jack and his wife, dainty Olive Thomas, sailed to Paris in the autumn of

1920. So far their marriage had been rocky. But they tried to heal it as they toured the sites – not the Eiffel Tower or the Louvre, but the bistros of Montmartre. Their favorite was the Dead Rat, a watering hole on the cutting edge of decadence. One Saturday night they returned to their hotel and wandered down the hallway, looking blurry and bright-eyed. Jack went to bed, but his wife was beyond sleep. A half hour later Olive groped for her sleeping pills in darkness, shook out the bottle, and took them all. But the suicide was unexpectedly gruesome. By mistake, Olive swallowed bichloride of mercury – in those days, a recommended cure for syphilis. Jack woke to Olive's screams as the pills burned through her throat and stomach. Or perhaps it was a maid who came to Olive's rescue – another story has it that Jack had slipped out for a last-minute round of drugs. Olive's death was ugly, and it took five days. Meanwhile rumors of her heroin addiction, the venereal disease she had acquired from Jack, and her husband's infidelity were front-page news. It was noted that before they sailed, Olive had made a will, leaving Jack Pickford all her money. The inference – that Jack had poisoned Olive – didn't hold water with those who knew him. After all, when Jack was broke, he had only to call his mother or older sister.

In October Jack sailed home with Olive's body. Mid-Atlantic, he grew morose and attempted to throw himself off the ship. Later, at her funeral, he turned to Charlotte. "That's the first time I ever had to watch anybody die." Mary tried to keep his mind off Olive by giving him co-directing jobs on *Through the Back Door* and *Little Lord Fauntleroy*. But Jack's contribution, according to Rosher, consisted of suggesting a gag or two – and that was on the days that he bothered to show up. He indulged in a wild wake, painting the town red and flying his plane in swoops over Los Angeles. One day when Mary was talking with a journalist, she heard a familiar sound above the studio. She ran outside screaming, "Oh, Jack, you promised!" Jack tipped a wing in recognition, and Mary shrieked, "Stop! You'll kill yourself!"

She guarded not only Jack but filmdom. It was as though her entire life had been rehearsal for this, her most demanding role – Queen Victoria of Hollywood. Adela Rogers St. Johns proposed the metaphor: "It was as though Mary said, as had young Queen Victoria on coming to the throne, 'I will be good,' and meant, 'I will live up to what is expected of me, and be *here* as long as my people need me.' And I am sure Queen Mother Charlotte backed her to the hilt. If Douglas said, 'I will be good,' I'm certain he meant, 'I'll go along with this as long as it amuses me,' and for a good many years it did."

Queen Mary was virtuous, sexless, pure. Hollywood, journalists wrote, was not. In 1921 they pilloried comic Fatty Arbuckle for the alleged rape and manslaughter of a bit-part actress (the supposed weapons were his weight and a liquor bottle). The comic endured a smear campaign, was tried by innuendo, and, though finally acquitted, was banned from film. This was the edict of Will Hays, a former postmaster general who became the industry's moral watchdog. In 1922 William Desmond Taylor was murdered in his bungalow, where it was said he kept pornographic photographs of Hollywood actresses. In the course of a fruitless investigation, the careers of actresses Mary Miles Minter and Mabel Normand were destroyed. In 1923 actor Wallace Reid died a morphine addict.

Pickford, more than ever, held film's reputation in her hands. Pickfair, which some called the second White House, had given the movies a social order. Its chatelaine was the essence of culture and civilization – and, in some opinions, a first-class bore.

She could sometimes be a snob. When Pickford and Fairbanks returned from their honeymoon, they were mobbed by reporters in New York. One proposed that silent-film actor Charles Ray, who was then at the height of his popularity, join them for a photograph. "Mary's nose went up, up, at the thought of sharing the publicity," wrote a journalist. "'Do you,' she asked with a touch of her new French, 'really think that would be *au fait*?'" (In fact, her newfound French was bad; the phrase she was seeking was *comme il faut*.)

On rare occasions, a Pickfair dinner was followed by dancing. "Only the waltz or two-step," said Mary. She was mindful of propriety. "We never 'jazz.'" Indeed, she rarely danced or swam in public, choosing to sit poolside at Pickfair while others shrieked and splashed about, and Fairbanks held contests to see who could hold his breath longest on the bottom. Fairbanks once arranged to have Maurice Chevalier pushed into the water, fully clothed. One doubts if even Fairbanks tried this trick on Mary. Years later Pickford prevented her husband, who was oily and bronzed from a day at their private beach, from watching a dance marathon on a pier. "Douglas, love, you know we can't be seen in a place like that." "Tupper, love," answered Fairbanks gently, "your steel hand is showing through your velvet glove."

But he joined her contentedly in civic duties, which took up a tedious amount of time and which Fairbanks probably enjoyed more than she did. It was the custom, in those days, for actors to stand when the movies' royal couple made a formal appearance. In return, they shook hands and posed for photos, cut ribbons, led parades, opened highways, met mayors, judged contests, laid cornerstones, and lent an air of dignity to all occasions. Too much dignity, thought some. "Don't say 'work,'" said actress Mabel Normand when asked by a journalist to name her hobbies. "That's like Mary Pickford." But Hollywood insisted that what Normand *really* said was, "That's like Mary Pickford, that prissy bitch."

"We'd go [to Pickfair] all dressed up," remembered actress Miriam Cooper, "and sit down at this huge table with the lovely china and servants falling all over themselves serving you, and not even get one lousy drop of wine." This can be blamed on Prohibition, which went into effect in 1920, and the Boy Scout habits of teetotaller Fairbanks. When Prohibition ended, he relaxed the rule and permitted weak drinks – only two per person, and the quality of the liquor was often poor. Sultans of the steam bath were allowed champagne.

Many were inspired by the new formality. But Marion, who hated it, lamented the loss of "the bungalow courts where once we had lived, when we barged in and out of each other's kitchens, often deciding to eat there, with the pot of stew sitting in the middle of the table and plates being passed hand over hand. Instead, we sat stiffly at Sheridan or Louis Quinze tables." Soon the film colony "learned to speak knowingly of vintage wines and with which courses they were to be served.... We ate caviar in ice swan boats, terrapin flown in from Florida, breast of pheasant under glass, hearts of palm salad, and elaborate desserts." Now actors built mansions – ersatz Tudor, Spanish, Moorish, and Italian – that littered the Los Angeles hills like stage sets. (Pickfair, Lord Mountbatten sniffed, was still "the best-taste house, I should say, in Hollywood.") They also acquired British accents. "Somewhat pathetic," wrote Marion tartly, "seeing how seriously they tried to conceal their lack of education and breeding."

For many, it was Little Mary's presence that made a visit to "the Big House" unforgettable. Pickford exuded, said Fairbanks's niece, Letitia, "this wonderful graciousness that smoothed everything." When novelist Elinor Glyn came to visit, she insisted that Pickford looked tired, and that, using psychic powers, she could make her sleep. "Show me the north," she intoned in Mary's bedroom. Glyn then placed a finger on Mary's brow. "Now she's fast asleep!" She plainly wasn't; Fairbanks and Chaplin, who were present, saw her lashes move. But Mary was unwilling to offend and lay still for an hour while Glyn hovered, hawklike, at her bed.

"She could be just a dynamo," laughed Letitia. "I remember one dinner party at Pickfair when they served filet mignon but it was tough. And afterward she gave the butler such a dressing-down you could hear it right down the hall. Boy, she had a temper when she really got to it. 'For the money I pay for you – *I want the best, and I want it now.*'" In fact, Pickfair's servants earned a modest wage.

Her kindness was equally swift and startling. British actress Wini Shaw recalled a depressing night in Hollywood, when, feeling homesick, she entered a restaurant and ordered a nostalgic meal of liver and bacon. But she soon found herself overwhelmed by tears. A waiter appeared beside her. "I beg your pardon, but what's your name?" Surprised, Shaw told him, and the waiter vanished. A few moments later he returned with a note: "Dear Miss Shaw: You look so lonesome sitting over there. I wonder if we may join you?" "It was signed, 'Mary Pickford,'" remembered Shaw. "I'll never forget that act of kindness till my dying day. Here I am, a punk kid, and she's the queen. So far as I'm concerned, she always will be. After that, I was invited to Pickfair for many informal dinners and for her very, very formal dinners.... It was beautiful."

Pickfair evenings ended early – the hosts were in bed by half past ten. There might be time for a round of bridge, not everyone's idea of a provocative evening. One lively night a well-known psychic told fortunes in Pickfair's Oriental Room. Most often everyone retired to watch a new movie, shown in the screening room downstairs. Mary hated steam heat; it brought back memories of slum hotels, and Fairbanks liked to emulate the cold-loving British. So the guests sat in easy chairs, covered with over-coats and blankets – a disappointment, surely, to anyone hoping to spend the night showing off a backless dress – while the majordomo offered fruit and cups of Ovaltine. Fairbanks often fell asleep before the closing credits, roused himself when the lights came up, and declared, "Best damned movie I ever saw!" Glamour star Gloria Swanson was disgusted, and when asked to dine with the Duke of York at Pickfair, she made off with him and selected guests for a wilder party at a nightclub. Then everyone, including the nightclub orchestra, drove out to Swanson's lavish mansion, where Chaplin cut capers and the duke ate breakfast. Swanson was naughtily pleased with herself, and Pickford rose above it all in silence.

Mary was proud; her position at Pickfair was her greatest challenge. But it made her a target. Often told was the probably apocryphal story, for instance, of "Princess Vera Romanoff," who rang up Doug and Mary from her room at the Biltmore Hotel in Los Angeles and asked if she could spend a few days at Pickfair. A Rolls-Royce promptly picked her up, and the princess was given a delightful weekend – after which she went home to Santa Monica, got a good night's sleep, and reported Monday morning to her typing job.

There were also rumors of penny-pinching. A local butcher, asked to put a steak on Pickfair's bill, protested, "Oh no! No more credit!" Fairbanks was known for his generosity, but Mary, gossips said, would wear a dress, then return it to the store with the claim that it didn't fit. Actress Madge Bellamy, who co-starred with Jack in *Garrison's Finish* (1923), was offended when Pickford, who had helped finance the movie, gave Bellamy her castoffs to wear onscreen. Even Helen Keller had a Pickford story. In 1925, on a fundraising mission for the blind, she visited Hollywood with her teacher, Anne Sullivan. Pickford was the only star who showed much interest, and she discussed how she might play a blind girl in a movie – her first such role since *A Good Little Devil*. Part of the movie's profits, she promised, would go to Keller's fund. But over the next few weeks, only silence came from Pickfair. Finally Keller and her teacher received an oddly small donation from the house on the hill. And Mary's plans to play a blind girl in another movie came to nothing.

It is difficult to govern, from a screen or from the White House, when the public mood changes with the wind. With postwar America's nerves in shreds, Woodrow Wilson asked the nation to commit itself to tolerance. Instead, a Communist witch-hunt swept the country, and the Ku Klux Klan swelled to four million members. In 1920 the public chose a different sort of president: Warren Harding, who never spoke of public duty or ideals.

Calvin Coolidge, who took office in 1923, made a god of business. Indeed, the expansion of mass production seemed a blessing in the twenties: consumers spent lavishly on cars, homes, radios, clothes, and Victrolas. Washing machines delivered women from the miseries of rough hands and backaches; refrigerators edged the icebox toward extinction. Hollywood tapped into this financial freedom, producing consumer-minded titles such as *Let's Be Fashionable*, *Extravagance*, *Charge It*, and *Money, Money, Money*.

The frenzy of spending reflected an impulse to live for the moment, trading soul for sensation and thought for thrills. The public fell head over heels for crazes: beauty contests, King Tut, monocles for women, and the game of Mah-Jongg. They also went sports-mad, tantalized by million-dollar matches such as Dempsey versus Tunney (two boxing titans). They watched, transfixed, as attention-seekers shivered on flagpoles and daredevils stood, arms outstretched, on the wings of flying planes. Hollywood, ever alert to trends, delivered finely crafted thrills: bespectacled comic Harold Lloyd lurching at dizzying height along a ledge or, most famously, dangling from a clock-face.

Eroticism was nothing new; Theda Bara had introduced it with a wallop in 1914. In private life, she was Theodosia Goodman, daughter of a tailor from Cincinnati. But that isn't how her studio, Fox, described her. According to publicists, Bara was the child of an Egyptian sheikh, weaned on serpent's blood, and married, symbolically, to the Sphinx. The actress's first film, *A Fool There Was* (1915), was based on Kipling's poem "The Vampire" – thus "vamp," or erotically voracious woman. The vamp divorced sex from any virtuous purpose; no good woman, after all, pursued pleasure so relentlessly. The vogue for Theda Bara had collapsed by 1919, but other vamps undulated through the twenties, alongside more subtle permutations – Swanson, Pola Negri, and Greta Garbo. And male stars, who often seemed bland in the teens, could now leer with abandon;

John Gilbert and Rudolph Valentino, for instance, turned the act of smelling flowers into passionate foreplay.

But issues of sex invaded less exotic movies; *Should a Wife Tell?* asked a twenties title. *Don't Tell Everything*, advised another. Women's social roles were re-examined when women won the vote in 1920 and moved in greater numbers toward the workplace. Cecil B. DeMille seized such moral ambiguities in eye-popping fantasies throughout the decade. They featured gorgeous, catlike women who lazily submitted their feet for pedicures and weighed infidelity from sunken bathtubs.

The audience knew no one who lived this way and assumed that DeMille was filming life in Hollywood. Soon the town was deluged with would-be celebrities, seeking to use their imagined talents as passports to the sweet life. Instead, so many lives were broken that in 1921 the chamber of commerce placed ads warning ingenues to stay away. "STREET SCENE IN HOLLYWOOD" ran a caption; the bloodcurdling photo shows bodies packed together like sardines. "This is a sample of the customary massed assault on the employment bureaus resulting from an ad for a very few men and women to work in an insignificant scene.... DON'T TRY TO BREAK INTO THE MOVIES IN HOLLYWOOD Until You Have Obtained Full, Frank and Dependable Information.... Out of 100,000 Persons Who Started at the Bottom of the Screen's Ladder of Fame ONLY FIVE REACHED THE TOP."

One who beat the odds was Clara Bow, who arrived in Hollywood in 1921 after winning a "Fame and Fortune" contest, sponsored by the publisher of *Motion Picture, Motion Picture Classic*, and *Shadowland*. A few years later she established her persona in flapper movies, a genre featuring modern girls who whacked their hair off, stepped out of corsets, raised their hemlines, and wore their unbuckled galoshes "flapping." They had flat hips and bosoms and rolled down their stocking tops. They smoked in public and drank cocktails they'd mixed up in shakers; in short, they acted and looked like boys. Onscreen, the spirited Colleen Moore, Louise Brooks, and Joan Crawford sampled fizzy drinks, cigarettes, the Charleston, and lipstick. But Clara Bow eclipsed them as "the girl who can't help it"; she was fresh, frank, vulgar, and as modern as tomorrow.

But the vogue of Little Mary still persisted. "A disillusioned nation," wrote Frederick Lewis Allen, "fed on cheap heroics and scandal and crime was revolting against the low estimate of human nature which it had allowed itself to entertain." Thus the adulation of Charles Lindbergh, the shy, self-effacing American whose stunt flight from New York to Paris made grown men and women blink back tears. According to Allen, Lindbergh offered "something that people needed, if they were to live at peace with themselves and with the world, [that] was missing from their lives." And thus, he might have added, the fame of Douglas Fairbanks, who embodied human nature at its healthiest, and his bride, the woman every man desired – as his sister.

In 1922 a writer for the *New Republic* noted that "sex appeal in movies" was "comparatively immature" in America. Pickford's attitude toward sex was that of "a healthy, humorous but by no means unsentimental girl of thirteen." Chaplin was even less mature – the magazine compared him to Jackie Coogan, who celebrated his sixth birthday while Chaplin was filming him as his co-star in *The Kid* (1921). And the more Fairbanks changed, the more he stayed the same; instead of vaulting furniture, he now vaulted moats. The actor distilled, wrote the *New Republic*, "that self-conscious age when boys affect to be indifferent to girls and to despise them; actually, of course, they are continually showing off for them."

Americans, it seems, were kids at heart – and as long as they were, the appeal of the trinity was invincible.

In 1923 Chaplin worked free of his First National contract and made his first feature for United Artists. Pickford and the others expected a box office smash along the lines of *The Kid*, a manipulative piece of comic pathos that, though it asks too obviously for tears, could break a heart of stone. Instead, Chaplin gave them *A Woman of Paris* (1923). Although his contract required that he star in his movies for United Artists, *A Woman of Paris* was a showcase for Edna Purviance, his long-overshadowed leading lady. Anticipating Hitchcock, Chaplin turned up in a walk-on as a porter while Purviance acted (beautifully) the acid-tinged tale of a fallen woman. Rather than pathetic, the film's tone is elegant and mordant. After it was screened at Pickfair, Mary raved, "I do not cry easily when seeing a picture, but after seeing Charlie's 'A Woman of Paris' I was all choked up – I wanted to go out in the garden and have it out with myself. Our cook," she added helpfully, "felt the same way." But as Chaplin's partner, she had hoped for his usual incarnation: in other words, the money-making Tramp.

UA's product shortage was causing a steady financial hemorrhage. Even the profits of films such as *Little Lord Fauntleroy* and *Robin Hood* could not make up for the lack of volume. The solution was to form, in 1922, a United Artists offshoot called Allied Producers and Distributors. Allied would distribute the work of other, less exalted artists; the added revenue would pay United Artists' day-to-day expenses. At least, that was the founders' hope. But the rush to Allied was at best a dribble. Charles Ray came with his production company; so did Max Linder, the gifted French comic whom Chaplin, among other silent clowns, revered. Mack Sennett signed a deal, and so did Jack Pickford, whose three films were bankrolled by his sister.

Mary Pickford was contemplating yet another change of pace. "To whom can we look for advance, for fresh vigor?" she once wondered aloud. "There are not so many [new directors], are there?" To many, the answer lay in Europe – especially Germany, where film seemed possessed of a "magic fire."

The Cabinet of Dr. Caligari (1919), one of the most influential films ever made, is also the best-known German silent and the apogee of expressionism. This and other European films had come by the boatful to postwar America and almost universally stunned the critics. Frederick James Smith of *Motion Picture Classic* declared that the 1920-21 season represented the "end of the glucose era of the photoplay. . . . Four or five productions of the studios of our late enemies, the Germans, succeeded in toppling the film god of banality." Smith put five German films on his ten-best list, and of these he rated *Passion* number one.

Its director, Ernst Lubitsch, is best known today for "the Lubitsch touch," the selection of spare and subtle detail that wittily illuminates a role or a relationship. But initially, Americans were more impressed by another thread in Lubitsch's work: his spectacle. *Passion*, released in the United States in 1920, told the story of Louis XV's mistress, with the sexual politics of Versailles – not to mention its conspicuous splendor – as an ostentatious backdrop. *Gypsy Blood*, which also reached North America that year, told the old tale of *Carmen* with panache and sweep; the crowd scenes and lurid themes unfold with the authority of flamenco. Film scholar Graham Petrie later described the reaction of American critics, as they raved about how Lubitsch brought history to life and humanized it. "The handling of crowds and mass action is vivid, spectacular and masterly; the sets are overpoweringly gorgeous and authentic; the pictorial effects are sensational; the pacing and tempo are controlled with superb skill; the characters leap to life on the screen through the quality of the acting; and dramatic tension and tragic events are skilfully interwoven with comic relief."

Mary must have read such reviews with interest. Historical films, as made in Hollywood, often served an actress's greater glory. In 1922 William Randolph Hearst produced *When Knighthood Was in Flower* (in its day, a famous novel and melodrama) as a showcase for the charms of his lifelong infatuation, Marion Davies. And indeed, an actress could hardly fail to impress when dressed in ruffs and farthingales, surrounded by Renaissance exotica, and seated on a splendid horse. Pickford, as it happened, had a script on hand called *Dorothy Vernon of Haddon Hall*. It concerned a British noblewoman who lived at the time of Elizabeth I and Mary, Queen of Scots, and whose love life played out against their conflict. She lost no time in asking Lubitsch to direct it.

The project was a bit of a risk for both. In 1921 Lubitsch had been invited by Famous Players–Lasky to direct in his costume-epic style. But the days in which Americans refused to eat sauerkraut and threw stones at dachshunds had not quite ended. Soon Lubitsch was receiving malicious phone calls; after a few weeks he sailed back to Germany. The seeming supremacy of German films also prompted a backlash from American workers who feared that their industry would suffer. The American Legion, Actors' Equity, and First National were among those who called for a ban on German films and opposed the employment of German artists.

But Lubitsch tried again for Mary Pickford, who hoped to slip him in with little fanfare. In October 1922 a United Artists lawyer named Nathan Burkan went to meet the new director as he disembarked. Could this be Lubitsch – a short German Jew in peg-top trousers, banana-yellow shoes, and a few gold teeth? The costume was a xenophobe's delight. At the lawyer's suggestion, Lubitsch was subjected to American-looking shoes and trousers, as well as a porcelain smile (courtesy of Burkan's dentist). "I want to cry when I think of it," said Mary, aware of the director's humiliation.

Before his arrival she endured an afternoon with the American Legion, sitting on a platform while an officer ranted about the filthy Huns. "I hear the son of the Kaiser is coming here. I would to God that the American Legion would go down to meet him – and throw him in the water. He doesn't belong here. He's still our enemy." He went on to complain about a German singer who was making an appearance in America. Pickford's blood ran cold. "He is going to turn on me," thought Mary, "and say to the audience, 'There sits a traitor.'" He never did, though Mary had prepared her answer, memorizing phrases such as "sick in the head" and "ill-bred and stupid."

When Lubitsch came to the lot, Pickford left her bungalow to meet him. After an official welcome speech, she shook his hand, which Lubitsch then dropped like "a hot potato." He turned to Edward Knoblock. "*Mein Gott*, she is cold!" Knoblock, a playwright who often wrote for Fairbanks, was present because he spoke fluent German. "*Ja*, cold!" said Lubitsch. "She cannot be an actress!" Knoblock, searching for an explanation, told Lubitsch, "Our actresses are paid to act. They don't act when offstage, or away from the camera. You're judging her by German actresses."

A few days later Mary looked through her window and saw Lubitsch, who was walking down the lot with Knoblock, waving his hands, his expression frantic as they discussed some creative problem. The *Robin Hood* set had been taken down and the empty lot had been sown with grain. As Pickford remembered the scene, "The wheat was chest high and they were swimming through it." Mary turned to Charlotte and said, "There goes trouble."

A few moments later Knoblock came to see her. Lubitsch, he explained, had decided he would not touch *Dorothy Vernon*. This was "a blow in the face" for Pickford, who had spent $250,000 on its preparation. She then met Lubitsch, who entered her office looking pale and sweaty. "Der iss too many qveens and not enough qveens!" he said of *Vernon*. Pickford assumed Lubitsch meant the competing plots sapped the movie's power. She was also upset by his lack of manners; Lubitsch, she claimed, kept touching her newly painted walls – and because he had been eating "German fried potatoes," he left a garland of greasy prints behind him. But she hid her distress and told Lubitsch she accepted his decision. In other words, Lubitsch said to Knoblock, she "took it standing up" – more proof, in his opinion, of Mary's coldness.

Swallowing hard, Pickford put aside her vision of Elizabethan beauty and tried to find a film more to Lubitsch's taste. The pair finally settled on Goethe's *Faust*. Mary was attracted to Marguerite, the heroine who kills her bastard child. The role would be strong meat for any actress. For Pickford, it was guaranteed to stun, and the about-face would eradicate Little Mary. Then Charlotte heard Lubitsch refer to the scene in which "you stringle the bebby" and stared him down. "Not my daughter!" she told him. "No sir!"

"Mother," said Pickford, "he's European."

But Charlotte glowered. "I absolutely forbid you doing that picture. And I've never said that to you before and I hope I never have to do it again."

So Lubitsch and Pickford renegotiated and came up with *Rosita* (1923). Adapted from a play called *Don Cesar de Bazan*, it told the story of a ragged street singer in old Seville. But Lubitsch had no interest in Mary's input. He followed his own internal vision, and the cast was expected to fulfill it. This is the way most directors work; it was not the way anyone directed Pickford. "Poor, dear Ernst," she said, shaking her head, though later she scorned him as "a perfect autocrat" and "very self-assertive, but then all little men are." Poor Ernst indeed.

"This is a love story," Pickford told Lubitsch. "You've got to put in a sequence that makes the ending important."

"I'm not making it!" Lubitsch answered.

Pickford thought it over, then went to see Lubitsch in his office. "This is the first time you've met me," she told him formally, "as the financial backer and producer."

"Vatt iss dis?" asked Lubitsch dimly.

"I'm telling you," said Pickford, "that I am the Court of Last Appeal. I'm putting up the money. I am the star, and I am the one that's known. I won't embarrass you," she continued. "I will never say anything before the company. If I have anything to say, I'll say it as I'm saying it now. . . . But you are not going to have the last word."

Lubitsch was astounded and told Pickford he would never consent to such an arrangement – not if she paid him a million dollars.

"I don't care if it's for ten million," Pickford told him evenly. "You are not going to have that privilege." She turned to leave, telling him, "That's final, Mr. Lubitsch." In response, Lubitsch threw a temper tantrum, tearing every button off his clothing: "And that was before zippers, if you know what I mean."

"My English was very poor then," remembered Lubitsch. "[Pickford's] kindness and cooperation made working with her a joy." A gallant statement. In fact, the director's fractured English became an increasing source of fun. "Now look, boys and girls," Pickford told the cast before Lubitsch reached the set one day. "If you went to Germany and tried to direct, you might say things that weren't proper yourselves. But you wouldn't like everybody to laugh at you. Now the first person that laughs on this stage will have to leave."

When Lubitsch arrived, cast and crew were stone-faced. Then Lubitsch spoke, and Charles Rosher hid his face behind the camera. The room was still – till Pickford exploded in gales of laughter.

She became an endless fund of anecdotes, all with Lubitsch's English as the punch line. "Komm, pliss," he once said commandingly. "Dis is de scene vere Miss Pickford goes mit der beckside to ze altar!" In another scene, Pickford keened dramatically over the body of George Walsh, who played her lover. Lubitsch tried to show her what he wanted by suggesting she throw herself on the body, pleading, "Don Diego, anschver me!"

Mary listened with a straight face, then cried, "Don Diego! Answer me!"

"Again, pliss," said Lubitsch. "Anschver me!"

Mary drew a deep breath, looked at Walsh, then threw herself into the scene, sobbing, "Anschver me!" Walsh's stomach began to ripple as the actor tried to bottle up his laughter.

"George," said Mary quietly, "I'll kill you!"

"Stop! Stop!" said Lubitsch. Then, reproachfully: "Miss Pickford – vat iss to laugh?"

Pickford swallowed. "Nothing, Mr. Lubitsch. I'm sorry."

"Don't make mit der laugh!" he told her sternly.

They filmed again; Pickford threw herself on Walsh and entreated him hysterically, "Anschver me!"

Lubitsch was the only one not laughing.

Somehow no one on the lot suspected that Lubitsch was making a brilliant movie, least of all Mary, who claimed she went home every night in tears. But *Rosita* is one of her finest films. "Nothing more delightfully charming than Mary Pickford's new picture, *Rosita*, has been seen on the screen for some time," raved the critic for the *New York Times*. "The photography is as perfect as the acting, and the sight of the interiors and exteriors elicits murmurs of admiration.... Exquisite is an adjective that fits this film as well as any, and it would be a quibbler indeed who could find much fault with it." The critic for *Variety* was astonished at "a Mary Pickford different and greater than at any time in her screen career," and thought the film superior to *Stella Maris*. And for a while, Mary seemed to know how great a gift she had been given. "I brought [Lubitsch] over here because I particularly wanted a new angle on myself. He had never seen any of my pictures and I didn't want him to see any. I placed myself completely in his hands."

In a way, Lubitsch saw what all directors saw: a straightforward, healthy, and humorous woman, possessed of a keen gaze, a mean punch, anger, and lots of hair. *Rosita* is a great deal like Tess of the Storm Country, grown up and singing in the streets of Spain. The poor folk adore her, especially when she takes up her guitar and sings like a silent-film Baez. In one of her lyrics, she savages Spain's immoral king, who, perversely, takes a sexual interest in her. But *Rosita*, unlike *Tess*, is more than a vehicle for its star.

In many of Mary's films, scenes without her seem mechanical, as though the director were waiting for Pickford to return and inspire him. But Pickford thought otherwise, stating she "relied upon my directors. They were hired for what they could contribute – new ideas and intelligent ways to make my pictures better. They weren't expected to 'yes' me, and I insisted they use their initiative and authority." But with few exceptions, Mary chose directors who were capable but passive. Through them, Pickford's vision would shape the film.

Mary was "a great comédienne," decided Lubitsch. She had "comedy touched with pathos"; he raved about her "courage and pluck" onscreen. But he also allowed her to show sophistication. Though virtue triumphs, the ethos of *Rosita* is decidedly modern; its heroine moves through the amoral court with a shrewd eye and matter-of-fact acceptance. And he gave her the requisite tragic moments, in which Mary did her utmost to upstage some gasp-inducing vistas. (These, as in *The Love Light*, are her weakest turns.) Most important, Lubitsch gave the film life beyond Pickford's presence – the comedy of manners at the court, for instance, or the queen who watches her straying husband and subtly lays a trap to win him back. Most of Pickford's movies are engaging cameos. But *Rosita* struck a new note: monumental.

The film made over a million dollars, and Pickford, elated, signed Lubitsch to direct her in three more pictures. Then something happened – a stray remark, perhaps, or a personal insult – and she severed the contract. Suddenly *Rosita* was "the worst picture, bar none, I ever made." Perhaps she was hurt by the small-town receipts. "A very fine picture," reported a Saranac Lake, New York, exhibitor, "and after you get through try and find the profit." "Not the type of picture Pickford fans like to see," was the verdict in Allentown, Pennsylvania. "Too long. Gets tiresome. Business opened big but fell off every day. Gave poor satisfaction. Price too high."

Through *Rosita*, Pickford reached a new, more sophisticated audience. It troubled her, however, that she'd lost the old one.

In 1924 Adolph Zukor paid a visit to the UA partners. He knew of their struggles and, paternally, offered them relief: reliable financing, splendid road shows, distribution through Paramount's sprawling chain of venues, and a blanket of publicity to match. But in one key aspect he fell noticeably short: he could not grant creative independence. UA's female founder had earlier expressed her opinion of such know-it-all bosses. "Neither Douglas nor I will ever again take dictation from business men who sit in their mahogany offices back East," said Mary, "with their big cigars, seeking to control a business which they do not understand." But the press was stunned when D.W. Griffith took Zukor's offer; the director's financial troubles were dire and he went off to Famous Players–Lasky, an unwilling slave.

UA replaced him with Joseph Schenck, who became not only a partner but chairman of the board. He had entered the business through Marcus Loew, who owned a massive exhibition chain, and rose to the company's highest ranks. In 1917 Schenck had left Loew's to become a producer, handling the films of Norma Talmadge (his wife), her sister Constance, Buster Keaton (his brother-in-law), and the doomed Fatty Arbuckle (no relation). Schenck had an excellent reputation; he was sensitive to artists, but shrewd and resourceful in business matters. On the creative side, his record with Keaton may be his most remarkable legacy, for the actor made a streak of astonishing films that, in later years, in other hands, he never equaled.

In typical fashion, Schenck brought United Artists a wealth of product by forming a division called Art Finance (reorganized two years later as Art Cinema; the cash-starved Allied had long since folded). Through it, Schenck would finance films for Talmadge and Rudolph Valentino, produce three films for Keaton that have since joined the ranks of silent classics, and distribute movies for Howard Hughes, the eccentric billionaire producer.

Schenck considered it his mandate to reorganize the company. Indeed, his administrative skills were just what the other partners lacked. Pickford's business experience, for instance, consisted of negotiating contracts, fashioning each to protect her artistic and financial interests. Through these arrangements she let the film industry know that, as an actress, she could not be exploited. Unfortunately, Mary and the other founders lacked the visionary skills to pilot an entire corporation. Chaplin, in particular, considered his own self-interests first and the health of United Artists second. And sometimes – often – the partners reversed themselves, arguing heatedly on a point, then taking the opposite view months later. Pickford and Fairbanks, for instance, criticized Griffith for arranging his own road shows, but on several occasions they did the same. With Schenck at the helm, the founders could devote themselves to what they did best: expressing their personal vision on film.

After *Rosita*, Mary thought nostalgically of *Dorothy Vernon* – and of Marshall Neilan, who made her laugh, never made remarks about "qveens and qveens," and conveniently needed a directing job.

Neilan's *Dorothy Vernon of Haddon Hall* (1924) was, according to

Pickford, a far better picture than *Rosita*. But then, "almost any film could have been." She noted that "people even professed to love it" – "professed" is the key word – and "it wasn't too badly received by the press." True – but apparently the press had a weakness for long, dull pictures.

The precarious state of United Artists made Pickford less sanguine when Neilan drank. "I would rather you put your hand in my pocketbook," she told him, "than steal the time and patience of my entire company, to say nothing of my own." Knowing Neilan's interest could flag mid-film, she began the shoot with *Dorothy*'s climactic scenes, to make sure they received his complete attention. But Neilan was a no-show for a massive piece of pageantry. All was ready: hundreds of horses and extras, decked out with cumbersome Elizabethan doodads, were standing restlessly in Golden Gate Park in San Francisco. Mary finally lost patience and directed one and all from the back of a horse. As she worked, Charles Rosher glanced over his shoulder to a crowd of passersby who had stopped to gawk and was astonished to see Neilan, just as curious, among them. "Say, you're doing pretty well!" the director said affably, then disappeared, presumably in search of a drink.

The result was, predictably, disjointed. The first reel of *Vernon* has some comic shtick – a chastity belt falls on Mary's foot, she nails a stool to the floor and later, in a tantrum, kicks it – all of it vintage Pickford business, and all of it strangely out of place. For *Dorothy Vernon* must stand or fall as a romantic epic, and in those terms it is stillborn, a seemingly endless ten-reel pageant, full of little figures who trot on horses, wave banners, and dance around a maypole. Lottie, billed proudly as Lottie Pickford Forrest, plays a small role with adequate results, and her husband, Allan Forrest, used his photogenic looks and a teaspoon of talent for the plum role of Mary's romantic interest. Mary's entrance is magnificent – her hair in close-up as Dorothy brushes it upside down, then peeks through its curtain like a blond Godiva. But nothing lives up to this erotic promise, nor to any standard one would care to name.

In her heart of hearts, Pickford knew the film had failed. "So many costume pictures just then," she said later, smiling bravely, "and most of them [were] done better than mine." "I was quite ready," she added in her memoirs, "to surrender to public demand and become a child again." Thus she would offer a kind of penance for deserting Little Mary's hard-core viewers – the immigrants and working class whose dollars had supported her since *Hearts Adrift*.

In 1925 the unpretentious *Little Annie Rooney* was the answer. One watches in amazement as Pickford, at thirty-three, fresh from the seductions of *Rosita* and the stiff declamations of *Dorothy Vernon*, slips into the body of a twelve-year-old slum kid, chugging her little legs, puffing up her flat chest, throwing punches. And one scene – when the child learns that her father has been killed – was a lachrymose link to Mary's past. In rehearsal, the melodrama so overwhelmed her that when Valentino dropped by the set, the actress was badly disoriented. "It took me hours to get back into the mood. . . . Had it been make-believe and nothing more, I could have turned it on and off at will. But I really was that bereaved little orphan."

Much of *Annie Rooney* is fresh and fun. But the film is a reel or two too long, and it feels more serviceable than inspired. In fact, Gloria Swanson, who saw Pickford in costume at about this time, thought she had not made peace with her return to childhood. "Mary'd come over to my bungalow," Swanson recalled, "with her little bee-stung lips and pout 'I want to do Sadie Thompson.'" (Swanson had Sadie, the temptress of Somerset Maugham's short story "Rain," in mind for a production of her own.) But Swanson had no patience with Mary's problem. "I'm exactly the same height as she is, maybe just a half inch taller, but she affected being a child, with her little Mary Janes and those damned curls, and I'd wear these enormous high heels and act like I towered over her." Swanson growled, "Get out of here, you little shrimp."

Just before the film's release, James R. Quirk, the editor of *Photoplay*, reported that Pickford was "distracted and unhappy" as she sat for an interview. "I know the magazine is read by two million five hundred thousand people . . . and that these constitute the essence of picture patronage. So I'm taking this direct route to ask for suggestions as to the type of stories I should do." "There is no one less sure of self, no one more open to criticism and advice than Mary," wrote Quirk of this cry for help.

Twenty thousand letters poured into the magazine, requesting (predictably) more children and young teens; Anne of Green Gables and Heidi were among the roles specifically mentioned. Fans also sought "confirmation of the belief that the sweet, wholesome things in life are worth while."

Stymied, Pickford wrote a syrupy response, thanking one and all for their loyalty and love. Then she made a move in the opposite direction by approaching a director named Josef von Sternberg.

His first film, *The Salvation Hunters* (1925), dramatized the sordid, hopeless lives of some seaside derelicts in California. It was dreary, stylized, self-indulgent, pretentious, daring, atmospheric – all on a shoestring budget, too. Fairbanks and Chaplin were wild about it, and the film was distributed by UA. And Mary, who also loved the film, immediately asked von Sternberg to direct her.

He was floored by the offer: "The charming lady was the chief representative of the saccharine spectrum of the popular film which I had vowed to denature." (Though one wonders if he'd ever seen Pickford act: "Curls and fidgeting" – in other words, the St. Vitus Dance – "no matter how charming, were anathema to me." But of course, these were anathema to Pickford, too.) Still, von Sternberg came up with the story of a blind girl who lives in Pittsburgh's industrial slums. The film, called *Backwash*, would contrast her fragile, imaginary world with the dismal realities around her. It all sounds a bit like *Stella Maris*, laced with von Sternberg's nihilism – an ingenious compromise, in other words, between Mary Pickford's traditional roles and the new-wave style of her daring director.

The potential alliance ran aground. "My star-to-be," wrote von Sternberg sarcastically, "asked me to wait ten weeks to accustom herself to the idea while she made a 'normal' film with a 'normal' director." "*Mon Dieu!*" Mary fumed years later, displaying, through her French, pretensions of her own as she criticized his. "He proved to be a complete boiled egg.. .. The business of *von* Sternberg [the "von" had been added] and carrying a cane, and that little moustache! I'm so glad I didn't do the film." Later von Sternberg found his ideal actress in Marlene Dietrich, whose image he honed into an icon of world-weary hedonism.

In 1925 Joe Schenck succeeded in connecting a moneymaker to United Artists: Sam Goldwyn.

Mary still loathed the man. Nine years before, he had crossed her at Famous Players–Lasky, disapproving of Charlotte's presence and voicing the opinion that Mary was overpaid and too powerful. He was eventually elbowed out by Zukor, and Mary had a hand in it. The story goes that after she heard Goldwyn speak slightingly of her Papa, she immediately reported the remarks to Zukor. The next day Zukor told Lasky coldly that he could not, and would not, work with Goldwyn. After Goldwyn was banished, he created Goldwyn Pictures with Edgar Selwyn. But in 1922 Goldwyn was ousted again, this time by his own stockholders, who had asked him in vain to keep his costs down. Indeed, he spent lavishly on his films; more often than not, the results were excellent. Goldwyn the producer left Goldwyn the company, after selling back his stock for a million dollars. The Goldwyn company then joined Metro and Mayer in a new conglomerate called MGM. And defiantly, Sam kept making movies with his own concern, Samuel Goldwyn, Inc.

The producer was prickly, vulgar, and almost pathologically hostile. It was as though he believed that no fight was worth winning unless he exacted the maximum blood, sweat, and tears from his opponents. He was also known for "Goldwynisms": "Include me out," "I would be sticking my head in a moose," and, after someone explained a sundial, "My God, what'll they think of next?" He seemed an unlikely mate for gracious, prestigious United Artists, but UA, like a down-at-heel aristocrat, needed money. In 1925 Schenck gave Goldwyn a contract to distribute his movies through UA, and Mary held her nose.

The year was also brightened by the arrival of Gloria Swanson, who, through sheer (and preposterous) glamour, had become a spectacular draw in her work for Zukor. With the film public fainting at her feet, she rejected his million-dollar contract renewal offer and decided to make fewer, more thoughtful pictures. To do so she became her own producer – and a new partner at United Artists (although she took little part in the business decisions).

Later in 1925 Schenck approached the partners with a bold proposal that he had developed with his brother. Nicholas Schenck was second in command at Loew's, the theater circuit that was now the parent company of MGM. Metro-Goldwyn-Mayer had a wealth of product, but its image was second-rate. On the other hand, United Artists could be nursed to health if it booked its product, as MGM did, through the vast Loew's chain. Joe Schenck told Chaplin, Pickford, and Fairbanks that a new distribution company to book both studios' films, with the name United

Artists–Metro-Goldwyn-Mayer, would benefit them all; MGM would gain a little glamour, and United Artists would no longer be in the money-losing business of booking films, screen after hard-won screen.

Chaplin immediately opposed it. He belittled MGM as "three weak sisters," somehow saw the plan as the creation of a trust, and complained that the result "would have been but a club for Metro-Goldwyn to force exhibitors into line, using the 'block booking' as a means to foist its film 'junk'" on the public. But Pickford and Fairbanks were enthusiastic. After all, they reminded Chaplin, the UA founders would continue, as producers, to control their films (and refuse block-booking). And there might be other benefits – MGM, for instance, might well help UA finance its endeavors.

Chaplin was adamant. "When Charlie came over to me," remembered Schenck, "and told me he would be very unhappy if the deal was made, I felt that we, as partners, had no right to make Charlie unhappy." Indeed, an unwritten pact required that the artists be united in both name and spirit – in other words, they had to make unanimous decisions. But often consensus was hard to come by. The price of Chaplin's truculence was high. According to Schenck, the joint distribution of UA and MGM films would have brought the partners five million dollars a year. And the proposal caused a rare clash between Chaplin and Fairbanks. The latter, at a meeting, called his friend a "kicker," for unreasonably kicking over UA's traces. Chaplin replied that Fairbanks was a "jumper," for his act first, ask questions later spirit.

Chaplin also refused to participate when the partners proposed that the company try to create a chain, primarily through big-city palace screens. Chaplin didn't need them; his films did well without road-show venues. But in this case he didn't care what the others did, so in 1926 Pickford, Fairbanks, and Schenck turned to Goldwyn to help them assemble a small chain, not technically part of UA but committed to distributing its films. Within a few years, the United Artists Theatre Circuit owned flagship venues in Los Angeles, Chicago, and Detroit. And eventually the circuit bought partial interests in New York's Rivoli and Rialto and a scattering of other screens coast to coast. The most exotic, not to say bizarre, were the Egyptian and Chinese Theatres in Hollywood.

The Egyptian arose in 1922, its courtyard lined with ominous tombstones, its interior etched with hieroglyphics. The feature was announced to the world at large each night by a Bedouin, chanting the movie's name as he strode across the parapets in billowing robes. Five years later, the magnificently odd Chinese Theatre would appear, with forty-foot obelisks, a red pagoda, ushers in Oriental tunics, and a great bronze lantern with crystal strands. Here, in the forecourt, was a homage to the deities – the footprints, handprints, and signatures of silent stars for all to gaze at. To silent-film fans, these marks were akin to religious relics – and Pickford and Fairbanks were the first to leave their imprints in the wet cement.

Indeed, when Pickford and Fairbanks went to Russia in 1926, they already found themselves worshipped like gods on earth. It began as they were whisked from the border in the former czar's railway car, while inside, Mary hid her hair in a babushka and threw kisses toward a camera. Thirty-five thousand people, shouting her Russian nickname, Marushka, greeted her train at the Moscow station and later mobbed the couple at the Hotel Metropole. A Russian film, *Potselui Meri Pikford* (*The Kiss of Mary Pickford*, 1927), wove documentary footage of their visit into a satire of film celebrity. The movie's hero, a woebegone usher named Goga, resents Douglas Fairbanks hugely; his girlfriend can't get enough of him, moons over his poster, and watches him onscreen, faint with love. When the pair visit Moscow the usher manages to get himself kissed by Pickford. (Mary participated in the scene as a gesture toward the struggling Russian movie industry.) The crowd is stunned, then interested. They begin to see a certain glow around the man who touched Marushka's lips, and they advance like hunting animals to tear his clothes off. When he locks himself into a room to eat, they line up one by one at the keyhole for the privilege of watching the marked man chew. Finally, when the usher's girlfriend removes Pickford's lipstick from his cheek, his adoring fans crumple to the ground en masse.

In 1926 the perfect evening's entertainment – Mary Pickford's *Sparrows* (with "a deeper note ... terrific suspense and power") and *The Black Pirate* (featuring "Buried Treasure! Pieces of eight!" and "Fairbanks!") – unfolded in a double bill at the Egyptian.

The Fairbanks feature was light as a feather; Pickford, for the first time, made a thriller.

She appeared as the teenage Mama Mollie, who lives on a "baby farm," a place where impoverished parents send their children, who work for food and board. They dress in rags, sleep on the barn floor, and are beaten by the terrifying Mr. Grimes, played by the cadaverous Gustav von Seyffertitz. In an ominous scene, he receives a letter. "Dear Mr. Grimes: I been very sick that's why I ain't sent the money regular for taking care of Amy. If I get well I'll send more. I read of a baby farm from where they was mean to children but I know you treat my Amy good." Amy's mother has sent her a doll. Grimes looks at it slowly, smiles like a death's-head, squashes its face in with his thumbs, then throws Amy's doll into some nearby quicksand. Slowly its body is tugged down, and slime closes over its mangled skull.

The swamp is the centerpiece of the film, along with its gaping alligators, a vicious dog ("Tree 'em!"), Grimes's dour wife, and his chubby son, Ambrose. This unholy trinity recalls the Squeers family in *Nicholas Nickleby*; the baby farm resembles their sadistic school, where parents send their children to be worked to death. In fact, the adjective "Dickensian" applies to *Sparrows* more than to any other Pickford film.

The *Sparrows* set is redolent of mud and muck, snaky vines, staleness, dust, and heat. The designer, Harry Oliver, blow-torched the tree stumps to give them their warped and withered look. Still, for all its creepy details, *Sparrows* has a strange, almost lurid beauty. A shot in which a child is dragged away and Mary and her charges wave goodbye, thrusting their fluttering hands through the cracks in a rickety barn wall, is often compared to an image in Cocteau's *Beauty and the Beast*, in which arms with torches thrust their way through a wall to light Beauty's way. And the children's final escape from Grimes – a night flight over quicksand and churning water – is a high-voltage getaway, complete with tree limbs breaking beneath them, snapping alligator jaws, and some slapstick involving falling pants. But even this sequence, like all of *Sparrows*, retains the morbid stillness of a trance.

The ominous, overcast look of the film was the work of cinematographers Charles Rosher, Karl Struss, and Hal Mohr, who labored to create several flawless trick scenes. The most eerie and touching involves a sick infant who dies in Mollie's arms. As she dozes with the dead child, a wall

of the barn dissolves to show Jesus in a vision, tending sheep. Every time
Rosher tried the shot, the nervous sheep wandered out of camera range. In
the end, he built a meadow on a high wooden platform, and the sheep,
terrified of falling off, stood rigid. Jesus then walks from the meadow to
the barn and the sleeping Mollie, from whom he gently takes the baby. A
ludicrous moment, if badly handled – but even today, this scene in *Sparrows*
plays to an audience of rapt believers.

The chase in the last reel could perhaps be trimmed. Otherwise,
Sparrows is horrifically good – a bad dream that wakens to a happy ending; a fairy tale told with brilliant style; a comedy; a Grand Guignol; an
expressionist thriller. And in 1927 Pickford matched, if not surpassed, it
in another genre altogether.

"Beyond its comic inventiveness,"
writes silent-film scholar Robert Cushman, "*My Best Girl* depicts the kind
of love affair that everyone, at least at one time, has wanted to have. The
scene in which Mary and Buddy [Rogers] walk through the rain without
realizing it is pouring is a statement in itself: the rain is drenching them,
but they just walk on slowly, looking into each other's eyes and talking,
jaywalking right across a busy street, oblivious to the interweaving cars,
trucks, people, and bicycles. Nothing affects them; nothing bothers them;
they notice only each other."

The movie glows contagiously. Viewers fall in with the story of a five-
and-dime salesgirl and her rich-kid beau with the automatic understanding
they would later give romances such as *Annie Hall*. And the film, like *Rosita*,
is richly balanced. Each character is fully drawn, the milieu (in this case, a
bustling American city) is effortlessly captured, and the love affair, the core of
the film, is electric. Indeed, Buddy Rogers had a crush on Pickford, an infatuation that no doubt sparked their onscreen rapport. Astonishingly, *My Best
Girl* presented Mary in her first extended love scene, located in a stockroom
packing crate. Pickford and Rogers, who are eating from a brown bag, have
changed it into a tiny dining room, complete with an alarm clock and vase
of flowers. The humor – some eccentric, some time-honored slapstick,
freshly used – is always effortless, always real. Deservedly, the film did smash-
ing business; its aim at the public's heart was true.

At last United Artists was showing signs of health. In 1927 the firm gained a partner – reluctantly admitting Sam Goldwyn to the inner circle – as well as a contract with D.W. Griffith, whose tenure at Famous Players–Lasky had been disastrous. He did not become a partner again, but Schenck took him under Art Cinema's wing, believing that, if sensitively handled, the director would find his creative footing. At the end of 1927, the partners were more than a million dollars in debt; twelve months later, they would show a $1.6-million profit.

Pickford had a vision of the movies' future; she called it "'canned' genius." "The culture and talent of Europe are at the command of Hollywood," she wrote; there was nothing, she believed, that film could not accomplish. After all, a generation had been born who would think automatically in terms of film. "Writers who have been taught to express themselves in the written word find difficulty in expressing themselves in action. It is like elderly persons learning to speak a foreign language – they speak the motion picture language with an accent. We will get away from this by using those from within who have grown up in the industry. They will know no other tongue." She was also inspired by what she called "the motion picture league of nations" – the Academy of Motion Picture Arts and Sciences, which she helped found in 1927.

Its original aim was to act as a forum for the resolution of conflicts in the movie business; the rise of unions in an industry that had previously relied upon an abundance of cheap labor was beginning to create bad blood. The brainchild of thirty-six titans of the studio system, the Academy, Mary wrote, would "end civil war within the industry," discourage "sharp practices," and become a "central laboratory" for technicians.

On May 11, 1927, Fairbanks, who had been voted the first Academy president (he would keep the position for the next three years), made the opening address at the founders' banquet. He was followed by Fred Niblo, who had recently directed the stupendous *Ben-Hur* and who euphorically tackled the theme of world peace and silent movies. This led him, in turn, to the subject of the seraph of silent film, who was sitting, with prepared notes, down the table. "The next speaker, my friends, needs no introduction. But I would like to mention that just her name and her personality is a symbol for all that is fine and splendid and unselfish – MARY."

Everyone stood up until Pickford reached the podium. Glowing, she spoke of "the millions of fan letters that pour into Hollywood" – and then proposed to make their authors "correspondent" members. The Academy, by sending regular bulletins, could educate the fans about the art of film. But her speech was more important for the way it showed how film had learned to think about itself. The silent pioneers were announcing their art's maturity. They were ready to pour its amorphous world of light and shadow into something more concrete, made of stone and steel. This building, as Mary imagined it, would assume almost biblical proportions as it looked upon film's calling and pronounced it good. "Inscribed therein will be the names of those who have blazed the trail, and in the walls of the academy will be the Roll of Honor. . . . It is you here tonight," she said, gazing out, "who represent the ultimate in motion pictures, the effort of twenty years." Then she sat down to a "great burst of applause, prolonged in its intensity, until at last Miss Pickford, her face radiating joy and pleasure, was compelled to stand up and take a bow."

Indeed, despite the complexities of producing, the downside of fame, and her personal demons, there was much happiness in Mary's life. By the late 1920s, United Artists had carved out a permanent, important place in the American moviemaking scene. Under its trademark, the actress made moving, intelligent films. Her public and highly idealized marriage was built on genuine respect and love. And for millions of people, she personified the heart of western culture; she comforted, inspired, and delighted millions.

Tongue in cheek, she deified herself at the United Artists Theatre in Los Angeles. The cinema (still standing, and fully restored) is a stunning fantasy: chandeliers, pillars, walls of mirrors, plaster stalactites dripping round the screen, as well as a vaguely Renaissance mural that sweeps around the audience like the Sistine Chapel. Cavorting among the clouds like cherubs are Chaplin, complete with bowler hat, a bare-chested Fairbanks, as *The Thief of Bagdad* – and Pickford, sitting lightly on a cloud, her pale locks tumbling down a pale blue dress, surveying the audience as though well pleased.

10

—

CUTTING TIES

While looking in a trunk for material that might be used for a costume in *Little Annie Rooney*, Charlotte let the lid slip shut. As it crashed down, it caught her breast. Doctors believed this trauma caused a lump that they discovered late in 1925. Horrified, Pickford blamed herself. "From the day I learned the truth about Mother's condition, I spent three long years in a hell that only a demon could conceive."

Charlotte refused surgery, citing the experience of an actress she had worked with on the road. "I've had three major operations in my life and I just can't face a fourth – not the kind that poor Josie had." A European tour, on which she was to have accompanied her daughter and son-in-law, was postponed while doctors tried futile nonsurgical solutions. Some of these may have been methods from Christian Science, of which Pickford was now a devotee.

In 1926 the three set off for Italy, France, and England, and Charlotte seemed healthy at the station in Santa Fe. Five days later, at Grand Central Station in New York, she detrained in a wheelchair. She was still in a chair when the travelers disembarked in Genoa. Mary sent her mother to a spa outside Florence. There she would be cosseted with fine food, nursing, and restorative waters, while Fairbanks and Pickford, who had promises to keep, made small talk with Mussolini and gave the fascist salute to photographers. Meanwhile the tumor grew.

Mary brought Charlotte to her private beach house late in 1927, and she remained at her mother's side for the next eighteen weeks. Charlotte's condition was hopeless. "We were both playing a game," remembered Mary, "she pretending that she didn't know and I concealing my terror from her." They spent hours reading aloud from the Bible. Then Pickford would excuse herself to go to the bathroom, turn on all the faucets, and cry her eyes out.

"Don't ask me to live any longer," said Charlotte. "Let me go, darling. . . . I can't go unless you promise you won't grieve and cry."

Pickford was in deep shock. "If that's the way you want it, I release you, Mama."

"You must never blame yourself for anything," said Charlotte. "You must never think that you ever displeased or upset me. You are the best daughter any mother ever had. I know how cruel and unjust you can be to yourself. You must promise never to condemn yourself for any imaginary wrong."

When Charlotte fell into a coma, Pickford sat at her bedside. She remembered how fragile Charlotte seemed; the blue of her eyes became truer and deeper, her skin was translucent and porcelain-smooth, and her hair had a strange, almost luminous health.

On March 21, 1928, Charlotte died. Finley Benson, who had married Lizzie's daughter Mabel, told Mary with the gentle phrase "She's gone." As she listened, the words made a rushing sound in Mary's head. She lost her vision; then she saw the phrase SHE'S GONE in a white-hot blaze, its letters toppling onto her body. Mary hurled her arms into the air, then found herself falling toward a plate-glass window. When Fairbanks caught her, she struck him in the face; she remembered that his lips turned white with shock. Hours passed – alone. No one dared come near her. Pickford heard the clock she had given her mother chime twelve. She could never bear to look at that clock again. When Jack and Lottie finally arrived, she cursed them. Where had they been as their mother lay dying?

Suddenly she focused on her cousin Verna, Lizzie's other daughter, who was eight months pregnant and sobbing deeply. Duty called and Mary finally took control. "You know my mother wouldn't want you to risk losing your baby." After a few more words of comfort, Verna was persuaded to retire, and Pickford, to everyone's relief, was rational.

Dully, she supervised the funeral and, aided by her lawyer, served as co-executor of Charlotte's estate. Charlotte had left her eldest a million dollars, and she provided two hundred thousand dollars each in trust funds for Jack, Lottie, and Gwynne, Lottie's daughter. (The child, about ten at the time, lived at Pickfair after Charlotte's death.) A few days later Pickford walked through her mother's house on Cañon Drive, surveying her fine china, silver, and crystal, her linens, rugs, and paintings. "I realized then . . . how futile it was to think of finding even the smallest part of my mother among them," remembered Mary. "I have never valued such things quite the same way since."

Pickford never recovered from her mother's death. "She was almost my very life," she said. "All that I have become, or achieved, I owe more to my wonderful mother than to anybody else in the world." Death struck with the force of an amputation, for Mary had always been an adjunct of Charlotte. Without her, she barely knew how to live.

But perhaps, in her initial bewilderment, she felt a disorienting touch of freedom. Adela Rogers St. Johns believed that Mary had long delayed cutting her hair out of regard for Charlotte's feelings. In *Pictorial Review*, Mary once asserted that bobbed hair was not beautiful but stylishly smart, and that the sight of "shaved necks" revolted her. She declared, in ambivalent terms, her devotion to the public, her husband, and her mother, who adored her as she was: "I haven't the courage to fly in the face of their disapproval. . . . If I am a slave, at least I am a willing slave." Perhaps her abandonment to grief unlocked this suppressed rage and made her reckless. Whatever the reason, on June 21, exactly three months after Charlotte's death, Pickford brutally attacked Little Mary – with scissors.

"Shall I ever forget that day at the hairdresser's on Fifty-seventh Street and Fifth Avenue in New York?" Pickford added, in italics, "*It was the first time scissors had touched my head.*" Photographers were present to record the execution. And though Mary and her hairdresser felt like fainting, "the most famous head of hair since Medusa's" was denuded while journalists stared and scribbled. Twelve curls lay shredded on the floor. The six remaining "shackles," as she called them, were carefully culled and preserved as souvenirs. Mary quickly stuffed them in her purse, swallowed when she saw herself in the mirror, and returned to her suite at the Sherry-Netherland. When Pickford removed her hat, Fairbanks wept.

"I had suspected, and probably secretly wished, that Douglas would react the way he did," wrote Mary – an enigmatic statement that hints at muffled anger in the marriage. Although she must have known that her newly shaved neck would offend her most fanatic devotees, she "wasn't at all prepared for . . . the avalanche of criticism that overwhelmed me." She received "the most indignant, insulting letters." Pickford lashed back, threatening retirement if nothing but a head of hair was keeping her in pictures. But her audience thought she had betrayed their trust. For Pickford had severed a symbolic cord to not only Little Mary but the holy days when film was virgin-fresh. "You would have thought I had murdered someone," she observed, "and perhaps I had, but only to give her successor a chance to live." Indeed, a new chemistry had entered entertainment that would end the era Pickford represented.

In the 1920s vacuum tubes caught waves of sound and released them through radios into homes. The audience that listened in their living rooms and kitchens felt connected to an unseen, nationwide community – working men and women, like themselves, smoking, sipping tea, holding hands, or sewing round their channel to the world at large. Radio was the flip side of silent movies: voices, dramatically presented, forcing the listener to imagine the bodies and lips that produced them. Odd as it seems from today's perspective, once the silents were established, the idea of mixing voices with moving images was of only passing interest to the industry.

The experiment had actually been tried. Edison had once married sound and image in a slot machine called the Kinetophone. But the silent Kinetoscopes drew more pennies, and he soon turned his talents toward a talking doll. In Paris, as early as 1900, audiences could see talkies of Bernhardt and the legendary actor Coquelin. Four years later, the Lubin studio's *Bold Bank Robbery* was released in America with two records and a phonograph to play them on. Chronophone, Fotophone, and Cinephone echoed Lubin's film with a gramophone positioned behind the screen. But the synchronization was imperfect; the projector, after all, was still hand-cranked. Cameraphone, Synchroscope, and Theatrephone followed, as well as Actologue and Humanovo, for which actors stood behind the screen, reciting.

In 1903 the Warner family of New England, whose son Sam had worked on a Hale's Tour, pooled their savings, hocked the family horse, bought a secondhand projector, and showed *The Great Train Robbery* in a tent in their backyard. By 1910 the four sons – Sam, Harry, Albert, and Jack – were making flickers, and in 1916 they launched into features with an anti-Hun film called *My Four Years in Germany.* For years Jack and Sam used the back door to slip past bill collectors. When the brothers bought Vitagraph in 1923, they needed cheap publicity and turned to radio. In 1925 the Warner Brothers station, built with secondhand equipment, joined the West Coast airwaves. In order to cut the cost of talent, Jack warbled songs on its maiden broadcast.

The engineer who built the station told Sam about a test film he had seen and heard in New York City. Two synchronized motors were used, one to move the film through a projector and another to turn a wax disk; thus the sound of music from a grand piano. The engineer had even heard the snap of buttons as the pianist peeled off his elaborate gloves.

Sam hurried to New York, where Bell Telephone technicians showed him a film with an orchestra accompaniment. Astonished by the horns and swooning strings, Sam walked behind the screen, half expecting to discover a real orchestra playing there. He didn't, and the brothers began to dream. Warner Brothers was a feisty but impoverished studio, scraping out a business in the majors' shadow. Now they envisioned new Warner products: films with their own recorded music. If Warner theaters, however modest, were converted to sound, they might find new viewers in the novelty market. "But don't forget," said Sam, inspired, "you can have actors talk, too." Harry would spend years living down his rejoinder: "Who the hell wants to hear actors talk?"

A few months and seven hundred thousand dollars later, the company unleashed its sensational *Don Juan* (1926), featuring John Barrymore's famous profile as it nuzzled Mary Astor's neck. True to form, the actors in the film were silent. But the Warner recording device, the Vitaphone, added sound effects and music. As the lights dimmed, someone cleared his throat. It was Will Hays, Hollywood's official censor, who stood onscreen with words of welcome. The audience response resembled that of the first silent viewers to a moving wave or train; their astonishment was childlike, the experience surreal. "There was no muffled utterance or lisping," raved the *New York Times*. Instead, it was undoubtedly "the voice of Hays." At the end of his pronouncements, Hays stood for a moment, and the audience applauded. They then received an unexpected jolt when Hays bowed graciously as though he had heard them.

Don Juan played New York for over seven months. Its popularity was partly due to the *Vitaphone Varieties*, a program of musical shorts that preceded it. At this point, all agreed that if sound had a future, it lay in sound effects and song. The audience was curious but uncommitted. Critic Walter Kerr later wrote of the *Varieties*: "We simply sat through them while we waited for the serious business of the evening, the silent feature: perhaps Josef von Sternberg's *The Last Command* or Buster Keaton's *Steamboat Bill Jr.*"

The feature film studios, like the trust before them, were resistant to what seemed an unnecessary change. Too much was at stake: in 1928 the value of America's movie studios (which made more than 80 percent of the world's films) was sixty-five million dollars. They employed vast numbers: 75,000 people in production, over 100,000 in exhibition, and 100,000 in distribution. Eighteen thousand actors were available as extras, and 16,500 were listed at the Central Casting Office. Of special concern were foreign profits, which accounted for 40 percent of the total. These numbers would diminish if language were allowed to limit film's appeal. Finally, showing talking movies would entail the dismantling and retooling of every movie theater in the world. Only the Fox studio took up the challenge with a process called Movietone, touting the result as *"Life* itself!"

"Wait a minute, wait a minute," shouted Al Jolson. "You ain't heard nothin' yet!" In 1927 Warner Brothers had induced him to star in *The Jazz Singer*, featuring some talking scenes as well as a handful of fervent songs. By the time Jolson sank to his knees to sing "Mammy," a new course for the movies seemed set in stone.

It wasn't what he said but how he said it. In one scene, Jolson chattered to his mother. "Mama darlin' – if I'm a success in this show, well we're gonna move from here. . . . Oh yes, we are. . . . We're gonna move up in the Bronx. A lot of nice green grass up there. A whole lot of people you know. There's the Ginsbergs, the Guttenbergs, and the Goldbergs. Oh, a lot of Bergs." (These lines were improvised.) "And I'm gonna buy you a nice, black silk dress. . . . Mrs. Friedman, the butcher's wife, she'll be jealous of you." Eugenie Besserer chatted back, her words tender but inaudible – the microphone was pointed at Jolson only. But her work seems natural and informal. In fact, when the dialogue is rehearsed, *The Jazz Singer* falls on its face – or its blackface. Its spoken segments, which make up about a third of the movie, disintegrate as self-conscious actors cope with microphones. But – to use a phrase credited to critic James Agate – the unrehearsed exchange had the aura of language *overheard*. It showed that sound was more than a stilted addition to an art form. Instead, it might trigger an entirely new one.

In December 1927 *The Jazz Singer* played in Los Angeles – to a moment of silence, then a ringing ovation. It occurred to Frances Goldwyn, wife of Sam, that the occasion was "the most important event in cultural history since Martin Luther nailed his theses on the church door." As the lights came up, she looked around at those applauding. They smiled, but their eyes were alive with terror. There was laughter and chatter in the aisles and lobby, but Frances felt sure that there was silence when viewers reached their cars. She admitted, "I know there was in ours."

Some emerged from the gloom in deep denial. Pickford, for instance, insisted that adding words to the art of silent film was a decadent frill, "like putting lip rouge on the Venus de Milo." Griffith boldly predicted that "speaking movies are impossible. When a century has passed, all thought of our so-called 'talking pictures' will be abandoned." This was false bravado, for *The Jazz Singer* sounded the silent movies' death knell. The rush to sound caused a financial panic that destroyed reputations, lives, and art. Studios were bulldozed, equipment junked, films burned and discarded, and careers cut short. Fear ripped through Hollywood, and by 1930 silent film lay on the trash heap.

Mary was visiting another studio "the day they tested Wallace Beery's voice. They'd built a sound experiment studio over there. He went in at about nine o'clock in the morning, and four hours later the doors opened and a young boy came running out and shouting, 'Wally Beery has a voice! Wally Beery has a voice!' " In other words, Beery had a voice that pleased the studio executives. They seemed to have forgotten that *The Jazz Singer's* high point involved Jolson's improvised, folksy speech. Neither did they heed the ads for Vitaphone ("Pictures that TALK like LIVING PEOPLE!"). Instead, the search was on for actors who spoke in formal, pear-shaped tones. Films such as *Singin' in the Rain* or Kaufman and Hart's play *Once in a Lifetime* make wonderful fun of silent actors who failed to survive the transition to the talkies. But they also imply that the talkies had exposed them all as frauds. In fact, they were artists – but masters of a different, now discarded, form.

"Off with their heads!" thought Frances Marion. She was watching as executives at MGM weighed the fate of the stars on their talent roster. Aileen Pringle – "sounds too ladylike." Ramon Novarro – "south-of-the-border accent." And the hapless drug-addicted Alma Rubens – "she's too sick anyhow." Often these judgments were ill advised (the aversion to accents) or simple vengeance on uppity actors whose box office future was now in doubt.

Laughter was the kiss of death, and viewers often laughed at early talkies. Much of the dialogue was inane. "Oh, beauteous maiden, my arms are waiting to enfold you" might succeed when written on a title card. In 1929, when John Gilbert spoke it, he brought the house down. *His Glorious Night*, the film in question, bestowed the coup de grâce on Gilbert's future. He was obviously terrified; his hyperalertness and wide, staring eyes make him look like the proverbial frightened deer. He was also the victim of bad recording: "All you heard is treble," confessed a technician, who "never turned up the bass when Gilbert spoke." Thus Gilbert's unctuous, bloodless voice. But perhaps any voice would have been rejected. Gilbert was required to have not only the right voice for film, but the voice that viewers had *imagined* for him. Indeed, with the notable exception of Garbo, few of the greatest silent actors made the journey into sound without disaster.

Even those performers who were new to film found that talkies often made them look – and sound – ridiculous. As directors rethought movie grammar, they rendered the talkies incoherent. Dialogue, for instance, was shot in close-up; with two or three people in a frame, directors feared the audience would be unable to distinguish who was speaking. A similar blunder had occurred in flickers, when actors moved slowly in the background lest they distract from the principal action. There was also the matter of audience inference. In flickers, directors had been loath to cut from location to location without a sequence in between to explain where the scenes were laid. Offscreen sound caused the same consternation. Would the audience always know what caused it? In 1928 *Interference* used a shot of actor William Powell listening to an actress sob off camera. And viewers successfully inferred that Evelyn Brent, not Powell, was in tears.

Film people's insecurity ran riot. Just as Zukor had once believed that Broadway would nourish the growth of silents, the talkies made talent raids on Broadway. Playwrights were hired to perform the rites of dialogue and didn't do it well, writing endless chat as though films were stage plays. Film actors with theatrical backgrounds found themselves starring in talking features. Critics wrote of voices "holding up," as though actors were breathless, tortured athletes. They spoke with exaggerated diction, followed by a pause in which the audience absorbed the shock of hearing voices. "Take him . . . for . . . a . . . ride," said a gangster in *The Lights of New York*, the first all-talkie, in 1928. "Ohhh," nods his buddy; another taps his chin. The effect is hilarious today, but the movie was a great success, and "take him for a ride" entered common parlance.

The whirring silent camera, with its reassuring grind and clicks, disappeared into a soundproof cabin, along with the cameraman and his assistant. This behemoth moved slowly, if at all. The effect resembled that of pre-Griffith flickers; the lens was reduced to stenographic duties, and the hard-won fluidity of film was lost.

Silent-film studios were destroyed. New ones were built mostly with brick and cement; only kiln-dried and rubber-sealed wood could be used. Others were encircled by moats of water that protected the stage against vibrations. Now actors worked in a pool of silence. No musicians played on site. No director spurred them with praise or insults; instead, he sat listening with the tension of a coiled spring. Actors were stripped of jangling jewelry, their hair combed with oil to combat static. They crept about the set as though walking on eggshells. Performances were pegged to the positions of the microphones, which were hidden, like land mines, around the set — behind a book or telephone, perhaps. Boom mikes dangled like the shadow of a guillotine. Actors glanced at them in panic as they tried to laugh and weep in even, well-measured tones.

"We would rehearse a dramatic scene," wrote actress Bessie Love, "and hear the play-back; the sound engineers would say, 'Too much echo.'" The set "would then be stripped of curtains, furniture, rugs – everything except the walls. Carpenters would swarm on to the set and hammer, hammer, hammer all the floorboards; everything would be replaced . . . curtains re-hung, thicker carpets laid; we would rehearse again – emotion and all; again hear the play-back, again hear the engineers' 'No!' and again try something different – more curtains, gauze walls." Spontaneity – the keynote of the silent actor – died. Pressure was intensified when more than one camera filmed a scene. Today several cameras are used in film when an event must be captured in a single take – say, blowing up a building. In early talkies, the same anxiety applied to getting scenes with decent sound. Thus one camera filmed in long shot, another in medium, and one was assigned to each actor for close-ups. Performers felt nerve-racked and besieged.

On March 29, 1928, the president of Dodge Motors in Detroit played host to a star-studded radio broadcast. At the time it seemed like a good idea: to expose the voices of United Artists first through sound waves, then through talkies. This would ease the transition for all involved. To ensure headlines and a sense of occasion, the event was broadcast not through homes but at specially wired cinemas. As the hour of the show approached, storm clouds moved ominously toward New England. And a sense of dread filled Mary's bungalow, which engineers had rigged into a broadcast studio.

After the sponsor's speech of welcome, Fairbanks joined the program through the cross-country hookup. He introduced the company – Pickford, Chaplin, Griffith, Swanson, Talmadge, and two new additions to United Artists, the exotic Dolores Del Rio and John Barrymore. Each gave a carefully tailored chat on some subject that suited his or her silent image. Fairbanks spoke of staying young at heart. Griffith, who put women on a pedestal, spoke of ideal love. Swanson, whose on- and offscreen glamour inspired many ingenues to gate-crash Hollywood, advised against it. Chaplin told jokes in a Cockney dialect. Barrymore recited a speech from *Hamlet*, Del Rio sang a song, and Talmadge spoke of fashion. Pickford gave a female heart-to-heart.

The reaction appalled them. The press, who had been barred from

Pickford's bungalow, listened at a distance in Fairbanks's gym. Now, in an unforgiving mood, they questioned the broadcast's authenticity, wondering if Talmadge and Del Rio had been "doubled." Blizzards marred the broadcast in New England. Those who heard it were rude and restless. A dispatch to *Variety* blamed "the dryness of the program and the length of the talks during which nothing much of anything was said that could be termed interesting." As the hour wore on, increasing static led to catcalls. It was a mistake, reported Baltimore, to "take the public behind the Hollywood scenes and let them listen to entertainers whose talents are essentially visual." "Bust in Rochester," droned the headlines. "Frisco Not Interested." "Detroit Depressed." In Memphis the razzing grew so loud that managers switched the power off. Then the audience settled back to watch a silent feature – none other than Pickford's *My Best Girl*.

If Mary was hurt, she would not admit it. "I never doubted my voice for a moment," she insisted, "because of my stage experience." One must add a grain of salt to this pronouncement. Even as a child, she had been overly conscious of what Charlotte called the "ornament of speech." "Pearls on a string," Pickford dutifully remembered. "Words that roll 'trippingly on the tongue.'" When she heard her first sound test, she was dismayed: "That sounds like a pipsqueak's voice!"

"I don't care," she whimpered in her first talkie, 1929's *Coquette*. Then, in a mean drawl, "I . . . don't . . . ca-yuh."

On Broadway *Coquette* had been a blue-chip production, produced by Jed Harris, who, according to Moss Hart, "flashed suddenly across the stodgy theatrical firmament of the early twenties with the hard white light of a winter star." *Coquette* was a solid, four-handkerchief hit. But *Theatre Arts* accused the play of "wringing tears for the sheer delight of torture without regard for either necessity or logic." No matter; it was fodder for bravura acting. George Jean Nathan, a New York critic, satirized the style with a checklist of how certain actresses played "fear": "Bending the stomach inward at the waistline, open hands pressed tightly against the breasts, mouth half open. This method may be varied by leaning against a table, fixing the gaze hard at the audience and saying, in a hushed voice, 'Oh, my Gawd!'"

Helen Hayes took the role of Norma, a Southern belle and irresponsi-
ble flirt who, when she falls in love, falls for someone several social rungs
below her. Her father, who believes his daughter has been ruined, shoots
her lover dead. The curtain falls when Norma, who discovers she is pregnant, ends her life with a pistol. Through roles like this, the five-foot Hayes
(who had appeared as Pollyanna in the 1917 Broadway tour) draped her
image with solemnity and mink.

This was the transformation Pickford wanted (though, in a last-minute
loss of nerve, she omitted Norma's pregnancy – even her suicide; instead,
Norma's father kills himself). She was also aware that when she spoke, her
public would expect the essence of a private, twenty-year communion.
And she gave it to them – or hoped she did – by drawling, groaning, pout-
ing, babbling, delivering attractively throaty shrieks, and, for tragedy, dropping to a moaning alto. I am trained, she told viewers between the lines.
Listen to me speak, pick up cues, and enunciate. But speech doused the
spark of inspiration. For Pickford had not yet divined – nor had anyone –
the right way to act in talking films. She wrongly assumed it was something like stage work and turned to the signals deplored by Nathan. Thus
her conventional, stagey Norma.

A sense of gloom settled over Mary's set. When a UA engineer,
Howard Campbell, made a film test of Mary with bad sound, he put it on
the discard pile. Unfortunately, Pickford asked to see and hear it. "When
Mary came to the projection room," remembered a technician, "and was
told that there was neither sound nor picture available, Campbell was as
dead as a man who had just been stabbed through the heart; he just hadn't
fallen down yet." There was no scene, no altercation. Campbell was
replaced, and a car was sent around to the studio's fire door to allow him to
remove his things discreetly.

Charles Rosher, who had shot every Pickford since 1918's *How Could
You, Jean?*, was head of *Coquette*'s cinematography; this made him one of
Pickford's key collaborators. "No cameraman," Pickford later wrote, "was
ever so solicitous of the face he was photographing as he was of mine.
There were times when I felt he was its true owner, and I only the
wearer." Rosher's challenge had grown more delicate through the years.
In 1925 he made his star (then thirty-three) look twelveish (or close
enough) as *Little Annie Rooney*. In *My Best Girl* she looked close to

twenty. These incarnations had been aided by the sensitive silent camera. But in talkies, an extra sheet of glass dulled the lens as it peered from the "icebox" window. Still, Pickford, at thirty-seven, had to look young and dewy-fresh.

Now, as she sobbed her way through a scene, Rosher stopped the camera. Pickford, who had worked herself into a frenzy, lost her concentration and "fairly trembled." "What's wrong?" she asked. "Did you run out of film?" No, answered Rosher. "A shadow fell across your face that I didn't like."

Mary lost her temper, claiming that in a tragic scene she hardly cared. Rosher, she remembered, was "completely unimpressed" and suggested they start again. "I'm afraid I cannot get the mood back," said Mary stiffly. She stormed off the set, and so did Rosher. The next day Pickford fired him — by letter. Tragedy, she told him, was "an ugly mask. I don't want to look like something on a candy box or a valentine." But her guilt was less cut-and-dried. "I didn't have the courage, the backbone, to face him," she confessed in an interview. She even dragged the tale into her autobiography. "Everybody else knew I was right," she pleaded. "Shadow or no shadow, he should not have stopped his camera." One suspects Mary knew she should not have fired Rosher.

On April 12, 1929, *Coquette* had its premiere at New York's Rialto. It began with a heart-stopping moment when a fuse blew; suddenly the talkie was completely silent. The film was rewound and shown again. Now there was bad, intermittent sound. Something in the background seemed like music, and a word or two emerged amid the rumble. Finally technicians solved the problem, and *Coquette* was displayed for viewers' judgment.

That night they were polite, and reviews were warm. But though *Coquette* is quite competent for its day, contemporary viewers might be pardoned for assuming the entire cast has just been resurrected from the morgue. Such is the effect of the monotonous pace, the hamstrung camera, and tinny sound. And the usually brilliant William Cameron Menzies could not create a set that accommodated microphones and pleased the eye.

But box office revenues were decisive: *Coquette* grossed $1.4 million. And on April 3, 1930, Mary won the second Academy Award for best actress (the distinction was not yet known as "Oscar"). Probably Mary convinced herself that she won on the basis of *Coquette*. More likely, the award was given to honor her seminal role in film – and, just as important, her contribution to the Academy's creation. Moreover, in what biographer Anthony Holden called the "first overt piece of campaigning" for an Oscar, the Academy's central board of judges had been invited by the actress to a tea at Pickfair.

At first Fairbanks tackled sound with gusto. His version of *The Iron Mask* (1929) was silent, but the actor recorded a talking prologue in which he recited a poem with such verve that he blew a sound tube. When properly recorded, his easy baritone dovetailed with the Fairbanks dash. In *The Iron Mask* Fairbanks appears as the old D'Artagnan, allowing him to weep, go gray, play father to a young king – even die.

He had learned to play father late in life. "I belonged to him reluctantly," wrote Douglas Fairbanks Jr., who willingly overlooked "slights and rebuffs . . . just because I didn't want to think they had happened." He correctly judged his father's problem: he had "built his career on a vision of himself as the ever-young champion." This champion was really a boy himself, incapable of nurturing another, unless it was a woman to whom he played the white knight. Nor was his youthful image helped by the presence of a rapidly maturing heir. Fairbanks rarely saw his son, remembered his birthday when prompted by others, and otherwise seemed blissfully oblivious to him.

Forgetting his son meant forgetting Beth. But luckily Beth was happily married to musical comedy star Jack Whiting. She raised Douglas with a vision of Mary as "a great and tender woman." In addition, she praised his "fine, great father," whose neglect was a puzzling, blameless riddle. But Mary and her husband's brothers eventually went to work on Douglas Sr.'s attitude. "You've got a wonderful son," said Robert sternly, "and it's time you started to realize it." Then he added, in a well-aimed blow, "I can't see that you've done much more for him than H. Charles [Ulman] did for you."

The oldest Fairbanks brother, John, died in 1927. Douglas, the youngest (at forty-four), was shaken, for John had been almost a father to him. His next film, *The Gaucho* (1927), was unusually dark and contemplative. And finally he reached out to Fairbanks Jr., who began to feel that "the genial barriers that still existed between us were now and then showing little cracks." Fairbanks *fils* was undeniably grown-up: seventeen, taller than his dad, and an actor since 1923, when he had starred in his first film, *Stephen Steps Out*. At about the time John Fairbanks died, he was poised to appear as Garbo's glamorously alcoholic brother in *A Woman of Affairs* (1928). "[Dad] couldn't exactly shake me off, or hide me," he remembered, and a bond developed. It was, as his cousin Letitia noted, more fraternal than paternal. Fairbanks called his son "Jayar." As requested, Jayar called him "Pete." In 1929 the relationship cooled, but only briefly, when Jayar, now nineteen, married Joan Crawford, his senior by about six years. Mary may have also disapproved, and Crawford, a social climber, sensed it. When she first went to Pickfair, she was paralyzed with terror and convinced that she would slip and fall at Mary's feet: "I even had on an extra pair of panties." But the meeting went well, and by the time Fairbanks Jr. was twenty-two, he rejoiced that his father accepted him as "companion, confidant, and teammate" – though he noted, with some surprise, that "I was the more responsible, even mature, of the two of us."

Pickford also saw a change in Fairbanks. A sense of anxiety, rather than joy of life, drove him forward. "There were spells when nothing satisfied him," Mary wrote. Fairbanks was a public personality – born to be famous, born for film. But perhaps Fairbanks sensed, as others did, that his viewers' gaze had begun to wander. For fifteen years, when the filmgoing public looked for an exemplar of the modern man, it saw Fairbanks, the man-child, "the public apostle of light" looking back at them. And Fairbanks, the extrovert, had thrived. He had no talent for introspection. He had only to look in the public's eyes to see his ideal self incarnate. Now he felt hounded by a nameless fear.

Mary felt him slipping out of reach – as early, she wrote, as 1925. Perhaps in response, she was finally overtaken by the family thirst.

There was an etiquette to alcohol among the Smiths: it was sometimes deemed excusable, sometimes not. Depending on who tells the tale, Mary sometimes played hooky from her

Pickfair duties, drove to Charlotte's, and sat down to share a glass. During Prohibition Charlotte's basement was renowned for its abundant stash; it is said she kept the door locked to prevent her son from making unexpected raids. And she often drank alone, which Jack and Lottie might have known. But it seems Charlotte feared Mary's disapproval. Gwynne remembered being posted as a lookout when she lived with Charlotte; she would call from the porch if Mary's car came down the street, giving Charlotte time to tuck the bottle out of sight.

Jack could drink and be forgiven, for he drank with style. He ran wild but in the company of Hollywood's top-drawer alcoholics – wits-about-town, with proven talent. On the other hand, it didn't seem to matter much to anyone if Lottie drank, or who shared her shabby misadventures. Lottie drank with hangers-on. She was at their level.

On November 9, 1928, reporters dined out on a story that Lottie had been kidnapped, beaten, and robbed while on a drive through the Hollywood Hills. She had divorced Allan Forrest a year before and was now involved with a Paramount actor named Jack Daugherty. After spending the evening at the Apex jazz club, she and Daugherty were stranded with engine trouble. Suddenly four men emerged from the shadows, beat Daugherty senseless, and drove off with Lottie, who screamed in protest as they pawed at her pearls and tore her lingerie. "I was desperate," she reported. "I heard one of the men say something in Spanish. So I screamed in Spanish, 'Mother of God, help me.'" The effect was startling: conscience-stricken, the Spanish-speaking bandit drove Lottie back to Daugherty, who was staggering, bewildered, around the road. Curiously, neither Lottie nor Daugherty could recall where these traumatizing incidents took place.

Seven weeks later Lottie was injured in a fight for her affections at a Christmas Eve party in her home. Daugherty attacked a guest – a romantic rival who, police noted, had been with them at the Apex – and "all but chewed [his] finger off." As the "fistic hostilities" continued, "an unidentified man in the roadway in front of the house is said to have pummeled Miss Pickford with one hand while throttling her with the other." Lottie's sidewalk and porch were splotched with blood.

Yet another marriage, in 1929 – wisely, not to Daugherty but to Russel O. Gillard, an undertaker from Muskegon, Michigan, whose hearse was often filled with bootleg liquor. When Lottie applied for the marriage license, she gave her name as Lotta Rupp and claimed that the marriage was her second. But the head of the license bureau checked the records. "Who told you Lotta Rupp was Lottie Pickford?" snapped Lottie. The clerk pointed out that the names on file were identical. "That's just a coincidence," said Lottie. "I've changed my mind, tear that application up." She and Gillard left the building, hurling insults at each other, and Lottie drove away, shouting, "Let it ride!" But she changed her mind again, and the squabbling lovebirds took the plunge.

Pickford's habit was, at first, far more controlled. In 1934 Margaret Case Harriman (whose father, Frank Case, owned the Algonquin) described her benignly as a social drinker: one who sometimes took an innocent nip of port. "And, when she goes out, [she] occasionally gets very funny on a couple of cocktails or – in another mood – volubly indignant about something or other." Actually, Harriman painted too bright a picture. "If you had seen Mary Pickford before noon in those days," said one of Mary's lawyers, Paul O'Brien, "you would have thought her still the beautiful, intelligent, clear-minded woman she had been for so many years." But by noon Mary's nerves demanded alcohol. After entertaining at a Pickfair dinner, she was known to retreat for a moment to the bathroom and return in a blur, her breath medicinal.

"One time," recalled director Eddie Sutherland, "Jack and I were on a drunk and we ran out of booze. Jack said not to worry, and we drove over to Pickfair. Mary wasn't home and Jack went right on in the front door, didn't even knock, and we went straight up to her room and into her bathroom. 'Gin or whisky?' he asked. 'The hydrogen peroxide bottle's gin, the Listerine bottle's scotch.' We sat down ... Jack on the tub, me on the commode, and finished off both bottles. I was worried about Mary. I know what it's like to go looking for a drink and not find it. But Jack said it was okay, there was plenty more where that came from."

Perhaps Charlotte's death encouraged Mary's problem. Or perhaps Mary knew, as Fairbanks did, that sound had dislodged her from the movie mainstream. Hollywood had never been kind to has-beens, as the case of Florence Lawrence illustrates. In 1915 she escaped a burning studio, then ran back in to help friends to safety. Her heroics left Lawrence temporarily paralyzed, and though she recovered, her career did not. "It's very hard," she said in 1924, "to be left forgotten by an industry you helped so hard to develop." When the actress tried to make a career in sound, she was ruthlessly rejected. She tried her hand at journalism, interviewing stars. In the 1930s, Lawrence finally signed a bit-part contract. In 1938 she killed herself.

Now, as a kind of creative insurance, Fairbanks and Pickford decided to appear side by side in a film. For years such a project had been rumored; at one point they had tried, before he filmed it, to persuade William Randolph Hearst to sell them the rights to *When Knighthood Was in Flower*. Then they had struck on the Children's Crusades as a theme: a ragged Mary would have led a band of urchins, and (presumably) Fairbanks would have played a knight. When their fame was still secure, the project was put on hold; why undercut profits with a two-for-one? But sound was an anxious, less predictable game, and the couple chose to maximize their assets. *The Taming of the Shrew* was a witty choice, for no one would dare criticize the lines. The result, premiered in 1929, was an excellent talkie (for its day). But before it was even released, Pickford knew she loathed it.

The movie contains several tracking shots — a remarkable feat in early dialogue films — one of which follows flying chairs, books, and broken china till it rests on Kate. Mary's tax accountant, Edward Stotsenberg, said later that Kate was the image of her offscreen anger. An alarming thought, for as Pickford fumes, supercharged with rage, she seems trapped by a hurt she barely understands.

Mary was dissatisfied with her performance. She had hired a vocal coach, actress Constance Collier, who was classically trained. They aimed for a formal grandeur, an impulse squelched by the film's director. "We don't want any of this heavy stage drama," advised Sam Taylor. Instead, he demanded the "Pickford tricks." Mary, simmering, gave the usual pratfalls, double takes, and pouts. And they almost all fall curiously flat, as she doesn't believe in them. In the silents, Mary Pickford was angry and amusing; as Shakespeare's Kate, she is merely angry.

Mary's voice is all right, though it *is* a bit small; it's her manner that's wrong. Terrified of verse, she declaims her lines, while her husband speaks them. He was better with verse, as Mary enviously noted, and he had a bit of Jolson's bounding ego. The result was not "mike fright" but insouciance. Petruchio is the class clown, and Fairbanks felt free to behave the way only a man sure of his virility can – wearing a jackboot on his head, for instance. Fairbanks also felt free to lampoon his lines. Mary didn't feel free unless her lines were removed. Indeed, her best moment is a silent sequence in which Kate enters from a rainstorm. She quietly removes her sopping cape and headdress, shuddering with cold, then sits, defeated. She looks lost and bewildered – then, as the seconds tick by, a little less so. Her rage begins to smolder as she ponders who has made her feel this way: Douglas Fairbanks, on and off the screen.

Throughout the shoot, Pickford found him infuriating. He would turn up for nine o'clock calls at noon (Mary totaled the delay at thirty dollars a minute), and she claimed he didn't know his lines. Take after take, Mary wrote in her memoirs, was ruined as Fairbanks read Shakespeare from a blackboard. (On the other hand, cinematographer Karl Struss said Fairbanks was never late; he did use cue cards, but this was rare.) When Pickford, unhappy with her work, asked, "Would you mind retaking it, Douglas?" he replied, within earshot of the crew, that he *would* mind. This was how Owen Moore had spoken to her.

She kept her hurt hidden. After all, "dozens of eyes" were watching. But the movie's expeditious schedule – it was shot in six weeks – suggests a serene set. The crew was familiar with the Fairbanks style, which included unplanned breaks, kidding around, and playing practical jokes. On *Shrew* he even used his electric chair. Mary, too, knew this rigmarole; still, with a "strange new Douglas" on her hands, she found his frolics perverse. Fairbanks, according to her memoirs, was baiting her, much as Petruchio baited Kate – "but without the humor." Soon she was projecting her tension everywhere, calling the *Shrew* set "a tragic change" from the usual Pickford esprit de corps. Plans to co-star with her husband in *Caesar and Cleopatra* died. George Bernard Shaw was inclined to grant the rights, with the proviso that not a word or line of dialogue be altered. The result, said Mary drily, would have been a film several weeks in length. And besides, Douglas Fairbanks could not sit still.

After completing *Shrew*, the couple took a trip around the world. The original intent had been to visit Gwynne in Lausanne, where she was attending private school. But

Fairbanks's wanderlust demanded they continue on to Athens, where their undimmed fame caused a gratifying riot. A group of stevedores who had climbed up on the running board of the car even asked the visitors to autograph their ears (they could then get the signatures tattooed). A mob of five thousand roared "Hola! Marie!" as the actors' boat crept up toward the wharf. A "splendid stimulant" to vanity, wrote Mary wryly, "except that Douglas and I had long since analyzed the personal element out of these receptions. Ovations, I have come to believe, are seldom or never accorded to persons, but to ideas." And the idea of Little Mary was about to vanish.

In Egypt they lumped along on camels, slept on the Nile, and climbed the pyramids. In Shanghai they ate a Chinese banquet, complete with thrush heads. Pickford, who hated foreign food, nibbled her way through fifteen courses. Later she would weep at the memory of Kobe, Osaka, and Kyoto, where Japanese women kissed her feet. In Tokyo a crowd of ten thousand nearly crushed her. Fearing for their lives, her husband hopped on the shoulders of Chuck Lewis, his trainer, and slipped through a window, then reached down and pulled Mary up behind him. They had tea with Emperor Hirohito, played golf with his Cambridge-educated cousin, and were deluged with tapestries, jade, and ivory. Then on to Hawaii and San Francisco.

The trip had shown Fairbanks at his best: plunging into crowds, eagerly investigating native habits (Mary watched, appalled, as he stuffed himself with goat stew). But his wife had grown tired of changing faces. She made every effort to remain in her hotel room, where she ate a few crackers and drank weak tea – and perhaps other liquids.

This was the last of the great royal tours, and the last celebration of the movies' innocence. At home, where talking film had spread, the bloom had at long last left the rose. The talkies had a way of making everyone smaller. "The more of life, the less of art," wrote Walter Kerr in 1980. He explained, "No painter or poet or dramatist in his right mind ever attempts to reproduce the abundance of life *in toto*. He may wish to evoke the *sense* of that abundance, in Brueghel's way or in Shakespeare's, but . . . he does it by constant subtraction. He limits the frame, sacrifices a dimension, chastens color, looks for absences, refusals." In 1934 Pickford noted that "the refined simplicity should develop out of the complex." Therefore, "it would have been more logical if silent pictures had grown out of the talkie instead of the other way round." But by 1930 the damage was done; only Chaplin would attempt another silent film. A New York reporter apologized for being "impious, but the truth must be told": a public that once was entirely Mary's was "forgetting — never knew — what her career has meant."

Pickford's solution was to work. She began a talkie called *Forever Yours*. When she saw the first rushes, she was devastated.

"The spirit of the thing had been missed," Mary thought, according to *Photoplay*, "some vague, remote motive was lacking, something intangible that made it all seem most unimportant." Mary herself hit the nail on the head: "No action." This was an odd flaw, considering that her director was Marshall Neilan. But Neilan had failed her on *Dorothy Vernon*, and since then he had lost his creative stride. He also taunted his producers, misspent their money, and topped it all off with witty insults. ("An empty taxi drove up to the studio today and Louis B. Mayer got out" was much repeated.) As Pickford knew, he was often too drunk to appear for work. For years Neilan got away with such behavior. Now, in the tense early days of sound, producers exacted their revenge. When Pickford brought Neilan to *Forever Yours*, he was living hand to mouth, directing two-reel slapstick.

Two alcoholics on one set: no wonder they quarreled. Supposedly Neilan insulted Pickford. Suddenly both were in hysterics. When Mary saw the rushes, she called them "the most stupid I ever saw." Rather than continue, she took a loss of three hundred thousand dollars and burned the film — or so she insisted at the time. (In fact, she couldn't part with all the footage, which she later donated to the Library of Congress.) The cause of the quarrel is still unknown, though Paul O'Brien once observed that alcoholics "change their mind. Then they change it back. It gets so that people working with them never know what to expect, and there's no stability, no confidence. Everybody's morale is shot, and the whole project — film business, marriage, whatever it is — goes to hell."

By 1930 the industry at large was recovering from the near death blow of the onset of the Depression. After the dust of introducing sound had settled, five studios — Famous

Players–Lasky (now renamed Paramount), MGM, Warner Brothers, Fox, and RKO – had ascended to the industry's top tier. In the shadow of the Big Five, which all owned exhibition chains, worked the Little Three – Universal, Columbia, and United Artists – which confined themselves mostly to distribution and production. Then, as the novelty of sound wore off, average weekly film attendance dropped from eighty million in 1930 to fifty million two years later. With higher production costs (sound had doubled them) and a dip in foreign profits, the bottom line was now dangerously low, especially for the Big Five, whose battles in the twenties for control of venues had left them swollen and overextended.

As the pioneers of talkies, Warners' had seen its profits soar. In 1929 Warner Brothers made seventeen million dollars, which it instantly plowed back into buying venues. But then Warners' fortunes turned a hairpin curve; in 1931 it lost eight million dollars. The next year, Paramount skidded into debt; in 1933, the mighty name went bankrupt. Fox was reorganized that year, RKO was thrown into receivership, and MGM hung on with modest returns of one million dollars. Of the Little Three, Columbia kept afloat, Universal went bankrupt, and United Artists – with far less overhead than any of the Big Five – cheated death.

In 1931 fortune smiled when the young Walt Disney signed a UA distribution contract. His Mickey Mouse, born in 1928, was considered in the vanguard of grown-up wit and style. And the shorts he released through UA were a godsend. They would reach their apogee in 1933 in *The Three Little Pigs*, with its dancing, prancing animals and lunatic jingle. This piece of animation, which still plays beautifully, was a staggering achievement for its time. It deservedly made ten times its production cost. In fact, Disney's eloquent animation seemed, like the silents, to transcend language; pigs, big bad wolves, and mice in pants disarmed everyone who saw them.

Pickford tried to be modern, too, with the madcap *Kiki* (1931). The gigantic loss incurred by *Forever Yours* had demoralized her; indeed, it is a sign of her creative malaise (not to mention her depression) that she asked Joe Schenck to produce the movie.

It was Schenck's idea that Mary film a sex farce, but she hesitated. Sex – especially the champagne and high-heels variety – had never been central to her image. Still, Schenck liked *Kiki* (he had produced a silent version for his wife, Norma Talmadge, in 1926). Pickford looked at *Kiki* closely, then signed with Schenck – for a flat fee of three hundred thousand dollars. In 1931 these were royal wages. But she had no contractual creative rights, nor a claim to a percentage of the movie's profits. For the first time since 1916, Pickford went to work as an actress on contract to another producer.

At first glance the casting seems pathetic – a middle-aged, somewhat desperate actress done up as a chorus girl, complete with French accent and a very tight skirt. Defying her age, Pickford brought it off, looking playfully attractive in men's pajamas and a blouse that apparently has the measles; somehow the star-shaped beauty mark, the dust-mop curls, and hat "like a restless question mark" suggest a mélange of Harpo Marx and Betty Boop.

As always, talkies made her anxious, and her preparation flirted with overkill. Although Beaudemère, Mary's maid at Pickfair, had a French accent, the actress asked to be tutored by Maurice Chevalier's wife and by Fifi D'Orsay, who was known for her Parisian floozy roles. And she didn't skimp on dance lessons: these were essential, for at one point Kiki tap-dances in a tux, loses her pants, and takes a plunge into a kettle drum. Still, despite the 1930s trappings, Kiki's nature is related to the Pickford hellcat. She fumes, swings her fists, and even bites another chorus girl. But Pickford couldn't capture the role's licentiousness. She goes through Kiki's motions with comic brilliance – fishing for a broken bra inside her blouse, slithering about in ostrich feathers, and wriggling on the floor with menstrual cramps. Here, though the slapstick is often brilliant, Kiki's sexual reckless-ness is elusive. The film meanders, the actors are pallid, the second half slumps, and the sets are dull. In the end, *Kiki* lost more than half its cost. "I presume," said Pickford a few months later, "I am not at the pinnacle of my success."

Fairbanks, too, was slipping. In 1930 he had also signed a contract with Schenck that put the burden of producing in Art Cinema's lap. Ironically, the actor once observed that the talkies would benefit from studying the quicksilver Mickey Mouse. *Reaching for the Moon* (1931) was a case in point. It badly needs some animation, for somehow it doesn't have a Fairbanks.

Letitia Fairbanks later wrote of her uncle's "increasing restlessness, his need of diversion. Pictures had ceased to be his dominant interest, and where before he had taken vacations between pictures, it was apparent that he was now making pictures between long trips." In fact, mere minutes into *Reaching for the Moon* it is painfully clear that the Fairbanks spirit has been extinguished.

The film had been designed not to translate his image into talking film but to exploit the sudden fad for all-singing, all-dancing celluloid. In a misbegotten moment, Schenck envisioned Douglas Fairbanks as a Wall Street baron who pursues Bebe Daniels, as a svelte aviatrix, on a gleaming ship. But their shenanigans are just a way of marking time; the film's star attractions were Irving Berlin's musical numbers, which, ironically, were excised (all but one) when the musical craze collapsed. What was left of the film didn't hang together, and Fairbanks's hollow laugh – which he uses, one assumes, as a stand-in for his usual acrobatics – seems unnervingly desperate. And in a scene in which he thinks he's lost the girl, Fairbanks stands alone, stripped of all bravura. "To an observer," Fairbanks Jr. later wrote of those days, "he was still the same energetic leader of the pack, the bouncing Scout Master, but that was sheer habit." Indeed, in this scene, Jayar's father looks small, damp, hopeless, and authentic.

After completing *Reaching for the Moon*, Fairbanks set off with Tom Geraghty to play golf in England. (Golfing was a passion. So was England.) No sooner had he returned than he was off on an all-boys trip with Chuck Lewis and director Victor Fleming. Four days out from Honolulu, Fairbanks set a record for ship-to-shore phone calls by contacting Mary at her New York hotel. *Photoplay* dared to satirize it, digging at Fairbanks's exhibitionism ("I'm jumping silly bully!" he declares of his athletics) and at penny-pinching Mary, who reverses the charges. When Fairbanks crows that the phone call will probably make the papers, Mary fusses, "Oh, I hope not! Our private lives are our private lives, it seems to me!"

In Japan Fairbanks plunged into swordplay and jujitsu. In Shanghai he visited opium dens. In Bangkok he dallied with king and court. On safari in India he shot three leopards, a tiger, and a panther from the back of an elephant. But often he was nagged by an encroaching dread.

He made two films – as an afterthought. Once again Fairbanks served as his own producer, though he clearly didn't care much about the results. *Around the World in Eighty Minutes* (1931) was a glorified travelogue, edited with trick shots of Fairbanks astride a map. The next year *Mr. Robinson*

Crusoe, a wafer-thin tale about conquering the elements, was made while he gamboled in Tahiti. Some who viewed these films were embarrassed. But the movies did not embarrass Fairbanks; instead, they helped him fulfill his purpose. "When a man finds himself sliding downhill," he reflected, "he should do everything to reach bottom in a hurry and pass out of the picture."

Pickford was miserable and afraid. She often didn't know her husband's plans. Neither did the press, for accounts of his travels disagree. Fairbanks improvised his trips. His mood was so frantic that his secretary learned to make daily reservations for train and plane travel in four directions. He spent several holidays at Pickfair and returned for the 1932 Olympics, but otherwise managed to stay away. Mary, in return, seldom went to meet him. "I just couldn't keep up the pace with a man whose very being had become motion, no matter how purposeless." She was wrong. Her husband had a purpose. He didn't want to think, or feel, or stop. And he wanted to be where Mary Pickford wasn't.

Throughout these years he escaped his demons by exploring the Philippines, the Suez, Siberia, Manchuria, Mongolia, and Morocco. Of course, he could have played golf at Pickfair. Instead, he played tournaments around the world, where his partners included the Prince of Wales. In England and Europe, he indulged his weakness for the upper classes, and a few more weaknesses besides.

"Doug is naive," declared a sidekick. "He doesn't even know a proposition when he hears one." "Well, he was human," said Chuck Lewis, "and there were lots of women willing to play. But that was when Mary wasn't around. He never hurt anybody, he was always discreet." It was often rumored that Fairbanks struck some offscreen sparks with Lupe Velez, his *Gaucho* co-star. And Douglas Jr. learned the hard way that his father had begun to stray. The young man was smitten with a guest at Pickfair, where Jayar made rare and awkward visits. She was only sixteen (he was not much older) and a Japanese aristocrat. Jayar took her for a drive to his father's studio and seduced her. He was nervous; mysteriously, she was not. In fact, she stopped him from apologizing: "Don't worry, please! You are very, *very* sweet." Then, after a moment: "You are *so* like your father!" For several days Douglas had a "difficult time . . . speaking normally to Dad."

In the spring of 1931 Fairbanks attended a party in London. The guest of honor was the King of Spain. Also on the scene was Lady Sylvia Ashley, known to her intimates as "Silky." "She had the manners of a duchess," laughed Letitia. "And she built that character out of nothing."

Born to a stableman named Hawkes (or perhaps he was a greengrocer, bobby, or footman — the press was never sure), Sylvia was lovely in the new way: tall, whippet-thin, with lofty cheekbones. "But her teeth!" said Letitia. "She had the English teeth that all need doing. And at times the Cockney would come out." In 1927 she slipped up the British social ladder through her marriage to Anthony Ashley-Cooper, the Earl of Shaftesbury's eldest son. This was a time-honored way of improving one's pedigree; Broadway showgirls often snagged rich, lovesick industrialists, and the British gentry also heard the siren call of showbiz. Unfortunately, Sylvia also welcomed the attentions of a dashing race-car driver named Dunfee, and in due course her marriage lay in shards. When Lady Ashley met Fairbanks, she was no longer living with Lord Ashley. Instead, she wore scandal like a string of pearls.

"Enchanting to chat with," said Letitia. "Sylvia had a marvelous sense of humor." Jayar — who, like Letitia, was a Pickford loyalist — agreed that Lady Ashley could be fascinating, and the gap in her teeth, he wrote, was "fetching." But to Cap O'Brien, father of Paul and also one of Mary's advisers, she was Lady Ashcan. He began to investigate her background, hoping to disillusion Fairbanks, who had fallen deeply for her soignée charms.

Sylvia was a swan, his wife a sparrow. Sylvia was born to wear gold lamé. Mary, on the other hand, sloshed through the rain in big galoshes, and sat around the house with her hair in pincurls. Short hair flattered Sylvia's frame. But it emphasized the flaw in Mary's build — the fact that her head was too large for her body. And if she looked bulky around the waist, it was because of her habit of rolling her skirts up rather than hemming them; then, Mary reasoned, she could simply roll them down again if styles changed.

Now she saw herself through her husband's eyes. She was thirty-nine, Sylvia was twenty-six; and the cameras recorded her gradually rounding face and arms, and at times her deeply tired eyes. She needed reassurance and began to send signals to Buddy Rogers, who was twelve years her junior and adored her.

She had always been impressed by Buddy's looks. When he came to audition for *My Best Girl*, she swooned as she once had for Owen Moore. "The handsomest man I'd ever seen," she cooed. "He had blue hair." The hair was "so like my mother's . . . [it] lay in thick waves on his beautifully shaped head." Buddy, at twenty-two, was slender, six foot one, and a self-described pretty boy with clothes to match. (His navy-blue coat matched his hair, remembered Mary.) His eyes were puppyish, his expression open. "Completely without guile," she wrote in her memoirs. "I knew at once that this was a man who would put the idea out of his mind if ever he thought the world was otherwise than good."

His hometown was wholesome Olathe, Kansas, where his father, B.H. Rogers, was a probate judge and edited Olathe's *Weekly Mirror*. Buddy grew up in a white frame house where his father presided over weddings in the living room; Mary later boasted that B.H. knew the names of every Johnson County family. B.H. loved his gorgeous boy, who attended the University of Kansas and became a campus star. "I had a racoon coat, a Model T Ford, two or three girls and I was in a fraternity. Heaven!" He also played several instruments and conducted a five-piece college band, which he toured through the Midwest Chautauqua circuit in 1922. But though Buddy wished for a musical future, his father had another kind of fame in mind.

In the summer of 1925, Famous Players–Lasky launched a nationwide search for movie talent; they were looking for twenty all-American faces to appeal to the jazz-age college crowd. B.H. submitted Buddy's photo. To his son's surprise, he was given a screen test; to his shock, he was one of the chosen twenty. The winners were paid fifty dollars a week while they studied at the New York studio. "It was six months," remembered Rogers, "and we learned two things – how to fall downstairs without hurting ourselves and how to hold a kiss for three minutes without laughing." In 1926 they appeared *ensemble* in *Fascinating Youth*, their graduation picture.

Though he made another 1926 release (*So's Your Old Man*, with W.C.

Fields), Rogers took it hard when he failed to win parts in the prestigious *Old Ironsides* and *Beau Geste* (both 1926). He was starting to panic when William Wellman cast him in the titanic *Wings* (1927), a breakthrough war film, with electrifying scenes of bombing raids, dogfights, crashes, and thousands of extras rushing headlong into World War I. It was long for a silent (thirteen reels) and long in production: eight months, during which Rogers logged ninety-eight hours of flying time, returning to the ground after each shot to vomit. All this for seventy-five dollars a week – sixty-five, really, with each check docked ten dollars by the studio to pay for a couple of suits they'd bought him.

Wings was awaiting release when Hope Loring, who had written the screenplay and was working on Pickford's *My Best Girl*, met Rogers at a Saturday-night dance in Los Angeles. She asked him what he was doing for lunch on Monday and arranged to meet him in front of Famous Players–Lasky. "She drove up in her car," remembered Rogers, "and we drove to another studio, not too many miles away . . . it was a new studio to me." (Any actor in Hollywood – with the exception, it seems, of Rogers – would have known the Pickford-Fairbanks lot.) "There was a big bungalow there," he continued, and Loring deposited the actor on the doorstep, asking him to ring while she parked the car. Thus the unworldly Buddy Rogers was delivered to Mary Pickford's door.

"My God, my time's coming," Rogers thought, as he watched other actors come and go. Finally he was asked to join Mary in another room. "We made a close-up of our two heads together and she put her head against mine and I sort of pulled away and thought to myself, 'Hey, she really wants me to get this part.'" In fact, their easy warmth onscreen was probably the result of their flirtatious offscreen. "She never threw her power around, I'll say that," Rogers recalled. "Never once in the three or four months that we worked did I hear her make a scene or stop anything. She was the perfect actress, the perfect friend." But in matters of the heart she was thoroughly human. Pickford was nettled, for instance, when Rogers told her that his favorite silent actress was Norma Shearer. "Didn't go over too well," he said drily. She was also unamused when Rogers proposed that she cast a friend of his, the struggling Carole Lombard, as her sister. "Oh fine," said Mary, looking at Lombard, "but I don't think so at all." And that was that.

In *Wings*, Rogers worked with the great Clara Bow. With fine direction and a sparkling actress, his presence onscreen was light but pleasing; he soon got the nickname "America's Boyfriend." And, with the exception of Douglas Fairbanks and the horse in *Suds*, he can claim to have been Pickford's strongest onscreen opposite. Unfortunately, his range was narrow, and too much ingenuousness can grate. Careful handling, time, and attention were needed to maximize his charm – and Famous Players–Lasky passed on these expenses. The studio began to give him second-rate productions: *Varsity, Someone to Love, Red Lips* (1928); *Close Harmony, Illusion, River of Romance, Half Way to Heaven* (1929) – the undistinguished list goes on. Many of these films were with first-time directors, used by Famous Players–Lasky to keep down expenditures on films that were already sold through block-booking. "All I knew," said Rogers later, "they'd get out their yearly folder, and I'd see, Oh, I'm going to make that film, that one. . . . I went through some of these pictures in the Thirties, and they were getting, you know, not four star rating, not three, but two-and-a-half. I thought, golly, am I that punk?" The studio asked him to be patient, assuring him that great roles were just around the corner. And Rogers, who often played one of six or seven instruments on the set while thinking, "Oh, to have a band," made more inferior pictures.

In 1931 he asked to be released from Paramount (the former Famous Players–Lasky), saying, "I have had a run of pictures that almost broke my heart." "They just said 'great,'" he remembered bitterly. "They didn't even beg me. But I had more fun in music than I ever had in films." He had long been dreaming of conducting music in the Paul Whiteman style: in other words, swanky orchestral versions of popular songs, and a little "hot" jazz. Soon, with financial help from Mary, he formed the California Cavaliers, the first of several orchestras, featuring Johnny Green on piano, Gene Krupa on drums, and singers Mary Martin and Marilyn Maxwell, all of whom easily eclipsed him as musicians. Buddy, on the other hand, was a showman, "a heavily handsome man," a critic noted later, who "supplied adequate dance-music and wowed the ladies with a dental smile." He turned down a contract with MGM because they wouldn't let him keep a band, but he made a few minor films from time to time.

Meanwhile his feelings for Pickford deepened. At one of the myriad events that honored the industry's royal couple, Rogers pointedly refused to stand when Fairbanks entered. And legend has it that Fairbanks had dropped by *My Best Girl*, only to see his wife and Rogers rehearsing the kiss in the packing crate. According to the story, he rushed away. "It's more than jealousy," he told his brother Robert. "I suddenly felt afraid." When asked about the story in his old age, Rogers said he didn't know if it was true. Then he grinned and confessed, "I'd like to think so."

"I never met Doug," he said, decades later. "I did not shake his hand ever. He always seemed to be somewhere else. It seemed to me this was not an accident." Certainly Fairbanks knew of the flirtation. In 1931 when Rogers and Pickford were both in New York, they set off down the Hudson in a motorboat. But the engine failed and Buddy had to summon help. When Paul O'Brien told Fairbanks the news, Fairbanks laughed. In fact, said O'Brien, "he laughed like hell." This was not the response his wife had hoped for.

"Separation? No, not now." Pickford smiled, but through most of the interview – a frank one with *Photoplay* in 1931 – she wept. She said she felt frightened, insecure, incompetent. She implied she would like to spank her husband. "I cannot deny that there may be a separation. I can only say there is none now." In six months or six years, who could say? She could promise nothing – not while she was caught "in this peculiar, shifting nightmare of a world." In July 1932 Mary hoped to find a few weeks' peace with Buddy in a cabin cruiser moored on the lower Hudson. Again the real world intruded – and spectacularly, too – when the ship caught fire and exploded. Luckily, the lovebirds were not on board.

But for Jack Pickford, luck was running out.

He had not been himself, Pickford later insisted, since Olive's death a dozen years before. (Mary stoutly maintained it was accidental. Jack, who would not have lied, had said so.) She indulged him endlessly, panicking when his dissipation led to breakdowns, paying his considerable legal fees, and financing several movies for him. Then, when his films did only middling business, she blamed her own fame for curtailing his.

In Mary's view, Jack, in his bereavement, was driven (through a series of unedifying love affairs) to find a love as pure as that of Olive Thomas. In

1922 he married the pink-and-gold Marilyn Miller, who had started her career in the Ziegfeld Follies and became a musical star on Broadway. Although Mary didn't like the bride, she gave them a lavish Pickfair wedding. (Deaf to irony, she remembered Miller as "the most ambitious human being I have ever met.") A few weeks later, Jack was named co-respondent in a divorce suit launched against Clara Kimball Young, a stage and screen actress, by her husband. No one was surprised when Jack abandoned Miller – to her relief; as Anita Loos told it, he often beat her. In 1927 Miller finally divorced him and, between drinks, applied her charms to Broadway. In 1936, at the height of her fame, she died suddenly after an operation. The cause was most probably an infection, but the explanation "syphilis" was also whispered.

In 1930 Jack wed his third steal from Ziegfeld, a pert, brunette showgirl named Mary Mulhern. "I'm the luckiest man in the world," said Jack. "I'm the luckiest girl in the world," said Mulhern. But the bride grew afraid of Jack within three months. He spent whole days abusing her and whiled away the others in drunken silence. In court she related how Jack once tried to break her door down, then chased her outside where she cowered in the bushes. "Mr. Pickford was a mighty nasty man," agreed the maid. "He sure is a hard man to get along with." The divorce occurred in 1932.

The last time Mary saw Jack, he was going down the staircase toward the door at Pickfair. Suddenly she saw him as he was: an emaciated shadow of his former self. "Don't come down with me, Mary dear," he told her. "I can go alone." Mary had the chilling intuition that this was the last time she would see her brother. On January 2, 1933, he fell ill in Paris, and Mary booked passage, begging him by cable to try Christian Science healing. But Jack died on January 3. He was reported to have announced on his deathbed, "I've lived more than most men and I'm tired – so tired!" Jack's death was variously attributed to neuritis (a nerve disease, but also a catchall term for a breakdown of the body), gastrointestinal problems, or a heart attack. But when all was said and done, the cause hardly mattered. As Biograph veteran Donald Crisp once observed, Jack never had a chance. "He was a drunk," he said bluntly, "before he was a man."

Mary fought bereavement with the dazzling idea of appearing as Lewis Carroll's "Alice" in a film by Walt Disney. The project, which took shape in 1933, would have used her as the only living figure – the Disney animation team would do the rest. Pickford's grasp of the concept was innate: It "is simple," she told the *New York Times*, "and it is sophisticated." In addition, a 1923 Disney series based on *Alice in Wonderland* had moved a human child through what appeared to be squiggling pen-and-ink. In effect, what viewers came to call *Alice in Cartoonland* could be used as a rehearsal for an up-to-date, wittier Pickford version.

The plan, at least at one point, was for Pickford and Disney to co-produce. But the project gripped Pickford, who badly needed to redefine herself onscreen, more deeply than it seems to have seized the artist. Alice was an assertive, no-nonsense child – in other words, the type of child Mary had acted for decades. And the stylized world of animation, like the stylized silents, would encourage the suspension of disbelief. But though Mary conceded that Disney had a number of movies on the boil (eighteen Mickey Mouse cartoons and twenty-eight "Silly Symphony" shorts – and the drawings for "Wonderland" would take two years), she thought she could make the film worth his while. To entice him, Pickford guaranteed certain profits: they would equal the usual amount Disney earned for the same amount of footage in his animated shorts; she would even pay the guaranteed sum in installments while the film was in production. These schemes, with their generous financial terms, were out of character for Mary, but the actress needed *Alice*, with its modern edge.

In 1933 Pickford made a Technicolor film test for *Alice*, as well as some stills in which she posed wearing ankle socks, flat shoes, a dress trimmed with rickrack, and loads of makeup. As a heavy hint to Disney, Mary also interacted with a stuffed Mickey Mouse, which stood half her height. The pair smile and wave at Uncle Walt, while a wall behind them bears the exclamation "TOYS."

Mary pushed; Disney dragged his feet; Disney said Pickford dragged *her* feet; and Pickford, finally, became aware that Paramount was planning an all-star *Alice*, which she claimed set the stage for a copyright conflict. And so she let the project tumble like a house of cards.

The balance of the year was sad and foolish. Fairbanks traveled but constantly sent his wife loving missives.

They expressed concern for her health and spirits and seemed to evince an undying devotion. But Beth had once received such cables. Indeed, a respect for his married past had endured throughout Fairbanks's affair with Mary. Now he felt tenderness for Pickford – a tenderness that vanished in Sylvia Ashley's presence. Still, he cabled that he loved her, missed her, valued his Hipper above all else. If only he could convince her there was nothing wrong, then perhaps he could believe it too.

Pickford, by way of reply, saw more of Rogers. She needed his approval, his adoration, his connection to a younger, more vital public. And he loved her blindly. He loved her flaws. ("The little dickens," he later smiled, "she gets to drinking and she just can't stop.") But Fairbanks refused to take the hint. Still a proud man, he could not believe he had a serious rival, especially a rival who was so young.

Besides, his wife was sending him other messages – at least through film. In 1932 she had produced, re-shot, and completed *Forever Yours*, released in 1933 as *Secrets*, with Frank Borzage stepping in for Marshall Neilan. It begins as Mary elopes with her lover, played by Leslie Howard. They travel to the West in a wagon train, and Mary stands bravely at Howard's side while outlaw bullets whiz around them. Time flies, and Howard, now rich, runs for senator. Mary stands by him, though the whole town knows of his infidelities. An excruciating scene shows Howard confessing his affairs; as Pickford listens, she looks like St. Sebastian taking arrows. "You want to tell me, don't you, John, that you never once stopped loving me, even when you were most unfaithful? . . . You want to tell me that these other women were nothing to you, and that I was everything, always." One hopes Mary found the scene therapeutic. This valentine to Pickford's sterling virtues closes with the couple, now jolly and silver-haired, taking a second honeymoon.

The movie has some excellent montage, and Borzage milks every wistful note. Sadly, its central flaw is Pickford. Her work lacks the wretched touch of tension that ruins her performances in *Shrew* and *Secrets*, and she's graceful and relaxed with comic banter. But she looks too old for the early segments. More important, the role is too passive for her take-charge spirit. And the need to speak quells her spontaneity; much of her work in the film feels *careful*. The only time Pickford scales the heights is in a sequence involving the death of her baby. Many silent actresses played such scenes, and Mary did them beautifully in *Sparrows* and *Daddy-Long-Legs*. Now, in *Secrets*, she blazes through the sequence with electrifying depth. Not incidentally, the scene is silent.

"Mary saw herself in those costumes," said Frances Marion, who wrote the screenplay. "She saw herself in a great dramatic role, making an impact on Doug as well as on her public. She would be faithful to one man on the screen, through three generations. I'm a woman, too. I understood."

In the early spring of 1933, Fairbanks went to Italy and wired his wife to join him. She did, and in a burst of chivalry, Fairbanks met her with a rented cruiser. But onshore the enchantment ended: it seems Mary asked him about his infidelity. Sadly, this scene had played better in *Secrets*, and Mary turned tail and booked passage home. Fairbanks, apparently unconcerned, struck back by playing golf in Rome and bedding for a night with a girl in his hotel room. But by May he was homesick and appeared at Pickfair, swearing he would not return to Europe. Unfortunately, Mary found his steamship tickets. The night before Fairbanks's fiftieth birthday, she left without warning for New York. Fairbanks, who couldn't bear to celebrate alone, caught up with the train at Albuquerque and presented himself at his wife's compartment. Of course, she was outraged and ordered him out, but he turned on the charm and got her laughing. He managed to persuade her that he loved her, that Sylvia meant nothing to him.

But as soon as the couple reached New York, he announced he was off to play golf in England. Now Mary's outrage was checked by pity, for never had Fairbanks seemed so panicked, so helpless in his need to get away. "Before sailing he asked me what I intended doing – would I wait for him until he came back? I replied that I would do nothing and that, while he was hurting me cruelly, he was like a man with a high temperature and even if he struck me in his delirium I would not blame him, knowing he was not responsible." Then a telegram arrived, stating that Fairbanks was *not* returning; that he no longer wished to live at Pickfair; if she lived there alone, he was indifferent.

Mary's first response was to fly to Chicago for the World's Fair, where Rogers and his band were playing. Her second was to lunch with Louella

Parsons — after tucking Fairbanks's telegram into her purse and collecting Frances Marion for moral support.

Parsons wrote gossip — breathless, brainless, frequently lethal — in a column that was syndicated coast to coast. Pickford called her a friend; in fact, all of Hollywood hoped to do so, for Louella held their reputations in her hands. She received lavish presents (jewels, cars, silver) and was asked to christenings, weddings, dinners. Parsons grew wealthy on bribes alone. And she often dined at Pickfair.

Mary showed her the fateful cable, stared at her plate, and said, "It's just — over."

"I had counted," she insisted later, "so trustingly on [Louella's] discretion . . . to treat the matter gently, without needless emphasis, to quote what could do no harm, and above all to treat the more intimate details as the confidence of a woman in sorrow who needed a friend and not a public advocate." Nonsense. Parsons made a living off indiscretion. And stars always kept her abreast of their love lives — if they didn't, she'd bide her time and destroy them. Showing Parsons the wire was, at best, a mixed signal on Mary's part.

The columnist's version has Pickford saying, "You are an old friend. You may write the story. The sooner it is known — and over — the better." "Honest little Mary," purred Louella, whose story on July 2, 1933, was the scoop of her career. And though Mary was furious, she didn't dare cross Parsons's poison pen. "I sometimes wonder," she mused in her memoirs, "whether, in the still, sleepless hours of the night, the consciences of these professional gossips do not stalk them."

Instead, it was Mary who was stalked, by photographers and newshounds who camped outside Pickfair until her manager, Mark Larkin, issued a statement that Pickford and Fairbanks loved each other. Yes, there might be a legal separation. But rumors of divorce were exaggerations. This last, of course, was nonsense, too.

Mary sued for divorce on December 8, 1933. The grounds were more or less "mental anguish"; she cited Fairbanks's constant travel and disregard for the pain it caused her. Two hours later she boarded a train for New York City, where she planned to spend Christmas alone with Gwynne. She emerged in Chicago, wrapped in mink, with a smile that left "her eyes unlighted." "There is no fight left in her," observed a journalist, "only a tight-lipped resignation." At New York's Pennsylvania Station, Pickford refused to speak of Fairbanks: "Good taste prevents." Then "she laughed and began talking in a grooved style, as if she were repeating lines she had rehearsed." Tactfully, no one forced the issue. "She was busy being famous for many years. Now when she isn't . . . any more, it is difficult for her to know what the substitute will be, or if there can be any." A few days after she reached New York, Pickford was spotted on Central Park Lake, where she skated repeatedly in figure eights.

Mary's problem child, United Artists, was picking a precarious path through sound. By 1933 Gloria Swanson was ruined (or so it seemed at the time); she had no choice but to sell back her stock. And D.W. Griffith had met disaster. His first three films since his return from Famous Players–Lasky – *Drums of Love* and *The Battle of the Sexes* (1928), followed the next year by *Lady of the Pavements* – had been painful failures.

Looking back, film scholar Iris Barry explained that Griffith worked "under conditions ill-suited to his temperament and experience, while business and financial problems of increasing complexity beset him. At the age of fifty, when he had already directed hundreds of films which include the most profoundly original films ever made, he was placed in competition with much younger men who inherited ready-made the technique he had perfected through arduous years. Obviously, they were far better able than he to adopt new methods, to adapt themselves to changing tastes and to represent the postwar age." He also drank, a fatal weakness when he needed to marshal his fading creative powers. The middling success in 1930 of *Abraham Lincoln* could not heal his rotting self-esteem. Griffith's final film – and perhaps his worst – was 1931's *The Struggle*, "a shiftless and pitiably stupid homily," wrote a critic, "which, esthetically and financially, should be an embarrassment to all concerned." *The Struggle*'s subject, ironically, was alcoholism. On April 19, 1933, Griffith's contract with United Artists ended.

Chaplin, on the other hand, had made *City Lights* (1931), a smash by any standard. Unfortunately, his previous release, *The Circus*, had appeared in 1928, and United Artists would wait until 1936 for the next Chaplin masterpiece, *Modern Times*. Artistically, Chaplin was a jewel. But because of their rarity, his films barely glinted on the ledger sheet.

The heroes of this period were Joe Schenck and Sam Goldwyn, who released forty-four pictures between them from 1928 through 1932, bringing needed millions to the company coffers. (Only three featured Schenck's wife, Norma Talmadge, whose career was obliterated by the talkies.) Goldwyn's other achievement was the singular enmity he inspired. His partners' contribution to UA's product was now next to nothing, which he thought a scandal, and at meetings the insults flew thick and fast. So did fists. In one encounter, Goldwyn called Fairbanks a crook, which so incensed the actor that he dove across the table for Goldwyn's throat. Goldwyn was advised to step out, where he steadied his nerves with whiskey, then returned to make amends. "I can't prove anything," he said sulkily to Fairbanks, "so I apologize."

In 1933 Art Cinema, which had recently sustained financial losses (not the least of which was *Kiki*), went out of business. But Alexander Korda was persuaded to join the UA fold. The producer/director had recently revived the film industry in Britain with *The Private Life of Henry VIII* (1933) and *Catherine the Great* (1934). Korda's high standing with British viewers was a godsend for United Artists' foreign market. And, in what seemed another stroke of luck, an enfant terrible named Darryl F. Zanuck had decided to become an independent producer – and United Artists hoped to capture him.

Zanuck was a knockabout sort who had worked at age eight in a silent western, lied about his age to fight in World War I, and worked, at various times, as a bantamweight boxer, clerk, waterfront laborer, and writer. At Warner Brothers he wrote scripts for a dog named Rin Tin Tin, who had also seen action in World War I (the dog had been rescued from a German trench and brought to California). These bright-eyed, wet-nosed films sustained Warners' in its hardscrabble years. In the talkie era, Zanuck's winning streak continued. As chief of production, he moved Warners' toward crime and social dramas – 1930's *Little Caesar*, for instance. In 1933 Zanuck branched out with *42nd Street*, launching the surreal world of Busby Berkeley. Then he suddenly bolted from Warner Brothers.

Everyone wanted him, but Schenck made the most attractive offer, by proposing they co-found Twentieth Century, which, like Art Cinema, would produce films and distribute them through United Artists. In his one-year contract, Zanuck promised to supply at least three films. Instead, he made a dozen and the profits flowed. Like Goldwyn before him, Zanuck felt he was entitled to become a UA partner. And Schenck, who was both his partner and UA's president, agreed, for the Twentieth Century product was not only plentiful but fine.

But Pickford immediately opposed the plan, for reasons unstated in the UA files. She may have thought Zanuck, who was loud and unrefined, would turn out to be as difficult a partner as Goldwyn. Her associates blew hot and cold, turning so many flip-flops on the issue that in 1935 the frustrated Zanuck took his company elsewhere.

Equally disastrous, UA lost Joe Schenck, who resigned as president, retained his position at Twentieth Century, and helped Zanuck merge the firm with Fox. Later he explained his resignation to Chaplin. "If you select a capable man for president and vest in him the necessary power to run the business without interference from the stockholders, I am absolutely certain that the company can and will be a success." He had had no wish to eliminate the partners' right to discuss or recommend UA policy. On the other hand, Schenck observed, "you cannot hog-tie a man at the head of a concern and put him in a position where he cannot make important decisions." Excessive quibbling by "people who know very little about the affairs of the distributing company" was bringing UA's growth to a standstill.

In a few years, the partners would prove him right.

The final nail in the Disney project's coffin was driven at Christmas 1933, when Paramount released its all-star *Alice in Wonderland*, a lumbering film that smothered such actors as Gary Cooper with cumbersome costumes and ornate masks. The film had a festive premiere on December 22 in New York. Ironically, Pickford was on the bill, performing in a playlet as a curtain-raiser.

In the days of silent palaces, playlets, revues, and dance exhibitions were often performed before the feature. These programs continued in early talkies, and Mary, who was aiming her career toward a return to Broadway, was using the tradition to get her feet wet again.

In *The Church Mouse* she appeared as Susie, who, looking adorable in collar and cuffs, confronts the president of a bank and finagles a job as his secretary. Mary approached this trifle as though she were training to play Medea, devoting four hours a day to recitations, breath control, scales, and songs. By the end she could recite "The Raven," wringing full value from all the vowels, and was apt to decant her champagne laughter, beginning at the bottom of the scale and burbling upward to a silvery trill. She was also inclined to read – not for pleasure but, anticipating long scripts, to sharpen her memorization skills.

But some found this busywork transparent – as much a cry for help as Fairbanks's life of roué pleasures. To literary critic Edmund Wilson, who met her that year to discuss a possible collaboration, she seemed "practical, clear in her mind. . . . I liked her." But he couldn't praise the surgery that had "tightened the skin so over all the lower part of her face that she couldn't smile with her mouth, which was nothing but a little stiff red-lined orifice in the face of a kind of mummy, nor change her expression at all. Only the upper part of her face was alive." Though Wilson called Mary's eyes "dark, agate-like blue" (they were hazel) and her chin, which was prominent, "recessive," much of his journal sketch rings true. Her eyes had the "power of energy and will," her brows were informed by "intelligent humor." But the lower part of her face was immobile. And at times he caught a flash of insecurity. "It seemed to me that for a moment when she first came into the room, and for a moment when I was leaving, there was a little despiteful [sic] look – or was it in the tightening of the skin around her mouth – as of resentment and disappointment against a world to which she was no longer irresistably winning."

But Pickford claimed she'd found the key to solving life's little problems. She could put it in a phrase: "Why not try God?"

At the time of her divorce from Owen Moore, Mary's faith in the church was severely shaken. And at some point she seized on Christian Science, which enjoyed a huge vogue in the 1910s and 1920s. Gradually she combined Mary Baker Eddy's teaching with her own think-positive, chin-up creed. "Her optimism has that quality of fierceness which is inseparable from her character," the *New Yorker* observed in 1934. "Good will prevail, her charming mouth will tell you, while something in her wide, uncompromising face adds silently that it damn well better." Mary's little sayings were bestowed upon friends like get-well presents. Or they were pressed into their hands in the form of her booklet *Why Not Try God?* (1934). "When our thinking is clear enough," the tract explained, "we become a transparency for God, or the Mind of the universe, to shine through." Mary also asserted, with equal vagueness: "Nothing in the world can make you conscious of failure or unhappiness unless you think about it."

Some were puzzled. Others grit their teeth and thought of Pollyanna. "Think how much more awful it would be if you had lost a leg," Mary said to an actor whose life lay in ruins. In 1935 Pickford's follow-up, *My Rendezvous with Life*, told how Mary helped a friend when her mother died. (The friend was almost certainly Elsie Janis, who, according to Letitia, was "as hooked on her mother as Mary was.") "Not a vibration, not an atom in the universe is lost for an instant," the book advises. "And so why should we suppose a personality – the most precious vibration of all – can be lost?" Janis finds the creed so powerful she dries her eyes and even cracks a joke about their mothers in heaven. (Charlotte lectures Elsie's mother on the value of a trust fund.)

Pickford, wrote the *New Yorker*, "likes to talk in generalities, which, with a disarming air of sincerity, she brings forth as great truths." Sometimes the tone – so naive, so confiding – verges on the infantile; in *Why Not Try God?* Pickford dramatizes doubt as two bad angels, Professor Poofinfoos and Madame Flitmajigger. Above all, the books stress joy through strength, the mental strength to beat back depression and look on the bright side. Beating down pain, rather than exploring it, hadn't worked particularly well for Douglas Fairbanks. Still, Pickford was determined to deny sad thoughts. And when she found herself failing to perform "right thinking," she would retire to the bedroom and scold Professor Poofinfoos aloud – then emerge a bit pale but with her faith renewed.

Still, at times she seemed bewildered. In January 1934, for instance, she announced that "an attempt to victimize me in some scheme of sinister, criminal purpose, has been thwarted." She had arrived in Boston (*The Church Mouse* toured a string of movie houses) and received a letter from a man who urgently wished to see her; the matter, he said, concerned a will. For the next two weeks he tried to make contact, and finally he was discovered with a female friend, listening at the door of the actress's hotel suite. (They would have heard her chattering with Lillian Gish.) They were ordered away but came back that night, when Pickford was entertaining guests. Mary's maid took them to a small adjoining room, where the strange man fixed her with a penetrating stare. Then Pickford swept in at her most imperious, demanding that the man and woman leave at once. Oddly, the man excused himself. But the woman remained and intoned at Mary, "I have a message for you. I've had spiritual guidance."

By midnight Mary had decided that the affair was an aborted kidnap; not only that, but that the strange man had tried to hypnotize her maid. She had been through this kind of thing before – an actual plan to kidnap Pickford, Pola Negri, child actor Jackie Coogan, and the heirs of an oil tycoon and banker. Police had warned her, and while Mary filmed *Little Annie Rooney*, her stand-in, Crete Skyle, was driven around in Mary's Rolls, wearing the actress's hat and coat. When the villains were arrested and appeared in court, Pickford gave them a contemptuous glare, sized up their attorney ("an insignificant pipsqueak"), then delivered herself of such scorn and fury that the judge had to silence her with a gavel.

Now she sped away to Falmouth, on Cape Cod, and the home of a friend, Charles Fulton Oursler, who edited *Liberty* magazine. "If anyone had the idea they can get me, they are wrong. I am surrounded by watchers and friends, am never alone and am amply taken care of." Her limousine was flanked by two policemen. There were also three guards watching Oursler's home.

A few days later Mary ventured on to New York and saw reporters, but only after trying all the doors in her hotel room and examining the locks. Management assured her that no one could reach her without a special pass to use the elevator. "But couldn't they walk up?" Pickford asked. Her suite was on the thirty-sixth floor, replied the management. Mary shot back: "They could rest on the way."

What was going on? Not much, according to Pickford's guests, who sued her for libel and told the press that they were merely Christian Scientists, hoping for a chat. Luckily, Mary hadn't named them, and a few years later she won the case.

"I don't feel at all afraid of you. You know, Canadians are so discreet." It was May 1934, and Pickford had arrived in Toronto with *The Church Mouse*. A month before, Lord Ashley had filed a divorce suit against his wife, naming Douglas Fairbanks co-respondent. At long last the rumors were public record. Fairbanks told Mary via long-distance phone call. She told him she sympathized, and she meant it.

But Toronto didn't seem to have heard the news. Instead, it turned the clock back to silent film – and more. At Union Station, where Mary detrained, she found G.B. Smith, her old doctor, waiting. G.B. wept as he joined her in her open car, which wound its way through downtown Toronto with a Scottish guard. Office workers waved from windows and showered the car with ticker tape. At City Hall a throng of people – more than had greeted the Prince of Wales – chanted for Pickford and drowned out the mayor's speech of welcome. Then Evelyn Pasen, a nine-year-old actress and a veteran of touring, offered Mary a nosegay.

The *Toronto Star* was most devoted. When Pickford visited its press room, she was offered flowers, and "the whole world's Queen of the May took the glowing blooms in her hands as though they had been a sceptre; and, with inevitable grace, buried her bonnie face in them." Later the writer met the Queen backstage. Her fans, he assured her, would be "interested in anything about you! If you were to brush off a fly from your cheek it would be quite acceptable to announce: 'The incomparable Mary struck to its death an insect on her peerless countenance.'" But even the incomparable Mary knew that purple prose like this was dated, and she cut the reporter off. "Don't be foolish."

"Do you remember the bicycle shop we used to have at Louisa and Yonge?" asked a member of the welcoming contingent. "Sure I do," responded Mary. "I bought the best bike I ever owned there." Gamely she rode another bike to her birthplace, though the fountains and chestnut trees were gone and her plain little house had been boarded up. Mary paused, leaned the bike against the porch, then tried the front door and found it locked. For a moment she seemed at a loss for words. "I don't think I'd exchange these days for the old ones," she finally told reporters. Probably the opposite was true.

These days she was increasingly beleaguered. Since the previous September she had suffered accusations from an Edward Hemmer, who claimed in a lawsuit (and in items in the press) to have once been her "guardian and foster-father." Apparently Hemmer's paternal duties included helping Mary convince Belasco she was too run down to tour *A Good Little Devil*. He recounted the skirmish when, in 1915, Charlotte asked him to remove her daughter from a New York apartment, probably Kirkwood's. Hemmer also recalled that, at Charlotte's behest, he protected Mary, then still Owen's wife, from the amorous attentions of Douglas Fairbanks. And after Jack's marriage to Marilyn Miller, she tried to keep tabs on her daughter-in-law by getting Hemmer to look into her intimate past.

In Hemmer's view, such personal errands were worth a lot of money. And, as a self-proclaimed family member, Hemmer thought he had a right to some of Charlotte's assets. The lawsuit claimed that at Mary's suggestion, he had put off asking for additional payment, expecting to be mentioned in Charlotte's will. When Charlotte left him nothing, he went back to Pickford, who refused to pay him. Five years later Hemmer sued her to the tune of $250,000.

Mary (who brushed aside reporters with the words "purely fictional") wouldn't budge and sought a court order to silence Hemmer. And it seems she got one, or decided to pay him off – for the final resolution was not revealed. If even a fraction of the claims were true, they showed the powerful Charlotte to be something more: unscrupulous. When Mary silenced Hemmer, she escaped a major scandal. But she must have wept in private – for Charlotte's sake.

In the fall of 1934, the Mary Pickford Stock Radio Company launched a nationwide series of stage and screen adaptations from its home base at WEAF, Los Angeles. Screen actors often did this kind of work; Clark Gable and Claudette Colbert, for instance, appeared in *It Happened One Night* on the airwaves. And though stage actors of the highest rank, including Ethel Barrymore and Helen Hayes, had radio "theaters," the venue notably lacked mystique. Pickford, who had once been borne aloft on Fairbanks's shoulders, now was being carried by Standard Brands, which trumpeted its gelatin through its "stink test." "Does Royal Gelatine in the raw stink? No. Do other competitive brands stink? They do."

Nervously, Mary chose *The Church Mouse* for her debut, and she floundered through rehearsal with a bad case of mike fright. Finally an engineer fitted a lampshade on the microphone to calm her. Still, she was panned on her maiden broadcast. "The voice is undistinguished," wrote a critic, "and there is a slight fuzz on the enunciation, something just this side of a lisp." Worse was her self-conscious, agitated acting. "Sentiment and comedy are better when they are burdened with no evidence of the laborious effort that might have gone into their creation. Miss Pickford brought to her performance a quality which baffled us for a few minutes but which we were at length able to identify as dogged determination. In her giggles there is a hint of hysteria, in her simple moments a haunting flavor of idiocy . . . she put every nuance into italics."

Mary soldiered on for several months – then wisely put her radio career aside.

Across the ocean, Douglas Fairbanks had his own distractions. Mary's husband had retreated from the British press to a grand estate with a pedigree dating to the Domesday Book. It was huge, a little way from London but close enough to welcome friends – new ones only. Jayar was in England, too, making films and doing plays. His premature marriage had soon dwindled away (Crawford filed for divorce in 1933), and he was now a social darling with a circle that often overlapped his dad's (the Astaires, Noël Coward, and the Prince of Wales). Still, he was absent from the Fairbanks revels – and confessed, looking back, that he was just as glad. Fairbanks was now seen publicly in casinos and nightclubs, just the kind of life he had once decried. At his residence there were hints of laxness. "Pomp and circumstance," wrote Letitia. "Mostly circumstance, the com promising kind."

In 1934 Fairbanks made his swan song, *The Private Life of Don Juan*. It seemed to hold his interest briefly, though only as an actor. The producer of the film was Alexander Korda, who became a UA partner the next year. It was shot in his studio in London. The script was both cerebral and picaresque – offering, in the package of a comic romance, a meditation on fame and its interplay with age. Fairbanks, as Don Juan, finds it hard to compete with the image of his younger self. Women who once fell hard reject him. Instead, they fall into the arms of a younger, more virile fraud. The movie touches as an act of reinvention and repentance. Don Juan –

and Fairbanks, one infers – has buried the past and wants a future, both as an artist and as a man. Indeed, in the last reel, the great lover wearies of the chase, passes the flame to his competition, and, vanquished, asks his wife's forgiveness. Mary must have watched these scenes with interest.

On January 10, 1935, she obtained her provisional divorce decree. Its terms were simple. Fairbanks kept the ranch and Santa Monica beach house, and Mary would continue to reign at Pickfair. Not that she intended to spend much time there. There were too many scripts to read, too many projects, so much to discover in her new career. Mary knew how to deal with grief. She was trouping.

On May 19, the play *Coquette* was presented at Seattle's Metropolitan Theatre. It featured Ann Kirby in a tiny role, and within a week, the actress was surrounded by reporters. "How do you know I'm Gwynne?" she asked. "No, I don't want to talk about it," she continued. "I don't think my aunt would want me to."

Mary, who was starring in the play, took over. "She's really only a high school girl and we didn't want to spoil her normal girlhood." Gwynne was in Seattle as a good-luck charm. And it seems to have worked. Mary's entrance was greeted with so much applause that the actress broke character and wept. "Her performance was superlative throughout," wrote a critic, and another declared she had carried him off "to the land of enchantment." One would think such reviews might carry Pickford off to the land of Broadway. But instead, she made light of the acclaim, described *Coquette* as a lark, and said that neither she nor Gwynne knew what they would do in the future. "This isn't her debut," said Mary gaily, "nor my comeback."

In the end, she might arrange to take *Coquette* on tour – a short one, up the northwest coast, with a stop across the border in Vancouver. (And in fact, the tour was planned, before Pickford lost her nerve and had the bookings canceled.) Or she might try a play called *The Demi-Widow*. She had written a novel by this name, and Belle Burns Gromer, who had ghosted it for her, met her in Seattle to discuss the project. But *The Demi-Widow*, which was published that August, seems to have been written with a rapturous eye not on the stage but on the worst of silent movies. It's a nightmare concoction of erotic clichés, and a transparent plea to Douglas Fairbanks. By day the heroine, a Pickfordish sparrow named Coralee, is all modesty, sweetness, and mother love. By night she is Coco, a pencil-slim showgirl – and "a brazen little hussy who receives men in her negligée." This shimmering sophisticate bewitches Camilo – the dashing Latin lover with "derisive dark eyes" (who seems not like Fairbanks, but like the man he once chased away from Pickfair: Valentino). "I've been a fool," Camilo says as he bares his soul to Coco. "I suppose you love hearing a man admit it." But when Coco, in return, must reveal her true identity, Camilo is even more entranced by her quaint little Pickfordish persona. The novel ends as "a masterful arm" (it belongs to the hero) draws Coralee "back into the circle of his embrace."

As if on cue, Douglas Fairbanks came to Pickfair.

According to Mary, this was "one of the strangest and most heartbreaking aspects of the whole affair. . . . He came back to California to try to prevent the divorce. I remember how shocked I was at his appearance; there was still the old vitality and physical glow, but something was gone. It was as though his spirit had fled. In the past I could always sense what Douglas was thinking and feeling. I could even read his face." Now, though her "heart wept," she refused him.

Fairbanks, undaunted, tried another route. He returned to England and sent Beth a wire, which he asked her to read aloud to Mary. It contained about two hundred words of guilt; he begged her, romanced her, on his knees. Beth read it to Pickford, who wouldn't bend. "What I knew personally about Douglas was one thing; but when the whole world was brought in on it, that was something else."

As the date of the final decree drew near, a dazed disbelief overtook their friends. It seemed inconceivable to all who knew them that a marriage so idealized could founder. But though Pickford and Fairbanks still loved each other, there was also a sense that events had overtaken them, that somehow their estrangement had a life of its own and must play itself out to its last, sad gasp.

On January 10, 1936, Mary's final divorce decree was granted. That night Fairbanks dined in New York at a night spot called Connie's Inn. Beside him sat Adele Astaire (Fred's dancing sister). The orchestra leader saw Fairbanks in the candlelight, sitting with a tall, rather glittering woman, and sent out a song in Sylvia's name. Then the nightclub watched, amazed, as the actor rose from his chair abruptly and hurried off before a note was played.

He had "rediscovered" Mary, he told his brother. He pronounced her his "one and only love." For the first time in years, his mind was clear. He would go to Los Angeles and win his wife back. He was tired and beaten, but he was single-minded, and as he trained west he felt newly sane.

Now he went every day to Pickfair, taking his ex-wife out for drives as he had in the old days before their marriage. She was kind, considerate – and asked for time. She refused the gift of a diamond bracelet. On some days she simply refused to see him. Then Fairbanks visited Jayar, who was living at the beach house in Santa Monica, or Mary Margaret Fairbanks, John Fairbanks's daughter. "He'd talk about settling down in a villa in Rome and reading books," she remembered later. As the twilight deepened, they played double solitaire, and Fairbanks held forth on his new philosophy. "When you've been every place, seen everything, there's nothing left to strive for." Such talk alarmed her. It alarmed Mary Pickford even more. "Why don't we go away together," he proposed, "and live in peace, perhaps in Switzerland, or if you like we can build on the ranch as we've always planned." Pickford rejected him once again.

Slowly he realized the truth. It was February 1936, and the time had come to "play the Arab, fold my tent, and sneak away" – or, in plain language, take a train to New York. At each stop, he sent his wife telegrams. Jayar, who was traveling with him, couldn't remember the words, "but I do recall the tone. He was pleading, beseeching, he crawled. He was prepared to take all the blame, not only for his own indiscretions but for hers." Often Fairbanks sat alone in his compartment while Jayar watched from a connecting room. In Chicago he asked the United Artists office if a telegram had come from California. Told there was none, he placed a call to Pickfair, only to be told by his old majordomo that the lady of the house was not at home. As Fairbanks boarded the Twentieth Century Limited, depression fell upon him like railway dust.

In New York, Jayar kept his father buoyant – or tried to – by dragging him off to Broadway shows. But when he was recognized by crowds, Fairbanks stared out with glaring eyes and scuttled off. Nor could he endure any backstage hubbub; he grew visibly frantic and retreated. Jayar watched with trepidation as Pete seemed to fall into a walking delirium. Still, he was cheered when his father agreed to meet him at breakfast to discuss working side by side in films. To the younger actor, who grew up watching Fairbanks in the movies and thinking, with wonder, "That's my father!" the plan seemed too splendid to be true.

Jayar appeared at his father's hotel the next morning at nine and asked the desk clerk to ring his father's room. "Your father has checked out," the clerk replied.

Fairbanks Jr. listened, stunned, as the clerk gabbled on that Fairbanks Sr. had left in the middle of the night for Europe. "Oh, sir!" said the clerk as he turned away. "There's something here in the box for him. . . . It must have come last night. Shall I give it to you?"

He saw it was a telegram, signed Hipper.

Jayar gathered his wits, took the key to his father's room, and searched it, hoping to turn up the name of his ship and destination. So did Tom Geraghty, who had also heard the news of Pete's strange departure. Finally they telephoned Frank Case, who reported that the actor had called after midnight, too agonized to sleep and strangely angry. Ever the hotelier, Case had booked him on a predawn voyage toward Sylvia. Jayar, growing slowly frantic, tried to reach the ship by phone. At last Fairbanks took the call and listened as his son read the wire in triumph. It said, in effect, that Mary forgave him. She was ready to take him back; come home.

Well, answered Fairbanks, it was all a plot, arranged by Mary's allies, for the pleasure of seeing him "jump through hoops." When Geraghty and Case took the phone, Fairbanks shouted that these, his oldest friends, had turned against him. Stunned, Jayar got in touch with Mary. Quickly she called her ex-husband's ship and repeated the contents of her wire. Now there was a long pause.

"It's too late." Another long pause, then Fairbanks mumbled: "It's just too late."

Sylvia had consented to become his wife. On March 7, 1936, Fairbanks married her in Paris.

A few years later he was living in semiseclusion at the beach house with Sylvia. There was no large studio, no playland of trampolines and mats. There was no glory, no films to make, no army of servants at his beck and call. Instead, Fairbanks mixed a few drinks (for others), played cards, and told a few old stories. He played the inevitable rounds of golf. But on certain afternoons Fairbanks stole away to spend some quiet hours at Pickfair. By the pool he sat at Mary's side, and sometimes she let him hold her hand. "What a mistake, Mary," he finally told her. Pickford looked at the horizon and said, "I'm sorry."

11

—

WHAT'S A MARY
PICKFORD FOR?

"When the spirit of the people is lower than at any other time during this Depression," said President Franklin Roosevelt, "it is a splendid thing that for just 15 cents, an American can go to a movie and look at the smiling face of a baby and forget his troubles." The baby with the smiling face was Shirley Temple.

Her career had begun as a glimmer in the eye of her mother, Gertrude, whose gaze first settled on silent star Pearl White's athletic spunk, then fastened, enraptured, on Little Mary. In 1931 she began to twist her three-year-old's hair into a mass of Pickford inspired ringlets. The next year Shirley left dancing school to join the "Baby Burlesk" one-reelers, a series that featured her in diapers and with, depending on the film, a pink garter or a rose behind her ear. From there she hopped, twinkling, into features, though in 1934 the six-year-old paused to sing and dance in *New Deal Rhythm*, a two-reel showcase for Buddy Rogers. In 1935 she was anointed with a special doll-sized Oscar. "When Santa Claus brought you down Creation's chimney," presenter Irvin S. Cobb informed her, "he brought the loveliest Christmas present that has ever been given to the world." Temple, like Santa, did her bit for the economy. Her face sold children's dresses, dishware, sheet music, sewing sets, pocket mirrors, playing cards, pads of paper, ankle socks, and candy molds.

"Shirley was the instrument on which her mother played," said Allan Dwan, who directed three Shirley Temple films. He was an old hand at managing strong, possessive mothers, as he'd seen it all before – "with Mary Pickford."

There were other parallels. Temple, like Pickford, played fix-it children. She melted the hearts of gruff old men and "healed" the repressed adults around her. She pouted, much in the O-shaped Pickford style. In 1935 an even more Pickfordesque image was fostered by a Fox film called *Curly Top*, based on *Daddy-Long-Legs*. In the Temple film, the heroine does a grown-up hula and executes a tap dance on a baby grand piano.

Following the birth of 20th Century–Fox, Darryl Zanuck took charge of Shirley's future. And, in a way, he took charge of Little Mary, continuing to piggyback Temple's image on the fading penumbra of Pickford's work. There were plans to revamp both *Fanchon the Cricket* and *Pollyanna*, but the adaptations never reached the screen. Instead, in 1936 *Poor Little Rich Girl* emerged with Shirley as the lonely Gwen – this time, the daughter of a soap tycoon. One day she wanders away from home and is sheltered by a poor but kind vaudeville team. And her latent talent for singing and tap dancing lands her on the radio, advertising soap for her father's rival. Two years later *Rebecca of Sunnybrook Farm* reprised the radio theme, allowing Temple's "cheerful little earful" to sing her way into America's hearts for Crackling Grain Flakes ("makes your tummy say yum-yum-yummy"). In 1939 *The Little Princess* diluted the power of the classic with pointless subplots, dance routines, and gurgling and burbling from its star.

"Oh, she was the cutest baby," Pickford sighed. And Mary saw herself in Temple – the curls, the fame, the working childhood. But she didn't understand that Shirley's image was polluting the memory of her own career. Neither did the critic who, in 1938, raved that Temple was "developing the same appeal, puffed sleeves, the ability to smile-through-tears, that made Mary Pickford 'America's Sweetheart.'" In fact, Little Mary was a far more complicated creature, informed by temper, violence, tragedy, street sense, optimism, and slapstick. And with few exceptions, these surfaced in adolescents, not prepubescent girls.

Each time Shirley played a Pickford role, she encouraged the impression that Mary had performed as children *only*. And she also changed the popular memory of how Mary had played them. In 1987 critic Molly Haskell complained that Pickford's "childish ebullience ... masks a calculating spirit. As the little hands clap in glee, the little mind is contriving how to get what it wants, how to charm the little boy or the disagreeable old man." But Haskell got it wrong. The description does not match Mary's work (and not all critics agree with Haskell), but it does reflect the aftertaste of Shirley Temple.

Temple left one critic cold. "Infancy is her disguise," raged novelist Graham Greene, who often wrote film reviews. "Her appeal is more secret and more adult." Greene claimed she "wore trousers with the mature suggestiveness of a Dietrich." In 1937 he called her performance in *Wee Willie Winkie* "completely totsy. Watch her swaggering stride across the Indian barrack-square: hear the gasp of excited expectation from her antique audience when the sergeant's palm is raised: watch the way she measures a man with agile studio eyes, with dimpled depravity. Adult emotions of love and grief glissade across the mask of childhood, a childhood skin-deep.... Her admirers – middle-aged men and clergymen – respond to her dubious coquetry, to the sight of her well-shaped and desirable little body, packed with enormous vitality, only because the safety curtain of story and dialogue drops between their intelligence and their desire."

None of this confusion was Temple's fault. She was talented, eager to please, and sweet. She performed as directed. Unfortunately, Shirley was directed to act, sing, and dance like a Ziegfeld girl. Mary had distinctly different gifts. She had not forgotten, as had Temple's directors, how a child thinks, feels, and moves her body. (Greene, who admired Pickford, never linked her acting to Temple's work.) Nevertheless, in the early thirties the impression grew that Pickford's films were a tainted brew of ringlets and infantile sexual signals.

Pickford didn't help by constantly referring to her own celluloid image as "the little girl." She had long since accepted that her hard-core viewers were obsessed with the children she played onscreen. And she no longer tried to counteract the image. Instead, the actress bowed her head and honored the roles that had once confined her, gushing that in "*Stella Maris* I played *two* young girls." Remarks like these implied that Pickford's darkest film had the hopping, skipping charm of "The Mickey Mouse Club."

Because silent film had lost its market, the real Little Mary could no longer be seen. Pickford, ironically, was glad. Her work, she claimed, was impossibly dated – a source of shame. In fact, her best films were "already old-fashioned. It is marvelous for me to remember *Daddy-Long-Legs*. I do not want to see it. I am more happy now in the memory of it than I was during the success of it." Her explanation, one she repeated throughout her life, implied that her films, in the light of the talkies, had failed as art. "I would rather be a beautiful illusion in the minds of people," she told – almost scolded – *Photoplay*, "than a horrible example on celluloid. I pleased my own generation. That is all that matters."

In February 1936 Mary began to host *Parties at Pickfair*, an ill-fated radio show that was broadcast coast to coast. The program supposedly unveiled a rarefied world of demigods, who swish past a butler in the latest clothes, greet Mary, and charmingly dish the dirt. "Grim," was the verdict of the *New York Post*. "Of virtually no entertainment value." And the critic detected a "note of hysterical desperation" as guests tried to imitate Noël Coward. With the show in trouble, the sponsors (Ice Dealers – "Cold Alone Is Not Enough") added Sidney Skolsky, a gossip columnist, who gave the show a little zest by lowering the tone. In April the *New York Post* heard improvement: "It was almost possible to develop the illusion that we were eavesdropping on Mary Pickford and her dinner guests. That illusion, however, was created at the expense of listening to an unconscionable amount of lip smacking and talk about the mouth-watering food."

There was another, more deadly flaw. The Pickford mystique had eroded badly. She was "alone, rich, and a little *passé* in her chosen field." Her fame had entered "the pathetic has-been." No one really cared about who she knew, what she thought, or what went on at Pickfair. Actors as well as listeners knew it.

She had fallen from grace as a producer, too. Creating silent movies had been instinctive; Mary knew what was right for her persona, and this touched the heart of the popular mainstream. Now she couldn't find the public pulse. Still, faced with United Artists' product crisis (which was greatly intensified by the loss of Zanuck), Mary tried, halfheartedly, to contribute.

She might have made a good film from "Little Liar." The story, which appeared under Pickford's name in *Good Housekeeping* (1934), echoed not only her early life but the lives of the children she had played onscreen. Its golden-haired heroine, Veronica, is a veteran "baby" actress who has played Little Eva and innumerable dog-eared melodramas. Veronica's mother, who has recently died, was a talented seamstress as well as a nurturing, empathic actress. Inevitably, Veronica is taken in by a humorless, unforgiving aunt, which leads to the patented clash of wills. The tale, with its links to the thin-skinned, impressionable Baby Gladys, might have truly engaged Mary Pickford, producer.

But she didn't produce it. Nor did Pickford pursue the truly awful idea of a singing *Dorothy Vernon of Haddon Hall* (Nelson Eddy and Jeanette MacDonald would have starred). She did not turn her hand to a talking *Suds* or put a hillbilly twang to *The Heart o' the Hills*. Her book *The Demi-Widow*, which reads like a bad movie, never became one. Instead, Mary paired up with Jesse Lasky, who had been fired by Paramount in 1932 and had spent the intervening years at Fox. In 1936 they released two films: *One Rainy Afternoon* and *The Gay Desperado*. They were frothy, improbable, and dreadful, and the producing team dissolved.

Luckily, Al Lichtman, who replaced Joe Schenck as president of UA in 1935, had a friend who was unhappy with the studio system. David O. Selznick had made his reputation at RKO, with *King Kong* (1933) among his credits. He worked similar wonders at MGM with literary films based on Dickens and Tolstoy. In 1935, after fielding offers, he established Selznick International Pictures and began to distribute through UA.

Lichtman resigned after only three months, his patience exhausted by the bullying Goldwyn. Mary took his place – and presided over one of UA's most embarrassing mistakes.

Apparently the company fussed so long over writing Disney's contract renewal that the artist accepted a counteroffer and announced his departure for RKO. The point of contention was minuscule: Disney's request to control the television broadcast of his films. Mary and Sam Goldwyn, in particular, worried this point to death, though in those days television was still a minor venue. But even if one credits United Artists with a farsighted vision of television's future, it should have been plain that Disney's talents were worth almost any price the artist asked.

After his departure Disney wrote to UA about a distribution buyout (he still owed them a raft of short cartoons and wished to give the rights to RKO). Mary, now shocked into a state of alertness, responded coldly that UA "would not consider it, not even for three times that sum as it would prove a serious loss of prestige." The addition of Walter Wanger, an accomplished producer, to the UA stable only slightly counteracted Mary's botch.

Industry watchers shook their heads – and perhaps a few recalled Mary's words in 1920, when she claimed that her mother was "the business brain. I just second the motion." And her partners may have echoed Pickford's depressed cry to a fan magazine in 1931: "If mother had only lived!"

"Poor Chuckie," wrote Mary, "she was never the same after Jack's going. . . . It was as though with my brother's passing the better part of her had died too." Lottie and Jack "were so very close in temperament and even in looks." And very close, too, in wasted promise.

"Once," remembered Mary, "Lottie and I were called for a theatrical engagement, as children. Lottie went back to the house to get something she had forgotten. I caught the street car and I got the job. I always think that if Lottie had been with me, she would have won it. Maybe that's what decided our fates." Here Pickford shows more guilt than sense. Lottie, like Jack, was a good enough actor but lacked brilliance, charisma, and self-discipline.

So did her third husband, Russel O. Gillard. In February 1933, after four years of marriage, Lottie went to divorce court, claiming, "I put him in business but it failed because of negligence. He wouldn't work." The judge agreed and gave her a provisional decree.

In June Lottie startled the press with the announcement that several months earlier she had married a Pittsburgh society man named John William Lock. Unfortunately, her divorce from Gillard was not yet final. Speaking from Chicago, Lottie giggled, "If this gets back to Los Angeles there'll be trouble.... But of course, the California authorities must prove where our secret marriage took place before they can separate us." She continued gaily, "I'm the one who would go to jail if we went back. Jack's never been married before."

Mary, who openly adored her brother, was far more closemouthed regarding Lottie. In her memoirs she defended Jack, gave the Pickford version of his various scandals, and called him an "infinitely superior" actor. At least Jack worked, in over forty features. Lottie, on the other hand, appeared in eight (in addition to the serial *The Diamond from the Sky*), and Mary remarked on none of them. Perhaps, like the press, she couldn't make much sense of her sister. And one can only speculate on Lottie's resentment of a sibling who not only raised her daughter but thoroughly eclipsed her in wealth, beauty, talent, and Charlotte's favor. ("Mary," she once asked, "how does it feel to have been able to give Mama everything her heart desired, and all the fame and honor besides?") One can speculate, too, on Mary's guilt – for when Lottie, showing rare ambition, tried to launch a children's radio program, her sister shouted, "One Pickford on the radio at a time is enough." "Auntie broke my mother's heart," remembered Gwynne.

The last time Mary saw her sister, they were listening to Lottie's piano teacher sing "Oh, Jesus, When I'm Sad and Lonely." Lottie had made a bet that Mary couldn't listen to the hymn without crying, and within a few verses Mary gladly paid the penalty of a dollar. The three then spoke about the Bible, for Lottie, too, had taken a religious turn. The scene, as it appears in Pickford's memoirs, is rendered in a suffocating moral tone, with Mary, in her piety, the haloed star. "Where two or three are gathered together in My name," said Pickford, in the Savior's words, "there am I in the midst of them." Then she closed, in her wisdom, with the immaculate pronouncement, "I'm sure He's been here with the three of us today."

On December 9, 1936, Lottie Pickford fell suddenly to the floor. She had suffered a heart attack and died, so her doctor said, standing up. And Mary's first reaction, as it often was in crisis, was a vividly detailed mental image. She was gripped by the memory of a saucy-sweet, laughing little girl. She and Lottie were young again, "out chasing sleds in Toronto, hooking our own to the big horse-drawn sleighs. Suddenly, Lottie was catapulted from her tiny sled into a bank of snow. I rushed to her side in terror, certain that she was dangerously hurt, and pulled her out of the snow. That lovely pink face of hers and generous mouth were covered with snow; even the long, dark eyelashes were white with it. I saw her brightly colored, tasseled stocking cap, and I became dizzy with the wave of love that came over me. I gave my unspoken thanks to God that Lottie was safe. I thought to myself, 'This is my very own little sister.'"

"They never should have divorced," said Gwynne of her Aunt Mary and Uncle Douglas. "Neither of them survived it, they both lost heart."

Fairbanks still felt intimately tied to Mary. His niece Letitia once recalled that at a UA meeting, an irritated partner shook his fist at Pickford. "How dare you talk to my wife like that?" shouted Fairbanks, although he and Mary were already divorced. Then he threw the offender out the door. Perhaps this slip of the tongue was encouraged by the fact that Mary, who was feeling ill, had called the group together in her bedroom at Pickfair.

As for Mary, her efforts to sparkle on the public scene seemed a transparent ruse. "Watching her dancing around the smart places of Manhattan with a young boy like Buddy Rogers, trying to be gay, making an effort to look romantic, the onlooker is more touched by the spectacle than by any of those sad little cinema tragedies of her past." And the age gap, in those days, strained credulity. "She was so much older," said Lina Basquette, a silent-film actress who married Sam Warner. "Everyone wondered how she got away with it. People said Buddy was after her money." Or perhaps he hoped to advance his fame by marrying film's most sacred symbol. If so, he chose his actress badly, for though Little Mary's allure remained, her aura was that of antique lace.

People knew, or thought they knew, what Mary wanted: Buddy's youth ("his damnable youth," in Fairbanks's eyes). Indeed, she seemed overly proud of his looks – this, too, a probable swipe at Fairbanks. And she may have hoped that, on Rogers's arm, she would emerge a younger, more 1930s woman. Unfortunately Buddy's fame sank to the middle ranks, a calamity for which the actor blamed himself. "I just jumped from stage, to band, to movie." The result: "I was neither fish nor fowl." Rogers once called his break with Paramount "the worst move I ever made" – sensing, perhaps, that his music was passable, nothing more. But he didn't think much of his acting either: "I was never any good," he said frankly. "I couldn't act worth beans."

But he always had fans in his faithful Olathe. The hometown paper recorded, for instance, his last-minute rescue of Connee Boswell. In May 1937 the jazz singer fell asleep in her dressing room, holding a cigarette. Rogers, who was playing on the same bill, snatched her from a burning couch, then personally beat out the flaming bedclothes. Six weeks later there were more heroics, as Buddy outdid himself with a feat some were betting he would never accomplish.

"At first," wrote Pickford in *Sunshine and Shadow*, "I put the thought of another marriage far from me." But Rogers, who began proposing as soon as she received her divorce decree, grew tired of prevarication. Like Fairbanks and Owen Moore before him, he finally had to issue an ultimatum. "It is foolish to go on this way," he told her. "You know exactly how I feel. It has never been a secret to you or to anyone else.... If you do not want to marry me, then in all fairness to us both you must let me know. It is entirely up to you now. I shall never bring it up again."

Pickford thought. Rogers loved her, promised to protect her. He was simple and ingenuous: even the Fairbanks family loved him. He was passive and conventional, and promised a more tranquil life than Fairbanks. And Mary valued loyalty above all else. Rogers, who had held her hand, adored, and supported her for years, had already demonstrated his commitment. And he thought her young and beautiful. It was enough.

To a *Liberty* reporter, Mary spoke of the difficult years behind her. "Do you know that I am finding it pleasant to shrink in the public eye, to recede from view? When my success was at its top I was pushed along at a terrific pace. There was no privacy. Look how silent this apartment is now." Indeed, she seemed magically at ease. "It's sort of a relief to have it over. At least, to get over the highest hurdles of fame." It would be easy, Mary thought, to reshape her life: "I think – in fact I'm sure – I shall sell Pickfair. For one thing, I want to get a small house on Lake Arrowhead. The sort of place where you can rough it by yourself." In Los Angeles she envisioned a carefree, unobtrusive home, where the hours would be whiled away at riding, horseshoes, archery, tennis, and "all kinds of games.... Everything will be less formal. I should like to live more within myself." And less, one infers, for Little Mary and her paralyzing load of obligations.

All this was said with a kind of wonder, as though Pickford had passed through the slough of despond and was still a bit awed by her own resilience. "I shall never present myself again in films. Neither am I going back to the theater. I have gotten rid of that ambition, along with others. Maybe I am growing sane." And she wished to share her newfound knowledge. "Living for self alone is not enough. You become narrow, selfish, limited." Through marriage she would realize life's completeness.

On June 17 she applied for the marriage license, holding Buddy's arm as they dashed through a gauntlet of bouquets and cameras. It was published that her wedding dress would be ice-blue crepe with a hat to match. "Very Mary Pickfordish," said a friend, who was struck by its oldfashioned halo brim. Mary, who wished to extinguish America's Sweetheart, changed the ensemble and went to the altar in a small, felt hat.

On June 24, 1937, she was married at the home of Hope Loring, who had brought the bride and groom together. Pickford kept them waiting for ten minutes or so; she had panicked while getting dressed at Pickfair. According to Gwynne, who danced in attendance, "the dress didn't fit right and had to be pinned. She kept stamping her foot and squealing – almost crying – 'I don't wanna' – like one of the little girls in her films." But when she appeared with a spray of orchids, Pickford looked younger than she had in years. The groom was waiting at a sycamore tree hung with calla lilies. Together they knelt on satin pillows and said their vows to love and honor – but not to obey, a phrase that the tempestuous bride deleted. Thirty guests attended, with only two representing Mary's family (Gwynne and Verna, Lizzie's daughter). John Lock was present as a bridge to Lottie. Then one and all flocked to a reception for three hundred, held at Pickfair.

For the next forty years, Buddy pointedly called his wife "Mrs. Rogers." "I'll get Mrs. Rogers..." "Mrs. Rogers says..." This, some thought, was a signal to the world that he had conquered not Pickford but Douglas Fairbanks. Nevertheless, the impression lingered that Fairbanks, not Rogers, was the victor. Douglas Fairbanks Jr., who admired Rogers and was genuinely glad to see Mary settled, wondered as late as 1988: "Was Mary's decision to marry Buddy revenge on Pete? Who could tell? Who could speak with real authority?" Gwynne thought she could, and her words were brutal. "She dangled [Buddy] in front of Douglas, kept him waiting in the wings, and married him out of spite."

Perhaps this was an element. And certainly revenge was sometimes sweet. Pickford glowed when, after she arrived at a United Artists meeting with Rogers in tow, Fairbanks said, "Well, you're a good picker, Mary; he certainly is a handsome guy." But he dreaded a confrontation between his ex-wife and the slinky Sylvia. Once, as Mary tried to leave a meeting, Fairbanks took her elbow. "Don't go out now, Hipper; you'll run into our current wife." (Hipper took the advice.) A few weeks later, when a mischief-making Gloria Swanson asked both women to a party of film folk, Fairbanks tried to intercede again. But this time Pickford steeled herself and asked her ex-husband to introduce them. When he refused, Pickford crossed the room to Sylvia, which was much admired. Feeling her height, Sylvia knelt on a chair so she could meet Mary's eyes, and, in deference, she fetched her a cup of tea. "I hear Pickfair is for sale," said Lady Ashley. (She was still known by the title although she could not legally claim it.) "What a shame." "Pickfair," Mary answered, "has served its purpose."

The women met again, much to Mary's shock. Pickford was sitting on a plane en route to Washington, holding her jewel box on her lap for safe-keeping. Then the new Mrs. Fairbanks, who was booked on the same flight, sashayed down the aisle with a familiar air and sat next to Pickford, intent on girl talk.

"Pickey, dear," said Sylvia, "let me see your jewels."

Mary flinched (no one called her "Pickey"), and the prospect of a tête-à-tête with Sylvia petrified her. Still, she gave her rival a wide-eyed smile. "Of course," she said smoothly, "I want you to see them, because Douglas gave them all to me."

Then she took them out, stone by dazzling stone. There were emeralds, sapphires (as big as quarters), a diamond set including huge teardrop earrings, and a ruby set worthy of czarist Russia. "This was for my birthday," said Mary idly, "and this one was for nothing at all — just a Tuesday present." Then she asked Sylvia to show *her* jewels. Sylvia stammered — all she had to show was a minor pin — and explained that she hadn't been married long.

By the time they reached Washington, where Mary deplaned, she was enervated after hours of not only matching wits but hiding the shock of sitting next to Sylvia. And, in her exhaustion, she forgot her jewels. But Sylvia didn't. She continued to New York to join her husband and didn't let the Tuesday presents out of her sight. Later she telephoned "Pickey, darling," assuring her "your jewels are safe with me." "Mary thanked her," remembered Colleen Moore, "thinking what a delicious scene there would be when Doug tried to explain that the fabulous earrings were not a present from him, and that he had not bought the rubies either – Mary had paid for them herself. An ex-wife does sometimes have her moments."

The *New York Times* announced the asking price for Pickfair: half a million dollars. It was rumored that Beverly Hills would be the buyer, and that Pickfair – always a draw for tourists – would be turned into a park or film museum. When Mary and Buddy returned from Hawaii, where they honeymooned, they moved into Rogers's home. It was near the Riviera Country Club, where the couple wore natty clothes and trotted down the bridle path; Rogers made use of the polo grounds and planned to raise ponies for the sport. But the reinvention didn't work; Pickford grew restless, and Buddy sensed it. There was no sustained effort to find the new home and new life they envisioned. One day Mary simply told her husband it was time to pack. And with that, she and Rogers drove up the mountain, where Pickfair's symbolic freight awaited.

In the summer of 1936 UA had elected yet another president, a financier named A.H. Giannini. He was both a sharp banker and a gentle soul, lending vast sums to film producers and often resolving the feuds and quarrels that regularly sprang up among the studios.

After his appointment he told the press, "The greatest need of the motion picture industry at the present time is peace.... There are many deals held up and never completed because one individual may not like another individual, no matter what the result may be. In the United Artists Corp., we shall never permit personal differences, either inside or outside the organization, to interfere with our work." But no one at UA paid him heed. "All my life I've been an adventurer," Giannini said later, "and have been in a lot of tough situations. But let me tell you, I never saw fights like the ones at U.A. board meetings in my life."

In 1937 Sam Goldwyn announced at a directors' meeting that the founding partners were "parasites." Indeed, he had made more films for United Artists than the total of the three remaining founders combined. Now, with near-maniacal anger, Goldwyn thundered that the founders should renounce their interests – to himself, of course, and he offered them half a million dollars each. Pickford, Fairbanks, and Chaplin laughed. But then they retired to another room, wondering if indeed they were ready to slip the reins. When they returned, they reported their price: two million dollars each. Frustrated, Goldwyn invited Korda to join him in raising the sum, but the two men failed.

In 1938 Mary frittered away her time by writing columns for the *New York Journal* – chitchat with celebrities, including Buddy, and innocuous comments on social problems. But this failed to have the impact of "Daily Talks," and one day the column disappeared. This was also the year of Mary Pickford Cosmetics – an unthinkable project when Mary's fame was pristine. But at age forty-six, it served a useful goal: the appearance of purpose, of moving forward. Ads showed the actress looking lustrously well brushed (the granite jaw, though, seems a bit forbidding). "When I had these products made up for my exclusive use, they actually cost me considerably more than the prices I have placed on them for you." But the advertising campaign cost more than the actress had planned to spend, and the production of lipstick and cold cream ended.

Goldwyn, on the other hand, was driven. While Mary was preoccupied with dusting powder, he kept up a furious pace producing. In 1939 he stunned the partners by demanding to be made the sole voting trustee. That way, though they still owned stock, Goldwyn could elect his own board of directors and turn UA into his personal fiefdom. Pickford, Fairbanks, and Korda sat numb with shock. Chaplin, who no longer came to meetings when he knew Sam Goldwyn would attend, had sent his proxy, lawyer Charles Schwartz. The meeting became a shambles as Goldwyn exercised his veto on all company business, swearing to continue till he got his way. At the meeting's end, Schwartz became incensed: "Get out, you punk," he shouted at the producer of *Wuthering Heights*, "and take your 'Murdering Heights' with you."

The crisis took two years to resolve. With the partners at an impasse, Goldwyn sued to be released from his distributing contract. But UA, which needed his movies, fought him. The case dragged on, incurring huge costs to all concerned, and ended only when Goldwyn's wife, Frances, drove up to Pickfair and threw herself, shaking, at Mary's feet. "I beg for my husband and child," she sobbed. Fear of destitution, love of family — these were the chinks in Pickford's armor. "Don't do that," she said, shocked and embarrassed. "I'll settle. But for God's sake, get up, Frances." From then on, work on the stalled matter picked up speed. On March 11, 1941, Sam Goldwyn sold United Artists back his stock, dissolved his contract, and went off to pick his distribution quarrels elsewhere.

"I'm not superstitious, not really," wrote Pickford, who regularly visited fortune-tellers. Apparently none of her psychic friends had predicted that Gwynne, who was feeling smothered, was planning to emancipate herself from Pickfair. On May 31, 1939, she allowed her aunt to believe she was spending the day at home. Instead, she eloped with a radio announcer — much older, incidentally — named Hugh Ernst. The couple were married in Las Vegas. Betrayed, Mary could not speak to Gwynne for weeks.

On June 11, 1939, Pickford asked an Irish maid to read her tea leaves. "I see someone stretched out lifeless," said the maid. "He is close to you and he is not close to you. He is either dying or dead, but I don't see you crying." The next day, Owen Moore, fifty-six, was found sprawled on his kitchen floor. Still a hard drinker, he had died, it was said, of a cerebral hemorrhage, and the body lay for two days before discovery.

Six months later, on December 12, Mary answered the phone in her suite at Chicago's Drake Hotel. It was four in the morning — an ominous hour, and as soon as she heard Gwynne's voice, she guessed.

Fairbanks had died of a heart attack. A few days before, he had suffered chest pains and hobbled to bed on doctor's orders. The next day the actor saw his brother Robert. Six years earlier, on his fiftieth birthday, Fairbanks had told Robert he was bored with life; he'd done everything he wanted, twice, and wished for nothing more than a sudden death. Fairbanks told

Robert that should he die, he would like him to give Mary Pickford a message. It was an old code: "By the clock."

On December 11, Fairbanks Jr. tiptoed into his father's room. It was dark, but he made out his father's mastiff, and Fairbanks, who feebly raised a hand. "It was never easy for us," recalled Jayar, "to be completely natural." Still, there had been almost intimate moments. Pete seemed unruffled by glowing reviews for Fairbanks Jr. in such picaresque fare as *The Prisoner of Zenda* (1937) and *Gunga Din* (1939). In the spring he had stood as best man at Jayar's marriage to Mary Lee Hartford (née Epling), who had recently divorced the heir to the A&P grocery fortune. "Now, as he lay there," wrote Jayar, "weak and dependent, it seemed as though we had exchanged relationships. I was the parent and he the child – the very ill child." They chatted, and Jayar volunteered to read. He cautiously took his father's hand and, after some passages from Byron and Shakespeare, Fairbanks fell asleep. Jayar kissed his father's forehead – the first kiss between them – and slipped out.

That night Fairbanks's nurse asked how he was feeling, and the actor flashed the old grin: "I've never felt better." A few hours later the nurse was in the hall and heard Polo, the mastiff, give a growl. He looked in and found his patient dead.

As Mary hung up, she checked her tears – she thought it was the least she could do for Buddy – and went to work on a formal statement. "I am sure it will prove a consolation to us all to recall the joy and the glorious spirit of adventure he gave to the world. He has passed from our mortal life quickly and spontaneously as he did everything in life, but it is impossible to believe that that vibrant and gay spirit could ever perish."

She would not attend the funeral: "I think it's barbaric to look at dead people. The second the spirit leaves the body, the body is nothing but an empty shell." Besides, there was Sylvia to consider. Cynically, actress Gladys Cooper described Lady Ashley, draped in black, but with bright red toenails peeping through her open-toed shoes – "which," she observed, "rather spoils the effect." But Letitia found Sylvia sincere. "I believe that she really loved Uncle Douglas. I never saw anyone collapse the way she did when Uncle Douglas died. And Sylvia grieved that way for months."

Mary wept alone on a train to New York. But first she dialed Chaplin, who had heard the news from Fairbanks Jr. Chaplin would not attend the funeral either: "I couldn't bear to see them put that heavy stone over Douglas." Instead, he observed a day of mourning by shutting down production on his current film. They spoke for an hour of the old days, of frolics on the Pickfair lawn and nights eating popcorn and peanut brittle as the trio watched and criticized one another's films. "You remember how I always showed my pictures first to Douglas," said Chaplin. (The actor, who always loathed his own films, had relied on Fairbanks for reassurance.) "I can still hear Douglas laughing so heartily he couldn't look at the screen," said Mary. "Remember those coughing fits he'd get at that moment?" But the truce was tenuous; as Mary listened, "it all came back to me, how Douglas used to treat Chaplin like a younger brother, listening patiently and intently, hours on end, to his repetitious stories." Now, as Chaplin spoke of their bereavement, she recalled how those same stories "bored me to extinction."

"God felt sorry for actors," declared Sir Cecil Hardwicke, who often left the London stage for film, "so he gave them a place in the sun and a swimming pool. The price they had to pay was to surrender their talent." To Hardwicke, Los Angeles was "Siberia with palms." Journalist Bruce Bliven, passing through, found a "prize collection of . . . placid creatures whose bovine expression shows that each of them is studying, without much hope of success, to be a high-grade moron."

These are typical remarks for the easterners and stage folk who could not abide stop-and-go moviemaking. But despite its somnambulant reputation, there were stirrings of intellect and conscience in the film world. Indeed, in the war years, Hollywood rivaled New York as a source of debate and activism, fueled partly by the presence of European artists who had fled the Nazis to live instead in "a mining camp in Lotus Land" (Scott Fitzgerald). They included writers Bertolt Brecht and Thomas Mann, actors Luise Rainer and Peter Lorre, composers Erich Korngold, Hanns Eisler, and Max Steiner, and directors William Dieterle, Fritz Lang, and Billy Wilder. Their plight, the Spanish Civil War, and the arrival of thousands of Jews in California inspired a lively anti-fascist faction — at least among the film world's liberal thinkers.

Pickford emphatically belonged to another, more right-wing set. She had met Mussolini in the 1920s, and in 1934 she attended an event in New York City to celebrate fascism's fifteenth anniversary. "The last time I visited Italy I found a different spirit there than on my earlier trip. That was because Mussolini had taken it over. Italy has always produced great men and when she needed one most Mussolini was there. Viva Fascismo! Viva Il Duce!" Three years later, after touring Europe, she repeated her praise, adding, "Adolf Hitler? He seems to be a very great fellow, too, for the German people. Things look much better over there."

Gradually Hollywood's left-wing tone was countered by a right-wing ideology so vicious that many liberal thinkers were smeared as Communists. Many were tainted in this anti-Red hysteria, and few suffered longer or more publicly than Chaplin.

Through the years he had become an easy target. In 1931 anti-Chaplin feeling began to swell when, during a publicity tour for *City Lights*, he began to speak freely on political subjects. Patriotism, for instance, he labeled "the worst insanity the world has ever suffered." The fact that Chaplin had not become an American citizen would worry, then inflame many Hollywood conservatives. In the depths of the Depression, critics waited to see if the actor would link the downtrodden Tramp with a political agenda. And indeed, the release of *Modern Times* (1936) led critic Richard Watts Jr. to declare, "Its suggestion of ideas is intermittent and rather vague, but they are definitely Left Wing in their sympathy and interest."

When *The Great Dictator* (1940) ended with a speech in which a poor barber, played by Chaplin, talks of peace and hope, the right-wing community thought it heard code words for Communism. Chaplin also supported a Soviet-American anti-fascist alliance — proof enough, for some, of his degeneracy. "After years of sly pretending," wrote reactionary columnist Westbrook Pegler, "when an open profession of his political faith would have hurt his business, now that he has all the money he needs and has lost his way with the public, [Chaplin] has frankly allied himself with the pro-Communist actors and writers of the theatre and the movies, who call themselves artists, but who are mostly hams and hacks."

Pickford wavered. She admired Pegler. She could work herself into a state about Chaplin, particularly after a drink too many. ("I have read and heard many harsh things about Charlie," she admitted, "and I've said a few myself.") Still, she knew he was no Communist. She also knew the actor could cling, self-destructively, to critical comment – or the slander that passed for it. Once he had carried a press clip in his pocket. It had something to do with the "underfed guttersnipes" who spawned him, and according to Mary, the repulsive prose was "the most scathing denunciation of Charlie Chaplin we had ever seen in print." She and Fairbanks tried in vain to make Chaplin throw the piece away. "Only some mean person suffering from envy and resentment could have written that, Charlie," said Mary indignantly. "Why must you hug a viper to your heart?"

But Chaplin thought Mary patronized him. "She had a reproving way of talking business," he wrote in his memoirs, "addressing me not directly but through the others, that made me feel guilty of gross selfishness." One suspects that this was Mary's intention, though she claimed bewilderment. "I finally became convinced he just didn't want what I wanted, that, somehow, particularly after Douglas' death, I rubbed him the wrong way."

She did her best not to – at least, in one particular disagreement. It was sparked by the activities of David O. Selznick, whose obsessive devotion to *Gone with the Wind* (1939) had transformed him into Hollywood's new colossus. (Unfortunately, *Gone with the Wind* was not distributed by UA. In exchange for the use of its star, Clark Gable, MGM got the contract to distribute the movie.) In 1941 Selznick joined Pickford and Chaplin as a partner, and the company advanced him some production money. Selznick used it up trading talent and properties; UA had thought it would result in films. Chaplin, incensed, launched a complex, venomously worded lawsuit. In 1943 Mary, who had done her share of bickering in the past, wrote Chaplin a forceful, clear-eyed letter. "Does it not strike you as being incongruous, Charlie, that you are suing David for not having produced a picture for three years and yet Douglas and I waited six years for the first Chaplin picture? And twenty odd years ago your picture was certainly as important, if not more so, than David's is to the organization today. Undoubtedly you, too, had reasons for not seeing fit to deliver the much needed product. ... [although] you were morally obligated to Griffith, Douglas and me to lend every possible assistance."

The impassioned letter pleaded for Chaplin to think in the long term, to act in United Artists' interests. "There has been nothing but dissension for the past fifteen years among the owners of the company ... dissension which has paralyzed the activities of the company. And now your lawsuit against David is not the least of these costly and public wrangles." Mary summarized their differences, point by point (blaming Chaplin, on each count, for lack of judgment), and revealed her weariness with the friendship. "You are the last person in the motion picture industry who should ever question my good faith and loyalty to you. But if after twenty-five years of such close partnership, you still don't know me, Charlie, it is useless for me to set forth the innumerable times I have stood loyally by you and have closed my eyes to the many hurts, rebuffs and humiliations I have endured at your hand."

This was followed by a meeting that October, a meeting marked by ill will and gritted teeth. Mary had been thinking about the bylaws. In the old days the founders had decided informally that action should be taken by unanimous vote. Later this requirement was enshrined in law. But "all for one and one for all" was no longer helpful; instead, with a single dissenting vote, a partner could frustrate UA's progress. This, decided Mary, was the root of all UA's recent evils, and she was suing to have unanimity ruled invalid.

"It has always existed," Chaplin said of the veto, "and we functioned."

Pickford said sarcastically, "And how we functioned."

"That is a question of ... opinion," said Chaplin. "You are doing very well," he told her. "So am I. I think we have done very well in the past," he continued, overriding her caustic "thank you." "I think your credit shows so."

Mary flared. "My credit is nothing to the United Artists. If my credit was run like that of the United Artists I would be penniless today." When the shouting died down, Mary declared, "Any business dealings I may be forced to have with him will be done as though with a total stranger."

Without Fairbanks to instigate their meeting, the pair seldom sought each other out. Instead, they nursed petty resentments that once they had checked, for Fairbanks's sake.

In the 1940s Mary Pickford was known to most people as a public-minded, wealthy matron. She had had a career, which some people remembered and others didn't. Most knew she was considered an aristocrat of some sort, and in some obscure way, embodied Good. When the General Federation of Women's Clubs selected its fifty-three women pioneers in 1941, the list included Helen Keller, Eleanor Roosevelt, and Mary Pickford.

Mary's shelf was also crowded with a trusteeship on the board of the Thomas Alva Edison Foundation, three honorary arts degrees, and continuing involvement with the Motion Picture Relief Fund. The Pickfair grounds were used for private functions – charities, mostly – but especially for a new cause, war amputees. In Washington, Pickford aligned herself with the National Youth Administration to provide jobs and guidance to needy students. Apparently FDR suggested that Mary extend her community involvement to a run for the Senate. ("I rejected the idea," she offered later, "because my thinking and his were so far apart.") But her most important contribution, in her own mind, was made in 1941, when she broke the ground for the Motion Picture Country House in Woodland Hills, California, turning over shovelfuls of earth for what would later become not only a residence for deserving performers but a full-scale hospital and a theater, set on rolling, landscaped grounds.

Among all these honors and activities something was still missing: a tribute for Charlotte. A film of her life might do it, with Mary producing. Her mind's eye assembled the heroic scenes: the death of John Charles, the long nights sewing, then the wearisome tours in demeaning plays. It would all end in triumph when Mary went to Biograph and, magically, changed the family's lives. In 1940 Pickford asked Shirley Temple – who was rapidly growing up and losing her audience – to re-create the childhood of America's Sweetheart. Luckily, Temple didn't take the bait; if she had, Mary's image might never have recovered.

Besides, after several disappointing films, Shirley's mother had signed her with a new producer, Edward Small, who distributed his movies through United Artists. Their short list of titles included two Pickford adaptations: *Little Annie Rooney* and *Stella Maris*. A Shirley Temple *Stella* is a terrifying concept – and one that, luckily, never took shape. But *Little Annie Rooney* was eviscerated. Now titled *Miss Annie Rooney* (1942), it concerned a bunch of jitterbugging, wholesome teens. Shirley, as Annie, got her first screen kiss, while her widowed, eccentric father found a way to turn milkweed into rubber.

In 1943 David O. Selznick bought Temple's contract. Undeterred, Mary asked her darling to star in a film called *Junior Miss*, a teen soap with previous incarnations as a *New Yorker* story and a Broadway play.

Temple was amused by all the fuss. After all, she had yet to meet Mary. And when she did – at a press event – Pickford swooped down like a hawk, embraced her effusively "as an old friend," then dragged her off toward a *Life* photographer. "What seemed just another innocent photo opportunity became an announcement," remembered Temple. "Confiding eloquently to the reporter, [Pickford] revealed my next film as *Coquette*, a re-make of her own 1929 starring role. . . . It was news to everyone but her." Pickford was boisterous that night. Temple, on the other hand, shrank from a venture that seemed "at best . . . a clumsy Pickford attempt at self-gratification, at worst her crude comeback attempt riding on my back."

The resulting photo not only sold four million copies of *Life* but, according to Temple, enjoyed "the greatest single-day news photo coverage in movie history." It showed two confident, round-faced women, the same height, walking arm in arm. They radiate confidence, health, and style. But the caption – "Two Greatest Has-Beens" – was gratuitously cruel.

Pickford, reportedly, was shocked. But she wisely took the high road and wrote *Life* a letter, dismissing a Hollywood gossip's claim that she wanted to sue as "stuff and nonsense." "How could I resent being labeled a has-been when I am placed in the same division as a junior miss of 15?" By the way, she added in a shameless plug, "*Junior Miss* is the title of the picture I am shortly to produce." Finally, "many of my friends complimented me and there were some who even said I looked like Shirley Temple's sister. Now tell me – after that would I think of suing *Life*?" The letter burbled on, "It never entered my head."

Onscreen, Little Mary was a friend to children, and in real life she instantly put them at ease. When she was first introduced to Fairbanks Jr., in the 1910s, she sat down immediately on the floor. "Are those your trains? May I play with them too?" Mary remembered later, "I had maternal designs on every baby that played with me on the screen." In the 1920s, she hoped to conceive a child and was on the alert for auspicious signs. ("Mary," Letitia told her drily, "when you're pregnant you will know it with a very *big* sign.") Pickford also told reporters that she hoped she and Fairbanks would adopt a child – if possible, a waif from their royal tours. But their lives were full, and Fairbanks, as Jayar knew firsthand, was too much a child himself to act the father.

In 1943 Mary was persuaded that the time was right. She was fifty-one, with time on her hands and a willing husband. She had also concluded she was sterile. "People say you can never love other people's children as much as you would love your own, but I think you can sometimes love them better." In fact, she had convinced herself she could love any orphaned child on sight. She was disillusioned; when she interviewed an eight-year-old girl, Mary found herself only slightly moved. Then Rogers saved the day by walking in with an apple-cheeked boy of six. He was dressed in a handsome little suit and saluted when Buddy introduced him. Mary watched, enthralled, as the boy climbed onto Rogers's lap. On the following Sunday he was brought for a day of play at Pickfair. He ate often and voraciously, and broke down when it was time to go. Mary fell so much in love she couldn't sleep. On May 2, 1943, she signed the required adoption papers, and Ronald Charles Rogers came to Pickfair.

About ten months later she was gazing at babies through an orphanage window as nurses held several up for inspection. One was a little girl, five months old, with a lively expression and a thatch of dark hair. According to authorities, her father had been killed on Guadalcanal, and her mother had died a few months later. The child, unknowing, fairly sparkled. "More than I ever wanted anything in my life, I wanted that baby," remembered Mary. For days she thought of nothing but Roxanne: her toothless smile, the tilt of her head, the weight of her body in her arms. A few weeks later the orphanage called to say that Roxanne's papers had finally been completed. Mary dashed down, received Roxanne, and drove home with the brakes on, running red lights and arriving at Pickfair in a cloud of dust. In her excitement she forgot to call Buddy, who had enlisted in the air force and was then on base, to inform him they had a second child. Mary hadn't made domestic preparations, either. When the child came to Pickfair, it was empty of baby clothes and bottles. In hindsight, the oversight seems prophetic.

Ronnie and Roxanne were shuttled from place to place, sent away to private schools, or left at Pickfair, entrusted to the hired help, while their parents traveled. Few of Mary's friends or relatives knew them, though Letitia thought Ronnie was a "smart, cute kid. He'd had a terrible life. When he was five, he was shining shoes; that way he could get himself something to eat while his mother was lying in the house in a stupor." Certainly Ronnie was fed at Pickfair. But Mary forgot that love must be forged through constant attentiveness and interaction. Charlotte ("her wisdom, her discipline!") had worked, played, and slept at her children's side. She had punished, listened, suffered, and protected. Mary, on the other hand, underlined discipline. "*Strict*," Roxanne explained in 1996. "If I misbehaved, I got one good heavy swat." (Pickford, to her credit, did this job herself.) But Roxanne remembers spankings above all else. Pickford gave the children rules and dollops of the luxuries that money could buy, but she neglected something vital in between.

"I was at Pickfair," recalled Letitia, "when Ronnie, who was seven, went running off the diving board, yelling out, 'Somebody catch me!' And you really had to be there because he couldn't swim." Alarmed, she drew the little boy aside. "I'm going to tell you about the dragon at the bottom of the pool," she said. "Have you seen it? He sits at the bottom, and if grown-ups are around he'll never bother you. But if a grown-up isn't here, and you put as much as your foot in the water, you'll see him." Ronnie, eyes wide, asked Letitia for a picture. Aware that she mustn't give Ronnie nightmares, Letitia drew the pool dragon, fierce but funny – just the sort of one-on-one, playful moment Mary seldom gave him.

It seems Mary yearned for physical perfection, too: "Ronnie," said Letitia, "had committed the sin of being just a little guy, and Mary couldn't stand that. She said, 'My God, he's just a runt, like me.' So things got off to a bad, bad start. Roxanne, this beautiful, tiny baby, grew up to have a big build. And her teeth needed straightening – they overlapped a bit. But for some reason Mary never had them fixed."

Still, the first years of family photos manage to dazzle. In one, Roxanne, a toddler, fondly gives her mother's ear a tug; both are dressed beautifully in tiny ruffles. In a family outing, they all look swank, but Roxanne easily steals the photo in her exquisite matching hat and coat. Others show the children overwhelmed by Christmas – Ronnie, eyes shining, takes possession of his brand-new rocking horse, and Roxanne, on the same horse, clutches a doll. There are fragments, too, of children's parties – an organ-grinder playing tunes while Pickford and the children dance around him; shots of Pickford and Roxanne, holding the organ-grinder's monkey. Candles are blown out, presents opened, and a movie shown.

And finally the entire family sits for a portrait in the main hall of Pickfair. Buddy, as usual, looks blandly handsome, and Mary is the perfect chatelaine in pearls. Roxanne, despite her perky bow, looks lost, and Ronnie sits alertly, with an easy smile. But all are overwhelmed by another presence. It is Little Mary's portrait in a gilded frame. Large as life, she hangs above them, as a constant reminder that Pickford's image, like an angel or a curse, would follow them all their lives.

In 1945 Fairbanks Jr. asked Mary, by letter, what she thought of his producing through United Artists. This wasn't entirely a new idea; in the mid-1930s, he had produced a few films and released them through UA. "He was making a desperate effort to create his own type of rôle," said Mary. "I had long ago decided that no one could follow in [my father's] footsteps," confessed Jayar. "They were so light they left no trace."

Many of Fairbanks Jr.'s films depended on his skill with airy give-and-take, although *The Prisoner of Zenda* had shown an inclination toward (in Mary's words) "wide gesture, poise and pose." So did *The Corsican Brothers* (1941). But by that time Pickford's stepson had competing interests. When the war began in Europe, his anglophilia had led him to join the White Committee, which advocated coming to the Allies' aid. Indeed, Jayar's social set now touched the White House, where he often spent the weekend as Roosevelt's guest. In 1941 he was sent on a good-will trip to South America – but its actual purpose was to gather information on the Nazi presence there.

Jayar served with distinction as a naval commander and was finally mustered out in 1946. At the time of his letter to Mary, he was casting about for a way to re-establish his old career. Mary loved the idea of a business connection to the younger Fairbanks – and then fondly advised him to avoid UA. "Between you and me," she wrote Jayar, "a dividend was declared in 1940 and I have yet to receive it." Indeed, World War II caused a box office boom for every Hollywood studio except United Artists, where times were tough. As usual, there weren't enough films to distribute, and most of those available were undistinguished.

Perhaps the worst offenders were Mary's own. In 1945 she enlisted her husband and Ralph Cohn, who had once produced films for Columbia, in a new venture called Comet Productions. Her intention was to give UA six B pictures. "B" defined production costs; in quality, the films fared somewhat worse. Next, through another production company, she attempted to film the play *One Touch of Venus*. But Mary's version never reached the screen, because of a million-dollar lawsuit launched by its director, Gregory La Cava, who claimed that Pickford had interfered at every level.

In what was now their wearily familiar style, UA's principals failed to pull together; they had quarreled through the war years with feuds and lawsuits. Mary wrote Jayar that she feared Selznick was intending to leave. "He is very frank in his lack of interests in United Artists, anything having to do with its policies or the building of its future." In addition, she and Chaplin hadn't spoken "in going on two years. He will not answer anyone's letters, telephone calls or wires. I suppose we must accord certain privileges to 'genius' and evidently this is one of them. His own director on the board came out here from New York to see him and he even refused to speak to him on the telephone."

Chaplin later admitted that his personal problems had preoccupied him. He had started the script for *Monsieur Verdoux* in 1942, then proceeded through the usual anxiety, self doubt, and mental blocks until the film's release in 1947. The ad campaign ("Chaplin Changes! Can You?") would challenge his viewers to accept him in the role of a licentious smoothie. But to some, the transformation was already accomplished, for an unseemly interest in the actor's sex life had become a new obsession among his right-wing foes.

"A little runt of a Svengali," snarled an anti-Chaplin lawyer, Joseph Scott. This vilification occurred in 1945, when Scott's client, a young, aspiring actress named Joan Barry, took the actor to court in a paternity suit. She was clearly unbalanced, and blood tests proved Chaplin was not the father of her child. But by then, there had been calls for his deportation, based on the actor's reputation as a leftie and the fact that he was often drawn romantically toward adolescent girls. (Two of his three ex-wives had been sixteen and pregnant when he took them to the altar.) In 1943 Chaplin, who was fifty-four, had wed Oona O'Neill, who was eighteen, had a famous father (playwright Eugene O'Neill), and displayed a fragile beauty that belied her remarkable inner strengths. She would stand by the actor until he died – and she stood loyally by him as Barry's lawyer ranted at the jury, calling Chaplin "a pestiferous, lecherous hound," "a cheap Cockney cad," and "a man who goes around fornicating ... with the same aplomb that the average man orders bacon and eggs for breakfast." Chaplin's first jury was hopelessly deadlocked. In a second trial, blood tests failed to save him. The "hoary headed old buzzard" was told to write twenty-one years of support checks for Barry's baby.

It is possible that somewhere, to someone, Mary raged at the injustice of it all. But she seems to have said nothing for the public record. Perhaps Pickford reasoned that, given the hysterical political climate, it was best to lie low and be discreet. It is possible, too, that she found herself affected by the sordid talk. Booton Herndon, who wrote a book about Pickford's romance with Fairbanks, claimed that Letitia and Lucile, Robert Fairbanks's beautiful daughters, were never left unchaperoned with Chaplin at Pickfair.

But for practical reasons, Mary could not turn against him. Ironically, the left-wing, pestiferous hound was her sole remaining partner at United Artists.

Jayar never joined UA, Korda had left in 1943, and Selznick abandoned ship, as Mary had feared, in 1947. Paying for Selznick's shares bled United Artists nearly dry. But Chaplin seemed strangely unaffected. "I was not too concerned," he remembered blithely, "because we had been in debt before and a successful picture had always pulled us out." Despite the repugnance with which some viewed him, the actor predicted that *Monsieur Verdoux* would come to the rescue with a profit in the twelve-million-dollar range.

Mary, who hoped to boost the movie's profile, attempted a rapprochement with Chaplin by attending the opening in New York. Charlie and

Oona were to meet her for dinner before the show. But the night began badly when she dashed to the table late, explaining she had lingered at a cocktail party. The trio then proceeded to the Broadway Theatre, where a radio announcer was at work in the lobby.

"And now Charlie Chaplin and his wife have arrived. Ah, and with them as their guest that wonderful little actress of the silent days who is still America's sweetheart, Miss Mary Pickford." Asked for her comments, Mary dragged Chaplin toward the mike. "Two thousand years ago Christ was born," she began, "and tonight..." Mercifully, the statement was interrupted as the jostling crowd swept them both away.

On the whole, the night was excruciating. Many of the viewers didn't like *Verdoux*, and many of them (those who hissed) didn't like Chaplin. During the year of the film's release, Senator William Langer asked why certain people were deported when "a man like Charlie Chaplin, with his communistic leanings, with his unsavory record of lawbreaking, of rape, or the debauching of American girls sixteen and seventeen years of age, remains?" Cinemas showing *Monsieur Verdoux* were picketed by anti-Chaplin groups. But Chaplin blamed the UA sales force for *Verdoux's* dismal box office performance. And, exhausted, he decided that he wanted out.

Astonishingly, Mary agreed to put the company up for sale. And equally strange, for she and Chaplin rarely saw eye to eye in business, they accepted an offer from a theater chain called Fabian. The terms were generous, with Chaplin making five million dollars in cash, and Pickford half again as much. Then, with the deal awaiting only their signatures, Chaplin broke it off, stating through a spokesman that the contracts had been drawn up while he watched with "humor and an eye for publicity."

This was unforgivable and threw United Artists into disarray. Its president, Ed Raftery, resigned. And Mary, who still wanted to sell, was stymied, for the Fabian chain wanted all of the available shares, or none.

UA's board of directors suggested that Joe Schenck be brought in to find a new president, reorganize the company, and reconcile the partners. Mary saw the sense of this and gladly gave him temporary power of attorney. As Chaplin resisted, Pickford swallowed her pride and made a personal visit. "I thought I had seen Charlie in a tantrum," she remembered, "but this beat everything."

Chaplin shouted, "I wouldn't give my power of attorney to my own brother. I'm perfectly capable of voting my own stock."

"But, Charlie, you know Schenck is a good businessman."

"I'm as good a businessman as anybody else!"

(This was debatable; as Mary wrote, "poor Charlie was no businessman at all.")

Pickford tried another tack. "Charlie, I'm not here as your partner today. I'm not even here as someone that's been your friend for so many years. I'm here as the voice of our thousands of employees the world over, of the producers and bankers – "

He cut her off. "If you're here as the voice of the bankers the interview is terminated."

Pickford, trying to hold her temper, strode to Chaplin's door. It stuck. Chaplin had to open it, and Pickford contemptuously sailed out.

In 1948 director Billy Wilder was dining with Sam and Frances Goldwyn in a Beverly Hills restaurant called Romanoff's. Suddenly a tall, hawk-nosed man came around the bar and stood swaying over them, furiously shaking his finger at Goldwyn. "Here you are, you son of a bitch," he growled. "I ought to be making pictures – ."
"Get away from here, you silly man," Frances hissed. The man lurched away and Goldwyn stared at his wife. When she asked him who the drunk was, he told her, shocked. "D.W. Griffith."

Although he hadn't made a film since 1931, Griffith was still seen around town, in old suits and frayed cuffs, alone or with somewhat seedy women. Linda Arvidson, his wife, had long since left him, and after their divorce in 1936 Griffith married a young, obscure actress named Evelyn Baldwin. A few days later Griffith was awarded an honorary Oscar ("For his distinguished creative achievements as director and producer and his invaluable initiative and lasting contributions to the progress of the motion picture arts"). Tears came to his eyes when he heard the ovation. After that he slipped out of the spotlight, dabbled in radio (a series called *Hollywood As Griffith Knew It* ran for fifteen weeks), and wrote poems (unfinished), his memoirs (unfinished), and screenplays (dreadful). Director Hal Roach took pity on him and in 1940 asked him to serve as consultant on *One*

Million B.C., a special-effects feature based on Griffith's *Man's Genesis* (1912). Griffith's contributions to the Roach film were small, but he did select the lithesome star, Carole Landis, and he supervised some trick shots. "I think he was confused at the time," said Roach. And Griffith complained to his chauffeur that "these young whippersnappers don't know what they're talking about, they don't even know the technique ... they try to ignore me ... but I really know. I was born with it, I started it, I invented it."

In 1946 his marriage foundered. Later that year the director was arrested as a common drunk. In 1947 Griffith moved to the Knickerbocker Hotel in downtown Hollywood, where a young journalist named Ezra Goodman got an interview by pushing an attractive woman in ahead of him. As Goodman listened, "the father of the American film sat in an easy chair in a hotel room in the heart of Hollywood guzzling gin out of a water glass and periodically grabbing at the blonde sitting on the sofa opposite.... It was Griffith, all right, his lordly, arrogant, aquiline features surmounted by sparse white hair, attired in pajamas and a patterned maroon dressing gown, and, at the age of seventy-two, sitting alone, drunk and almost forgotten in a hotel room in the town he had been instrumental in putting on the map." Drink made the old man lachrymose. "They will not print any of this," Griffith predicted. "But I don't care. I am seventy-two years old and I can say anything I like about this movie business."

He spoke of directors he admired: Frank Capra, Preston Sturges, and Leo McCarey. He called *The Birth of a Nation* a lousy picture – waiting, thought Goodman, to be contradicted – and spoke a bit pointedly of Orson Welles ("I loved *Citizen Kane* and particularly loved the ideas he took from me.") And he spoke almost yearningly of early film. "We did Browning and Keats then, *Pippa Passes*.... Imagine anyone doing Browning today. [The movies] have not improved in stories. I don't know that they've improved in anything." He regretted, too, that a certain sterility had entered film. "The moving picture is beautiful; the moving of wind on beautiful trees is more beautiful than a painting. Too much today depends on the voice.... In my arrogant belief," said Griffith, "we have lost beauty."

The great man died on July 24, 1948. Three days later a formal service was held at the Hollywood Masonic Temple. But the turnout was small, for to many, D. W. Griffith was as pointless as the relics in museums that are tagged and displayed as "use unknown." Even some artists of Griffith's era had lost their understanding of silent film. In 1978 critic Alexander Walker pointed out that King Vidor, who had directed several silent classics, recalled his technique "as if he was the slowly recuperating victim of amnesia."

> I wondered exactly what I had told [actors] to do and just how they had accomplished what they did.... Some directors talked during the scene more than others. Commands had to be sharp and clear so that they would penetrate an actor's consciousness without causing confusion. But to what extent was the director responsible for the performance of the actors as compared with today's talk-oriented performances?

"This," wrote Walker, "is an extraordinary confession coming from one of the great silent film-makers; no wonder we lack so many first-hand accounts of the pre-talkie era. Sound seems in many cases to have been like a trauma, expunging it from recollection."

Despite her aversion to funeral services, Mary couldn't miss this one and took a pew. (She did not view the body as it lay at the funeral parlour. It is said that only six people went to do so.) At the church, some attendees were recruited from the crowds who came to gawk at Griffith's mourners. Mae Marsh, Lionel Barrymore, Mack Sennett, Dell Henderson, Blanche Sweet, and Donald Crisp, all Biograph alumni, bowed their heads. A eulogy was given by screenwriter Charles Brackett, who was then Academy president (he had never known Griffith). He spoke a bit stiffly for a dialogue writer: "When you've had what he'd had, what you want is the chance to make more pictures, unlimited budgets to play with, complete confidence behind you. What does a man full of vitality care for the honors of the past? It's the present he wants, and the future. There was no solution for Griffith but a kind of frenzied beating on the barred doors."

Donald Crisp followed with a bitter and heartfelt accusation. "It was, I believe," said the actor/director, "inevitable that the very momentum which he generated carried the industry ahead at a pace which finally left him behind. It was the tragedy of his later years that his active, brilliant mind was given no chance to participate in the advancement of the industry. Difficult as it might be for him to have played a subordinate role, I do not believe that the fault was entirely his own. I cannot help feeling that there should always have been a place for him and his talent in motion pictures..."

Someone sobbed abruptly, "Yes, yes – why not!"

Crisp was startled and tried to go on. "It is hard to believe," he said, steadying his voice, "that the industry could not have found some use for his great gifts in his later years."

No one knows which listener cried aloud. It is probable, though, that as she listened to Crisp, Pickford recognized the shape of her own artistic dilemma.

As a mother, she was well on her way to disaster. Gwynne, who had lived with both Mary and the hard-drinking Charlotte, was an expert in coping with alcoholics. Once, at twelve, she had stopped her Aunt Verna from approaching Mary: "Don't go in there now," she piped. "Auntie is in one of her quiet, dangerous moods." (Gwynne herself began to drink in high school, though, like Charlotte, she could hold her liquor.) After her divorce in 1944, Gwynne often came to Pickfair to see her aunt. Once she heard Roxanne talking loosely in front of guests: "Let me see, that was *before* she got drunk that night." "For God's sake," said Gwynne, "don't say those things."

"It became a tragedy," said Letitia. "Ronnie got older and they had a lot of set-to's." In the late 1940s Mary sent him to a prep school, one with a reputation for hazing, sex, and drinking. According to Letitia, Ronnie entered the school wearing childish short pants – this when the other boys were wearing long ones. Humiliated, Ronnie locked himself in his room. Mary, when she heard the news, was mystified: "He'll just have to wear short pants, that's all." Finally the headmaster lost his patience. "Miss Pickford, you'll have to get that child into long pants or take him out of school." "Then she *had* to do it," said Letitia. "She bought Ronnie new clothes, delivered them herself – and the kid just grabbed the pants and ran." But Pickford thought this story was about herself. "He didn't even thank me," she complained to friends.

On the other hand, Pickford was instantly drawn to a vulnerable young man named Malcolm Boyd. In the 1940s Boyd opened an office to act as a link between radio and the movies; in other words, he put actors on the air to plug their films. In 1948 one of his star clients was Buddy Rogers.

"I was in my twenties," Boyd remembered, "a young gay boy who didn't know what gay meant. I knew who Mary was, but on the other hand, I didn't want anything from her. I was much more caught up with myself and what I wanted to do with my life. I didn't have a lot of guile. I had no program; there was no agenda. From the very beginning, she was motherly to me, and very caring. She was never too busy or too important."

Boyd intuitively grasped that this angel had a wounded wing. Years before, as a boy in Colorado, he had noticed her photo in the paper and was transfixed by its "aura of royalty. . . . Mary, dressed in white from head to toe, walked alone a few steps ahead of two or three other people. Crowds quietly watched from a distance out of deep respect and in actual awe. . . . There was almost a sense of the numinous, an insinuation of the godlike in the incredible scene. Mary's face and body invoked images of purity and innocence, somehow unapproachable. Yet she was as regal, her straight back a marvel, as Queen Mary of England ever was."

Now she was enduring a living death – loved, when not ridiculed, for something she had been, not for what she was. Often when she entered a room – the posture still regal, the head held high – there was applause (some people still stood up), and cries of "Mary! Mary! Oh, Miss Pickford!" It was tiresome, sometimes – always wondering what the public thought Little Mary would do, what the public thought Little Mary would say, what the public expected Little Mary to think. Sometimes Little Mary took a drink to get through it.

She drank through the first night of *Sleep My Love* (1948). *Junior Miss* had come to nothing, as had *Girls Town*, another Temple project. But *Sleep My Love*, with Claudette Colbert, was a not-bad update of the classic *Gaslight*. Buddy was nominally her co-producer.

Mary took the premiere to the country of her birth. A showing was arranged in Ottawa on January 13, 1948; it would benefit a United Nations/Unesco project known as the Canadian Appeal for Children, and the Canadian prime minister, W.L. Mackenzie King, and the governor general were the crown jewels atop an impressive guest list.

She arrived at Union Station. "Grandmothers and middle-aged matrons were there in large numbers," reported the *Ottawa Citizen*, and "many an oldster choked back a nostalgic sigh." And Canada, it seemed, was still all agog at Pickford's hair, which had grown long enough to be drawn into a rippling, girlish topknot. "It was like turning back the clock a quarter century to see [it]," gushed the *Citizen* reporter, for the people who knew Mary from "their courting days."

Pickford endured the interviews, scheduled back-to-back throughout the day. She chattered brightly, then seemed to fade. But after a respite in her hotel room, Pickford was back, more relaxed and garrulous.

The evening was planned with pomp and circumstance; dinner with the prime minister and the governor general, at which alcohol was served. Afterward, the governor general's party piled into a sleigh and set off for the gala at the Elgin theater, with Mary looking striking in a white fur coat – and the governor general's hat. When the lights went down, she strode onstage, gave what was meant to be a graceful curtsy, then struggled with her footing on the way back up. Her speech was appropriate at the start, but soon took some unexpected turns. A United Artists publicity man switched off the mike when the actress began to list her favorite recipes.

"I think the job of being Mary Pickford, the perfect, sexless angel, was just about impossible," said Malcolm Boyd. "And somewhere along the line she ran out of gas." On some days, alcohol alone could fuel her. She would drift through the hours neither drunk nor sober (displays such as at *Sleep My Love* were rare) – sweet and tender, a little bit excitable, perhaps, and vague. On other days she couldn't relax and adopted what Boyd called "the persona."

In 1949 he joined Mary and Buddy in P.R.B. (Pickford-Rogers-Boyd), a TV and radio production company. Mary took the unprecedented step of closing Pickfair and moving to Manhattan, where she opened an office in the Squibb Building penthouse and rented a sumptuous suite in the Pierre and later an apartment on Park Avenue. Slowly Boyd was exposed to every side of Pickford: her pain, her humor, bewilderment, fear – and the days when (he winced) "nothing worked at all."

Throughout the forties, Pickford had continued to work in radio – determined, one assumes, to get it right. But she seldom did. A nativity scene in 1940 paired Mary (as the Virgin) with Ronald Colman. But

Colman, as Joseph, sounds more like a dashing fighter pilot, and Mary an elocution teacher. ("*It was* as *if* the *rooooom* had suddenly been *streeeewwwwn* with *pawm brawnches.*") A scripted chat with Eleanor Roosevelt assumed the pallid tones of a tale from the crypt: "I have *always* ... been *interested*," Pickford announces, "in the fight ... against ... INFAN-TILE PARALYSIS."

One of P.R.B.'s endeavors was a radio show called "Theatre of American Valor," a tribute to the heroes of World War II. When NBC declared its interest, Pickford went to Washington to meet with the secretary of defense in order to gain access to the best material. She was sober as a judge and emerged triumphant. But the New York denouement was disastrous. The trial broadcast was scheduled for May 20, 1950, and a sixty-piece orchestra was waiting in the studio. But Pickford, her secretary, Bess Lewis, and Boyd were delayed when they ran into a massive parade through midtown. Mary, Boyd recalled, had been "off" all day. When it came time to record the introduction, the persona of the grand lady reared its head. She had mike fright, badly – aware that she was speaking as an icon, and overly aware of such technical issues as breath and diction. The result was her formal, sepulchral tone. When Boyd heard the playback, he destroyed the tape and told Pickford that the program had been "bad, an embarrassment." In another attempt, Pickford interviewed Lillian Gish for the show, and her guest was a chatty, informal delight. But Gish couldn't disarm her stilted host. This tape, too, was destroyed by Boyd, who recalled that Mary "didn't fight it"; she had learned to trust his judgment, and no more was said.

"New York was so wonderful then," said Boyd. He was not yet thirty but, because of his ties to Mary, was soon taking tea with Lillian Gish, chatting over cocktails with Adele Astaire, or attending a brunch with Mrs. William Randolph Hearst. As they strolled Fifth Avenue one night, he and Pickford passed Garbo and Louis B. Mayer. Suddenly he felt Mary grip his arm. "I've got to have money," she implored him. "You must find me a way to earn some money." Boyd was intrigued by "this millionairess who was incongruously, and often humorously, frugal." But sometimes the effects were cruel. Often Pickford didn't pay her bills to "little people" – seamstresses or plumbers who were owed perhaps several hundred dollars but had to go to small claims court to get it.

Pickford gave generously to beggars – or, because she seldom carried cash, encouraged her companions to do it for her. Some nights she drove in her limousine from Pickfair to a mission or soup kitchen, delivering the remains of dinner. "It was odd," said Boyd, who was often in the car. "She was acting out a role. Why not write out a check and say, 'Here, feed ten thousand people'? Of course, so much philanthropic work was done in Mary's name – all by rote. I don't think she gave of herself too deeply – unless, of course, an old friend was involved." Or unless an issue touched her guilty streak.

Behind his back, Pickford called Goldwyn "Shylock." And to Fairbanks, whose grandfather had been Jewish, Mary sometimes said, "That's the Jew in you." But she topped these comments in the presence of actress Carmel Myers, to whom she explained that the Jews had invited Hitler's persecution. Forgetting that Myers was a rabbi's daughter (in fact, Myers had refused a studio executive's request to change her last name to something glamorously gentile), Pickford chirped that avaricious Jews had snapped up German property at bargain prices after World War I. She added that a syndicate of Jews would repeat the conspiracy after World War II.

"I will make only one comment to that," Myers told her. "You must never forget that before we are Jewish or gentile, we are all human beings." Mary's heart sank. Overwhelmed with guilt, she "went home that night and got down on my knees. I asked God to forgive me and show me the right path to help these persecuted people." And, as she rose, Pickford told herself, "You're not a poor Christian; you're no Christian at all." For years, she tried to compensate by giving till it hurt to Jewish causes. Her greatest triumph was the Mary Pickford Building at L.A.'s Jewish Home for the Aged, to which she became a devoted patron. But her shame burned long, and an abject description of the incident with Myers fills four pages in her autobiography.

Pickford rolled up her sleeves and went to work when Billy Bitzer had a heart attack. For years, she had sat on the Motion Picture Relief Fund's case committee. Mary arranged to have Biograph's cameraman moved from a public to a private hospital; the relief fund not only paid his bills in full but agreed to give Bitzer a regular stipend. But Mary wasn't finished; to tide him over, she sent the photographer a check for clothes. She also suggested that Bitzer proceed directly to the men's store Barney's, which was having a sale, and was open on Mondays till ten o'clock.

Mary also took up the cause of John Mantley, her second cousin. They had first met in the late 1930s, when Pickford, who was breezing through Toronto on publicity errands, organized a party for the Smiths at Mantley's home. He was about sixteen, a self-styled rebel, and refused to join the fuss. Instead, he watched disdainfully as Mary's limo, flanked by a motor-cycle escort, rolled grandly down the street. Then he hid in his room. Soon there came a knock, and a gentle scold: "It's your cousin," said Mary. "*Will you open the door, please?*" "I opened the door, and there she was, in a porkpie hat with a veil," said Mantley. "She looked absolutely ravishing." After a long chat in which they discussed Fairbanks's feats as a gymnast, Mary coaxed the boy into a goodbye kiss. "You *stop* that," she said when at first he demurred. "Smiths kiss and hug."

By 1950 Mantley was an actor, scraping out a living and eating in the Automats of New York. The sympathetic Pickford often took him to dinner, and her ravenous cousin would eat three entrées. She was marvelous company, he remembered, though at dinner parties she would throw out a line or two from *The Taming of the Shrew*, turn to Mantley, and expect him to respond as Petruchio. "It got to be quite a game," said Mantley, who finally had to sit down and learn the play. Pickford also helped the actor out with loans. Once, when Mantley couldn't afford to join his mother at Christmas, Mary gave him a round-trip airplane ticket. In the interim, he kept track of his accumulating debt. And Pickford kept track, too; many years later, she informed Mantley by letter that he owed her over six hundred dollars – in other words, the cost of the Christmas trip. "I insisted I did not," remembered Mantley, "that the plane fare had been given to me as a present. I had worked very hard under rigorous circum-stances to return every penny she ever loaned me. I was *not* going to give back my Christmas present!" (He let Pickford know, and she dropped the matter.)

Often Malcolm Boyd marveled at Mary's strength – or, at least, her commanding air. At times she wore royalty with humor. In San Francisco, for instance, she refused to leave town before climbing on a trolley car. "Aren't you Mary Pickford?" asked a rider, amazed. "Yes, my good man, I am!" said Pickford, grandly, as the trolley car clanged and rolled downhill.

"Ultimately," reflected Boyd, "it got very tiring to go out being queen for the umpteenth time. Someone who is hungry for it eats it like raw meat: it's drinking blood. But there's also a point when it all becomes boring beyond redemption." With trusted staff and a few friends at Pickfair, Mary let her hair down – or put it up in pincurls and sat around with cold cream on her nose. She would clown, do impressions, or engage her French maid in a pillow fight. Once she capriciously suggested that she and her secretary wear each other's clothes. But in public, she seldom forgot herself. When she did, Boyd found her behavior touching.

He remembers, with something akin to wonder, a day in New York when Pickford left her limousine, saying, "It's such a beautiful day, let's walk!" She was hardly dressed for walking. She was wearing her rubies: "There were ruby earrings, there was a ruby in her hair, a ruby something at her throat, there were rubies on the shoe buckles and the belt, there was a ruby bracelet and a ring. She was in her mid-fifties and extremely handsome, and besides, many people knew Mary's face. The sunlight was catching all her jewels, and everyone around us was becoming hysterical. But Mary was unaware, oblivious." There was also a disastrous parade in Denver, held to inaugurate a new local theater. The actress was insecure and tired, and refused to leave her suite as the parade assembled. Finally the procession, which had other stars in tow, began without her. Mary, swathed in fur, made it in time to be put into the last car – an open convertible, despite the cold weather and a squall of snow. Suddenly, said Boyd, the event "seemed to bring up some memory from Mary's past." Pickford, insensible to winter blasts, let her furs slip and stood up to wave, bare-shouldered. "A performance," Boyd remembered, "but alcoholic."

At first, Boyd didn't know she drank. "Well, I did and I didn't," he elaborated. But he knew she had mood swings, of the cruelest kind.

"I will *destroy* you," Mary snarled. She and Boyd were in New York and had eaten in her suite at the Pierre hotel. "We'd had a charming dinner," Boyd remembered, "and Mary couldn't have been more delightful. I got back to my room at the Gotham and the phone rang." It was Pickford – raging, abominable. "Who invited you into my life?" she screamed. "How dare you! Shut up! Don't talk to *me*! You're nothing. You're nobody. I'm going to drive you out of this business." She ended as she'd started. "*I'll destroy you.*"

"This went on for fifteen minutes," Boyd remembered, describing the phone call as "one of the most difficult moments of my life." But throughout the relationship, he learned the hard way that alcoholics betray and humiliate even those they love. And the next day, Mary had no memory of it. This often happened. Pickford sober was denied the revelations of Pickford drunk.

There were nights of pure fear, remembered Boyd. There were burglars in the shadows, as well as Reds. "Mary would lock herself into her room, locking, locking, locking, and she'd call the Beverly Hills police and tell them the house was being robbed." The police caught on after coming out night after night to find Pickfair safe and sound.

Later Boyd and Mary drank together. "I was totally inexperienced, and searching for something. Mary was searching for something, too. I think we were trying to help each other. We'd had intimate times when we were drinking. I mean drinking deeply – the kind of drinking where you don't get drunk but you do become perceptive. We would drink at Pickfair, late into the night, and Mary would go deep within herself. And she knew herself better in those moments than she did at any other time." What did she find in those moments? Boyd recalled the quality, not the facts. "She was haunted. She was lost. Her image was a burden, but she couldn't find a meaningful other life. To me she was the image of the mother in Eugene O'Neill's *Long Day's Journey into Night*."

"Fifty-four, about medium height," wrote O'Neill when he described Mary Tyrone. "A young, graceful figure, a trifle plump.... [Her face] must once have been extremely pretty." Her laugh and her appearance are vaguely Irish, but the essence of Mary Tyrone's appeal lies in a "youthfulness she has never lost – an innate unworldly innocence." With the aid of morphine, the fictional Mary escapes the "contempt and disgust" of the present to her convent girlhood, to the day she fell in love, to her wedding dress. Pickford, in a similar state, spoke of Toronto, of Charlotte, Jack, and Lottie, of the father she had barely known. Often her eyes shone, she laughed, and a flush mounted in her cheeks. But often she felt harrowingly alone. She had lost not only her family but something she could barely identify: purpose. "I've become such a liar," Tyrone tells her son. "I never lied about anything once upon a time. Now I have to lie, especially to myself. But how can you understand, when I don't know myself. I've never understood anything about it, except that one day long ago I found I could no longer call my soul my own."

In the late 1940s Billy Wilder and Charles Brackett wrote a script that seemed the ideal film for Mary. It told the story of Joe Gillis, an embittered Hollywood writer so down on his luck that he accepts a commission from a once-mythic silent-movie star. He knows the project – a spectacular, cast-of-thousands *Salomé* – and her comeback in the title role are ludicrous notions, but he's fleeing debt collectors and needs the money. Eventually he also needs the suits, ties, cigarette cases, and champagne that the actress, Norma Desmond, presses on him; he needs the bed beneath her roof (eventually, one understands, it becomes *her* bed). At the time *Sunset Boulevard* was written, the silents had been gone for only twenty years. But Wilder, through the viewpoint of the Gillis character, presented them the way the public saw them at the end of the 1940s: laughable, foolish, and as distant as the prehistoric age. "You're Norma Desmond!" says Joe Gillis when he meets her. "You used to be in silent pictures. You used to be big!" He could not be more astonished, implies the subtext, had he found himself conversing with a brontosaurus.

Wilder thought of Mae West as Norma Desmond, but she turned down the role in its planning stages. His next inspiration was Mary Pickford. He had reason to believe that, like Desmond, Pickford felt ripe for a comeback; a few years earlier, she had been tested for the lead role of Vinnie in *Life with Father* (1947). (For reasons unknown, the part was finally awarded to Irene Dunne.) The director went to Pickfair, explained the story, and tried to act out several scenes. Mary watched, listened, and imagined herself as the desperate Norma: bossy, suicidal, self-deluded, and, in the movie's spectacular last shots, completely and eerily insane. She would play Norma Desmond, she declared, eyes glistening. But with one important caveat: she thought the role of Gillis should be reduced. Why not wrap the entire film around Norma Desmond's rich emotional life? Gradually Wilder came to see that Mary was accustomed to far more creative participation than the average actress; he began to think about giving the role to Pola Negri, and the offer was retracted.

When Pickford saw the finished film in 1950, she was shattered. Gloria

Swanson, who accepted the role after Negri refused it, gave an unnerving, spidery performance – so chilling (and admirably unsentimental) that her place in talkie history was assured. Mary dried her eyes, then began to tell her version of her differences with Wilder. "I said, 'You don't want me.'" He insisted, claimed Mary, but she stood her ground. "There are two actresses that could do this part better. One is Gloria Swanson – that's my first choice – and the next one is Pola Negri. But if you want to put me into that role, people will come expecting me to do something like, oh, my former performances, and they'll go away disappointed. And the people who couldn't stand my curls would stay away from the theatre. So I said, you'll have a failure both ways."

Maybe she did say something along these lines, to save face when Wilder withdrew the script. She also gave prissier explanations: "I wouldn't do that kind of picture; why, she kills a man." (Ironically, Mary's silent movies often featured her wielding a gun or rifle. She shot a man dead in *The Heart o' the Hills* and shot a woman at the climax of *Stella Maris*.) There were more complaints; Wilder's film was "too satirical. I don't approve of my people, of the picture industry, doing anything that would harm the reputation of motion pictures." But assuming that Wilder could have made a great (though radically different) film with Pickford – she was Swanson's superior as an actress, but had a less tigerish persona – he might have accomplished the reinvention she had found with Lubitsch, abandoned, and never again recaptured.

Then, miraculously, Pickford had another chance. In 1951 writer Daniel Taradash and producer Stanley Kramer brought a script to Pickfair. Called "The Librarian," it told the story of a middle-aged woman who insists that a book called *The Communist Dream* remain available to readers, despite a campaign by right-wingers to remove it. It included a particularly touching scene in which the librarian tells a young boy about the principles of free speech. "The script was very bold for the time," remembered Taradash. Neither Taradash, Kramer, nor director Irving Reis knew if Pickford was still capable of giving a performance. "We were taking a big chance," Taradash admitted. "We knew that Pickford might be awful." But if she wasn't the ideal actress, Mary was undoubtedly the ideal *person*. "No one," the writer remembered wryly, "could say that Mary Pickford was a Communist."

Married in 1920, mobbed in London on their honeymoon: Pickford's new husband, Douglas Fairbanks, carries his terrified wife on his shoulders.

America's second White House: a view of Pickfair's lawn, 1921.

The couple go a-rowing in their backyard pool.

Domestic bliss, c. 1922. "This is a happy house," Mary said of Pickfair. "This is a house that has never heard a cross word."

Pickford reprising her role as the hellcat *Tess of the Storm Country* (1922).

Pickford, in costume as *Dorothy Vernon of Haddon Hall* (1924), and Fairbanks, as *The Thief of Bagdad* (1924), made films on adjoining sets.

Douglas Fairbanks, who was rarely still, pauses for a moment in *The Black Pirate* (1926).

Fairbanks, as *The Black Pirate*, relaxes between takes with his wife (dressed for *Sparrows*), 1926.

The slapstick *Suds* (1920), with Pickford up to her neck in collars.

Pickford as *Rosita* (1923):
"Different and greater than at
any time in her screen career."

The street–smart *Little Annie Rooney*
(1925, with Pickford at left).

Buddy Rogers when he first
came to Hollywood, c. 1926.

Flirtation on and off camera: Buddy Rogers and
Mary Pickford in *My Best Girl* (1927).

Before and after: Pickford's hair (above, c. 1920) was once worshipped like
a religious relic. When she cut it in 1928 (right), she signaled the end of an era.
The watershed event made the front page of *The New York Times*.

Mary Pickford with George Irving and Louise Beavers in *Coquette* (1929), her first talkie.

Reginald Denny romances a modern, madcap Pickford in *Kiki* (1931).

Actress Mona Maris, Douglas Fairbanks, Leslie Howard, and Mary Pickford on the set of *Secrets* (1933).

Pickford, with a "strange new Douglas" on her hands, found it easy to embody Kate's bewildered rage in *The Taming of the Shrew* (1929).

Fairbanks as Petruchio and Pickford as Kate.

Douglas Fairbanks Jr., Pickford's stepson,
with Greta Garbo in *A Woman of Affairs* (1928).

Fiancés
Mary Pickford
and Buddy
Rogers at the
theater, 1937.

A test shot of Pickford as *Alice in Wonderland*, an aborted Disney project, 1932.

Pickford on the radio, c. 1934. Lines were drawn on the photo to suggest potential retouching.

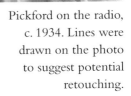

Mary Pickford (left), divorced from Douglas Fairbanks, and Lady Sylvia Ashley, Fairbanks's new wife, 1941. Such meetings were awkward. Here, the actress Norma Shearer stands between them.

The Rogers family beneath Mary's portrait at Pickfair, c. 1946.

Rogers and Pickford with their adopted children, Ronald and Roxanne, 1941.

Malcolm Boyd, Pickford's "spiritual son," graduates from seminary with Mary at his side, 1953.

Mary Pickford (second from left) at the burial of D.W. Griffith, 1948. Lillian Gish and actor Richard Barthelmess are at the far right.

Mary Pickford in
Toronto, 1963.

Mary Pickford
with Buddy Rogers,
1976: a troubled
marriage that lasted
forty-three years.

Taradash read aloud and Mary listened. "I almost lost my voice," he remembered later. "I was reading aloud for at least two hours. But Pickford was transfixed. I couldn't believe my eyes, when I took them off the page, to see how intent she was, how totally involved and how emotionally excited. Within about ten minutes after I'd finished, she said, 'I want to do this picture.' Of course, we were thrilled, and I think she felt pretty good about us, too."

Indeed, Pickford took up the movie's cause, agreeing to make certain enigmatic statements that would keep its inflammatory subject secret while igniting public interest. "This is a picture which stands for everything we Americans hold dear," she said earnestly. "It is the most important subject in the world today." But the announcement that Pickford was returning to the movies was the most important subject in many papers; there was front-page jubilation in the *New York Times*. Kramer's studio, Columbia, was elated; Columbia had never really wanted to make the film, but with Pickford on board it was a viable project.

Unfortunately, Hedda Hopper disapproved. In the 1930s, the former silent actress ascended from providing tidbits to Louella Parsons to writing her own gossip column in a rival paper. Like Louella, she cheerfully wrecked careers, and the Red scare increased her taste for blood.

Hopper decided that producer Stanley Kramer was too liberal for her liking; she also hadn't liked Mary's off-again, on-again bond with Chaplin. She made a threatening call to Pickfair: was Mary going to work for that Red, Stanley Kramer? And it seemed she wasn't. Three weeks before the film was due to start, Pickford stated that she wished to make a Technicolor comeback (*The Librarian*, she regretted, would be in black and white). The excuse was concocted by committee: "We didn't want to say that she pulled out because she was afraid of being labeled a Red," said Taradash. Happily for the writer, *The Librarian* lingered on; first Irene Dunne, then Barbara Stanwyck considered the project. Finally Taradash became the director, called the movie *Storm Center*, cast Bette Davis, and released the film in 1956.

But Mary had less fortitude. "This was a beloved actress, and she needed an outlet," said Malcolm Boyd. "Naturally people thought all they had to do was come up with the vehicle. But that was wrong. Mary had shifted gears." Even a dinner with old friends was often too much to bear.

One night, when Lillian Gish and Boyd were at Pickfair, Mary got up, left the table, and wandered off. After an hour, Boyd and Gish went to find her. They searched the grounds to find Pickford, still glittering in jewels and taffeta, lying unconscious on the guest-house bed. Her understanding guests turned out the lights and left her.

12

—

LETTING GO

No place in Los Angeles, next to Pickfair, was more redolent of Fairbanks than the sprawling lot where Doug and Mary, as husband and wife, had made films in the 1920s. Here, despite film production's relentless pace, they could steal a few intimate moments: phone calls, tea breaks, and sunny walks in costume, hand in hand. The work also allowed for spontaneous romance. It is believed that Mary, in a wig, stood in for the dark-haired Billie Dove, who played *The Black Pirate*'s resident princess, for a last scene requiring an amorous clinch. Pickford also appeared as the Virgin Mary — a walk on, but a pretty one — in Fairbanks's *The Gaucho*. (A penny sparkler burned behind her to create the appropriate celestial glow.) And legend has it that Fairbanks dashed over like a "wild, wounded bull" when he heard that, during a rehearsal for *Sparrows*, his wife was running barefoot past lunging alligators — not only that, but while carrying a baby on her back. Mary loved this story of her husband's chivalry, although the danger to her was probably not that great. The gators were on the set, but not as close to her as they appear in the film: that moment of terror was accomplished through a complicated trick shot.

When Pickford and Fairbanks weren't making films, the lot was a cash cow, bringing in a handsome rental income. Joe Schenck, for instance, filmed Art Cinema productions there; he also bore the cost of retooling for sound. Goldwyn, who had been given a fifth of the shares when he became a UA partner, also used the lot and acquired more shares as they came on the market. (After the death of Fairbanks, for instance, he relieved Sylvia of Douglas's holdings.) By 1949 the producer had collected thirty-nine of the lot's potential eighty shares. And, Mary, who had forty-one, liked to rub his nose in her winning hand – driving to the studio with Boyd, for instance, then parking her car in Goldwyn's space. She promised "Mal darling" she would return in "just a minute," then sailed into the studio to do some business. "That was her deviltry," remembered Boyd, who had to make peace when Goldwyn found him in the car.

Such malicious diversions may have passed the time, but Mary Pickford was fiddling while her company burned. By 1949 the clock had wound down for United Artists. There were only a few B movies to distribute – but at least it had a president, Gradwell Sears. He had been chosen by the board, a necessary measure when the two remaining partners weren't on speaking terms.

Sears sent Pickford and Chaplin a letter that was meant to shock:

> Your company is in a most perilous predicament ... without credit, working capital or any guarantee of forthcoming production. Theatre receipts are declining and, in your President's opinion, will continue to do so due to inferior pictures and the competition offered by television. The foreign markets are rapidly depleting and will undoubtedly get worse.... The United Artists Corporation has a great name, but it must have working capital in order to inspire confidence of banking institutions and worthwhile production. Without capital, credit or proper production, it cannot now long continue to meet its obligations.

Selmer Chalif, a UA lawyer who was married to Pickford's cousin Verna, made his own assessment. He wrote to Sears, "I've had several conversations with Madam and she seems to still be playing around with mysterious plans. She now says there are two [potential offers] that might mean something but she always winds up with a little touch of discouragement.

... I don't know what her ultimate goal is ... but I do have a distinct feeling that both she and Chaplin are waiting for a miracle."

United Artists stock was now virtually worthless. The company at that point was hemorrhaging a hundred thousand dollars a week, and funds due to producers were being diverted into day-to-day operations. But in 1950 two lawyers, Arthur Krim and Robert Benjamin, each of whom had worked in the movie industry, looked at the books and thought UA could squeak through with proper management. Mary, Krim discovered, was in deep denial. She had entertained some unrealistic offers, from people who knew little of the film world, and believed that her company was worth as much as twelve million dollars. Each time an offer was made, said Krim, "she had to be given a dash of cold water to realize that this was pie in the sky and while she was delaying in coming to grips with the reality of the situation ... the company was getting sicker and sicker." Pickford's latest (and last) effort as producer, *Love Happy* (1950), with the Marx brothers, was not the hoped-for cure. Her co-producer was a relative nonentity named Lester Cowan, and the film ran out of funds before completion. Critics greeted the result with flat reviews.

In February 1951 she and Chaplin let the lawyers take control of United Artists by making them trustees for its stock. And just in time, according to Krim, who claimed they were days from receivership. They immediately raised about half a million dollars, which they used as capital, and also found product – at first, some B movies from the bankrupt Eagle-Lion Classics, and then two windfalls, the western *High Noon* and *The African Queen*. Miraculously, UA was out of debt by 1952, and Krim and Benjamin collected their reward, half ownership. But the bad blood continued between the founders. They rarely spoke, unless to engage in petty spite, and the silliest displays were about a cat. The Pickfair pet often nipped down the road to Chaplin's home, where it knew it could count on extra food. Mary deemed this alienation of affection, even theft, and would often phone Chaplin, demanding the wandering pet's return.

Chaplin's farewell to UA was *Limelight* (1952), an attempt to put into words what the Tramp had communicated in silence. The movie is filled with self-conscious speeches espousing his smile-through-tears philosophy, and some allude to his recent traumas. "As a man gets on in years," he sighs, "he wants to live deeply. A feeling of sad dignity comes upon him and that's fatal for a comic. It affected my work. I lost contact with the audience." The sympathetic, ravishingly young Claire Bloom sits, hanging on the white-haired actor's words. "What a sad business," she exclaims, "being funny!"

In September Chaplin sailed with his wife and their children to attend *Limelight's* world premiere in London. His departure entailed tense negotiations to obtain the essential re-entry permit. He had been at sea only two days when he heard that the permit had been revoked. And when Chaplin learned that in order to return to the United States he would have to endure an investigation, he decided he would not return at all.

Good riddance, according to Hedda Hopper, who claimed that thousands of people in Hollywood were "dancing in the street for joy." There was more of the same from Westbrook Pegler: "He has lived among us and imposed upon us by flouting our ideals and degrading our morals and standards in entertainment for almost half a century." When *Limelight* was released in the United States, the American Legion brought out vociferous picket lines. The film did poorly – many bookings were canceled – and it failed to play Los Angeles, a necessary engagement if the film were to be eligible for an Oscar.

The Oscars went ahead without Chaplin but with Pickford. On March 19, 1953, the queenly Mary swept onstage, jewels aglitter, at the Pantages Theatre in Los Angeles. The Academy Awards were being broadcast to a television audience for the first time, and "the accent," according to *Life*, "was on nostalgia." Indeed, *The Greatest Show on Earth* was declared best picture, an award conferred on its producer/director, Cecil B. DeMille. When he accepted, noted *Life*, he trailed forty years of moviemaking in his wake. And it was another oldster, Mary Pickford, who gave DeMille the golden hardware.

Her terror of the man had long ago subsided. But she was still in awe of him, for Cecil had not only weathered talkies but triumphed in them – striding, like the prophets he loved to film, through the corridors of power, making great pronouncements. He considered himself a great artist, and some took him at his word. When Pickford was a girl, she had listened to David Belasco's bombast and received it as profundity. Now, at age sixty, she sang DeMille's praises with the breathtaking dullness of a dutiful schoolgirl: "He's one of the finest metaphysicians I've ever met. He knows the Bible from cover to cover. I'm sure that he's just as conversant with all of the great philosophical and metaphysical works."

Mary's next public performance was just as successful. In April her down-to-earth manner and promptness (rare for a secret drinker) made a bond-selling tour a seamless triumph. The project, co-chaired by Mamie Eisenhower, hoped to encourage good saving habits. Mary kicked off the tour in the nation's capital, sold her first bond to Mamie's husband, then finessed a seven-week, twenty-six-city tour of speaking engagements.

But at other times drink made her play the fool. In 1950 Malcolm Boyd had enrolled in an Episcopal seminary in Berkeley, California. Soon after the bonds tour Mary drove down to watch him graduate. "She was wonderful, fine at first," said Boyd. "Then she went to the ladies' room and came back drunk." After dinner, she addressed his classmates. "Yooouuuu ... future ... men ... of ... God," she drawled, her persona distorting every word. "Yoooooou are crusaders ... of truth ... in the world." The effect was theatrical, superficial. "Everyone hated her," said Boyd, who had praised Mary's brilliance to the other students. "Later they talked about her cruelly. Mary had just smashed three years of my life. On the other hand," he added ruefully, "why would her behavior be different this time?" Mary was beyond embarrassment. A photograph shows her, arms flung out, face turned to the sun, looking lost in bliss.

In 1954 Chaplin tempted fate by accepting a peace prize that the right wing labeled "Communist-sponsored." Worse, he went to dinner with Chou En-lai. The predictable Chaplin-bashing followed, and – despite their quarrels, despite the cat – Mary finally felt goaded into speaking out. "I am no Communist but I don't think that anybody, including Chaplin, should be condemned without his day in court." Speaking on a New York radio show, she continued, "I'm going to fight for the right – for his right, your right and my right to stand up for what we believe in.... I'm going to risk the wrath of people that are so poisonous that if you will disagree with them they would have you thrown in jail. And that is the hole in the dike that I spoke about. It is the crumbling of the ramparts we watch."

This swipe at the notorious Westbrook Pegler so inflamed the columnist that he now turned virulently anti-Pickford. At one time, he fumed, the actress had written him a self-described "fan letter," praising his attacks on FDR. Now he considered her imbecilic, suggesting that because she had written an article for *McCall's* (this was a left-wing publication, Pegler hinted), Mary Pickford had gone pink around the edges.

McCall's transgression was to run "My Whole Life," an unpretentious series of memoirs that appeared in book form a year later as *Sunshine and Shadow* (1955). Mary found "writing" the first draft delightful: six months of talking to a tape recorder. But sweeping cuts were made to the manuscript when Mary's chat became contentious. The result was a sticky-sweet, wholesome read, leavened by revealing veins of black moods, family love, and lacerating guilt. Still, it was astonishingly well reviewed. Today few people would agree that the book is "one of the best histories of the American movies" – but at the time, few scholars wrote seriously of the silents, and much of what appeared in the book was new. Predictably, Mary found time to brood. "It nearly drives me mad leaving out so many things I know but can't print," she fretted to one reporter. "I couldn't tell the worst and the best," she told another, remembering that she "tried to fight the publisher" and lost.

There was another defeat when, in 1955, Goldwyn finally won the fight to own the old production lot. A showdown became inevitable when he announced he would remove "improvements" he had made there for his various films. A game of suit-countersuit ensued, until a judge slapped the opponents' wrists and ruled that the lot should be sold at auction. "They acted like children," said Boyd, amazed, who knew what the property meant to Mary. But throughout, "she didn't seem to think this thing was real."

Pickford was determined to crush Sam Goldwyn, and even posed for photos with her fist in the air. First out of the gate at the auction, she opened with a $1.5-million bid. Goldwyn then matched her, tit for tat, till the sum hovered just below two million. Then Mary unaccountably lost her nerve. When Goldwyn upped the bid another twenty thousand dollars, there was a pause. Pickford watched as the gavel dropped. Only then did she seem to realize she'd lost another fragment of Douglas Fairbanks. Emerging from court, Mary seemed subdued: "I want to forget business for a while." Later, said Boyd, she sobbed in private.

In March 1955 Chaplin finally sold his shares in United Artists. "I cried my eyes out over that," said Pickford later, "though I wouldn't let Charlie see me. A woman should never take unfair advantage of a man that way." For all their quarrels, his departure shocked her, for the business alliance with Chaplin was a link both to Fairbanks and to a sweeter, more familiar era. Later, when Mary's grief subsided, she allowed the old vitriol to return. "I never wanted Chaplin in the company," she fretted. "That was Douglas's idea." Still, at public events, she wished him well.

Now the sole remaining founder of United Artists, she was consummately charming to Robert Blumofe, an associate of Arthur Krim and Robert Benjamin, who was charged with delivering constant updates. "What are you boys doing with my company?" she asked him, like a dig in the ribs, when he visited Pickfair. They were making it flourish. The game plan included a practice that had always been avoided by the previous regimes: financing independents and, in essence, becoming co-producers. In this setup, the producer and United Artists would agree on the choice of director, story, cast, and budget. United Artists then stepped aside, giving the creators of the film free rein; in addition, the producer owned a share of the movie and the right to participate in the profits. Not surprisingly, UA was soon overwhelmed with suitors, and in 1956 it showed a profit of six million dollars – a spectacular improvement over 1950's deficit, which had veered close to the million-dollar mark.

Mary should have been grateful and relieved. But instead she felt only fatigue and loss. United Artists, her "pride and joy and also, at times, my despair," was becoming too heavy a cross to bear. Finally, in February 1956, Mary followed Chaplin's lead and burned her bridges, selling back her shares for a cool three million. "I sold because there were too many problems and nothing was the same," she told a writer later. "Mr. Griffith was dead." Then she added, heartsick, "So was Douglas."

"That is my life up to now," *Sunshine and Shadow*'s final pages had declared – but Mary had fiddled with the truth. Six-year-old Ronnie and the baby Roxanne appear, magically charming, at the close. But alert readers also found them magically young, for their actual ages were probably nineteen and thirteen when *Sunshine and Shadow* was published. By that time, the family had much to hide.

Pickford showered attention on Roxanne. "She was treated like a princess, like a doll," said Boyd. "But I think that in some way, Roxanne lacked the experience of direct, real love." Roxanne's first words were French, as she often was attended by the French-speaking maid. To adults, she seemed lost amidst the parties, the formal occasions, and Mary's first love, alcohol. And as she aged, Roxanne grew rambunctious. "I was always a rebel," she remembered, looking back. "I was never a *bad* child" – but often up to mischief, and "imaginative. I could figure out ways of getting around things quite well." This included how to raid Mary's costume collection (for dress-up games) and between-meal snacks from the Pickfair fridge. Mary often caught Roxanne with her fingers in a tray of hors-d'oeuvres at midnight but couldn't reproach her, since Mary had arrived there with the same intention. Such incidents cast Roxanne as the incarnation of Mary's old character Rebecca – and Pickford, in turn, as the tetchy parent who doesn't dare reveal the smile she feels inside. But often Mary's wrath was deep and real. "My mother was very, very strong-willed, and I am very stubborn at times," said Roxanne. "We did have our differences. But," she added earnestly, "we always made them up." And then more differences would begin, as Roxanne "never went along with anything I was supposed to." In her teens, Mary's daughter was enrolled at a lycée in Barcelona (there she lived with Gwynne, who was married to Bud Ornstein, a UA executive) and later at a private school in Lausanne. Her isolation – or perhaps her liberation – had begun.

A scan of the papers reveals that at sixteen, Ronnie was at prep school in New York State. Mary flew to his side when she heard he'd hurt his back in a football game. But despite such gestures, the relationship had rotted beyond repair. Ronnie seemed insolent, wrapped in fury. "He hated being Mary's son," remembered John Mantley. "From the day he came to Pickfair, the boy was rough-hewn, curt, and surly. And he absolutely refused to take on any round edges." Boyd also found Ronnie remote, though he sensed that his disdain was, in part, a frightened pose. "I think that Ronnie learned a survival technique. Even as a child, he was unapproachable. I'd be at most of Mary's big events, like Thanksgiving dinner, and Ronnie would be there, so cold, so distant." But in private, fury shattered Ronnie's enigmatic surface. On at least one occasion, he struck his mother. Boyd, who saw the incident, recalled that they were quarreling on the stairs of a New York hotel – and that Mary, relaxed from a round of drinks, tumbled limply to the ground.

If Ronnie could not love his mother, he thought he could love the young Lenore – his bride, whom he married in the fall of 1954. He was probably only eighteen years old when he stood at the altar, and a baby girl, Jamie, was born soon after. But apparently the new life did not take hold. Ronnie tried hard to shoulder responsibility, working day and night as an apprentice mechanic at an aircraft plant in Hawthorne, California. But his mood was still volatile, and neighbors heard shouts through the door of the family's cramped apartment. In the summer of 1955 Lenore gave birth to their son, Tommy. His arrival taxed the marriage beyond endurance. Twice Lenore packed her bags and left. Twice she returned, and the frayed, exhausted family soldiered on.

Within the year Ronnie tried to kill himself. In late March 1956 police found him in his apartment, unconscious, with a photo of Lenore dangling from his hand. A neighbor had been tending the children when he wrote a final note to his wife, who had left him and, this time, not returned.

The contents of the letter: "My Dearest Darling. What I am about to do is one of the hardest things I've done but it has to be this way. This is not a quick decision because I've thought about it over and over. I've tried to love you, darling, but you wouldn't let me. I've loved you more each day until my love for you got so deep that I could never lose it. I figured I am lucky to have just had your love if even for a moment." Ronnie also assured her he had written a letter to Mary Pickford: "I'm sure she will give you enough to start a very happy life." (If she got the letter, Mary never told a soul.)

At the hospital, doctors pumped Ronnie's stomach. Fenton, Mary's butler, brought Lenore to Ronnie's bedside, where she said some tender words and the patient wept. Pickford, who had her son transferred from a hospital in Hawthorne to the tonier St. John's in Santa Monica, arrived at his bedside in a state of shock. "This is terrible," she said. "I was resting in Palm Springs. It was a rest I needed." "Madam," said the doctor, "*your son has tried to commit suicide and he nearly succeeded.*"

Now the children disappear – from the press, from the memory of

Mary's friends. But oddly, Douglas Fairbanks lived. It was as though he were caught, mid-leap, over Pickfair, casting his shadow on Buddy Rogers and inspiring his wife to new heights of admiration. "No matter how many people were in the room, when he left, the room was empty," she rhapsodized. Well and good, but she often called her present husband "Douglas" – a forgivable slip if it happened once. But it happened many times, drunk or sober, behind Rogers's back and to his face. Once, on the street, she heard, "Oh! Mrs. Fairbanks," and instinctively turned around. In fact, the remark was addressed to Jayar's second wife, who was shopping with her in Manhattan. At Pickfair Mary often launched, unasked, into paeans to the legendary Fairbanks dash ("like an arrow in full flight"). Guests were afraid to meet Buddy's eyes. "It was always 'Douglas,'" one listener recalled, "as if he was with her, at that moment. A completely different look was on her face, a different sound came to her voice. When she talked about Fairbanks, she was passionate." A Canadian film critic, Gerald Pratley, was amazed when Mary greeted him at Pickfair with a stiff drink, raved about her fabulous Fairbanks (in the background, Buddy tinkled the piano), then opened a closet and showed him several rows of Fairbanks's suits.

Then there was Jayar, the glittering stepson – now Sir Douglas Fairbanks. It seemed fitting that Fairbanks Jr. should be knighted; at one time Fairbanks Sr. had been nearly royal himself. Jayar's award was for good works, especially with CARE, which sent food to the needy in postwar Europe. When he was knighted in 1948, he was scheduled for a three-minute audience with King George. Instead, he spent forty, sharing cigarettes and sherry. Some in Britain thought Jayar was an interloper. Some Americans, confused, began to think he was British. But a man who could entertain in *Sinbad the Sailor* (1947) and five years later give a dinner for the young Queen Elizabeth in London was, to say the least, uniquely situated.

How did Buddy cope? "He played golf," said Boyd. "He was good at it, too. He built his lifestyle around it." On the links, Buddy Rogers was his own man; at Pickfair he seemed something less. In 1950 he had hosted a television show called *Cavalcade of Bands*. "Don't worry, dear," said his wife when he fluffed a comic's name. "You don't have to work." The news struck Buddy like a revelation. "That was it. I wasn't lazy, but I didn't have to work." Instead, he explained, he and Mary kept their spirits up with "little things" and travel. This included several trips to see Gwynne and Roxanne in Spain. There were other trips to Europe throughout the decade. It is hard to imagine Mary liking these tours; she had loathed being dragged around the world by Fairbanks. But the vacations kept up appearances and masked her increasing inner drift. They may also have been bonuses for Buddy – sweet, supportive Buddy, who was younger and less worldly, and who, above all, endured.

"I don't always understand him," she confided in her memoirs. "At times I find him aloof, self-contained, undemonstrative; a complete introvert. I am just the contrary, a complete extrovert." This attack, both public and unprovoked, seems a bit cockeyed; most friends of the couple would have switched the labels. Perhaps, at times, Mary saw her long-suffering husband recoil, or refuse to take the bait, when she unleashed her rage. Indeed, "she could be hard on him," admitted Mantley. "One night at Pickfair I said something, and Buddy interrupted, and then Mary interrupted *him*: 'Oh, why don't you *stop*, Buddy! He has more intelligence in his little finger than you have in your whole body!' At a moment like that, the whole room would freeze. Later Buddy would remember, and just chuckle and say, 'That little dickens.'"

Rogers was a kind man. He loved his wife. If he suffered, almost no one saw it. "He was gallant and gracious, all the time," said Mantley. Malcolm Boyd agreed: "There was mutual caring." But he also saw a dangerous undercurrent. "Each wanted to hurt, and each knew where the hurt was. There were very sharp words at the dinner table." Worse, he saw "knockdown fights and rage. But my heart goes out to Buddy. I would never judge him. It can't have been easy to be married so long to an alcoholic."

And it couldn't have been easy to deny to journalists, for over fifty years, that Mary Pickford drank.

She could still rise, formidably, to the occasion, doing flawless work as silent film's head of state. She was endlessly kind and amusing at "the Georges" – a night of silent-film awards held at George Eastman House, a film and photographic archive, named for the celluloid stock tycoon and located in his former home in

Rochester, New York. The event was inspired, at least in part, by the death of Clyde Bruckman, a silent-film screenwriter and director who, in his work with Buster Keaton, made a series of superlative comic films. In 1955 he had not had a directing job in twenty years. One night, after eating in a West Coast restaurant, Bruckman saw the bill, realized he couldn't pay it, and went quietly to the washroom, where he shot himself.

This was not the first suicide to strike the silents, but it shocked James Card, the director of the Eastman House film department, into action. Determined to give credit to the long-neglected artists of silent film, he mailed ballots for best actor, actress, director, and cameraman to every silent veteran he could find. Both Pickford and Chaplin were easy winners, with the lion's share of votes in their categories. Mary, who attended the event in November, kept the crowd in stitches as she spoke, off the cuff, about the old days. (Chaplin, still barred from the country, was absent.) This was Pickford the Figurehead – regal but approachable, and still, after forty years, custodian of silent film's reputation.

On Easter morning, 1956, the Pickfair grounds overflowed with film folk: two hundred silent-film alumni, summoned by the Figurehead to wallow in nostalgia. "You could almost eat it with a spoon," announced Mary proudly. Wandering on the emerald-green lawns of Pickfair were contingents from Biograph and Pickford's features, and a smattering of Fairbanks's leading ladies; these guests made the gathering especially touching. Pickford also hoped that the attendant press would increase the visibility of the actors. "A lot of these darlings," she confided in an interview, "need the money." Humorously, actor William Bakewell called the gathering "a waxworks," though the keynote was laughter and auld lang syne. Only Irving Sindler, a prop man on *Rosita*, felt a touch of chill. It was Mary, ironically, whose mood seemed to dampen the atmosphere. The actress, he remembered, had become "an old lady. There was something bitter in her life and it was showing."

Neither Lillian nor Dorothy Gish attended; they were busy on the East Coast. Just as well. Mary's mood, concerning Lillian, could be tinged by envy. Once, with her guard down, she snapped, "I hate her!" She was sitting with Kemp Niver, a film historian, and Niver had shown her a picture of Lillian. Niver was shocked and asked, "How can you say that? She's your oldest and dearest friend."

Gish was a woman of exceptional good sense who guessed correctly, at the dawn of talkies, that her studio was preparing to cut her loose. In response, she stepped fearlessly back on stage, appearing in 1930 in a Broadway *Uncle Vanya* and in John Gielgud's *Hamlet* six years later. She continued to act onstage for decades, returning to the camera for prestigious films such as *Duel in the Sun* (1947), *The Night of the Hunter* (1955), Robert Altman's *A Wedding* (1978), and, claiming the age of ninety-two, a co-starring role with Bette Davis in *The Whales of August* (1987).

Gently she tried to encourage Pickford to continue her career, in some way, at some level. Trouping, for the Gishes, was a point of honor. In 1939, after Lillian saw Broadway's *Life with Father*, she quickly took herself backstage, accosted the co-author, Howard Lindsay, and asked if she and Dorothy could each tour a company. And in fact, both Gishes toured the play. A few years later, when Mary was approached about a *Father* tour, she declined because the set had a modest staircase, and running up and down it would be too exhausting. There is no known comment on this from Lillian. But she later told the tale of heroic Dorothy, who, stricken by cancer in the 1950s, could still pull herself together and get on stage. Her preparation often involved lying down in the wings, face white, fists clenched, until her cue was called. The hint from Lillian to Mary was obvious: Why can't *you*?

"[Lillian] still acts and she's too old to act," said Mary. This was nonsense. All an artist needs is inspiration, opportunity, and will; both Dorothy and Lillian Gish had all three, plus humility, self-discipline, and endless curiosity about the world and their changing place in it as performers. On the other hand, their fame was of a different kind: both (but especially Lillian) were worshipped by the highbrow crowd because of their long association with D.W. Griffith. In Lillian's case her continuing prominence was also due to intellect; Eugene O'Neill once declared she was the most intelligent woman he had ever met. Also undeniable was her acting brilliance, which her fans claim outstrips the skills of any silent actor. According to Canadian critic Urjo Kareda, Gish "seemed to hold within [her] all the possible ages of a woman, young and old, girl and adult." At sixteen her face, with its large eyes, long neck, tiny mouth, and hint of a double chin, fused her delicate, just-grown beauty with the down-to-earth sanity of a spinster. Later, at sixty, Gish's gaze could be steady, determined, serene, or wrathful. It also seemed as helpless as a soft, young girl's. Watching Lillian Gish grow old seemed not a violation but a trust fulfilled. But an old Little Mary? To her acolytes, the notion was grotesque.

In 1956 Lillian sailed, unruffled, through a television performance of a best-selling book, *The Day Lincoln Was Shot*. She adored going "live" before the cameras, comparing the adrenaline rush to the thrill of early film. Then she toured with Dorothy in the play *The Chalk Garden*. But when Pickford made the news, she was less impressive: the unfortunate incident in May, for instance, when a gun went off near Pickfair's door. Mary was returning, after midnight, from a party with a group of friends. These included her husband and Marion Davies, a fine silent actress and an even more legendary alcoholic. After living with William Randolph Hearst for forty years, Davies married a Captain Horace Brown. (At the wedding in Las Vegas, Davies had to be held up to say "I do.")

Brown, who was also in Mary's party, had been showing Buddy Rogers how to handle a gun – a professional matter, Mary's butler told reporters, for his master had just acted in a western. Unfortunately, Brown stepped in some oil on the Pickfair drive and took a fall to the pavement, and the gun went off. A bullet hit Pickfair, then ricocheted to Mary's head – or so she thought. At the hospital, doctors found a small lump, caused (they supposed) by a bit of flying plaster. This was just the sort of press Lottie had once received.

Meanwhile Buddy's minor westerns came and went. The last, called *The Parson and the Outlaw*, was released in 1957. Mary was believed to have put up the money – not much, as the film was shot in seventeen days, and rehearsals were held by the Pickfair bar. "My Buddy," cooed Mary, as she patted his cheek, "he's going to make a picture!"

Perhaps Buddy, too, was growing bored.

The death of Marshall Neilan left Mary stunned. His directing career had declined with the silents, and for years he lived penniless, squeaking by on an extra's pay and loans. The tide seemed to turn, for a moment, when Elia Kazan cast the actor in *A Face in the Crowd* (1957). "I have never seen a man who had once been as big as Mickey behave with so little bitterness," said Kazan. "He seemed to have no resentment or hatred in him." But cancer of the throat prevented Neilan from continuing his career. Desperately ill and destitute, he checked into the Motion Picture Country House, assuring Pickford, "I'll beat it yet." Instead, he began to waste away. Following some futile treatments, Neilan died there in 1958.

In his will he left Pickford some unfinished story ideas and scripts. And specific instructions: she was not – repeat, not – to attend the burial (nor was anyone). Instead, she was one of fifteen people whom he asked to attend a wake at Hollywood's Knickerbocker Hotel. There, at the end of the bar, was an open bottle of beer, a glass, and a tag: "Reserved for Mickey Neilan." At first Mary tried to disobey, leaving the funeral and proceeding toward the cemetery in her Rolls. But her car, unaccountably, coughed and died. "I had the most weird sensation that Mickey was playing his last diabolical joke on me for disobeying his instructions! I could almost hear him saying to himself in glee, 'Look at the Tad – thought she was so elegant in her Rolls-Royce, but I outfoxed her!'" Pickford, chastened, took a taxi to the wake.

Jesse Lasky died that same year, with a huge outstanding debt to the tax department. A few years later, a request for aid was submitted to the board of the Motion Picture Relief Fund. The applicant's husband had been broke when he died, and his widow was penniless. No name was revealed (this was customary), and as Mary heard the story, she shook her head, scolded the deceased for being bad with money, and expressed only limited sympathy for him. At the suggestion of her fellow board member William Bakewell, a vote was taken to reveal the name. It was Lasky's widow, Blanche, and Pickford blushed. "Oh my God. I cannot tell you how sorry I am. How could I . Jesse was my partner, my friend." Another vote was taken – in Lasky's favor.

Pickford's last great cause was the care of the elderly. She had once told *Photoplay* that wealth sapped the urge to do creative work, or "to make good in anything. . . . Wealth and place weaken endeavor, weaken the will to sacrifice, weaken passionate enthusiasm." But the loss of old friends brought her own enthusiasm back to full strength, and in 1961 Pickford threw her support behind a state bill to house the old and sick. She spoke well on the issue. This was lucky; when asked in 1960 about Khrushchev and Castro, Mary answered with "a real gusty snort," suggesting, "Shoot 'em."

Mary's comments were both reasoned and from the heart. "It is a shame and disgrace," she declared. "It upsets me. . . . Most of these people have lived gainful lives and find their savings wiped out, mainly by the costs of medical care and serious illnesses. I am not for socialized medicine, but there should be some way to stop waste in government and provide the dollars necessary to take care of our poor old people."

Or her poor old friends. In 1963 James Kirkwood died. His last directing jobs had been forgettable films – *In Wrong* and *Bill Apperson's Boy*, which had starred Jack, forty-four years before. Both films were made with Pickford funds, and it is commonly believed that Kirkwood's presence as director was the family choice. When directing dried up, Kirkwood found himself back before the cameras, and he spent the next decade on stage and screen. But the stock market crash wiped out his fortune, and he couldn't find work in the talkie era. Still a hard drinker at the age of eighty, he refused Pickford's offer of a place at the Motion Picture Country House. He was "gallant in adversity," declared a friend, though much of the notorious Kirkwood charm was now blotted out by temper and ethnic slurs.

At the funeral, Pickford was overwrought. She went to view the body (which was not her habit) and had to be supported as she made her approach, cried Kirkwood's name, threw roses on the face of the corpse, and swooned. Two days later she sat with Kemp Niver, who had dipped into his archives and pulled out an old Biograph, *Sweet and Twenty*. They watched James Kirkwood, large as life. In the film, a frisky comedy, he played Mary's father (though the difference in their actual ages was only nine years). Mary, who is waiting for her beau to arrive, tries to show she's doing nothing of the sort. A game of "loves me, loves me not" with a flower becomes, under Kirkwood's gaze, a badly faked botanical investigation. Kirkwood isn't fooled; he looks at Mary, at the flower, and then walks on, smiling.

Another loss: Roxanne had deserted Pickfair. No one seems to know how or when this happened, though Boyd recalls vaguely that she married, in her teens, a young man who worked at a filling station. The marriage was a mismatch and didn't last. Still, it achieved Roxanne's purpose: to distance herself from Pickfair. Indeed, it soon seemed as though she had never existed. Mary's friends had the impression that Ronnie and Roxanne were to be blotted out, Stalin-style, from discussion. And in a senseless, vengeful moment, Pickford tried to burn another bridge, with Frances Marion. The screenwriter, asked to a Pickfair dinner in the early 1960s, was astonished when her hostess came down the staircase, glimpsed Marion among the other guests, and ordered her to leave the house at once. The reason: forty years before, Marion had written the screenplay for *Anne of Green Gables*, starring Mary Miles Minter. Marion quietly left the dinner. Two days later, Pickford sent her an incoherent note: "I am terrible afraid I hurt your feelings the other evening. I so frightfully sorry and appologeties." Generously, Marion forgave her. But as the years went on, the friendship was reduced to bouquets on their birthdays and occasional notes. For emotional connection, Mary Pickford lived increasingly in the past. The memories she chose were of a better world.

"She would speak of events as if they happened only yesterday," said Douglas Kirkland. In 1963 he was a *Look* photographer, sent to take pictures of the actress for an article. Pickford was elated, "even girlish." And she put herself entirely in Kirkland's hands, "going on location with the boys" in her Rolls, singing "God Save the King" at the top of her lungs if it would make a good photo. Kirkland shot in the morning, because his subject grew listless by half past eleven. In the end the *Look* piece never ran, and "I heard that that was hard on her. Very hard." In 1989, when a book of Kirkland's work was published, a photo from the session finally surfaced. In it Mary stands by the pool, with her hands crossed before her in a dolorous pose. Her blond wig resembles a stiff meringue, and her eyes look down. The effect is desolate.

Mary traveled to Toronto for the last time in 1963, declaring that she wore her hometown "like a beautiful mantle. I feel safe." She admitted to age seventy (she was seventy-one), refused to pose holding a drink in her hand ("not me, I'm a hypocrite"), and turned up on a television quiz show called *Front Page Challenge*. Buddy, now a silvery Lorne Greene look-alike, joined her as she chatted in a panel segment – and caused ripples of excitement (more than Mary did) from the audience.

In 1965 Mary Pickford was given a more meaningful honor when the Cinémathèque Française staged a massive retrospective of her work. Pickford cherished the occasion; she had always had a crush on France. The response – to over fifty of her films – overwhelmed her. "The French never forget an artist who has pleased them," she responded. "I have received many honors in my life and have had audiences with kings and queens and the world's great. But this tribute touches me most of all."

Then she went back to Pickfair and closed the door.

"Somewhere," Mary wrote in *My Rendezvous with Life*, "I have read that 'Happy lives are little lives. They do not live beyond their rose-wreathed walls.'" For the next fifteen years Mary lived at Pickfair — sleeping, dreaming, reading the Bible, and drinking whiskey throughout the day. On occasion she and Buddy watched television sports. "And I'm going to start a movement to resist it. Football, golf, tennis — where does that leave a wife?" Sometimes Buddy took her out for drives, and Roxanne, who came for visits, also played chauffeur. Occasionally Pickford would slip downstairs for a movie in her private screening room. But she soon grew disgusted with modern Hollywood. When Buddy arranged a Pickfair showing of *Bob and Carol and Ted and Alice*, a 1969 "swinging" comedy, Mary called it off after several reels. "You boys get that stag movie out of here."

When she was lucid, "she was quick as a whip," said Roger Seward, who was hired as Pickfair's security guard after Sharon Tate's murder in 1969. His job was to check the doors at night. "Then they told me to sit on the landing by their bedrooms and make sure I had a gun and knew how to use it. It was the rattiest chair in the world," he added. "Buddy said he didn't want me to fall asleep." There was a lot to stay awake for: through the bedroom door, Seward often heard Pickford giving Buddy a tongue-lashing.

In 1970 Gwynne arranged for her daughter, Mary Charlotte, to be wed at Mary's home. The estate was still lovely, with a breathtaking view (though the twelve-acre lot had been sold, bit by bit, till it was down to four). First Aunt Mary announced she would attend, and had a special wig made, for her hair was sparse. But she canceled at the last minute, claiming that a rare appearance outside her room would steal the spotlight from the bride. And indeed, Pickford rarely left her bed. Gwynne, who came from Spain from time to time, claimed that Mary sometimes slipped from her room at night and drifted through the house, looking over her possessions. If she did, Roger Seward never saw it.

She adored Douglas Fairbanks Jr. – from afar. He spent most of these years at his London home, but a steady stream of flowers, cards, and photos arrived at Mary's door. It took only his signature ("from your son") to reduce "Mama Mary" to a flood of grateful tears. Still, when this paragon came to visit, he was banished to the guest house. Even Gwynne spent her nights outside the mansion and, like others, saw Pickford by appointment.

"I'm not Garbo," said Mary. "I don't *vant to be alone.*" But she always had excuses: she had fallen, for instance, and hurt her leg – so badly, it seems, that she required constant bed rest and her legs began to atrophy from lack of use. About 1970 she endured a cataract operation. "That was upsetting," she conceded. "More to my nerves than to my eyes." "She's fine," echoed Rogers. But he sometimes grew wistful. "I only wish she had more energy. I wish I could give her some of mine."

Few people were allowed to see Pickford now. Fairbanks Jr., Lillian Gish, Colleen Moore, and Adolph Zukor's daughter Mildred were among the few allowed into the inner sanctum. John Mantley (who was by then the producer of television's *Gunsmoke*) and Gwynne were allowed, with their children in tow. Adela Rogers St. Johns, who made the pilgrimage, wrote that "reports and dark rumors to the contrary," Pickford was "still very much alive and doing well, thank you." St. Johns stoutly maintained, "I can promise you that any vicious tales of Mary's 'secret drinking,' any tales that she spends her life in seclusion *because* of this dark secret, are not only vicious but untrue. Lies. Mean, petty, criminally careless lies." But other friends admitted that the chatelaine of Pickfair was drunk in bed.

Mary spoke to reporters on the phone if they called when she was brightest (in the early afternoon). She would often fade away in mid-conversation, at which point Rogers interceded. She promised many people she would speak to them, write them, remember or see them. For Robert Cushman, then at UCLA (where he spent years studying Mary's films), the actress wrote letters of introduction, and she lent him her personal clipping book. She gave him a watch when he graduated, and two of her letters invited him to visit her. But each time Cushman telephoned, he was told by a secretary, Esther Helm, that the actress was indisposed; call again another day. The days grew into months – then approached a decade.

In May 1971 Rogers warned his wife, "Honey, all your friends are coming, all those wonderful members of the press." The occasion was the exhibition of ten Pickford features and a sampling of her Biographs at the Los Angeles County Museum of Art. Robert Cushman, who curated the show, wrote memorable program notes. This was part of a worldwide celebration: Pickford's films were shown in Washington, San Francisco, New York, and Dearborn, Michigan; Stratford, Ontario; London, Brighton, and some European cities. In what was meant to be a festive kickoff, a group of reporters were asked to come to Pickfair for a press event.

But the mood was wrong; the house seemed sealed and drained of life. The third-floor Oriental Room lined with treasures from Pickford's heyday seemed utterly unused, and other items (Napoleon's dinnerware, for instance) were displayed in glass museum cases. Champagne, served in antique crystal, failed to take the edge off. For at this point, Mary's retreat to the bedroom had entered film mythology. She seemed the living essence of *Sunset Boulevard* – the mythic star who, unable to rule the world at large, had retreated to a dream world, where she reigned supreme.

Buddy, ever jovial, came to greet them – not with Mary Pickford but with a tape recorder. "Mary's so happy you're all here," he assured them, then he started the tape. According to reporter Aljean Harmetz, who wrote about the day's events at length, it emitted a "musty, unused" voice, which seemed "cracked and faded, like a piece of velvet ruined by the sun." "She's a million times better than that," said Rogers as he pushed the stop button. "She's been sick, you know." Then he ended on a trademark bit of treacle: "She was 'My Best Girl' in 1927 and she's still my best girl." His listeners nodded.

Buddy then led the troops upstairs. "Darling," he called into Mary's room, "all your friends are here." A faint murmur inside. "Give them what?" asked Rogers. More murmurs, which everyone strained to hear. "Give them your love?" asked Buddy, peering in. "Mary says to give you her love," he repeated, and reporters scribbled. (To Harmetz, the effect was an unholy marriage of Edgar Allan Poe and Edgar Bergen.) As the press followed Buddy down the hall, some glanced at the haunting, half-closed door.

How much easier, and truer, to show the films. There, rather than a disembodied voice at Pickfair, Mary was an image alive with joy and fire. Before the 1971 screenings, confessed critic Rhonda Koenig in the *Village Voice*, "my image of Mary Pickford was that of a curly-headed blonde, all ruffles, ribbons, and Ivory soap." Afterward she wrote about the close of *Sparrows*: "The camera stays on her lovely face long enough for us to see everything in it; it is a look of hard-won achievement, of gratitude, a face illuminated with happiness. We have a great many actresses whose stock in trade is sexiness or kookiness or beautifully blank expressions. But an actress you can rest your eyes on while she looks radiantly happy? There are not so many of those that we can afford to overlook Mary Pickford."

But the world did overlook her, and in turn Mary Pickford overlooked the world. She preferred Douglas Fairbanks and her mother (whom, she claimed, she saw at night as ghosts). One day, as Adela came down from Mary's bedroom, she found Buddy Rogers waiting on the landing. "What did you talk about today," he asked. "Douglas?" "I suppose I looked guilty," St. Johns remembered, "for actually we very often did." "I've been married to her now for almost forty years," said Buddy, "and she still thinks, half the time, she'll always be married to Douglas Fairbanks. So do lots of other people, I guess."

Not everyone forgave her her nostalgia. The singer Pearl Bailey was a friend of Fairbanks Jr., and like Pickford, she was interested in spiritualism. She'd heard macabre tales of Mary's seclusion. In 1971, when Douglas gave a party at Pickfair, the extroverted Bailey asked to see Mary Pickford in the flesh. To everyone's astonishment, Pickford invited her to enter the forbidden bedroom (she had heard of Bailey's interest in ESP). Immediately Bailey asked about "the doll" – "the one I dreamed about, with the broken head."

Stunned, Mary pointed to her doll collection. There lay her prop doll from *The Warrens of Virginia*. It was old, made of china, and its head was broken. Gently Bailey took it in her hands, then reproached her hostess for being like a shattered doll herself – her spirit defeated, her body wasted. "When this doll is mended," predicted Bailey, "you will be too. You've got to pull yourself together and get up and get out again, and you will."

Bailey took the doll away to be repaired, and soon it was returned, good as new, to Pickfair. Its owner, on the other hand, never healed.

"I don't ever want to see him again ... and you can print that!" The occasion for this outburst was Chaplin's second Oscar (the first had been in 1928 for *The Circus*). In 1972 the Academy belatedly brought back the Tramp to honor "the incalculable effect he has had on making motion pictures the art form of this century." Chaplin, spooked by past experience, had steeled himself for a chorus of hisses. Instead, his entrance, the last of the evening, received a tumultuous ovation; thunderstruck, he clutched at words and managed an old Tramp trick with a bowler hat. A year later there were even more hosannas, when *Limelight*, which had at last found a venue in Los Angeles, won an Oscar for Chaplin, as composer of its score.

Pickford sulked. While the rest of the industry engaged in mass repentance, Mary's streak of compassion had at last run dry. "He wasn't grateful for his career," she complained to a reporter. "It's disgraceful that he never became a citizen." Sinking lower: "I think they should ask some of his wives what they think of him." (Chaplin married four times; of course, Pickford married almost as often.) Her resentment deepened when the actor was knighted in 1975. Still, even Douglas Fairbanks Jr. hoped that peace between the artists could be restored. He once sat with Mary in her pastel bedroom and decided that some meddling was in order. He invented a story that Chaplin was anxiously asking after Mary, telling Jayar how much he cared for her, and how sorry he was that the partnership had been broken up. "I went on and on," he remembered. "I laid it on with a trowel." Mary lay quietly, apparently believing Jayar's fabrication. When her stepson ran out of things to say, Pickford turned her gaze on him balefully. "I still say he's an s.o.b."

Pickford's second Oscar came in 1976, but she was far too fragile to attend. Her legs, after years of disuse, were crippled, and she needed a wheelchair. And she often found it hard to follow what went on around her; according to Seward, she was living on tranquilizers, light food, and watered booze.

Her acceptance of the Oscar was taped at Pickfair. Two men carried Mary down the steps – a tiny, light figure, her body wrapped tightly in something satin, with a white fur collar and ropes of jewels. Only the day before, Mary had been sitting up in bed in a pink gown, a pink flower peeking through her wisps of hair, which she wore combed and natural.

Now her face peered out below a childish wig of yellow curls, the eyes behind the false lashes looked astonished, and her mouth had been painted vermilion red. She seemed alternately fearful, amazed, and insensible — though her gaze became suddenly as bright as a bird's as she told a technician how she wished to be lighted.

"Mary," said Academy president Walter Mirisch, "I present this to you with great pride and with the love and admiration of the whole Academy." Mary nodded, eyes glacial, with her old hands steepled in the prayer position. "You've made me verrry, verrrry happy . . . and thank you," she drawled, her voice corroded. Pickford grappled with the Oscar and stroked its head. "I shall treasure it always," she assured him, wobbling. Then a tear left her left eye on perfect cue.

Her acceptance, when broadcast, caused an uproar. "I didn't think it was possible," wrote Mike Royko in the *Los Angeles Times*, "but Mary Pickford, the one-time screen darling of America, has managed to offend lots of people. She did it by growing old. . . . For some reason it doesn't bother people nearly as much when an elderly actress has her breasts propped up like the bow of a ship, her facial skin stretched out like a drumhead, her siliconed body girdled and buttressed into preposterous curves and lumps. . . . Many of those who saw Mary Pickford said they would rather remember her as she once was. Why? She's not dead. She may be old but she is a living, breathing human being."

But Mary's aged body was not the only issue, at least for the Oscars' more thoughtful viewers. It was the hint of incompetence that made the taped tribute seem exploitive and cruel. As a critic complained in the *New York Post*, "I wouldn't be surprised if that video-taped interlude were sold as a short to be packaged with a double-bill re issue of *Sunset Boulevard* and *What Ever Happened to Baby Jane?* . . . I felt I was watching the most pornographic moment in the history of television."

"It was after the Oscar," said Roger Seward, "that she started to go downhill. She began regressing, thinking she was young again and on the road." When Douglas came to visit, he held her hand ("skin-and-bones," he wrote). She was fairly alert and told jokes with her usual bawdy humor. She recalled their first meeting, when Jayar was six and they'd sat on the floor together, playing with toy trains. Another day she murmured something vague, and he strained to listen. Then suddenly he understood. "Oh no, dear," said Jayar. "It's not him, it's me."

Seward listened for thumps and crashes. He respected Pickford; he knew her life, and believed that no one else at Pickfair really cared. "She couldn't walk, but in the night she would forget that. She would try to get up but she would fall on the floor."

She was content to dream – imagining herself before the cameras, for instance, and fretting that her famous hair should be redone. And as she slept, she was once again an eight-year-old, speeding on her bike by the chestnut trees. She was "coming down University Avenue, turning west, I think, on Queen. I got right in front of a pair of horses and I put the brakes on the best I knew how and I gouged my ankle and I still have the marks there." The scar, which she treasured, was a point of pride.

Mary Pickford was dying, and perhaps she knew it. At any rate, it was suddenly important that she see Malcolm Boyd. He came, unprepared for Mary's derelict appearance. They talked for an hour and she pointed to pictures of John Charles and Charlotte. "There's Mama. There's Daddy." And the crucifix on the wall: "There's Jesus." She began to run her hands on the lines in Boyd's face, chanting like an incantation: "Love. Love. Love." She half laughed and half wept at her hands; they were veiny, she said, and resembled a monkey's. He replied that his hands did, even more.

Seward, as usual, kept his nightly vigil. One night he heard Pickford, quite alone, babbling on about selling bonds.

On May 25, 1979, Buddy Rogers rushed his wife to the Santa Monica Hospital. She had suffered a stroke, and she slipped into a coma two days later. Death came, painless and quiet, to Mary Pickford on the 29th.

EPILOGUE

The press was careful in its eulogies, explaining why Pickford's was a notable death – though the emphasis was often on her business sense. "She was a good staunch fighter," remembered her accountant, Edward Stotsenberg, "a brilliant woman, and a determined one. And you had better not tell her anything and then hope she'd forget in 10 or 15 years, because she never did." "America's Sweetheart" was invariably mentioned, as well as a few films – usually *Rebecca of Sunnybrook Farm* and *Pollyanna*, for the titles were familiar through their talkie remakes. But one wonders how much of this touched the readers, few of whom remembered the birth of film, or could imagine Mary's place in its creation.

On the last day of May, a hundred people crammed into the Wee Kirk o' the Heather, a chapel at the Forest Lawn cemetery. As they filed in, a violin and organ played "My Buddy," "Let Me Call You Sweetheart," and George M. Cohan's "Mary." Douglas Fairbanks Jr. and Lillian Gish, who arrived late, sat quietly in the back. Some mourners observed Pickford's "gentle admonition" that there be no weeping. Others couldn't manage. John Mantley, for instance, fought back tears as he delivered the eulogy. And at the end, friends took Buddy, eyes streaming, from the chapel.

Mary Pickford was interred in a special locked section of the cemetery,

365

alongside Charlotte, Jack, Lottie, Aunt Lizzie, and Lizzie's children. A titanic marble monument, top-heavy with angels, shone white in the sun, and soft, piped-in music joined the breeze – a far cry indeed from the crumbling graveyard that shelters Grandma Hennessey's grave in Toronto.

On October 8, 1979, the Academy of Motion Picture Arts and Sciences organized a tribute to the actress. It included a screening of *My Best Girl* and a thoughtful speech from Fairbanks Jr., who described the intensity of Mary's fame. Rogers read a telegram from Lillian Gish (who, as usual, was working and could not attend). "It's very difficult for me," he confessed, "but those years that I had, it was like a dream come true."

Meanwhile Mary's will was being processed. Her estate, which was valued for filing purposes at ten million dollars, was said to be worth five times as much. Most of this was earmarked for the Mary Pickford Benevolent Trust; its trustees were Pickford's longtime lawyer, Sull Lawrence, and Edward Stotsenberg. To her husband, Mary left a yearly income of forty-eight thousand dollars, some valuable stocks and real estate, and the use of her jade and Napoleonic dishes. (The University of Southern California will inherit these items after Rogers's death.) Rogers also received "that portion of the real property known as Pickfair . . . which is southwest of the presently existing swimming pool." There Rogers planned to build a brand-new home, using, as the will allowed, a selection of articles and furniture from the old one.

Gwynne received two hundred thousand dollars. In what seems like a furious slap from the grave, Mary gave relatively little to her children. Her original will left fifteen thousand dollars each to Ronnie and Roxanne. Mary upped the sums over the years but in the end bequeathed each only fifty thousand dollars – mere tokens from a multimillionairess. Her vengeance was somewhat offset by a trust fund for Roxanne's and Ronnie's children, and for Gwynne Ornstein's several children, too.

In 1980 an unseemly tug of war about the will's intentions began between Rogers and the other two executors of Mary's estate. It was Mary's intention that proceeds from the sale of her possessions go to benefit her charitable foundation. But Buddy, whose newly built home was more lavish than the trustees or Pickford had envisioned – 7,500 square feet, precisely, complete with pool and tennis court – laid claim to nearly all of Pickfair's furniture. "We were placed in an awkward position," said

Lawrence, who claimed that "Mary would never have gone along" with Rogers taking "every single stick" from Pickfair. A few months later a probate court awarded Rogers a gift of a million dollars – compensation for his role in helping Mary sell her UA shares. (Buddy's role in this seems to have been symbolic.) Eventually Rogers's home contained Pickfair's western bar as well as its black-and-white Remingtons and watercolors by Rodin. (The Pickfair legend dimmed a little when appraisers decided these works were fakes.)

Everything else – save her papers, scrapbooks, and photographs – was destined for the auction block. Methodically, Pickfair was catalogued, tagged, and allegedly looted. While appraisers dug into nooks and crannies, executors believed that small pieces were swiped – hidden in the shrubs "during clean-up operations and picked up later." Chaos reigned. The Smithsonian sent an employee to receive the star sapphire Mary left them. But another bequest to the museum – six vintage guns in a priceless gun box – left the house unsupervised and disappeared. One day a van pulled up in the driveway, and two strange men began to load it. When asked who had sent them, one replied, "Mrs. Rogers." "But she's been dead for nearly two years," replied an appraiser. "Mrs. Rogers," it turned out, was Beverly Ricono, who was shortly to marry Buddy.

Later that year Jerry Buss, then owner of the L.A. Lakers basketball team, bought Pickfair for just over five million dollars. Buss declared that he "idolized Mary Pickford" and, modest renovations aside, would leave the historic home intact. (He couldn't stop the locals from re-dubbing it "Buss-fare.") As he moved in, sorting of the mansion's former contents continued, and on March 13, 1981, a three-day auction of the dream began.

Mary's trademark straw hat from *Rebecca of Sunnybrook Farm*, Fairbanks's black wool cape from *The Mark of Zorro*, and a corduroy suit, trimmed with yellowing lace, that Mary wore as Lord Fauntleroy reached the block. A Petruchio costume from *The Taming of the Shrew* and a dress from *Rosita* were also sold. There was even a bit of Valentino, for whom Pickford had always nursed a fondness. Thus a magnificent emerald cape with a crust of gold leaf from *Blood and Sand* joined the rack and was going, going, gone.

Some of Pickfair's furnishings were rare and sumptuous – in particular, a Chinese bed, lacquered red and gold, for use while smoking opium.

More redolent of legend were Pickford's personal autograph book, her makeup box, a four-foot Kabuki fan bearing her portrait, her mended prop doll from *The Warrens of Virginia*, and — most central to her royal years — her Vuitton steamer trunk, which was plastered with stickers from the Far East and Europe. Even more poignant were her twelve-inch curls, keepsakes from the haircut that shook the world. Most intimate were the contents of her honeymoon box, found at the back of a musty closet: Mary's size-four wedding dress, delicate negligées, a man's kimono monogrammed "DF," a photo of the sevenish Gladys Smith, and an ancient rag doll and teddy bear. Heartbreaking, too, was a bundle of agonized, pleading letters, written by Pickford to Fairbanks as their marriage moved inexorably toward divorce.

But to some, Pickford's keepsakes were merely kitsch. At the preview, an auction house employee watched as Mary's tiny satin shoes, her feather fans, and an intricate ball gown worn in *Secrets* were tossed about by "carelessly curious" people who behaved like "garage sale patrons." When the auction was half over, prices dropped. "Oh, you're kidding. From Pickfair!" moaned the auctioneer, selling off a breakfast set for thirty-five dollars. Mary's monogrammed silk bedspread sold for sixty dollars. "Listen, folks," he pleaded as the bidders sat listlessly, "you understand you're not renting these things — you're buying them."

A few weeks later, in a ghastly footnote, the auctioneers learned that two buyers from Seattle had stopped payment on a check. They had bought several costumes from Mary's films, then tossed them in the washer, where they fell apart. The loss was calamitous, for any relic from a silent is a key to reconstructing how the films were made. But the ultimate blame must be borne by Pickford, who, for the most part, made no provisions that such items be donated to appropriate archives and museums.

In 1988 Pickford's home was sold again. Jerry Buss, who had once envisioned picnics on the lawn, had found the home and grounds too sweeping for his bachelor needs. It was bought by an eccentric multimillionaire and trader of junk bonds, Meshulam Riklis, who had once had his private jet painted to resemble a Tootsie Roll. Riklis's representative, Bruce Nelson, praised the buyer's intention to leave Pickfair's character untouched. "Many people are tearing down these old properties, but this has such history and tradition."

In 1990 Riklis and his starlet wife, Pia Zadora, submitted the tradition to the wrecking ball. Today, where Mary's home once stood, looms a massive marble pile, with a theater, beauty parlor, gym, dance studio, massage room, two living rooms, twenty bathrooms, replicas of ceilings at Versailles, and a special wing built for Zadora's agent. Some, including Riklis, still refer to this gleaming palazzo as Pickfair. Others know the real Pickfair's mystique has been annihilated.

Buddy Rogers remarried in 1981. The bride was born Beverly Ricono, and her brother built the couple's home on Pickfair Way. It not only shares Pickfair's stunning view but has a room set apart to honor Mary. There, carefully displayed, are mementoes of her travels and a portrait of her posing as Betsy Ross. At the mention of her name, Rogers often weeps. These are usually nostalgic, happy tears. But they are puzzled and wounded when the subject of alcohol is raised.

Fairbanks Jr.'s second wife, Mary Lee, died in 1988. In 1991 he wed Vera Shelton, a merchandiser for a home shopping network. Aside from the occasional stage appearance, Fairbanks Jr. continues his career of good works. In 1988 he published *The Salad Days*, an unpretentious memoir with an off-the-cuff elegance to the prose. He speaks frankly of Pickford and his father, and remains a major spokesman for silent film.

Pickford's children remain out of the public eye. When queried, Buddy Rogers falls immediately silent, and Mary's friends profess not to know their whereabouts. It was rumored that Ronnie spent some time in Alaska in the 1970s, and in 1973 the *New York Daily News* alerted readers that Roxanne was a waitress in Las Vegas. Indeed, that is where Malcolm Boyd once found her, when he passed through the city after Mary's death. She was married to a cook in an Italian restaurant, and her daughter had enrolled at university. "She had forgiven the past — totally," remembered Boyd, who believed that Mary's daughter had somehow dealt with the family trauma and emerged, free of bitterness and serene. Since leaving Pickfair, she had married three times; Roxanne's third marriage lasted twenty-three years and ended with her husband's death in 1996. That March Roxanne sat for an interview with filmmaker Nicholas Eliopoulos and smiled. When asked what Pickford might say if she were listening from the grave, Roxanne answered promptly, "Never listened to me, did you? Always did your own thing!"

In 1929 film scholar Paul Rotha wrote an influential book called *The Film Till Now*. It was comprehensive and, like most early books that viewed film as art, sometimes stiff and self-consciously academic. It included such chapters as "The Aim of the Film in General and in Particular" and "The Preconception of Dramatic Content by Scenario Organisation," as well as assessments of film's influential artists. He devoted several pages to the masterful Fairbanks, then continued, in oddly stumbling prose, "Of Mary Pickford I find difficulty in writing, for there is a consciousness of vagueness, an indefinable emotion as to her precise degree of accomplishment." One assumes that, for Rotha, Little Mary's iridescence blotted out his attempts to judge the actress who created her on the screen.

The neglect has continued – and the fault is, to large degree, Pickford's own. When she declared in 1931 that she intended to burn her films, she faced outraged opposition from her friends. "They don't belong to you," Lillian Gish insisted. "They belong to the public." "Well, time's passing," answered Mary, "and people will compare me to modern actresses."

Mary feared that the world would laugh at her. She may also have imagined that the silents were inferior, as an art form, to the talkies. Indeed, most people thought they were. Silent films may well be the only art form to be discovered, developed, and rejected by a single generation. Even at their height, they were regarded as disposable products. In the 1920s, for instance, Pickford burned twenty-one prints of *Rosita* and seventeen prints of *Pollyanna* to recover the silver in the film stock. Meanwhile the negatives of her films were locked in vaults, where the unstable nitrate cracked and rotted.

Mary Pickford knew better than to let it happen. As far back as the 1930s, she was approached by Iris Barry, who was setting up the film department at New York's Museum of Modern Art. At the time the idea was fairly new: "The only great art peculiar to the 20th Century," explained a pamphlet, "is practically unknown to the American public most capable of appreciating it." When Barry came to Hollywood to look for funds, she was allowed to use Pickfair for a reception (Mary later sent a bill for the cost of the firewood). The highlight of the night was a screening of *All Quiet on the Western Front* (1930). One of its stars, Louis Wolheim, had recently died of cancer. It occurred to those assembled that film preservation could ensure that they, too, might achieve an afterlife. The evening was successful and donations soared.

Few felt committed to acquiring Mary's own work, however, and the actress was reluctant to provide it. Even Barry – who wrote in her book *Let's Go to the Pictures*, "the two greatest names in the cinema are, I beg to reiterate, Mary Pickford and Charlie Chaplin ... and from an historical point of view they always will be" – could not acquire the films for her department.

In 1945 Pickford finally relented and gave cans full of negatives to the Library of Congress. Work began immediately to preserve the legacy, but the gesture came too late for her early features. Numerous cans had the ominous smell that precedes decomposition, and a shocking ninety reels were beyond redemption. Among the missing was *A Good Little Devil* – a bad film, according to those who saw it, but a valuable record of the stage production. *Fanchon the Cricket*, which featured Jack and Lottie in supporting roles, was another film mottled beyond repair. These, like the fairy-tale plays on Broadway, were thought in their day to be as deep as Greek mythology. Unfortunately, Mary's efforts in this genre, other than *Cinderella*, had rotted through.

Such a Little Queen (1914), *Behind the Scenes* (1914), and *The Eternal Grind* (1916), all totems from Pickford's early work, had disintegrated. Also hopelessly corroded were *Hulda From Holland*, the William Desmond Taylor films *How Could You, Jean?* (1918) and *Captain Kidd, Jr.* (1919), and, unluckily, *A Girl of Yesterday* (1915). This was a film by Frances Marion (who also took the role of a society vamp), and its theme of social mores struck a rare note of satire in the Pickford canon. As for James Kirkwood, fully half his films with Pickford were among the missing. Perhaps most novel (and reduced to dust) was the Inuit drama *Little Pal*, which Kirkwood had directed from a plot by Marshall Neilan. In a stroke of luck, a print of *Little Pal* turned up in France. There a writer noted Pickford's "challenging manner" as well as her nuanced style of acting: "she absorbs misfortune as a destiny read only in her face." Two films from 1915, *The*

Dawn of a Tomorrow, in which Mary played what many thought her quintessential guttersnipe, and the romantic *Esmeralda*, were also ravaged. These, from the work of Frances Hodgson Burnett, were the springboard for a decade's association between Pickford and the novelist. But Mary's first features for Famous Players – *In the Bishop's Carriage*, *Caprice*, and *Hearts Adrift* – were the most devastating losses, for these films contained the genesis of her fame.

Many of Pickford's classic films were saved by transferring them to acetate "safety" stock. But often they were in spotty, even scarred condition. And although she had the negative, Pickford flatly refused to hand over *Rosita*. "That's a dirty word to Mary," said Matty Kemp, who oversaw the handling of her films for almost fifty years. "She told me, 'If you ever restore that film, I'll not only fire you, I'll sue you.'" Later a *Rosita* print was found in Russia, foiling Mary's plan to keep the film from view.

In 1947 the U.S. Congress slashed the library budget, and work on Mary's films did not resume for years. In the meantime, her movies were absent from the festivals and film exhibitions that are key to sustaining reputations and that would have kept the memory of her work alive. "Looking at these films," wrote James Card, who saw the movies in 1959 after Eastman House helped Congress in their restoration, "one is immediately struck by the enormity of the gap in all film history that now exists." Scholar Arthur Knight, who finally saw the films in the 1970s, issued a public mea culpa (he had skimmed over Pickford in his own 1957 film history, *The Liveliest Art*). "By a cruel irony, one of the greatest and most contributive pioneers to the movies, both as an art and as an industry, has been unforgivably ignored." He pleaded for a "true, full appreciation of Mary Pickford's artistry and genius. All it would take," he complained, "is her movies."

Today the Mary Pickford Company (part of her foundation, and custodian of the films) is restoring and distributing Mary's work. But the damage to her fame has been insidious. After her death, for instance, the London *Times* wrote baldly that "no one has ever maintained that Mary Pickford was a great actress, or anything like it." And the "Little Mary" image is cut adrift – a small, smiling woman in heavy curls, dancing on the fringes of the public psyche, increasingly simpering and grotesque. The words "Little Mary" and "America's Sweetheart" seem unpleasantly saccharine when divorced from the newness of her fame and the naive culture in which films were born. In 1970 a rare screening in Toronto of *Pollyanna* (a poor choice if meant to epitomize Mary's work) played directly into popular misconceptions. "There was the whole thing up there," wrote a critic, "that insipid insufferably sweet girl singing her darling daddy to his eternal rest in the Ozark mountains." After fifteen minutes, the reviewer "had the feeling that I had already seen not only the whole picture but every movie Mary Pickford ever made."

Another view prevails, among feminist critics, that Pickford's roles as children are, in fact, case studies of repression – a refusal, by both Mary and an infantile public, to allow her sexuality to unfold. But the yardstick is wrong, for the silents are less literal than the talkies. Indeed, modern viewers often watch them as though silents were attempting to be talkies and, mysteriously, not succeeding. A more accurate comparison is to dance: specifically, narrative ballet, which, like the silents, tells a story, free of speech, with music phrased to underscore and shape the drama. Viewed this way, Mary's onscreen children seem real and right – as genuine, say, as today's ballerinas who, at age forty, dance the childish Juliet.

At least works of ballet are correctly presented. Silents, on the other hand, are not. There are exceptions: magnificent restorations, shown as special events, with a live, orchestral score. Far more often, they are seen in appalling prints in which the image, once diamond-sharp, is badly blurred. The play of light and shadow and the textures of the monochrome have been lost, and what's left is a confusion of smears and glare. In addition, they are dubbed with mindless music – not a film score that dovetails with the action, but a grind of tootling ragtime or organ chords.

These look and feel like travesties, which they are. And worse, such copies lie about the past. The Directors Guild of America once warned that "no civilization worthy of the name can afford to promulgate lies about itself. If we do not preserve with fidelity images of how we once viewed ourselves, we increase the likelihood that we will arrive at a distorted understanding of who we are and how we got that way." And indeed, the silents tell us about ourselves. Silent-film scholar and restorer Kevin Brownlow once explained why silent movies ought to be preserved. "Directly or indirectly, the kaleidoscope of dreams, aspirations, prejudices, loves and loathings of a dead epoch comes to life again with undiminished authenticity on the screen. A precious factor of a film, say, 1921, was that it was made in 1921. It is not a period confection like *The Sting*, which depends on instantly recognisable signals and symbols to induce nostalgia. You may see a still from a film of 1921 and recognise nothing about it. The clothes may seem exaggerated, the make-up overdone, the urban landscape that of another planet. But once the picture itself gets under way, you will experience a distillation of another time. This is beyond value, whether you care about film technique or not."

Most people do care about film technique, though they may not think about it in such terms. Film and its cousin in the field of moving images – television – dominate our lives. They have affected how we think about ourselves, how we filter our reality, and how we dream. To fully understand them, we must look for their roots in silent film. And there, as though in a secret garden, lies the seminal career of Mary Pickford – a woman of unstoppable power and purpose, whose genius still floods the screen, fierce and sweet.

NOTES

Full citations for sources given in the Notes can be found in the Bibliography.

ABBREVIATIONS

AMPAS Margaret Herrick Library, Academy of Motion Picture Arts and Sciences, Los Angeles

BF Biographical File

DWG Papers Barnett Braverman Collection, Griffith Papers: 1897–1954, Museum of Modern Art, New York

DT "Daily Talks" by Mary Pickford, *Detroit News*, Nov. 8, 1915–May 14, 1917

Eastman Richard and Ronay Menschel Library, George Eastman House, Rochester, New York

Fairbanks Coll. Douglas Fairbanks Jr. collection, Special Collections, Mulgar Library, Boston University

JM John Mantley, interviewed by the author in 1995

LAT *Los Angeles Times*

LFS Letitia Fairbanks Smoot, interviewed by the author in 1989

MB Malcolm Boyd, interviewed by the author in 1992

MP Mary Pickford

MP/Friedman Mary Pickford interviewed by Arthur Friedman, May 1958;

Richard and Ronay Menschel Library, George Eastman House, Rochester, New York

MP/Pratt Mary Pickford interviewed by George Pratt, 1957, 1958; Richard and Ronay Menschel Library, George Eastman House, Rochester, New York

MP/Shaw Mary Pickford interviewed by Grace Lydiatt Shaw, 1977; National Archives of Canada, Ottawa. By permission of Grace Lydiatt Shaw.

MP/Thomas/TN Mary Pickford interviewed by Tony Thomas, mid-1950s or early 1960s. Broadcast on *Tuesday Night*, CBC Radio, 1974. CBC Archives, Toronto.

MP/Thomas/V Mary Pickford interviewed by Tony Thomas, mid-1950s or early 1960s. Broadcast on *Venture*, "The Magnificent Silents," CBC Radio, July 9, 1961. CBC Archives, Toronto.

NYDM *New York Dramatic Mirror*

NYPLPA Robinson Locke Collection, New York Public Library for the Performing Arts

NYT *New York Times*

PP *Photoplay*

S&S *Sunshine and Shadow* by Mary Pickford

SB Scrapbook

PROLOGUE

2 "Why not?" *NYT*, Oct. 13, 1966
2 "a flash of sunlight" *PP*, Sept. 1914
2 "her tender human sympathy" *PP*, Feb. 1916
2 "the spirit of spring" *PP*, June 1918
2 "We who loved you" Wagenknecht, *The Movies in the Age of Innocence*, 139
3 "I can't imagine" *Philadelphia Inquirer*, Apr. 13, 1934, Mary Pickford Clipping File, Museum of Modern Art, New York
3 "When I go" *NYT*, Mar. 16, 1976

CHAPTER ONE

5 "A spirit stronger"... "fiery ancestors" *PP*, May 1931
5 "Does your mother know"... "the warrior" *S&S*, 26
6 "Oh faith" *S&S*, 25
6 "I don't know where" MP/Thomas/TN
6 "Never again" *S&S*, 61
9 "Why doesn't He kill" *S&S*, 30

9 "back there" MP/Friedman

10 "I want to go back" *S&S*, 30

11 "I can close my eyes" *S&S*, 37

12 "lived with husbands" *Seattle Daily Times*, May 24, 1935

13 "flashing bit of sunlight" *S&S*, 33

13 "those graceful hands" *S&S*, 31

14 "She's a beautiful baby" *S&S*, 40–41

14 "spoiled and pampered" ... "We're quarantined" *S&S*, 42

15 "When Father died" *S&S*, 42

15 "Father had been" *S&S*, 38

15 "After a very sad time" ... "And so we were" MP/Thomas/TN

15 "Mama, have you" *S&S*, 42

16 "Lottie, you've just got" ... "Mother was never" *S&S*, 42–43

17 "The next time" *S&S*, 61

19 "felt a terror" ... "A determination" *S&S*, 46

CHAPTER TWO

21 "I'm sorry" *S&S*, 50

22 "I respect your misgivings" *S&S*, 50

22 "sob music" *Boston Traveler*, June 10, 1919, Pickford SB II, AMPAS

23 "lure of money" *S&S*, 31

23 "If there are any" DT, Feb. 18, 1915

24 "Helpless and unprotected" Smith, *Victorian Melodramas*, xi

24 "was my playhouse" *Pictorial Review*, Mar. 1931

25 "Oh, Will" Bailey, *British Plays*, 336

25 "Sleep on" ibid., 349

25 "a *nasty* little girl" MP/Shaw

25 "Let me play with you!" Bailey, *British Plays*, 351

25 "Don't speak to her" *S&S*, 50

27 "Take her to see" *S&S*, 56

28 "ferocious whiskers" *Boston Traveler*, June 19, 1919, Pickford SB II, AMPAS

29 "I don't see any reason" *S&S*, 57

29 "Please, lady" *S&S*, 57

29 "Where I was born" unsourced clipping, Apr. 15, 1916, Pickford SB 2, NYPLPA

29 "deeper tone" Marion, *Off With Their Heads!*, 9

29 "Well, there can't be" *S&S*, 57

30 "Little Gladys Smith" *NYDM*, Feb. 2, 1901

31 "Do you like chicken" *S&S*, 66

31 "What were you thinking about" MP/Shaw

31 "Rise, put hat on" Weaver, *Duse*, 18

32 "Don't think about your hands" MP/Shaw

32 "Each word is like" ... "There may be" MP/Shaw

33 "donkeys and bloodhounds galore" *Toronto Globe*, Nov. 17, 1898

33 "real coloured people" *Toronto Globe*, Dec. 20, 1898

33 "18 Real Georgia Plantation Shouters" ... "10 Cuban and Russian" Hughes, *A History of American Theatre*, 301

33 "sticks closely to the text" *Toronto Globe*, Apr. 6, 1901

34 "I'm so glad to see" *S&S*, 60

34 "Oh! love! joy! peace!" Gerould, *American Melodrama*, 107

34 "Oh, Evangeline!" ibid., 90

34 "It is nothing to die" Bailey, *British Plays*, 323

34 "These things *sink into my heart*" Stowe, *Uncle Tom's Cabin*, 220

35 "Her face was remarkable" ibid., 147

35 "Gorgeous clouds" Gerould, *American Melodrama*, 133

CHAPTER THREE

37 "Gladys – only Gladys" *S&S*, 66

38 "No one can have" *S&S*, 69

38 "The too eager" Hart, Moss, *Act One*, 94, 95

39 "rudeness of the receptionists" *S&S*, 69

39 "You'll be down in five" *S&S*, 68

40 "aged countenance" ... "a pirouette" Dickens, *Nicholas Nickleby*, 283–84

40 "a typical theatrical brat" *S&S*, 89

41 "While the child's back" Wagenknecht, *As Far As Yesterday*, 90

41 "The idea of expecting me" *S&S*, 75

41 "I want that speech repeated" ... "From that moment" *S&S*, 76

41 "a mischievous, fun-loving" ... "You bad girl" DT, Dec. 13, 1915

42 "Mother was a very beautiful woman" *S&S*, 79

43 "In our fondest dreams" *S&S*, 79

43 "so tightly that every finger" *Good Housekeeping*, Aug. 1934

44 "small, hopeless theatres" *New York Telegraph*, Jan. 22, 1913, Pickford SB 1, NYPLPA

44 "We know the theatre is rotten!" Lewis, *Trouping*, 114

44 "Well, now we'll get" ibid., 119

44 "Now you *stop* that" ibid., 117

44 "hooting, jeering galleries" *Ladies Home Journal*, July 1923

45 "pricked and bleeding" *Liberty*, circa 1935, Mary Pickford BF, AMPAS

46 "You can lock" *S&S*, 73

46 "You'll have to do" ... "And what would you" *S&S*, 71

46 "He felt very inferior" ... "I just freeze" MP/Friedman

46 "the only one of" *S&S*, 71

47 "That was the only" *S&S*, 78

47 "Nonsense is not" *Ladies Home Journal*, July 1923

47 "If you complained" Lewis, *Trouping*, 120

48 "Do you recognize" Gish, *The Movies, Mr. Griffith, and Me*, 20

49 "the unbelievable courage" *S&S*, 79

49 "didn't mind" ... "had a wonderful time" MP/Shaw

49 "[We] scrunched down" *S&S*, 85

49 "in the old days" *NYDM*, Oct. 14, 1905

49 "charming and lovable" ibid.

50 "We were playing" ... "When I saw things" *Ladies Home Journal*, July 1923

50 "Dear God" ibid.

50 "its cheap tinsel worst" ... "the furniture" *Pictorial Review*, Mar. 1931

50 "My heart was filled" ibid.

51 "Death will be" Peters, *The House of Barrymore*, 146

51 "defies description" Vardac, *Stage to Screen*, 115

52 "The audience heard" Winter, *The Life of David Belasco*, 2:206

52 "a plenitude of needless talk" Bronner, *The Encyclopedia of the American Theatre*, 137

52 "the glow of intellectual excitement" Eaton, *The American Stage of To-Day*, 3

52 "a stale conventionality" ibid.

52 "could buy the materials" Atkinson, *Broadway*, 47

53 "The only vow" Edwards, Anne, *The DeMilles*, 21

53 "big, imported yellow automobile" DT, July 13, 1916

53 "Never mind, Mabel" *S&S*, 101

54 "a sensitive, poetic face" MP/Friedman

54 "Then I saw myself" DT, Jan. 12, 1916

54 "might as well try" *Toronto Globe and Mail*, Apr. 19, 1975, 29

54 "Week after week" DT, Jan. 12, 1916

55 "I've never asked you" ... "All right" *S&S*, 91

55 "My life depends" *S&S*, 92

55 "What's your name?" *S&S*, 92

55 "I saw him then" *Theater*, June 1913

55 "At home in Toronto" ... "Mother always says" *S&S*, 92–93

56 "I'm getting a splendid salary" ... "She looked straight" PP, Dec. 1915

56 "buoyancy of youth" *NYT*, Dec. 2, 1906

56 "An empty theatre" DT, Jan. 14, 1916

57 "I would like a chair" *S&S*, 94

57 "blind mother in the cottage" *Boston Traveler*, June 12, 1919, Pickford SB II, AMPAS

57 "My voice did not" DT, Jan. 14, 1916

57 "So you want to be" ... "No, sir" *S&S*, 94

57 "Frances, here's a young" *S&S*, 95

57 "Yes, Miss Starr" DT, Jan. 14, 1916

57 "That will not be difficult" ... "GLADYS SMITH" *S&S*, 105

58 "little ray of feminine sunshine" *NYT*, Oct. 20, 1907

58 "the worn, ill, suffering" Winter, *The Life of David Belasco*, 2:264

58 "Dear Brother Arthur" de Mille, William C., "The Warrens," Act II, 1–2

58 "What a magnificent sight" *S&S*, 100

59 "special charm" Winter, *The Life of David Belasco*, 2:261

59 "outdoor scene" Eaton, *The American Stage of To-Day*, 210

59 "Hold everything" ... "This is a great secret" *S&S*, 96–98

59 "I liked [him] immensely" *Boston Traveler*, June 12, 1919, Pickford SB II, AMPAS

60 "unmentionables" episode: *S&S*, 99

60 "loved by everyone" ... "all repose" *PP*, Dec. 1915

60 "Gladys Smith is not" *Toronto Daily Star*, Jan. 16, 1909

61 "Don't answer yet" Yurka, *Bohemian Girl*, 51

61 "made a kind of Roman Holiday" ... "You were all" ibid., 52

61 "Belasco thinks" *Toronto Daily Star*, Jan. 16, 1909

61 "loathsome" *S&S*, 103

61 "worse than a come-down" MP/Pratt

CHAPTER FOUR

63 "They [the lower class] talk" *Nation*, Aug. 28, 1913

64 "Would you be very much" ... "I'll let you wear" *S&S*, 102

65 "recorded the color" *Ladies Home Journal*, July 1923

65 "finally managed" *Christian Science Monitor*, Apr. 3, 1928

67 "The effect was the same" ... "Wave after wave" *NYDM*, May 2, 1896

69 "No longer are the protagonists" Barry, *Let's Go to the Pictures*, 30

69 "They all started" *Hollywood*: "The Pioneers"

70 "soaring up and down" ... "There is snow" Hart, James, *The Man Who Invented Hollywood*, 27

70 "What a grand invention" ibid., 29

71 "No one else among his associates" DWG Papers

71 "Don't lean" Arvidson, *When the Movies Were Young*, 27

71 "Ah me! but the wind" *Leslie's Weekly*, Jan. 10, 1907

71 "The world was full" Hart, James, *The Man Who Invented Hollywood*, 69

72 "What happened" Knight, *The Liveliest Art*, 23

72 "To watch [Griffith's] work" Agee, *Agee on Film*, 313

73 "Changes in scenes" *NYDM*, Sept. 4, 1909

73 "How can you tell" Arvidson, *When the Movies Were Young*, 66

74 "laughingly called" Hart, James, *The Man Who Invented Hollywood*, 77

74 "She stands with eyes" Ellman, *Oscar Wilde*, 114

74 "Deep lines on the face" *PP*, Dec. 1918

74 "Please send us" Gish, *The Movies, Mr. Griffith, and Me*, 90

75 "a good-looker" Hart, James, *The Man Who Invented Hollywood*, 77

75 "All my life" ibid., 37

75 "Too jaunty and familiar" ... "Only ten years in the theatre" *S&S*, 105

75 "Small, cute figure" Hart, James, *The Man Who Invented Hollywood*, 77

75 "You're too little" *S&S*, 105

75 "Well, Miss – " ... "When that little girl" Hart, James, *The Man Who Invented Hollywood*, 77-78

76 "Pompous and insufferable" *S&S*, 105

78 "To arms, men" Marion, *Off With Their Heads!*, 14

78 "the floor kept going" DWG Papers

78 "Who's the dame?" ... "With that, Mr. Griffith" *S&S*, 109

79 "Will you dine with me?" ... "Till tomorrow" *S&S*, 109-10

80 "They're going to pay me" *S&S*, 110

CHAPTER FIVE

81 "never so reluctant" *S&S*, 111

81 "That girl was simply" *Moving Picture World*, Feb. 19, 1918

82 "There was no coaching" Arvidson, *When the Movies Were Young*, 31

82 "Will you gentlemen" Walker, *Stardom*, 4

82 "One day I was called" ... "I advised him" Bitzer, *Billy Bitzer*, 63-64

83 "[Duse] plays only" Weaver, *Duse*, 95

83 "An actress of lesser genius" ibid., 356

83 "People in the pictures" ... "attempts to introduce" *NYDM*, Dec. 28, 1910

84 "Gaga-baby" Gish, *The Movies, Mr. Griffith, and Me*, 167

84 "St. Vitus dance" ... "How else can I get" ibid., 99

85 "Buy this child" *S&S*, 111

85 "it is not one" Schickel, *D.W. Griffith*, 163

85 "cost all of $10.50" ... "less irksome" *S&S*, 111

86 "lesser persons" ... "From the first day" *Ladies Home Journal*, July 1923

86 "Will you play" ... "vulgar in the extreme" *S&S*, 111-12

87 "Miss Pickford has had" . . . "After ten years" DT, Dec. 27, 1915

87 "more spiritual than material" Niver, *Mary Pickford, Comedienne*, 6

88 "A sobriety of speech" Weaver, *Duse*, 70

88 "It isn't what you do" . . . "The art of [film] acting" PP, Dec. 1918

88 "what moving picture acting" PP, Dec. 1919

89 "something sacred" Brownlow, *The Parade's Gone By*, 147

90 "happy way of working" Arvidson, *When the Movies Were Young*, 58

90 "Let the notes fall" . . . "We all fairly ached" DWG Papers

91 "You have expressive bodies" Gish, *The Movies, Mr. Griffith, and Me*, 37

91 "Go to hell!" . . . "You're standing amid" DWG Papers

92 "one little touch" Arvidson, *When the Movies Were Young*, 125

92 "Everything's fun" MP/Thomas/V

92 "Do you think" Bitzer, *Billy Bitzer*, 74

93 "Made up for her part" PP, Jan. 1916

93 "I think in his way" Brownlow, *Parade*, 142

93 "one who was not exactly" Hart, James, *The Man Who Invented Hollywood*, 37-38

93 "keen perception" DWG Papers

93 "Griffith said" MP/Thomas/V

94 "He'd exaggerate" DWG Papers

94 "I will not exaggerate" *S&S*, 115

94 "like a goose" Brownlow, *The Parade's Gone By*, 142

94 "I'm a young girl" . . . "I'll go home" MP/Friedman

94 "Turn your head" DWG Papers

94 "like an automatic doll" Goldwyn, *Behind the Screen*, 33

94 "two dominant rulers" St. Johns, *Love, Laughter and Tears*, 76

94 "middle range of feeling" Agee, *Agee on Film*, 315

94 "was not and never" Eyman, *Mary Pickford*, 48

94 "the most miserable-looking" . . . "Now you're a heroine again" MP/Shaw

95 "For one thing" . . . "Come on, now" *S&S*, 116-17

98 "I shall never forget" *S&S*, 112

98 "not because I was afraid" PP, Dec. 1915

98 "stood apart" Bitzer, *Billy Bitzer*, 74

98 "Five-feet eleven inches tall" *S&S*, 131

99 "We're the Black Irish" MP/Thomas/TN

99 "darling Arthur Johnson" MP/Pratt

99 "To my mind" Arvidson, *When the Movies Were Young*, 49

99 "He nearly killed us" . . . "had an unfriendly way" ibid., 90, 101

99 "I hate to tell you this" *S&S*, 133

100 "How little we know" Arvidson, *When the Movies Were Young*, 101

100 "not only mid-Victorian" *S&S*, 133

100 "Not on company time" . . . "Don't you *dare*" Eyman, *Mary Pickford*, 56

100 "Why waste time" Bitzer, *Billy Bitzer*, 75

100 "I'm not certain" *Toronto Star*, Mar. 29, 1979

102 "Don't be silly" *S&S*, 127

102 "The grass there" Brownlow, *Hollywood*, 91

103 "There was hardly" *Ladies Home Journal*, Aug. 1923

103 "I had to take care" MP/Pratt

104 "the sweet little Irish-American kid" DWG Papers

104 "Stage money" *S&S*, 130

105 "How do you feel" Fell et al., *Before Hollywood*, 60

105 "Miss Lawrence is" Jacobs, *The Rise of the American Film*, 87

105 "the buttons from" Drinkwater, *The Life and Adventures of Carl Laemmle*, 141

105 "If you don't promise" ... "I'll give you" *S&S*, 123

106 "I used to think" Arvidson, *When the Movies Were Young*, 179

106 "I scarcely know him" ... "I lived in the dreadful" *S&S*, 136–37

107 "standing at the rail" *S&S*, 138

108 "no one during my entire career" Croy, *Starmaker*, vii

108 "Go to one of the actors" *S&S*, 138

108 "I felt that if" MP/Pratt

109 "affront to her art" ... "Her spontaneity" *NYT*, Oct. 15, 1911

110 "Don't put on any" ... "It was an inadmissible" *S&S*, 139

110 "Where is *she* staying?" *Chicago Herald-Examiner*, May 9, 1920

111 "mischievous Mary" *Moving Picture News*, Jan. 1911

CHAPTER SIX

112 "one of the loveliest things" MP/Pratt

112 "made me think" DT, June 28, 1916

112 "Oh, was I happy!" MP/Pratt

112 "You – criticizing Billie Burke!" ... "And you're not privileged" Brownlow, *The Parade's Gone By*, 143

113 "I'm sure my mother" MP/Friedman

114 "Do you remember" *S&S*, 146

114 "wanted Mae to work" DWG Papers

114 "a little girl" *S&S*, 146–47

114 "Cold reason" MP/Pratt

114 "Do you suppose" *S&S*, 147

114 "Gladys Smith has fallen" *S&S*, 148

115 "great between stage jobs" Gish, *The Movies, Mr. Griffith, and Me*, 33

115 "You have courage" *S&S*, 148

115 "Look at your friend" Gish, *The Movies, Mr. Griffith, and Me*, 76

115 "He wants to get me" *S&S*, 148-49

115 "It's too bad" . . . "So long, Mary" *S&S*, 149-50

116 "Mary Pickford was famous" . . . "I have a beautiful part" *PP*, Dec. 1915

116 "Why do you bedevil me" MP/Pratt

116 "It can't wait" . . . "he turned and scrutinized" *S&S*, 152

117 "Well, Pickford, bless you" Brownlow, *The Parade's Gone By*, 143

117 "something of life's experience" *NYT*, Jan. 26, 1913

118 "lived the part" *Brooklyn Daily Eagle*, Jan. 9, 1913

118 "I had every reason" *S&S*, 159

118 "From now on" . . . "the exciting jigsaw puzzle" *S&S*, 157

119 "A new pair of shoes" Irwin, *The House That Shadows Built*, 15

119 "a newborn person" Zukor, *The Public Is Never Wrong*, 32

120 "belonged entirely to technicians" Gabler, *An Empire of Their Own*, 30

120 "If you run Queen Elizabeth" *Moving Picture World*, Oct. 19, 1912

121 "the most important thing" *Ladies Home Journal*, Aug. 1923

121 "felt instinctively" *S&S*, 160

121 "one of the worst" MP/Pratt

121 "the eyes must speak" *Christian Science Monitor*, Mar. 27, 1928

121 "What salary would you" Zukor, *The Public Is Never Wrong*, 98

122 "Three hundred" Gish, *The Movies, Mr. Griffith, and Me*, 82

124 "What right have you" . . . "God, I want" *S&S*, 140

125 "You were apt to see" Marion, *Off With Their Heads!*, 4

126 "revealed unsuspected" *PP*, Feb. 1916

126 "Her tragedy" *PP*, Feb. 1916

126 "waves of perfect understanding" *NYDM*, Sept. 15, 1915

126 "Here was feminine fascination" *PP*, Feb. 1916

126 "Silent enchantress" *NYDM*, Aug. 13, 1915

127 "I move, like a Fairy" *New York Review*, Nov. 28, 1914, Pickford SB 1, NYPLPA

127 "It has come" Lindsay, Vachel, *The Art of the Moving Picture*, 317

127 "weird magnetic grip" *PP*, Oct. 1917

127 "[Mary] has the saddest" *PP*, July 1918

127 "She gives one the impression" *Bioscope* (England), June 24, 1920, Pickford SB V, AMPAS

128 "A simpler and more diffident" *Pittsburgh Leader*, Dec. 27, 1914, SB 141, NYPLPA

129 "I think shorn" Carey, *Doug and Mary*, 181

129 "appeared to have grasped" Winter, *Other Days*, 258

129 "Our Mary is Coming" Wilson, Garff B., *A History of American Acting*, 65-66

129 "a rare and wholly" *PP*, Feb. 1916

130 "Instead of becoming" Kerr, *The Silent Clowns*, 12

130 "the intimate possession" *PP*, Nov. 1914

131 "expressive-eyed" *Variety*, Apr. 3, 1914

131 "the slightest interest" Spears, *Hollywood*, 154

131 "the best known woman" *Hollywood*: "In the Beginning"

132 "If everybody were" *PP*, Oct. 1917

132 "Do you remember Lowell's" *PP*, Apr. 1919

132 "Dear Miss Pickford" DT, Feb. 10, 1917

133 "drab little wren" *S&S*, 162

133 "The mere fact" *Variety*, June 16, 1916

133 "Calling Mary" . . . "I was standing" Schulberg, *Moving Pictures*, 37

134 "The press is as much" *Toronto Telegram*, Feb. 6, 1934

134 "People . . . consider me" *Boston Traveler*, June 14, 1919, Pickford SB II, AMPAS

134 "was not yet on speaking terms" *New York Telegram*, Oct. 16, 1916, Pickford SB 1, NYPLPA

134 "We did a little washing" *Los Angeles Examiner*, Apr. 30, 1915, ibid.

134 "I've worked since" . . . "one bit rich" *Pittsburgh Leader*, Dec. 27, 1914, SB 141, NYPLPA

135 "I was only" Irwin, *The House That Shadows Built*, 245

135 "Mary, I want you" . . . "That dear, sweet man" *S&S*, 163–64

136 "Zukor kills" Talmey, *Doug and Mary and Others*, 50

136 "A seizure of pity" *S&S*, 140

137 "No longer was he" DT, Dec. 8, 1916

137 "A wedding should be something" unsourced clipping, 1916, Mary Pickford file, Eastman

137 "Real, unselfish devotion" DT, Jan. 27, 1917

137 "He called my mother" *Chicago Herald-Examiner*, Mar. 31, 1920

139 "You'll have to change" *S&S*, 129

140 "what my mother used to call" MP/Thomas/TN

140 "a cheap, hamfat comedian" Wagner, *You Must Remember This*, 18

140 "Pickford was" Ramsaye, *A Million and One Nights*, 746

140 "a fascinating thing" *Motion Picture Classic*, Aug. 1918

141 "Her mannerisms" Bodeen, *From Hollywood*, 35

141 "had me down" . . . "an amusing, charming" MP/Friedman

142 "As for the balcony" *S&S*, 169

142 "Square-souled" *PP*, Feb. 1916

142 "furious quarrel" . . . "He assured me" Spears, *Hollywood*, 169–70

143 "Personal feelings" Irwin, *The House That Shadows Built*, 246

143 "Let's get the business" Slide, *The Big V*, 32

143 "I'm going to give you" Irwin, *The House That Shadows Built*, 248

143 "We have the same" ibid.

144 "Thank you. We'll build" DeMille, Cecil, *The Autobiography of Cecil B. DeMille*, 152

145 "I was astonished" Chaplin, *My Autobiography*, 222

145 "That pretty little thing" Arvidson, *When the Movies Were Young*, 106

145 "In appearance so typically" Goldwyn, *Behind the Screen*, 42

145 "Mary is the most practical" Carey, *Doug and Mary*, 141–42

145 "I don't think" *Toronto Telegram*, Feb. 6, 1934

145 "I'm not the money-lover" … "I never enjoyed" MP/Friedman

146 "It may sound rather" MP/Pratt

146 "dry, dead meetings" MP/Friedman

CHAPTER SEVEN

148 "Probably he believed" DeMille, Cecil B., *The Autobiography of Cecil B. DeMille*, 61

148 "proving, first" de Mille, Agnes, *Portrait Gallery*, 164

148 "I'm pulling out" Lasky, Jesse K., *I Blow My Own Horn*, 91

148 "real Indian country" ibid., 92–93

149 "Want authority" … "Don't make" Edwards, Anne, *The DeMilles*, 51

149 "I can break you" DeMille, Cecil B., *The Autobiography of Cecil B. DeMille*, 153

149 "high-hat and snooty" MP/Pratt

149 "completely bewildered" … "an intimate little family" *S&S*, 176, 173

150 "adhesive relatives" Goldwyn, *Behind the Screen*, 63

150 "I am not going" MP/Friedman

150 "it often took longer" Goldwyn, *Behind the Screen*, 37

150 "My God" … "And the next time" *S&S*, 177

151 "You can talk" DT, Apr. 22, 1916

151 "I just begged" *Motion Picture Classic*, July 1918, Pickford SB 2, NYPLPA

151 "eerie feat" *PP*, Sept. 1916

151 "Oh, Miss Pickford" *S&S*, 173

152 "a strange watchfulness" Marion, *Off With Their Heads!*, 9, 11

152 "expressive little talent" Beauchamp, *Without Lying Down*, 32

152 "in all the articles" Marion, *Off With Their Heads!*, 10

153 "Brush those cobwebs" DT, June 15, 1916

153 "do not think much" DT, May 1, 1916

153 "Would you have me send" DT, Feb. 1, 1916

153 "Yes, I am married" DT, Apr. 1, 1916

154 "That phase of my life" … "walled up" MP/Pratt

155 "Mlle. Pickford" Spears, *Hollywood*, 172–73

155 "It is not in the play" *S&S*, 179

155 "I am a dignified man" Cushman, *A Tribute to Mary Pickford*

156 "masterpiece of comedy" *S&S*, 179

156 "spontaneous combustions" Marion, *Off With Their Heads!*, 44

156 "But I had to live" *S&S*, 180

156 "stocky and straight" de Mille, Agnes, *Dance to the Piper*, 33

157 "was a man who" Lasky, Jesse K., Jr., *Whatever Happened to Hollywood?*, 133

157 "Here comes the Celestial" Marion, *Off With Their Heads!*, 48

157 "A commanding general" DeMille, Cecil B., *The Autobiography of Cecil B. DeMille*, 181

157 "Now, Mary" . . . "Now, let me see" *S&S*, 180

157 "Make it plenty humble" MP/Pratt

157 "I have no desire" *S&S*, 180–81

157 "unending marathon" *S&S*, 181

157 "a shop girl" *NYT*, Nov. 28, 1915

158 "Oh, my dear" unsourced, undated clipping, Mary Pickford BF, Eastman

158 "She is telling" *PP*, Nov. 1917

159 "Poor Owen is worried" . . . "You and Charlie" Marion, *Off With Their Heads!*, 40

159 "I thought he was" MP/Thomas/TN

159 "tongues stilled" *NYDM*, Mar. 10, 1915

159 "holds the eye" Slide, *Selected Film Criticism*, 156

160 "Keep Your Hero Smiling" Brownlow, *The Parade's Gone By*, 316

160 "are the greatest assets" Fairbanks Jr., *The Fairbanks Album*, 56

160 "Dammit, I can't play" Loos, *The Talmadge Girls*, 35

160 "yields instantly to any" Fairbanks Jr., *The Fairbanks Album*, 56

160 "A sort of Ariel" Cooke, *Douglas Fairbanks*, 24, 23

161 "To me, he was" MP/Thomas/TN

161 "We're not going to" *S&S*, 197

161 "Do you mind?" *S&S*, 197

161 "that I saw" MP/Thomas/TN

161 "When the party" Marion, *Off With Their Heads!*, 41

162 "You do less apparent" . . . "a breath of new life" *S&S*, 198–99

162 "dear Mary" Fairbanks Jr., *The Salad Days*, 33

162 "He was a little boy" MP/Thomas/TN

162 "sound and fury" Fairbanks Jr., *The Salad Days*, 24

164 "couldn't help falling" . . . "Everyone must be" ibid., 34–35

164 "Room to expand" Hancock and Fairbanks, *Douglas Fairbanks*, 137

164 "a myth and a surety" Lejeune, *Cinema*, 56

165 "It was the first" Hancock and Fairbanks, *Douglas Fairbanks*, 137

165 "Tu-Tu would have understood" Herndon, *Mary Pickford and Douglas Fairbanks*, 151

165 "If [Cecil] lost his temper" de Mille, Agnes, *Dance to the Piper*, 34

165 "He'd get her shaking" *Hollywood*: "The Autocrats"

166 "DeMille was a great" Brownlow, *The Parade's Gone By*, 147

166 "Mary, darling!" Marion, *Off With Their Heads!*, 45

166 "Smart enough" Wiggin, *Rebecca*, 209

167 "one of the most delightful" Spears, *Hollywood*, 288

167 "Do you know" Goldwyn, *Behind the Screen*, 41

167 "he would dream up" Spears, *Hollywood*, 288

167 "To my way of thinking" MP/Thomas/TN

167 "such as being called" ... "Before the afternoon" Spears, *Hollywood*, 288

168 "a trapped little animal" Marion, *Off With Their Heads!*, 50

168 "mutt expression" *Motion Picture Classic*, July 1918

168 "What *is* this" MP/Pratt

169 "nearly eleven" Harte, *Selected Stories*, 97

170 "Mary's so sneaky" Herndon, *Mary Pickford and Douglas Fairbanks*, 171

170 "that family" Loos, *A Girl Like I*, 168

171 "No male is quite so" ibid., 158

171 "that faker Douglas Fairbanks" St. Johns, *Love, Laughter and Tears*, 113

171 "vile and revolting" *Moving Picture World*, Jan. 17, 1914

171. "Pickford the Second" *PP*, June 1915

172 "Oh, boy" Carey, *Anita Loos*, 48

172 "Any good?" Hancock and Fairbanks, *Douglas Fairbanks*, 130

173 "Whatever the stunt" *S&S*, 228

173 "tiresome" *Toronto Star Weekly Magazine*, Oct. 8, 1960

173 "It behoves us" Chaplin, *My Autobiography*, 222

173 "That's nothing but spooks" *S&S*, 232

173 "the little angel" Weaver, *Duse*, 353

173 "I am an atheist" ... "Let the heathen drown" Windeler, *Sweetheart*, 137

174 "There is but one place" DT, Mar. 8, 1916

174 "Can you imagine women" DT, Mar. 10, 1917

174 "America wages no wars" DT, Mar. 8, 1916

175 "Viewed as drama" *Hollywood*: "Hollywood Goes to War"

176 "a conflict of emotion" *New Republic*, Feb. 15, 1919

177 "heads erect" DT, June 17, 1916

177 "a special couturier's outfit" ... "like a little soldier" *Hollywood*: "Hollywood Goes to War"

178 "make the world" ... "This is not a time" *St. Louis Globe*, Apr. 2, 1918, Pickford SB III, AMPAS

178 "The clean life" *PP*, Feb. 1918

178 "an avalanche" Chaplin, *My Autobiography*, 212

179 "Each bond you buy" ibid., 213

179 "Every bond you buy" *New York Evening-World*, Apr. 13, 1918, Pickford SB III, AMPAS

180 "her small figure" *PP*, July 1918

180 "If all the world" *St. Louis Globe-Democrat*, June 4, 1920.

180 "I have always felt" *Boston Traveler*, June 9, 1919, Pickford SB II, AMPAS

180 "I'm tired of make-up" *Chicago News*, May 1, 1918, Pickford SB III, AMPAS

CHAPTER EIGHT

182 "Terribly hot trip" telegram, Aug. 3, 1917, "Albums and Memories" Box, Fairbanks Coll.

182 "no more paternal feeling" Fairbanks Jr., *The Salad Days*, 30

182 "Wired you affair was off" telegram, Oct. 9, 1917, "Albums and Memories" Box, Fairbanks Coll.

183 "Owen came to me" ... "I won't have it" *S&S*, 200–2

183 "Imperative. Meet me" Bogdanovich, *Allan Dwan*, 45

183 "Your friend Owen Moore" Herndon, *Mary Pickford and Douglas Fairbanks*, 168

184 "I have come to realize" ibid., 174

184 "For 12 years" unsourced clipping, Box 85, Fairbanks Coll.

184 "that theirs was" *Pittsburgh Leader*, 1918 (datelined Apr. 12), Pickford SB 3, NYPLPA

184 "is associated with my husband" ibid.

184 "My wife and I" *NYT*, Apr. 12, 1918

184 "Not quite playing" unsourced, undated clipping, Pickford SB MWEZ + n.c. 6145, NYPLPA

184 "We are simply associated" ibid.

184 "The other woman" Carey, *Doug and Mary*, 62

184 "little more than a child" ... "repugnant and distasteful" Carey, *Doug and Mary*, 62-63

184 "too busy working" unsourced, undated clipping, Pickford Clipping File, MWEZ + n.c. 6145, NYPLPA

105 "startled the cashier" "were so greatly" *NYT*, Apr. 17, 1918

185 "And I want you to know" *Front Page Challenge*, CBC Television, May 21, 1963

185 "At dinner" *LAT*, May 5, 1918, Pickford SB III, AMPAS

185 "I was really slipping" MP/Pratt

186 "sheltering arm" Zukor, *The Public Is Never Wrong*, 196

186 "the silver cord" Irwin, *The House That Shadows Built*, 251

186 "I answered that" Zukor, *The Public Is Never Wrong*, 195

187 "Let her go" *S&S*, 187

187 "A charming individual" MP/Pratt

187 "had carved out" *S&S*, 198

187 "I'll tell you what" *S&S*, 185

187 "Mary, it is too big" ... "No. We've done the best" Zukor, *The Public Is Never Wrong*, 195

187 "saying good-by forever" ... "I have given my word" *S&S*, 187

187 "God bless you" ... "I can't either" MP/Pratt

188 "I'm going to turn my back" *S&S*, 187

188 "not only come up" ... "She is working" *PP*, June 1920

188 "If no statement is made" unsourced, undated clipping, Pickford SB MWEZ + n.c. 6145, NYPLPA

188 "nothing has been said" ... "Again, nothing is said" unsourced clipping, Aug. 27, 1918, Pickford SB I, AMPAS

189 "beautiful girls" ... "a certain escapade" *NYT*, Dec. 1, 1918

189 "Not a soul" Fairbanks Jr., *The Salad Days*, 54

189 "Pride means a lot" St. Johns, *Love, Laughter and Tears*, 105

190 "looked very 'nifty'" *Oakland Examiner*, Jan. 4, 1919, Pickford SB I, AMPAS

190 "Oh folks" *San Francisco Chronicle*, undated, ibid.

190 "I've brought Mother Pickford" unsourced, undated clipping, ibid.

191 "Doug has signed up" ... "Mary may" Balio, *United Artists*, 3

191 "We believe [United Artists]" ibid., 13

192 "The lunatics have taken charge" ibid., 14

192 "Actually, the founders" *Films in Review*, Nov. 1959

192 "Dear boy" ... "Had it been typed" Fairbanks Jr., *The Salad Days*, 53

194 "creative frenzy" ... "popped with excitement" Spears, *Hollywood*, 178

194 "coated and permeated" *NYT*, Dec. 1, 1918

196 "Mary Pickford's threatened retirement" *Chicago News*, July 7, 1919, Pickford SB III, AMPAS

196 "My whole life" ... "Just at a time" *PP*, June 1919

196 "I can see her now" ... "I believe" Brownlow, *Hollywood*, 157

197 "wanted all of Mary" Fairbanks Jr., *The Salad Days*, 46

197 "Think what you mean" Marion, *Off With Their Heads!*, 73

197 "You don't know" *PP*, Dec. 1919

197 "If any spark of tenderness" *S&S*, 202

197 "Oh, sure, Mrs. Pickford" *S&S*, 202

198 "The world smiled" *PP*, June 1919

198 "Information has it" *Chicago News*, Mar. 31, 1920

198 "I was haunted" *S&S*, 203

199 "I am happy" *Los Angeles Record*, Mar. 6, 1920, Pickford SB VIII, AMPAS

199 "If I have done anything" ... "I have learned" *Toledo Blade*, Mar. 22, 1920, Pickford SB MWEZ + n.c. 6145, NYPLPA

199 "If the world" ... "I love you" *S&S*, 204–5

200 "Charlie!" ... "Let's tell him" unsourced clipping, Apr. 11, 1920, box dated 7/14/82, Fairbanks Coll.

200 "not at all worried" *Toledo Blade*, undated, Pickford SB 1, NYPLPA

201 "Ask the real ones" Carey, *Doug and Mary*, 81

201 "There is nothing to hide" *Weekly Record*, June 26, 1920, Pickford SB V, AMPAS

201 "rose with the eager anticipation" *Daily Express*, June 22, 1920, ibid.

201 "[Their idols] had materialized" *Daily Mail*, June 22, 1920, ibid.

201 "Famous people glow" Braudy, *The Frenzy of Renown*, 6

201 "Even at the distance" *Daily Mail*, June 22, 1920, Pickford SB V, AMPAS

202 "thousands and thousands" *S&S*, 208

202 "a lynch mob" *Midland Daily Telegram*, June 23, 1920, Pickford SB V, AMPAS

202 "I say, please unhand" *S&S*, 213

203 "I've seen her" *Liverpool Evening Express*, June 23, 1920, Pickford SB V, AMPAS

203 "You British people" *Times* (London), June 23, 1920

203 "London professes to love" *Daily Herald*, June 24, 1920, Pickford SB V, AMPAS

203 "A fat woman" *NYT*, July 21, 1920

204 "prisoners of the crowds" St. Johns, *Love, Laughter and Tears*, 116

204 "The amazing reception" *Pall Mall Gazette*, June 24, 1920, Pickford SB V, AMPAS

204 "One must not ask" *Aberdeen Free Press*, June 25, 1920, ibid.

204 "every 'nice boy'" ... "By the alchemy of a machine" *Times* (London), Jan. 24, 1920

CHAPTER NINE

206 "This is a happy house" Herndon, *Mary Pickford and Douglas Fairbanks*, 202

207 "to meet a man" Lockwood, *Dream Palaces*, 102

207 "it is a promise" *S&S*, 217

207 "Douglas and I" *S&S*, 218

207 "To Till de Pewr" *New Yorker*, Apr. 7, 1934

207 "I wanted nice things" *Ladies Home Journal*, July 1923

207 "an exquisite thing" Herndon, *Mary Pickford and Douglas Fairbanks*, 204

208 "enjoyed a status" Fairbanks Jr., *The Salad Days*, 151

208 "real pleasure" ... "watching that vast sea" Coward, *Autobiography*, 122-23

209 "*We're delighted*" *The Magnificent Silents*

209 "I would like to concentrate" *PP*, Jan. 1924

210 "Two-fifths" Seabury, *The Public and the Motion Picture Industry*, 60

210 "The stories were sudden" *Ladies Home Journal*, Aug. 1923

210 "funny, fat little girl" *Christian Science Monitor*, Mar. 20, 1928

211 "a small talent" Chaplin, *My Autobiography*, 198

211 "Poetry in motion" MP/Thomas/TN

211 "If reincarnation should prove" ... "sickening" *S&S*, 190-91, 192

212 "Why have the people" Wagenknecht, *Stars of the Silents*, 21

213 "the most immoral story" Rosen, *Popcorn Venus*, 39

213 "I am sick" Walker, *Sex in the Movies*, 60

214 "A wild impulse" *S&S*, 252

214 "[He] said he never knew" MP/Friedman

214 "serious, reserved" *Boston Traveler*, June 9, 1919, Pickford SB II, AMPAS

214 "an exquisite Russian type" DT, June 29, 1916

215 "was very ambitious" Spears, *Hollywood*, 185

215 "No woman should ever play" PP, Mar. 1928

216 "charming love-locks" Burnett, *Little Lord Fauntleroy*, 8

216 "The more ragged" PP, Sept. 1914

216 "It's hard work" . . . "If somebody drops" *San Francisco Daily News*, Mar. 28, 1921, Pickford SB VIII, AMPAS

216 "all very lovely" *NYT*, Nov. 13, 1922

216 "It is a better production" *Ladies Home Journal*, Sept. 1923

217 "Can you guess" Pickford Collection, Photograph 221, Bison Archives, Los Angeles

217 "Do you think that enough?" PP, Jan. 1924

217 "No one ever worked for me" MP/Pratt

217 "The look she gave me" . . . "I just can't cry" MP/Pratt

218 "I'll say definitely" . . . "The director would often" Brownlow, *The Parade's Gone By*, 262

218 "Bill, I am the producer" Spears, *Hollywood*, 191

218 "We called her" Herndon, *Mary Pickford and Douglas Fairbanks*, 230, 229

218 "funny people" *NYT*, June 2, 1920

219 "The Duke of Alba" Chaplin, *My Autobiography*, 288

219 "Hello, Doug" Lockwood, *Dream Palaces*, 115

219 "a *dégagé* familiarity" Chaplin, *My Autobiography*, 288

220 "Your Royal Highness" Case, *Tales of a Wayward Inn*, 89

220 "When a man" Chaplin, *My Autobiography*, 288

221 "The great have no friends" Peters, *The House of Barrymore*, 310

221 "I never saw Douglas" . . . "Since it was all" *S&S*, 308

221 "a man of superficial" Marion, *Off With Their Heads!*, 226

221 "Doug" Schickel, *His Picture in the Papers*, 63

221 "He'd kowtow" Herndon, *Mary Pickford and Douglas Fairbanks*, 201

222 "He was jealous of *me*" Lockwood, *Dream Palaces*, 104

222 "Mary was always" Windeler, *Sweetheart*, 145

222 "She was very lonely" . . . "She explained" Herndon, *Mary Pickford and Douglas Fairbanks*, 277

222 "even if the man" unsourced clipping, July 17, 1929, Lottie Pickford BF, AMPAS

223 "Lottie was a tramp" Herndon, *Mary Pickford and Douglas Fairbanks*, 250

223 "At least I married" Windeler, *Sweetheart*, 170

223 "This little girl" May, *Screening Out the Past*, 133

223 "The big night" Brownlow, *Hollywood*, 108

224 "That's the first time" Loos, *A Girl Like I*, 168

224 "Oh, Jack" Carey, *Doug and Mary*, 104

224 "It was as though Mary" St. Johns, *Love, Laughter and Tears*, 132

225 "Mary's nose went up" Eyman, *Mary Pickford*, 157

225 "Only the waltz" Lockwood, *Dream Palaces*, 104

226 "Douglas, love" St. Johns, *Love, Laughter and Tears*, 133

226 "Don't say 'work'" Fussell, *Mabel*, 108, 109

226 "We'd go [to Pickfair]" Lockwood, *Dream Palaces*, 112

226 "the bungalow courts" Marion, *Off With Their Heads!*, 115

226 "the best-taste house" *Hollywood*: "In the Beginning"

226 "Somewhat pathetic" Marion, *Off With Their Heads!*, 115

227 "the Big House" Fairbanks Jr., *The Salad Days*, 151

227 "this wonderful graciousness" LFS

227 "Show me the north" Chaplin, *My Autobiography*, 201

227 "She could be" LFS

227 "I beg your pardon" ... "I'll never forget" Rosenberg and Silverstein, *The Real Tinsel*, 267

228 "Best damned movie" Herndon, *Mary Pickford and Douglas Fairbanks*, 199

228 "Oh no! No more credit!" Carey, *Doug and Mary*, 95

230 "This is a sample" Torrence, *Hollywood*, 88

230 "A disillusioned nation" ... "something that people needed" Robinson, *Hollywood in the Twenties*, 23-24

231 "sex appeal in movies" ..."that self-conscious age" *New Republic*, Nov. 16, 1927

231 "I do not cry easily" PP, Jan. 1924

232 "To whom can we look" PP, Jan. 1924

232 "magic fire" Knight, *Liveliest Art*, 65

232 "end of the glucose era" Petrie, *Hollywood Destinies*, 18

233 "The handling of crowds" ibid., 63

234 "I want to cry" MP/Pratt

234 "I hear the son" Brownlow, *The Parade's Gone By*, 149

234 "He is going to turn" ... "sick in the head" MP/Pratt

234 "ill-bred and stupid" Brownlow, *The Parade's Gone By*, 149

234 "a hot potato" MP/Pratt

234 "*Mein Gott*" ... "Our actresses are paid" Brownlow, *The Parade's Gone By*, 150

234 "the wheat was chest high" ... "There goes trouble" ibid.

234 "a blow in the face" MP/Pratt

234 "Der iss too many qveens" S&S, 252

234 "German fried potatoes" Brownlow, *The Parade's Gone By*, 150

235 "took it standing up" MP/Pratt

235 "you stringle the bebby" MP/Pratt

235 "Not my daughter!" Brownlow, *The Parade's Gone By*, 154

235 "Mother, he's European" . . . "I absolutely forbid you" MP/Pratt

235 "Poor, dear Ernst" *S&S*, 255

235 "a perfect autocrat" Spears, *Hollywood*, 190

235 "very self-assertive" ibid., 154

235 "This is a love story" . . . "That's final, Mr. Lubitsch" ibid., 153-54

236 "And that was before zippers" MP/Pratt

236 "My English" *PP*, Aug. 1933

236 "Now look, boys and girls" ibid., 151

236 "Komm, pliss" ibid.

236 Don Diego anecdote: ibid., 153

237 "Nothing more delightfully" *NYT*, Sept. 4, 1923

237 "a Mary Pickford" *Variety*, Sept. 6, 1923

237 "I brought [Lubitsch] over" *PP*, Dec. 1924

237 "relied upon my directors" Spears, *Hollywood*, 156

237 "a great comédienne" *PP*, Aug. 1933

238 "the worst picture" *S&S*, 253

238 "A very fine picture" *Moving Picture World*, May 10, 1924, Pickford SB IX, AMPAS

238 "Not the type of picture" ibid.

238 "Neither Douglas nor I" *PP*, Jan. 1924

240 "almost any film" *S&S*, 255

240 "I would rather you" Spears, *Hollywood*, 178

240 "Say, you're doing" Brownlow, *The Parade's Gone By*, 408

240 "So many costume pictures" *PP*, Mar. 1928

240 "I was quite ready" *S&S*, 263

241 "It took me hours" *S&S*, 264

241 "Mary'd come over" . . . "Get out of here" Windeler, *Sweetheart*, 151-52

241 "distracted and unhappy" *PP*, Sept. 1925

241 "confirmation of the belief" *PP*, Oct. 1925

242 "the charming lady" . . . "My star-to-be" von Sternberg, *Fun in a Chinese Laundry*, 206-7

242 "*Mon Dieu*" Brownlow, *The Parade's Gone By*, 220

243 "Include me out" Berg, *Goldwyn*, 396

244 "three weak sisters" . . . "jumper" Balio, *United Artists*, 61-62

245 "a deeper note" *Ladies Home Journal*, Oct. 1926, 226

247 "Beyond its comic inventiveness" Cushman, *A Tribute to Mary Pickford*

248 "'canned' genius" . . . "the motion picture league" *Christian Science Monitor*, Apr. 10, 1928

248 "end civil war" ibid.

248 Banquet speeches: Verbatim Transcript of Organization Banquet of Academy of Motion Picture Arts and Sciences, May 11, 1927, AMPAS

CHAPTER TEN

250 "From the day I learned" *S&S*, 299

250 "I've had three" *S&S*, 300

251 "We were both playing a game" *S&S*, 299

251 "Don't ask me" . . . "You must never blame" *S&S*, 301

251 "She's gone" *S&S*, 302

252 "You know my mother" *S&S*, 302

252 "I realized then" *S&S*, 304

252 "She was almost" *Toronto Daily Star*, May 19, 1934

252 "shaved necks" . . . "I haven't the courage" *Pictorial Review*, Apr. 1927

252 "Shall I ever forget" *S&S*, 293-94

252 "the most famous" *NYT*, May 30, 1979

252 "shackles" MP/Pratt

253 "I had suspected" . . . "wasn't at all prepared" *S&S*, 294

253 "the most indignant" MP/Pratt

253 "You would have thought" *S&S*, 294-95

254 "But don't forget" . . . "Who the hell wants" Warner, *My First Hundred Years*, 168

255 "There was no muffled" *NYT*, Aug. 7, 1926

255 "We simply sat" Kerr, *The Silent Clowns*, 8

255 "*Life* itself!" *PP*, Jan. 1929

256 "the most important event" . . . "I know there was" Berg, *Goldwyn*, 173

256 "like putting lip rouge" *New York Daily News*, Mar. 13, 1934, Pickford SB MWEZ + n.c. 6145, NYPLPA

256 "speaking movies" Flexner, *Listening to America*, 404

256 "the day they tested" Wagner, *You Must Remember This*, 19

257 "Pictures that TALK" *PP*, Jan. 1929

257 "Off with their heads!" . . . "She's too sick anyhow" Marion, *Off With Their Heads!*, 182-83

257 "All you heard is treble" Fountain and Maxim, *Dark Star*, 184

259 "We would rehearse" Love, *From Hollywood with Love*, 111

260 "the dryness of the program" . . . "Detroit Depressed" *Variety*, Apr. 4, 1928

260 "I never doubted" Wagner, *You Must Remember This*, 19-20

260 "ornament of speech" *Pictorial Review*, Mar. 1931

260 "That sounds like" MP/Pratt

260 "flashed suddenly" Hart, Moss, *Act One*, 243

260 "wringing tears" Bronner, *The Encyclopedia of the American Theatre*, 105

260 "Bending the stomach" Nathan, *Another Book on the Theatre*, 358

261 "When Mary came" Eyman, *Mary Pickford*, 188

261 "No cameraman" *S&S*, 295

262 "fairly trembled" ... "I'm afraid I cannot" *S&S*, 297

262 "an ugly mask" ... "I didn't have" MP/Pratt

262 "Everybody else knew" *S&S*, 297

263 "first overt piece" Holden, *Behind the Oscar*, 99

263 "I belonged to him reluctantly" Fairbanks Jr., *The Salad Days*, 151

263 "a great and tender woman" ibid., 106

263 "fine, great father" ibid., 47

263 "You've got a wonderful son" Hancock and Fairbanks, *Douglas Fairbanks*, 230

264 "the genial barriers" Fairbanks Jr., *The Salad Days*, 119

264 "[Dad] couldn't exactly" ibid., 151

264 "I even had on" St. Johns, *The Honeycomb*, 157

264 "companion, confidant" Fairbanks Jr., *The Salad Days*, 210

264 "There were spells" *S&S*, 309

264 "the public apostle" Talmey, *Doug and Mary and Others*, 30

265 "I was desperate" unsourced clipping, Nov. 9, 1928, Lottie Pickford BF, AMPAS

265 "all but chewed" unsourced clipping, Dec. 26, 1928, ibid.

265 "fistic hostilities" unsourced clipping, Dec. 30, 1928, ibid.

265 "an unidentified man" unsourced clipping, Dec. 26, 1928, ibid.

266 "Who told you" ... "Let it ride!" ibid.

266 "And, when she goes out" *New Yorker*, Apr. 7, 1934

266 "If you had seen Mary" Herndon, *Mary Pickford and Douglas Fairbanks*, 276

266 "One time, Jack and I" ibid., 278

266 "It's very hard" Walker, *Stardom*, 20

267 "We don't want any of this" *S&S*, 311

268 "Would you mind retaking" *S&S*, 312

268 "dozens of eyes" ... "a tragic change" *S&S*, 311–12

269 "Hola! Marie!" ... "splendid stimulant" *Saturday Evening Post*, Aug. 23, 1930

269 "The more of life" Kerr, *The Silent Clowns*, 3

269 "the refined simplicity" *Toronto Star*, May 19, 1934

269 "it would have been" Brownlow, *The Parade's Gone By*, 667

270 "impious, but the truth" Carey, *Doug and Mary*, 188

270. "The spirit of the thing" *PP*, Jan. 1931

270 "No action" *PP*, May 1931

270 "An empty taxi" Spears, *Hollywood*, 299

270 "the most stupid" *PP*, May 1931

270 "change their mind" Herndon, *Douglas Fairbanks and Mary Pickford*, 276

272 "like a restless" *NYT*, Mar. 6, 1931

272 "I presume I am not" *PP*, May 1931

272 "increasing restlessness" Hancock and Fairbanks, *Douglas Fairbanks*, 211

273 "To an observer" Fairbanks Jr., *The Salad Days*, 209

273 "I'm jumping silly bully!" "Oh, I hope not!" *PP*, Apr. 1931

274 "When a man finds himself" Schickel, *His Picture in the Papers*, 130

274 "I just couldn't keep up" *S&S*, 309

274 "Doug is naive" Hancock and Fairbanks, *Douglas Fairbanks*, 217

274 "Well, he was human" Herndon, *Mary Pickford and Douglas Fairbanks*, 283

274 "Don't worry, please" Fairbanks Jr., *The Salad Days*, 119

275 "She had the manners" LFS

275 "But her teeth!" LFS

275 "Enchanting to chat with" LFS

275 "fetching" Fairbanks Jr., *The Salad Days*, 213

276 "The handsomest man" Wagner, *You Must Remember This*, 18

276 "so like my mother's" *S&S*, 341

276 "Completely without guile" *S&S*, 342

276 "I had a racoon coat" *LAT*, Oct. 24, 1987, Buddy Rogers BF, AMPAS

276 "It was six months" *Toronto Star*, Apr. 18, 1970

277 "She drove up" . . . "My God" *Silent Cinema*, Summer-Autumn 1971

277 "We made a close-up" Eyman, *Mary Pickford*, 178

277 "She never threw" . . . "Oh fine" *Silent Cinema*, Summer-Autumn 1971

278 "All I knew" . . . "Oh, to have a band!" ibid.

278 "I have had a run" unsourced clipping, Sept. 5, 1931, Buddy Rogers BF, AMPAS

278 "They just said 'great'" *Toronto Star*, Apr. 18, 1970

278 "a heavily handsome man" *Billboard*, Dec. 24, 1936, Pickford SB X, AMPAS

279 "It's more than jealousy" Hancock and Fairbanks, *Douglas Fairbanks*, 201

279 "I'd like to think so" Buddy Rogers, author's interview, 1994

279 "I never met Doug" *LAT*, Oct. 19, 1980, Buddy Rogers BF, AMPAS

279 "he laughed like hell" Herndon, *Mary Pickford and Douglas Fairbanks*, 285

279 "Separation? No, not now" . . . "in this peculiar" *PP*, May 1931

280 "the most ambitious human being" *S&S*, 337

280 "I'm the luckiest man" . . . "I'm the luckiest girl" unsourced clipping, Aug. 13, 1930, Jack Pickford BF, AMPAS

280 "Mr. Pickford" unsourced clipping, Feb. 23, 1932, ibid.

280 "Don't come down" *S&S*, 337

280 "I've lived more" *Los Angeles Daily News*, Jan. 4, 1933, Jack Pickford BF, AMPAS

280 "He was a drunk" Herndon, *Mary Pickford and Douglas Fairbanks*, 251

281 "is simple" *NYT*, May 31, 1933

282 "The little dickens" *Silent Cinema*, Summer-Autumn 1971

283 "Mary saw herself" Herndon, *Mary Pickford and Douglas Fairbanks*, 289

283 "Before sailing" *S&S*, 317

284 "It's just – over" Parsons, *The Gay Illiterate*, 125

284 "I had counted" *S&S*, 319

284 "You are an old friend" Parsons, *The Gay Illiterate*, 125-26

284 "I sometimes wonder" *S&S*, 314

284 "her eyes unlighted" "There is no fight" *New York American*, Dec. 12, 1933, Mary Pickford BF, AMPAS

285 "Good taste prevents" . . . "she laughed" *New York World-Telegram*, Dec. 12, 1933, Pickford SB MWEZ + n.c. 6145, NYPLPA

285 "She was busy" *Pictorial Review*, Jan. 1934

285 "under conditions ill-suited" Barry, *D.W. Griffith*, 32

285 "a shiftless and pitiably stupid" *Time*, Dec. 21, 1931

286 "I can't prove anything" Berg, *Goldwyn*, 274

287 "If you select a capable man" . . . "you cannot hog-tie" Balio, *United Artists*, 124-25

288 "practical, clear" . . . "It seemed to me" Wilson, Edmund, *The Thirties*, 359-60

288 "Her optimism has" *New Yorker*, Apr. 7, 1934

289 "When our thinking" Pickford, *Why Not Try God?*, 11-12

289 "Nothing in the world" ibid., 13

289 "Think how much more awful" *New Yorker*, Apr. 7, 1934

289 "as hooked" LFS

289 "Not a vibration" Pickford, *My Rendezvous with Life*, 22

289 "likes to talk in generalities" *New Yorker*, Apr. 7, 1934

289 "an attempt to victimize" *New York American*, Jan. 28, 1934, Pickford SB MWEZ + n.c. 6145, NYPLPA

290 "I have a message" unsourced clipping, Jan. 28, 1934, Mary Pickford BF, AMPAS

290 "an insignificant pipsqueak" *S&S*, 273

290 "If anyone had the idea" unsourced clipping, Jan. 28, 1934, Mary Pickford BF, AMPAS

290 "But couldn't they walk" unsourced clipping, Jan. 29, 1934, ibid.

291 "I don't feel" *Toronto Daily Star*, May 10, 1934

291 "the whole world's Queen" *Toronto Daily Star*, May 11, 1934

291 "interested in anything" . . . "Don't be foolish" *Toronto Daily Star*, May 19, 1934

291 "Do you remember" *Toronto Daily Star*, May 10, 1934

291 "I don't think" *Toronto Daily Star*, May 17, 1934

292 "guardian and foster-father" *NYT*, Sept. 8, 1933

292 "purely fictional" unsourced clipping, Aug. 11, 1934, Mary Pickford BF, AMPAS

292 "stink test" *Variety*, Oct. 9, 1934, Pickford SB MWEZ + n.c. 6145, NYPLPA

293 "The voice is undistinguished"... "Sentiment and comedy" *New York Evening Post*, Oct. 4, 1934, ibid.

293 "Pomp and circumstance" Hancock and Fairbanks, *Douglas Fairbanks*, 235

294 "How do you know"... "She's really only" *Seattle Post-Intelligencer*, May 25, 1935

294 "Her performance was" *Seattle Daily Times*, May 21, 1935

294 "This isn't her debut" *Seattle Post-Intelligencer*, May 25, 1935

295 "a brazen little hussy" Pickford, *The Demi-Widow*, 142

295 "derisive dark eyes" ibid., 48

295 "I've been a fool" ibid., 260

295 "a masterful arm" ibid., 272

295 "one of the strangest" *S&S*, 323

295 "What I knew personally" *S&S*, 324

296 "rediscovered"... "one and only love" Fairbanks Jr., *The Salad Days*, 252

296 "He'd talk about"... "When you've been" Herndon, *Mary Pickford and Douglas Fairbanks*, 294

296 "Why don't we" Hancock and Fairbanks, *Douglas Fairbanks*, 241

296 "play the Arab" Fairbanks Jr., *The Salad Days*, 252

296 "but I do recall" Herndon, *Mary Pickford and Douglas Fairbanks*, 294

297 "Your father has checked out"... "Oh, sir!" Fairbanks Jr., *The Salad Days*, 254

297 "jump through hoops"... "It's too late" Hancock and Fairbanks, *Douglas Fairbanks*, 243

298 "What a mistake"... "I'm sorry" Moore, *Silent Star*, 169

CHAPTER ELEVEN

299 "When the spirit" Black, *Child Star*, 59

299 "When Santa Claus" Osborne, *60 Years of the Oscar*, 39

300 "Shirley was the instrument" Edwards, Anne, *Shirley Temple*, 65

300 "Oh, she was" *Toronto Star*, Mar. 11, 1974

300 "developing the same appeal" Edwards, Anne, *Shirley Temple*, 105

301 "childish ebullience" Haskell, *From Reverence to Rape*, 61

301 "Infancy is her disguise"... "completely totsy" Parkinson, *The Graham Greene Film Reader*, 233-34

301 in "*Stella Maris* I played" *S&S*, 241

302 "already old-fashioned"... "I would rather be" *PP*, May 1931

302 "Grim"... "It was almost possible" *New York Post*, Apr. 8, 1936, Pickford SB MWEZ + n.c. 6145, NYPLPA

302 "alone, rich"... "the pathetic has-been" *Pictorial Review*, Jan. 1934

304 "would not consider it" Balio, *United Artists*, 137

304 "the business brain" *NYT*, June 2, 1920

304 "If mother had only lived!" *PP*, May 1931

304 "Poor Chuckie" *S&S*, 338

304 "Once, Lottie and I" unsourced clip, Jan. 4, 1933, Mary Pickford BF, AMPAS

304 "I put him in business" unsourced clip, Feb. 17, 1933, Lottie Pickford BF, AMPAS

304 "If this gets back" *LAT*, June 9, 1933, Mary Pickford BF, AMPAS

305 "I'm the one" unsourced clip, June 9, 1933, Lottie Pickford BF, AMPAS

305 "infinitely superior" *S&S*, 329

305 "Mary, how does it feel" *S&S*, 351

305 "One Pickford on the radio" . . . "Auntie broke" Windeler, *Sweetheart*, 170

305 "Where two or three" *S&S*, 339

305 "out chasing sleds" *S&S*, 338

306 "They never should have divorced" Windeler, *Sweetheart*, 180

306 "How dare you talk" Hancock and Fairbanks, *Douglas Fairbanks*, 245

306 "Watching her dancing" *Pictorial Review*, Jan. 1934

306 "She was so much older" Lina Basquette, author's interview, 1994

306 "his damnable youth" Schickel, *His Picture in the Papers*, 139

306 "I just jumped" . . . "the worst move" *Silent Cinema*, Summer-Autumn 1971

307 "I was never any good" *Toronto Star*, Apr. 18, 1970

307 "At first, I put" *S&S*, 344

307 "It is foolish" *S&S*, 344

307 "Do you know" . . . "all kinds of games" *Liberty*, Jan. 5, 1934

308 "I shall never" . . . "Living for self alone" ibid.

308 "Very Mary Pickfordish" *Kansas City Times*, June 26, 1937.

308 "the dress didn't fit right" Windeler, *Sweetheart*, 185

308 "Was Mary's decision" Fairbanks Jr., *The Salad Days*, 255

309 "She dangled [Buddy]" Windeler, *Sweetheart*, 184

309 "Well, you're a good picker" *S&S*, 348

309 "Don't go out now" *S&S*, 326

309 "I hear Pickfair" *S&S*, 326

309 "Pickey, dear" . . . "Mary thanked her" Moore, *Silent Star*, 169-70

310 "The greatest need" Balio, *United Artists*, 142

310 "All my life" Berg, *Goldwyn*, 273

311 "parasites" ibid., 306

311 "When I had these products" *Women's Home Companion*, Nov. 1938

311 "Get out, you punk" Berg, *Goldwyn*, 338

312 "I beg for my husband" ibid., 349

312 "I'm not superstitious" *S&S*, 348

312 "I see someone" *S&S*, 348

313 "It was never easy" Fairbanks Jr., *The Salad Days*, 1

313 "Now, as he lay there" ibid.

313 "I've never felt better" Hancock and Fairbanks, *Douglas Fairbanks*, 255

313 "I am sure" Schickel, *His Picture in the Papers*, 152

313 "I think it's barbaric" *New York Post*, Dec. 13, 1939, Pickford SB MWEZ + n.c. 6145, NYPLPA

313 "which rather spoils" Kidd, *Debrett Goes to Hollywood*, 51

313 "I believe that" LFS

314 "I couldn't bear" . . . "bored me to extinction" *S&S*, 226

314 "God felt sorry" Peters, *House of Barrymore*, 277

314 "prize collection" Farber and Green, *Hollywood on the Couch*, 23

314 "a mining camp" Peters, *House of Barrymore*, 277

315 "The last time I visited" *NYT*, Mar. 24, 1934

315 "Adolf Hitler?" *New York World-Telegram*, May 3, 1937, Pickford SB X, AMPAS

315 "the worst insanity" *Literary Digest*, May 23, 1931

315 "Its suggestion of ideas" Maland, *Chaplin and American Culture*, 156

315 "After years of sly pretending" *New York World-Telegram*, Dec. 21, 1942

316 "I have read and heard" *S&S*, 231

316 "the most scathing denunciation" . . . "Why must you" *S&S*, 233

316 "She had a reproving way" Chaplin, *My Autobiography*, 292

316 "I finally became convinced" *S&S*, 234-35

316 Mary's letter: Balio, *United Artists*, 194-96

317 Pickford-Chaplin exchange: ibid., 196-97

318 "I rejected the idea" *Hollywood Citizen-News*, Sept. 23, 1968, Mary Pickford BF, AMPAS

319 "as an old friend" . . . "the greatest single-day" Black, *Child Star*, 355-56

319 "Two Greatest Has-Beens" *Life*, Oct. 4, 1943

319 "stuff and nonsense" *Life*, Nov. 29, 1943

319 "Are those your trains?" Fairbanks Jr., *The Salad Days*, 35

320 "I had maternal designs" *S&S*, 351

320 "Mary, when you're pregnant" LFS

320 "People say you can" *Toronto Telegram*, Feb. 6, 1934

320 "More than I ever" *S&S*, 354

321 "smart, cute kid" LFS

321 "her wisdom, her discipline" MP/Pratt

321 "*Strict*" Roxanne Monroe, interviewed by Nicholas Eliopoulos, 1996

321 "I was at Pickfair" LFS

321 "Ronnie had committed" LFS

322 "He was making" Connell, *Knight Errant*, 88-89

322 "I had long ago" Fairbanks Jr., *The Salad Days*, 217

322 "wide gesture, poise and pose" Connell, *Knight Errant*, 89

323 "Between you and me" letter dated June 26, 1945, "Albums and Memories" Box, Fairbanks Coll.

323 "He is very frank" ibid.

323 "A little runt" . . . "hoary headed old buzzard" *Time*, Jan. 8, 1945

324 "I was not too concerned" Chaplin, *My Autobiography*, 440

325 "And now Charlie Chaplin" . . . "Two thousand years ago" ibid., 443

325 "a man like Charlie Chaplin" Maland, *Chaplin and American Culture*, 259

325 "humor and an eye" Balio, *United Artists*, 215

325 Pickford–Chaplin exchange: *S&S*, 235

326 "Here you are" . . . "D.W. Griffith" Berg, *Goldwyn*, 447

326 "For his distinguished" Osborne, *60 Years of the Oscar*, 43

327 "I think he was confused" . . . "these young whippersnappers" Schickel, *D. W. Griffith*, 592–93

327 Goodman–Griffith interview: Goodman, *The Fifty-Year Decline*, 1, 5, 10–11

328 "as if he was" Walker, *The Shattered Silents*, 202

328 "I wondered exactly" Vidor, *King Vidor on Film Making*, 63–64

328 "This is an extraordinary" Walker, *The Shattered Silents*, 202

328 "When you've had" Goodman, *The Fifty-Year Decline*, 14

328 Crisp's speech: Goodman, *The Fifty-Year Decline*, 14–15; Schickel, *D. W. Griffith*, 605

329 "Don't go in there now" *S&S*, 351

329 "Let me see" . . . "For God's sake" LFS

329 "It became a tragedy" . . . "He didn't even thank me" LFS

330 "I was in my twenties" MB

330 "aura of royalty" *Los Angeles Times Calendar*, June 10, 1979

330 "Grandmothers and middle-aged matrons" . . . "It was like" *Ottawa Citizen*, Jan. 12, 1984

331 "I think the job" MB

331 "nothing worked at all" MB

332 "*It was* as *if*" . . . "I have *always*" Mary Pickford

332 "bad, an embarrassment" MB

332 "didn't fight it" MB

332 "New York was" MB

332 "I've got to have money" . . . "this millionairess" *Los Angeles Times Calendar*, June 10, 1979

333 "It was odd" MB

333 "That's the Jew" Berg, *Goldwyn*, 110

333 "I will make" . . . "You're not a poor Christian" *S&S*, 360

334 "It's your cousin" . . . "Smiths kiss and hug" JM

334 "It got to be" . . . "I insisted I did not" JM

334 "Aren't you Mary Pickford?" MB

335 "Ultimately, it got" MB

335 "It's such a beautiful day" . . . "A performance" MB

335 "Well, I did and I didn't" MB

335 "I will *destroy* you" . . . "one of the most difficult" MB

336 "Mary would lock herself" MB

336 "I was totally inexperienced" . . . "She was haunted" MB

336 "Fifty-four, about medium height" . . . "I never lied" O'Neill, *Long Day's Journey into Night*, 12, 13, 95, 93

338 "I said, 'You don't want me'" . . . "There are two actresses" *Front Page Challenge*, CBC Television, May 21, 1963

338 "I wouldn't do that kind" *Toronto Globe and Mail*, Mar. 30, 1972

338 "too satirical" *Front Page Challenge*, CBC Television, May 21, 1963

338 "The script was very bold" . . . "I was reading aloud" Daniel Taradash, author's interview, 1994

339 "This is a picture" unsourced clipping, 1951, Mary Pickford clipping file, Museum of Modern Art

339 "We didn't want to say" Daniel Taradash, author's interview, 1994

339 "This was a beloved actress" MB

CHAPTER TWELVE

341 "wild, wounded bull" MP/Pratt

342 "Mal darling" MB

342 "Your company is" Balio, *United Artists*, 229

342 "I've had several conversations" ibid., 232

343 "she had to be given" ibid., 234

344 "dancing in the street" Maland, *Chaplin and American Culture*, 151

344 "He has lived among us" *New York Journal-American*, Sept. 29, 1952

344 "the accent was on nostalgia" *Life*, Mar. 30, 1953

344 "He's one of the finest" MP/Pratt

345 "She was wonderful" MB

345 "I am no Communist" *Los Angeles Examiner*, July 27, 1954, Mary Pickford BF, AMPAS

346 "fan letter" ibid.

346 "one of the best histories" *San Francisco Chronicle*, June 5, 1955

346 "It nearly drives me mad" *Ottawa Journal*, Apr. 23 (no year), Mary Pickford BF, AMPAS

346 "I couldn't tell" MP/Friedman

346 "They acted like children" MB

346 "I want to forget" Berg, *Goldwyn*, 448

347 "I cried my eyes out" Kirkland, *Light Years*, 28

347 "I never wanted Chaplin" Wagner, *You Must Remember This*, 17

347 "What are you boys" Robert Blumofe, author's interview, 1990

347 "pride and joy" unsourced clipping, Feb. 24, 1956, Mary Pickford BF, AMPAS

347 "I sold because" Wagner, *You Must Remember This*, 17

347 "That is my life" *S&S*, 382

348 "She was treated" MB

348 "I was always" ... "never went along" Roxanne Monroe, interviewed by Nicholas Eliopoulos, 1996

348 "He hated being Mary's son" JM

348 "I think that Ronnie" MB

349 "My Dearest Darling" *LAT*, Apr. 1, 1958, Mary Pickford BF, AMPAS

349 "I'm sure she will give you" unsourced, undated clipping, ibid.

349 "This is terrible" ... "Madam" LFS

350 "No matter how many" MP/Thomas/TN

350 "Oh! Mrs. Fairbanks" Connell, *Knight Errant*, 17

350 "like an arrow" MP/Thomas/TN

350 "It was always 'Douglas'" Douglas Kirkland, author's interview, 1989

350 "He played golf" MB

350 "Don't worry, dear" ... "little things" *Toronto Star*, Apr. 18, 1970

351 "I don't always" *S&S*, 347

351 "she could be hard" JM

351 "He was gallant" JM

351 "There was mutual caring" MB

352 "You could almost eat it" MP/Friedman

252 "A lot of these darlings" MP/Pratt

352 "a waxworks" William Bakewell, author's interview, 1993

352 "an old lady" Eyman, *Mary Pickford*, 289

352 "I hate her!" ibid., 295

353 "[Lillian] still acts" ibid.

353 "seemed to hold" *The Arts Tonight*, CBC Stereo, Mar. 25, 1994

354 "My Buddy" Eyman, *Mary Pickford*, 291

354 "I have never seen" ... "I'll beat it yet" Spears, *Hollywood*, 311-12

355 "I had the most weird" ibid., 312-13

355 "Oh my God" William Bakewell, author's interview, 1993

355 "to make good" *PP*, Mar. 1928

355 "a real gusty snort" *Hollywood Citizen-News*, Sept. 22, 1960, Mary Pickford BF, AMPAS

356 "It is a shame" ibid.

356 "gallant in adversity" Spears, *Hollywood*, 167

357 "I am terrible afraid" Beauchamp, *Without Lying Down*, 368

357 "She would speak" Douglas Kirkland, author's interview, 1989

357 "like a beautiful mantle" *Toronto Daily Star*, May 22, 1963

357 "not me, I'm a hypocrite" *Toronto Globe and Mail*, May 22, 1963

357 "The French never forget" Windeler, *Sweetheart*, 200

358 "Somewhere, I have read" Pickford, *My Rendezvous with Life*, 35

358 "And I'm going to start" *Philadelphia Daily News*, Jan. 13, 1971, Mary Pickford BF, AMPAS

358 "You boys get" unsourced, undated clipping, Fairbanks Coll.

358 "she was quick as a whip" Roger Seward, author's interview, 1994

358 "from your son" Fairbanks Coll.

359 "I'm not Garbo" Wagner, *You Must Remember This*, 12

359 "That was upsetting" Harmetz, *Rolling Breaks*, 9

359 "She's fine" . . . "I only wish" *Film Fan Monthly*, Dec. 1970, Buddy Rogers BF, AMPAS

359 "reports and dark rumors" . . . "I can promise you" St. Johns, *Love, Laughter and Tears*, 96

360 "Honey, all your friends" Harmetz, *Rolling Breaks*, 3

360 "Mary's so happy" . . . "Mary says to give you" Harmetz, *Rolling Breaks*, 3-5

361 "my image of Mary Pickford" *Village Voice*, Nov. 18, 1971

361 "The camera stays" ibid.

361 "What did you" . . . "I've been married" St. Johns, *Love, Laughter and Tears*, 90, 99

361 "the doll" . . . "When this doll" Windeler, *Sweetheart*, 203

362 "I don't ever want" Wagner, *You Must Remember This*, 18

362 "the incalculable effect" Osborne, *60 Years of the Oscar*, 219

362 "He wasn't grateful" . . . "It's disgraceful" Wagner, *You Must Remember This*, 18

362 "I think they should ask" *Toronto Globe and Mail*, Mar. 30, 1972

362 "I went on and on" . . . "I still say" A Centennial Tribute to Mary Pickford, May 25, 1993, Samuel Goldwyn Theatre, AMPAS

363 "Mary, I present" . . . "You've made me" 1976 Academy Awards, AMPAS

363 "I didn't think" *LAT*, Apr. 2, 1976, Mary Pickford BF, AMPAS

363 "I wouldn't be surprised" *New York Post*, Apr. 3, 1976, Box 88, Fairbanks Coll.

363 "It was after the Oscar" Roger Seward, author's interview, 1994

363 "skin-and-bones" Fairbanks Jr., *The Salad Days*, 35

364 "Oh no, dear" Douglas Fairbanks Jr., author's interview, 1989

364 "She couldn't walk" Roger Seward, author's interview, 1994

364 "coming down University Avenue" MP/Thomas/TN

364 "There's Mama. There's Daddy" MB

EPILOGUE

365 "She was a good staunch fighter" *NYT*, Mar. 12, 1981

365 "gentle admonition" Mary Pickford, Last Will and Testament, June 7, 1971, Los Angeles Superior Court, Santa Monica

366 "It's very difficult for me" clipping, illegible source and date, Mary Pickford BF, AMPAS

366 "that portion" Mary Pickford, Last Will and Testament, June 7, 1971, Los Angeles Superior Court, Santa Monica

366 "We were placed" *Toronto Globe and Mail*, Jan. 24, 1981

367 "during clean-up operations" ibid.

367 "Mrs. Rogers" "But she's been dead" ibid.

367 "idolized Mary Pickford" *Los Angeles Herald-Examiner*, Sept. 21, 1980, Homes/Pickfair file, AMPAS

368 "carelessly curious" . . . "Listen, folks" *LAT*, Mar. 15, 1981, Mary Pickford BF, AMPAS

368 "Many people are tearing down" *Hollywood Reporter*, Jan. 13, 1988, Homes/Pickfair file, AMPAS

369 "She had forgiven" MB

370 "Never listened to me" Roxanne Monroe, interviewed by Nicholas Eliopoulos, 1996

370 "Of Mary Pickford" Rotha and Griffith, *The Film Till Now*, 176

370 "They don't belong to you" . . . "Well, time's passing" Harmetz, *Rolling Breaks*, 6

370 "The only great art" Roud, *A Passion for Films*, 33

371 "the two greatest names" Barry, *Let's Go to the Pictures*, 103

371 "challenging manner" Program, The Sixth Annual Festival of Preservation, University of Southern California, 1994

372 "That's a dirty word" *Variety*, Apr. 14, 1976

372 "Looking at these films" *Image*, Dec. 1959

372 "By a cruel irony" *Hollywood Reporter*, Apr. 16, 1976, Mary Pickford BF, AMPAS

372 "no one has ever" *Times* (London), Nov. 19, 1979

373 "There was the whole thing" *Toronto Globe and Mail*, Apr. 21, 1970

373 "no civilization worthy" *Saturday Night*, Aug. 1987

373 "Directly or indirectly" Brownlow, *Hollywood*, 9

BIBLIOGRAPHY

Abbott, George, and Ann Preston Bridgers. *Coquette*. Toronto: Longmans, Green, 1928.

Agee, James. *Agee on Film*. Toronto: George J. McLeod Limited, 1958.

Arthur, Eric. *Toronto: No Mean City*. Toronto: University of Toronto Press, 1964.

Arvidson, Linda. *When the Movies Were Young*. New York: E.P. Dutton & Co., 1925.

Atkinson, Brooks. *Broadway*. New York: Macmillan, 1970.

Bailey, J.O. *British Plays of the Nineteenth Century*. New York: Odyssey Press, 1966.

Bakewell, William. *Hollywood Be Thy Name*. Filmmakers No. 25. Metuchen, NJ: Scarecrow Press, 1991.

Balio, Tino, ed. *The American Film Industry*. Madison, WI: University of Wisconsin Press, 1985.

Balio, Tino. *United Artists: The Company Built by the Stars*. Madison, WI: University of Wisconsin Press, 1976.

Banner, Lois W. *American Beauty*. Chicago: University of Chicago Press, 1984.

Barry, Iris. *D.W. Griffith: American Film Master*. Garden City, NY: Doubleday & Company, 1965.

———. *Let's Go to the Pictures*. London: Chatto & Windus, 1926.

Beauchamp, Cari. *Without Lying Down: Frances Marion and the Powerful Women of Early Hollywood*. New York: Scribner, 1997.

Berg, A. Scott. *Goldwyn*. New York: Ballantine Books, 1989.

Bergan, Ronald. *The United Artists Story*. New York: Crown Publishers, 1986.

Bergreen, Laurence. *As Thousands Cheer: The Life of Irving Berlin*. New York: Penguin Books, 1990.

Birdoff, Harry. *The World's Greatest Hit: Uncle Tom's Cabin*. New York: S.F. Vanni, 1947.

Bitzer, G.W. *Billy Bitzer: His Story*. Toronto: Doubleday Canada, 1973.

Black, Shirley Temple. *Child Star*. New York: Warner Books, 1989.

Blum, Daniel. *A Pictorial History of the Silent Screen*. London: Spring Books, 1953.

Bodeen, DeWitt. *From Hollywood: The Careers of Fifteen Great American Stars*. South Brunswick, NJ: A.S. Barnes, 1976.

Bogdanovich, Peter. *Allan Dwan: The Last Pioneer*. New York: Praeger, 1971.

Bordwell, David, Janet Staiger, and Kristin Thompson. *The Classical Hollywood Cinema: Film Style and Mode of Production to 1985*. New York: Columbia University Press, 1985.

Bowser, Eileen. *The Transformation of Cinema*. Toronto: Collier Macmillan Canada, 1990.

Braudy, Leo. *The Frenzy of Renown: Fame and Its History*. New York: Oxford University Press, 1986.

Bronner, Edwin. *The Encyclopedia of the American Theatre 1900-1975*. New York: A.S. Barnes & Company, 1980.

Brown, Karl. *Adventures with D.W. Griffith*. New York: Da Capo Press, 1976.

Browning, Robert. *Pippa Passes & Men & Women*. London: Chatto & Windus, 1908.

Brownlow, Kevin. *Behind the Mask of Innocence: Sex, Violence, Prejudice, Crime: Films of Social Conscience in the Silent Era*. New York: Alfred A. Knopf, 1990.

———. *Hollywood: The Pioneers*. London: Collins, 1979.

———. *The Parade's Gone By*. New York: Ballantine Books, 1970.

Burnett, Frances Hodgson. *A Little Princess*. New York: Dell Publishing, 1975.

———. *Little Lord Fauntleroy*. Toronto: William Bryce, 1887.

Butler, Ivan. *Silent Magic*. London: Columbus Books, 1987.

———. *The War Film*. New York: A.S. Barnes and Company, 1974.

Campbell, Craig W. *Reel America and World War I*. Jefferson, NC: McFarland Publishers, 1985.

Card, James. *Seductive Cinema*. New York: Alfred A. Knopf, 1994.

Carey, Gary. *Anita Loos*. New York: Alfred A. Knopf, 1988.

———. *Doug and Mary: A Biography of Douglas Fairbanks and Mary Pickford*. New York: E.P. Dutton, 1977.

Carringer, Robert, ed. *The Jazz Singer*. Madison, WI: University of Wisconsin Press, 1979.

Case, Frank. *Tales of a Wayward Inn*. New York: Frederick A. Stokes Company, 1938.

Chaplin, Charles. *My Autobiography*. New York: Viking Penguin, 1987.

Coe, Brian. *The History of Movie Photography*. Westfield, NJ: Eastview Editions, 1981.

Connell, Brian. *Knight Errant: A Biography of Douglas Fairbanks, Jr.* London: Hodder and Stoughton, 1955.

Cook, David A. *A History of Narrative Film*. New York: W.W. Norton and Co., 1981.

Cooke, Alistair. *Douglas Fairbanks: The Making of a Screen Character*. Film Library Series No. 2. New York: Museum of Modern Art, 1940.

Cooper, Miriam. *Dark Lady of the Silents: My Life in Early Hollywood*. New York: Bobbs-Merrill, 1973.

Coward, Noël. *Autobiography*. London: Methuen, 1986.

Croy, Homer. *Starmaker: The Story of D. W. Griffith*. New York: Duell, Seran and Pearce, 1959.

Cushman, Robert B. *A Tribute to Mary Pickford*. Washington, DC: American Film Institute, October 1970. Event program.

de Mille, Agnes. *Dance to the Piper*. Boston: Little, Brown and Company, 1952.

———. *Portrait Gallery*. Boston: Houghton Mifflin, 1990.

DeMille, Cecil B. *The Autobiography of Cecil B. DeMille*. Englewood Cliffs, NJ: Prentice-Hall, 1959.

de Mille, William C. *Hollywood Saga*. New York: E.P. Dutton & Co., 1939.

———. "The Warrens of Virginia." Playwright's typescript, 1907. Special collections, New York Public Library for the Performing Arts.

Dickens, Charles. *Nicholas Nickleby*. London: Collins, 1977.

Drew, William M. *Speaking of Silents: First Ladies of the Screen*. Vestal, NY: Vestal Press, 1989.

Drinkwater, John. *The Life and Adventures of Carl Laemmle*. New York: G.P. Putnam's Sons, 1931.

Eaton, Walter Prichard. *The American Stage of To-Day*. Boston: Small, Maynard and Company, 1908.

Edwards, Anne. *The DeMilles: An American Family*. New York: Abrams, 1988.

———. *Shirley Temple: American Princess*. New York: William Morrow and Co., 1988.

Edwards, Murray D. *A Stage in Our Past: English-Language Theatre in Eastern Canada from the 1790s to 1914*. Toronto: University of Toronto Press, 1968.

Ehrenkranz, Anne, Willis Hartshorn, and John Szarkowski. *A Singular Elegance: The Photographs of Baron Adolph de Meyer*. San Francisco: Chronicle Books, 1995.

Ellman, Richard. *Oscar Wilde*. Toronto: Penguin Canada, 1987.

Endres, Stacey, and Robert Cushman. *Hollywood at Your Feet: The Story of the World-Famous Chinese Theatre*. Universal City, CA: Pomegranate Press, 1992.

Epstein, Jerry. *Remembering Charlie: The Story of a Friendship*. London: Bloomsbury Publishing, 1988.

Everson, William K. *American Silent Film*. New York: Oxford University Press, 1978.

Eyman, Scott. *Mary Pickford: From Here to Hollywood*. Toronto: HarperCollins, 1990.

Fairbanks, Douglas, Jr. *The Fairbanks Album*. Introduction and narrative by Richard Schickel. Boston: New York Graphic Society, 1975.

———. *The Salad Days*. New York: Doubleday, 1988.

Farber, Stephen, and Marc Green. *Hollywood on the Couch*. New York: William Morrow and Company, 1993.

Fell, John. *Film Before Griffith*. Berkeley, CA: University of California Press, 1983.

Fell, John L., Stephen Gong, Neil Harris, Richard Koszarski, Jay Leyda, Judith Mayne, Brooks McNamara, Russell Merritt, Charles Musser, and Alan Trachtenberg. *Before Hollywood: Turn of the Century American Film*. New York: Hudson Hills Press, 1987.

Flexner, Stuart Berg. *Listening to America: An Illustrated History of Words and Phrases from Our Lively and Splendid Past*. New York: Simon and Schuster, 1982.

Fountain, Leatrice Gilbert, and John R. Maxim. *Dark Star*. New York: St. Martin's Press, 1985.

Fussell, Betty Harper. *Mabel: Hollywood's First I-Don't-Care Girl*. New York: Ticknor & Fields, 1982.

Gabler, Neal. *An Empire of Their Own: How the Jews Invented Hollywood*. New York: Crown Publishers, 1988.

Gates, Eleanor. *The Poor Little Rich Girl*. New York: Grosset & Dunlap; Duffield & Company, 1912.

Gerould, Daniel C., ed. *American Melodrama*. New York: Performing Arts Journal Publications, 1983.

Gilbert, Douglas. *American Vaudeville: Its Life and Times*. New York: McGraw-Hill, 1940.

Gish, Lillian. *Dorothy and Lillian Gish*. New York: Charles Scribner's Sons, 1973.

————. *The Movies, Mr. Griffith, and Me*. With Ann Pinchot. Englewood Cliffs, NJ: Prentice-Hall, 1969.

Goldwyn, Samuel. *Behind the Screen*. New York: George H. Doran Company, 1923.

Gomery, Douglas. *The Hollywood Studio System*. New York: St. Martin's Press, 1986.

Goodman, Ezra. *The Fifty-Year Decline and Fall of Hollywood*. New York: Simon and Schuster, 1961.

Graham, Cooper C., Steven Higgins, Elaine Mancini, and Laoa Louiz Vieira. *D. W. Griffith and the Biograph Company*. Filmmakers, No. 10. Metuchen, NJ: Scarecrow Press, 1985.

Grau, Robert. *The Stage in the Twentieth Century*. New York: Broadway Publishing Company, 1912.

Guiles, Fred Lawrence. *Marion Davies*. Toronto: McGraw-Hill, 1922.

Gunning, Tom. "D.W. Griffith and the Origins of American Narrative Film: The Early Years at Biograph." Dissertation, University of Illinois, 1991. Copyright 1991 by the Board of Trustees of the University of Illinois.

Hall, Ben M. *The Best Remaining Seats: The Golden Age of the Movie Palace*. New York: Da Capo Press, 1988.

Hampton, Benjamin B. *History of the American Film Industry: From Its Beginnings to 1931*. New York: Dover, 1970.

Hancock, Ralph, and Letitia Fairbanks. *Douglas Fairbanks: The Fourth Musketeer*. London: Peter Davies, 1953.

Harmetz, Aljean. *Rolling Breaks and Other Movie Business*. New York: Knopf, 1983.

Hart, James, ed. *The Man Who Invented Hollywood: The Autobiography of D.W. Griffith*. Louisville, KY: Touchstone, 1972.

Hart, Moss. *Act One*. New York: Random House, 1959.

Harte, Bret. *Selected Stories*. Chicago: Puritan Publishing Co., undated.

Haskell, Molly. *From Reverence to Rape: The Treatment of Women in the Movies*. Chicago: University of Chicago Press, 1987.

Haver, Ronald. *David O. Selznick's Hollywood*. New York: Bonanza Books, 1980.

Henderson, Robert M. *D.W. Griffith: His Life and Work*. New York: Oxford University Press, 1972.

———. *D.W. Griffith: The Years at Biograph*. New York: Farrar, Straus and Giroux, 1970.

Herndon, Booton. *Mary Pickford and Douglas Fairbanks: The Most Popular Couple the World Has Ever Known*. New York: W.W. Norton & Company, 1977.

Holden, Anthony. *Behind the Oscar: The Secret History of the Academy Awards*. Toronto: Penguin Canada, 1994.

Hollywood. 13 episodes. Thames Television Production, 1980. Written, directed, and produced by David Gill and Kevin Brownlow.

Hoyt, Harlowe R. *Town Hall Tonight: Intimate Memories of the Grassroots Days of the American Theatre*. New York: Bramhall House, 1955.

Hughes, Glenn. *A History of American Theatre: 1700-1950.* Toronto: Samuel French, 1951.

Irwin, Will. *The House That Shadows Built*. Garden City, NY: Doubleday, Doran and Company, 1928.

Izod, John. *Hollywood and the Box Office, 1895-1986*. London: Macmillan, 1988.

Jackson, Kathy Merlock. *Images of Children in American Film: A Sociocultural Analysis*. Metuchen, NJ: Scarecrow Press, 1986.

Jacobs, Lewis. *The Rise of the American Film*. New York: Teachers College Press, Columbia University, 1971.

Janis, Elsie. *So Far, So Good!* New York: E.P. Dutton & Co., 1932.

Jesionowski, Joyce. *Thinking in Pictures: Dramatic Structure in D.W. Griffith's Biograph Films*. Los Angeles: University of California, 1987.

Kahn, E.J., Jr. *Jock: The Life and Times of John Hay Whitney*. Garden City, NY: Doubleday & Company, 1981.

Kerr, Walter. *The Silent Clowns*. New York: Da Capo Press, 1980.

Kidd, Charles. *Debrett Goes to Hollywood*. London: Weidenfeld and Nicolson, 1986.

Kirkland, Douglas. *Light Years*. New York: Thames and Hudson, 1989.

Knight, Arthur. *The Liveliest Art: A Panoramic History of the Movies*. New York: New American Library, 1979.

Kobal, John. *Hollywood: The Years of Innocence*. New York: Abbeville Press, 1985.

Koszarski, Richard. *An Evening's Entertainment: The Age of the Silent Feature Picture, 1915-1928*. Toronto: Collier Macmillan Canada, 1990.

Lash, Joseph P. *Helen and Teacher: The Story of Helen Keller and Anne Sullivan Macy*.

New York: Delacorte Press/Seymour Lawrence, 1980.

Lasky, Jesse K. *I Blow My Own Horn*. With Don Waldon. London: Victor Gollancz, 1957.

Lasky, Jesse K., Jr. *Whatever Happened to Hollywood?* New York: Funk & Wagnalls, 1975.

Laurie, Joe, Jr. *Vaudeville: From the Honky-Tonks to the Palace*. New York: Henry Holt and Company, 1953.

Lee, Raymond. *The Films of Mary Pickford*. New York: Castle Books, 1970.

Lejeune, C.A. *Cinema*. London: Alexander Madehose & Company, 1931.

Lewis, Philip C. *Trouping: How the Show Came to Town*. New York: Harper and Row, 1973.

Lindsay, John. *Turn Out the Stars Before Leaving: The Story of Canada's Theatres*. Foreword by Mary Pickford. Erin, ON: Boston Mills Press, 1983.

Lindsay, Vachel. *The Art of the Moving Picture*. New York: Macmillan, 1922.

Lockwood, Charles. *Dream Palaces: Hollywood at Home*. New York: Viking Press, 1981.

Long, Bruce. *William Desmond Taylor: A Dossier*. Metuchen, NJ: Scarecrow Press, 1991.

Loos, Anita. *A Girl Like I*. New York: Viking Press, 1966.

———. *The Talmadge Girls*. New York: Viking Press, 1978.

Love, Bessie. *From Hollywood with Love: An Autobiography of Bessie Love*. London: Elm Tree Books, 1977.

Lurie, Alison. *Don't Tell the Grown-ups: Subversive Children's Literature*. Toronto: Little, Brown and Company, 1990.

MacGowan, Kenneth. *Behind the Screen*. New York: Dell Publishing, 1965.

The Magnificent Silents. Written and produced by Bud Greenspan. Narrated by Henry Fonda. Choral Records CRL 57303.

Maland, Charles J. *Chaplin and American Culture: The Evolution of a Star Image*. Princeton, NJ: Princeton University Press, 1989.

Marion, Frances. *Off With Their Heads! A Serio-Comic Tale of Hollywood*. New York: Macmillan Company, 1972.

Marsh, Mae. *Screen Acting*. Los Angeles: Photo-Star Publishing Company, 1921.

Mary Pickford: America's Sweetheart. Original Radio Broadcasts. A George Garabedian Production. Mark 56 Records, Anaheim, CA 92805. 1975.

May, Lary. *Screening Out the Past: The Birth of Mass Culture and the Motion Picture Industry*. Chicago: University of Chicago Press, 1983.

Merritt, Russell, and J.B. Kaufman. *Walt in Wonderland: The Silent Films of Walt Disney*. Baltimore: Johns Hopkins University Press, 1993.

Moore, Colleen. *Silent Star*. Garden City, NY: Doubleday & Company, 1968.

Morddan, Ethan. *Movie Star: A Look at the Women Who Made Hollywood*. New York: St. Martin's Press, 1983.

Mosley, Leonard. *Zanuck: The Rise and Fall of Hollywood's Last Tycoon*. Toronto: Granada, 1984.

Musser, Charles. *The Emergence of Cinema: The American Screen to 1907*. Los Angeles: University of California Press, 1990.

Nathan, George Jean. *Another Book on the Theatre*. New York: B.W. Huebesch, 1915.

Naylor, David. *American Picture Palaces: The Architecture of Fantasy*. Toronto: Prentice-Hall, 1981.

Negri, Pola. *Memoirs of a Star*. Garden City, NY: Doubleday & Company, 1970.

Niver, Kemp R. *Mary Pickford, Comedienne*. Los Angeles: Ocare Research Group, 1969.

O'Dell, Paul. *Griffith and the Rise of Hollywood*. New York: Castle Books, 1970.

O'Neill, Eugene. *Long Day's Journey into Night*. New Haven: Yale University Press, 1989.

Osborne, Robert. *60 Years of the Oscar: The Official History of the Academy Awards*. New York: Abbeville Press, 1989.

Paine, Albert Bigelow. *Life and Lillian Gish*. New York: Macmillan Company, 1932.

Parkinson, David, ed. *The Graham Greene Film Reader: Reviews, Essays, Interviews & Film Stories*. New York: Applause Books, 1995.

Parsons, Louella O. *The Gay Illiterate*. Garden City, NY: Doubleday, Doran and Co., 1944.

Pearson, Roberta E. *Eloquent Gestures: The Transformation of Performance Style in the Griffith Biograph Films*. Los Angeles: University of California Press, 1992.

Peters, Margot. *The House of Barrymore*. Toronto: Simon & Schuster, 1990.

Petrie, Graham. *Hollywood Destinies: European Directors in America 1922-1931*. Boston: Routledge & Kegan Paul, 1985.

Pickford, Mary. *The Demi-Widow*. New York: Bobbs-Merrill, 1935.

———. *My Rendezvous with Life*. New York: H.C. Kinsey & Company, 1935.

———. *Sunshine and Shadow: An Autobiography*. New York: Doubleday and Co., 1956.

———. *Why Not Try God?* New York: H.C. Kinsey & Company, 1934.

Porter, Eleanor H. *Pollyanna*. New York: Puffin Books, Viking Penguin, 1987.

Powell, Michael. *A Life in Movies: An Autobiography*. New York: Knopf, 1987.

Pratt, George C. *Spellbound in Darkness: A History of the Silent Film*. Greenwich, CT: New York Graphic Society, 1966.

Rahill, Frank. *The World of Melodrama*. University Park, PA: Pennsylvania State University Press, 1967.

Ramsaye, Terry. *A Million and One Nights: A History of the Motion Picture Through 1936*. New York: Simon & Schuster, 1986.

Rhode, Eric. *A History of the Cinema from Its Origins to 1970*. New York: Hill and Wang, 1976.

Robinson, David. *Chaplin*. Toronto: Collins, 1985.

———. *Chaplin: The Mirror of Opinion*. Bloomington, IN: Indiana University Press, 1984.

———. *Hollywood in the Twenties*. New York: A.S. Barnes & Company, 1968.

Rosen, Marjorie. *Popcorn Venus*. New York: Avon Books, 1973.

Rosenberg, Bernard, and Harry Silverstein. *The Real Tinsel*. New York: Macmillan, 1970.

Rotha, Paul, and Richard Griffith. *The Film Till Now*. Middlesex: Hamlyn Publishing, 1967.

Roud, Richard. *A Passion for Films: Henri Langlois and the Cinémathèque Française*. New York: Viking Press, 1983.

Saddlemeyer, Ann, ed. *Early Stages: Theatre in Ontario 1800-1914*. Toronto: University of Toronto Press, 1990.

St. Johns, Adela Rogers. *The Honeycomb*. Garden City, NY: Doubleday & Co., 1969.

———. *Love, Laughter and Tears: My Hollywood Story*. Garden City, NY: Doubleday & Company, 1978.

Schickel, Richard. *D.W. Griffith: An American Life*. New York: Simon and Schuster, 1985.

———. *The Disney Version: The Life, Times, Art and Commerce of Walt Disney*. New York: Simon and Schuster, 1968.

———. *His Picture in the Papers: A Speculation on Celebrity in America Based on the Life of Douglas Fairbanks, Sr.* New York: Charterhouse, 1973.

———. *Intimate Strangers: The Culture of Celebrity*. New York: Fromm International Publishing, 1986.

Schulberg, Budd. *Moving Pictures: Memoirs of a Hollywood Prince*. New York: Stein and Day, 1981.

Seabury, William. *The Public and the Motion Picture Industry*. New York: Macmillan, 1926.

Simmon, Scott. *The Films of D.W. Griffith*. New York: Cambridge University Press, 1993.

Slide, Anthony. *The American Film Industry: A Historical Dictionary*. New York: Greenwood Press, 1986.

———. *Aspects of American Film History Before 1920*. Metuchen, NJ: Scarecrow Press, 1978.

———. *The Big V: A History of the Vitagraph Company*. With Alan Gevinson. Metuchen, NJ: Scarecrow Press, 1987.

———. *The Griffith Actresses*. Cranbury, NJ: A.S. Barnes and Company, 1973.

Slide, Anthony, ed. *Selected Film Criticism 1912-1920*. Metuchen, NJ: Scarecrow Press, 1982.

Smith, James L., ed. *Victorian Melodramas*. Totowa, NJ: Rowman and Littlefield, 1976.

Spears, Jack. *Hollywood: The Golden Era*. New York: Castle Books, 1971.

Stanley, Robert. *The Celluloid Empire: A History of the American Movie Industry*. New York: Hastings House, 1978.

Starr, Kevin. *Inventing the Dream: California Through the Progressive Era*. Toronto: Oxford University Press, 1985.

Stenn, David. *Clara Bow: Runnin' Wild*. Toronto: Doubleday, 1988.

Sterling, Anna Kate. *Cinematographers on the Art and Craft of Cinematography*.

Metuchen, NJ: Scarecrow Press, 1987.

Stowe, Harriet Beecher. *Uncle Tom's Cabin*. New York: Harper & Row, 1965.

Talmey, Allene. *Doug and Mary and Others*. New York: Macy-Masius, 1927.

Tibbets, John C., and James M. Welsh. *His Majesty the American: The Cinema of Douglas Fairbanks*. New York: A.S. Barnes and Company, 1977.

Torrence, Bruce T. *Hollywood: The First Hundred Years*. New York: New York Zoetrope, 1982.

Vardac, A. Nicholas. *Stage to Screen: Theatrical Origins of Early Film, David Garrick to D.W. Griffith*. New York: Da Capo Press, 1987.

Vidor, King. *King Vidor on Filmmaking*. New York: David Mackay, 1972.

von Sternberg, Josef. *Fun in a Chinese Laundry*. New York: Macmillan, 1965.

Wagenknecht, Edward. *As Far as Yesterday: Memories and Reflections*. Norman, OK: University of Oklahoma Press, 1968.

———. *The Movies in the Age of Innocence*. Norman, OK: University of Oklahoma Press, 1962.

———. *Stars of the Silents*. Filmmakers, No. 19. Metuchen, NJ: Scarecrow Press, 1987.

Wagner, Walter. *You Must Remember This*. New York: G.P. Putnam's Sons, 1975.

Walker, Alexander. *Sex in the Movies: The Celluloid Sacrifice*. Baltimore: Penguin Books, 1966.

———. *The Shattered Silents: How the Talkies Came to Stay*. London: Harrap, 1978.

———. *Stardom: The Hollywood Phenomenon*. Markham, ON: Penguin Books, 1974.

Warner, Jack, and Dean Jennings. *My First Hundred Years in Hollywood*. New York: Random House, 1964.

Weaver, William. *Duse: A Biography*. London: Thames and Hudson, 1984.

Webster, Jean. *Daddy-Long-Legs*. Scarborough, ON: New American Library, 1988.

Westmore, Frank, and Muriel Davidson. *The Westmores of Hollywood*. New York: J.B. Lippincott Company, 1976.

Wiggin, Kate Douglas. *Rebecca of Sunnybrook Farm*. New York: Grosset & Dunlap, 1917.

Wilson, Edmund. *The Thirties*. New York: Farrar, Straus and Giroux, 1980.

Wilson, Garff B. *A History of American Acting*. Bloomington, IN: Indiana University Press, 1966.

Windeler, Robert. *Sweetheart: The Story of Mary Pickford*. New York: Praeger, 1974.

Winter, William. *The Life of David Belasco*. 2 volumes. New York: Moffat, Yard and Company, 1918.

———. *Other Days: Being Chronicles and Memories of the Stage*. New York: Moffat, Yard and Company, 1908.

Yurka, Blanche. *Bohemian Girl: Blanche Yurka's Theatrical Life*. Athens, OH: Ohio University Press, 1970.

Zolotow, Maurice. *Billy Wilder in Hollywood*. New York: G.P. Putnam's Sons, 1977.

Zukor, Adolph. *The Public Is Never Wrong*. With Dale Kramer. New York: G.P. Putnam's Sons, 1953.

FILMOGRAPHY

Films listed here are those that featured Mary Pickford as a performer. For her feature films, credits for source material, scenario, photography, and cast have been included when the contributors were significant members of Pickford's creative team, or when their work is of anecdotal interest.

Sources include *The American Film Institute Catalogue of Motion Pictures Produced in the United States; Magill's Survey of Cinema (English Language Films, First Series)*; Graham et al., *D.W. Griffith and the Biograph Company*; and the Paramount production files at the Margaret Herrick Library, Academy of Motion Picture Arts and Sciences, Los Angeles.

SHORT FILMS, 1909–1913

Listed by production company and release date.

AMERICAN MUTOSCOPE AND BIOGRAPH COMPANY

Two Memories	May 24, 1909
His Duty	May 31, 1909
The Violin Maker of Cremona	June 7, 1909
The Lonely Villa	June 10, 1909
The Son's Return	June 14, 1909
The Faded Lilies	June 17, 1909
Her First Biscuits	June 17, 1909
The Peachbasket Hat	June 24, 1909
The Way of Man	June 28, 1909
The Necklace	July 1, 1909
The Country Doctor	July 8, 1909
The Cardinal's Conspiracy	July 12, 1909
Tender Hearts	July 19, 1909
The Renunciation	July 19, 1909
Sweet and Twenty	July 22, 1909
The Slave	July 29, 1909
They Would Elope	Aug. 9, 1909

His Wife's Visitor	Aug. 19, 1909	*The Newlyweds*	Mar. 3, 1910
The Indian Runner's		*The Thread of Destiny*	Mar. 7, 1910
Romance	Aug. 23, 1909	*The Twisted Trail*	Mar. 24, 1910
"Oh, Uncle"	Aug. 26, 1909	*The Smoker*	Mar. 31, 1910
The Seventh Day	Aug. 26, 1909	*As It Is In Life*	Apr. 6, 1910
The Little Darling	Sept. 2, 1909	*A Rich Revenge*	Apr. 7, 1910
The Sealed Room	Sept. 2, 1909	*A Romance of*	
"1776" or, The Hessian		*the Western Hills*	Apr. 11, 1910
Renegades	Sept. 6, 1909	*The Unchanging Sea*	May 5, 1910
Getting Even		*Love Among the Roses*	May 9, 1910
(also author)	Sept. 13, 1909	*The Two Brothers*	May 12, 1910
The Broken Locket	Sept. 16, 1909	*Ramona*	May 23, 1910
In Old Kentucky	Sept. 20, 1909	*In the Season of Buds*	June 2, 1910
The Awakening		*A Victim of Jealousy*	June 9, 1910
(also author)	Sept. 30, 1909	*Never Again*	June 20, 1910
The Little Teacher	Oct. 11, 1909	*May and December*	
His Lost Love	Oct. 18, 1909	(also author)	June 20, 1910
In the Watches of		*A Child's Impulse*	June 27, 1910
the Night	Oct. 25, 1909	*Muggsy's First Sweetheart*	June 30, 1910
Lines of White on		*What the Daisy Said*	July 11, 1910
a Sullen Sea	Oct. 28, 1909	*The Call to Arms*	July 25, 1910
The Gibson Goddess	Nov. 1, 1909	*An Arcadian Maid*	Aug. 1, 1910
What's Your Hurry?	Nov. 1, 1909	*When We Were*	
The Restoration	Nov. 8, 1909	*In Our 'Teens*	Aug. 18, 1910
The Light		*The Sorrows of*	
That Came	Nov. 11, 1909	*the Unfaithful*	Aug. 22, 1910
A Midnight		*Wilful Peggy*	Aug. 25, 1910
Adventure	Nov. 18, 1909	*Muggsy Becomes*	
The Mountaineer's		*a Hero*	Sept. 1, 1910
Honor	Nov. 25, 1909	*Examination Day*	
The Trick		*at School*	Sept. 2, 1910
That Failed	Nov. 29, 1909	*A Gold Necklace*	Oct. 6, 1910
The Test	Dec. 16, 1909	*A Lucky Toothache*	Oct. 13, 1910
To Save Her Soul	Dec. 27, 1909	*Waiter No. 5*	Nov. 3, 1910
The Day After		*Simple Charity*	Nov. 10, 1910
(author only)	Dec. 30, 1909	*The Song of the Wildwood*	
All On Account		*Flute*	Nov. 21, 1910
of the Milk	Jan. 13, 1910	*A Plain Song*	Nov. 28, 1910
The Woman		*White Roses*	Dec. 22, 1910
From Mellon's	Feb. 3, 1910	*When a Man Loves*	Jan. 5, 1911
The Englishman		*The Italian Barber*	Jan. 9, 1911
and the Girl	Feb. 17, 1910	*Three Sisters*	Feb. 2, 1911

A Decree of Destiny	Mar. 6, 1911
Madame Rex	
(author only)	Apr. 17, 1911
The Mender of Nets	Feb. 15, 1912
Iola's Promise	Mar. 14, 1912
Fate's Interception	Apr. 8, 1912
The Female of the Species	Apr. 15, 1912
Just Like a Woman	Apr. 18, 1912
Won by a Fish	Apr. 22, 1912
The Old Actor	May 6, 1912
A Lodging for the Night	May 9, 1912
A Beast at Bay	May 27, 1912
Home Folks	June 6, 1912
Lena and the Geese	
(also author)	June 17, 1912
The School Teacher	
and the Waif	June 27, 1912
An Indian Summer	July 8, 1912
The Narrow Road	Aug. 1, 1912
The Inner Circle	Aug. 12, 1912
With the Enemy's Help	Aug. 19, 1912
A Pueblo Legend	Aug. 29, 1912
Friends	Sept. 23, 1912
So Near, Yet So Far	Sept. 30, 1912
A Feud in the	
Kentucky Hills	Oct. 3, 1912
The One She Loved	Oct. 21, 1912
My Baby	Nov. 14, 1912
The Informer	Nov. 21, 1912
The New York Hat	Dec. 5, 1912
The Unwelcome Guest	Mar. 15, 1913
The Heart of an	
Outlaw	(filmed 1909, unreleased)

INDEPENDENT MOTION PICTURE COMPANY (IMP)

Their First	
Misunderstanding	Jan. 9, 1911
The Dream	Jan. 23, 1911
Maid or Man	Jan. 30, 1911
At the Duke's	
Command	Feb. 6, 1911

The Mirror	Feb. 9, 1911
While the Cat's Away	Feb. 9, 1911
Her Darkest Hour	Feb. 13, 1911
Artful Kate	Feb. 23, 1911
A Manly Man	Feb. 27, 1911
The Message	
in the Bottle	Mar. 9, 1911
The Fisher-Maid	Mar. 16, 1911
In Old Madrid	Mar. 20, 1911
Sweet Memories	Mar. 27, 1911
The Stampede	Apr. 17, 1911
Second Sight	May 1, 1911
The Fair Dentist	May 8, 1911
For Her Brother's Sake	May 11, 1911
The Master and the Man	May 15, 1911
The Lighthouse Keeper	May 18, 1911
Back to the Soil	June 8, 1911
In the Sultan's Garden	July 3, 1911
For the Queen's Honor	July 6, 1911
A Gasoline Engagement	July 10, 1911
At a Quarter of Two	July 13, 1911
Science	July 24, 1911
The Skating Bug	July 31, 1911
The Call of the Song	Aug. 13, 1911
The Toss of a Coin	Aug. 31, 1911
'Tween Two Loves	Sept. 29, 1911
The Rose's Story	Oct. 2, 1911
The Sentinel Asleep	Oct. 9, 1911
The Better Way	Oct. 12, 1911
His Dress Shirt	Oct. 30, 1911
From the Bottom	
of the Sea	Oct. 20, 1911

THE MAJESTIC COMPANY

The Courting	
of Mary	Nov. 26, 1911
Love Heeds Not	
the Showers	Dec. 3, 1911
Little Red	
Riding Hood	Dec. 17, 1911
The Caddy's Dream	Dec. 31, 1911
Honor Thy Father	Feb. 9, 1912

FEATURES, 1913–1933
Listed by distributor and release date.

STATE RIGHTS
(negotiated state by state)

In the Bishop's Carriage (September 10, 1913)
Producer: Famous Players Film Company
Director: Edwin S. Porter and J. Searle Dawley

Caprice (November 1913)
Producer: Famous Players Film Company
Director: J. Searle Dawley
With Owen Moore as the male romantic lead.

Hearts Adrift (February 10, 1914)
Producer: Famous Players Film Company
Director: Edwin S. Porter
From a scenario by Mary Pickford.

A Good Little Devil (March 1, 1914)
Producer: Famous Players Film Company
Director: Edwin S. Porter
From the Broadway production, starring Mary Pickford. With a special appearance by David Belasco.

Tess of the Storm Country (March 20, 1914)
Producer: Famous Players Film Company
Director: Edwin S. Porter

PARAMOUNT PICTURES

The Eagle's Mate (July 5, 1914)
Producer: Famous Players Film Company
Director: James Kirkwood
With James Kirkwood (as the male romantic lead) and Jack Pickford among the cast.

Such a Little Queen (September 21, 1914)
Producer: Famous Players Film Company
Directors: Edwin S. Porter and Hugh Ford

Behind the Scenes (October 26, 1914)
Producer: Famous Players Film Company
Director: James Kirkwood
With James Kirkwood as the male romantic lead.

Cinderella (December 28, 1914)
Producer: Famous Players Film Company
Director: James Kirkwood
With Owen Moore as Prince Charming.

Mistress Nell (February 1, 1915)
Producer: Famous Players Film Company
Director: James Kirkwood
Scenario: Frances Marion
With Owen Moore as the male romantic lead.

Fanchon the Cricket (May 10, 1915)
Producer: Famous Players Film Company
Director: James Kirkwood
Scenario: James Kirkwood and Frances Marion
Jack and Lottie Pickford were among the cast.

The Dawn of a Tomorrow (June 6, 1915)
Producer: Famous Players Film Company
Director: James Kirkwood
Based on the novel and play *The Dawn of a Tomorrow*, by Frances Hodgson Burnett.
Some sources credit Frances Marion with the scenario.

Little Pal (July 1, 1915)
Producer: Famous Players Film Company
Director: James Kirkwood
Story: Marshall Neilan
Scenario: Frances Marion and Marshall Neilan

Rags (August 2, 1915)
Producer: Famous Players Film Company
Director: James Kirkwood
With Marshall Neilan as the male romantic lead. Some sources credit Frances
Marion with the scenario.

Esmeralda (September 6, 1915)
Producer: Famous Players Film Company
Director: James Kirkwood
Scenario: Frances Marion
Based on the short story "Esmeralda," by Frances Hodgson Burnett,
and the play by Burnett and William Gillette.

A Girl of Yesterday (October 7, 1915)
Producer: Famous Players Film Company
Director: Allan Dwan
With Jack Pickford, Marshall Neilan, and Frances Marion among the cast.
Mary Pickford is believed to have written the scenario.

Madame Butterfly (November 8, 1915)
Producer: Famous Players Film Company
Director: Sidney Olcott
With Marshall Neilan as Pinkerton.

The Foundling (January 3, 1916)
Producer: Famous Players Film Company
Director: John B. O'Brien
Scenario: Frances Marion

Poor Little Peppina (February 20, 1916)
Producer: Famous Players Film Company
Director: Sidney Olcott
With Jack Pickford in the cast.

The Eternal Grind (April 17, 1916)
Producer: Famous Players Film Company
Director: John B. O'Brien

Hulda from Holland (July 31, 1916)
Producer: Famous Players Film Company
Director: John B. O'Brien

ARTCRAFT PICTURES

Less Than the Dust (November 6, 1916)
Producer: Pickford Film Corporation
Director: John Emerson

The Pride of the Clan (January 8, 1917)
Producer: Pickford Film Corporation
Director: Maurice Tourneur
Scenario: Frances Marion
With Matt Moore, Owen Moore's brother, as the male romantic lead.

The Poor Little Rich Girl (March 5, 1917)
Producer: Pickford Film Corporation
Director: Maurice Tourneur
Scenario: Frances Marion

A Romance of the Redwoods (May 14, 1917)
Producer: Pickford Film Corporation
Director: Cecil B. DeMille

The Little American (July 2, 1917)
Producer: Pickford Film Corporation
Director: Cecil B. DeMille

Rebecca of Sunnybrook Farm (September 22, 1917)
Producer: Pickford Film Corporation
Director: Marshall Neilan
Scenario: Frances Marion

A Little Princess (November 5, 1917)
Producer: Pickford Film Corporation
Director: Marshall Neilan
Scenario: Frances Marion
Based on the novel by Frances Hodgson Burnett.

Stella Maris (January 21, 1918)
Producer: Pickford Film Corporation
Director: Marshall Neilan
Scenario: Frances Marion

Amarilly of Clothes-Line Alley (March 11, 1918)
Producer: Pickford Film Corporation
Director: Marshall Neilan
Scenario: Frances Marion

M'Liss (April 18, 1918)
Producer: Pickford Film Corporation
Director: Marshall Neilan
Scenario: Frances Marion

How Could You, Jean? (June 23, 1918)
Producer: Pickford Film Corporation
Director: William Desmond Taylor
Scenario: Frances Marion
Photography: Charles Rosher

Johanna Enlists (September 29, 1918)
Producer: Pickford Film Corporation
Director: William Desmond Taylor
Scenario: Frances Marion
Photography: Charles Rosher
Featuring the 143rd California Field Artillery, of which Pickford was honorary colonel.

Captain Kidd, Jr. (April 6, 1919)
Producer: Pickford Film Corporation
Director: William Desmond Taylor
Scenario: Frances Marion
Photography: Charles Rosher

FIRST NATIONAL EXHIBITORS CIRCUIT

Daddy-Long-Legs (May 11, 1919)
Producer: Mary Pickford Company
Director: Marshall Neilan
Photography: Charles Rosher, Henry Cronjager
Mary Pickford is credited with assisting Agnes C. Johnston with the scenario.

The Hoodlum (September 1, 1919)
Producer: Mary Pickford Company
Director: Sidney A. Franklin
Photography: Charles Rosher

The Heart o' the Hills (November 17, 1919)
Producer: Mary Pickford Company
Director: Sidney A. Franklin
Photography: Charles Rosher

UNITED ARTISTS

Pollyanna (January 18, 1920)
Producer: Mary Pickford Company
Director: Paul Powell
Scenario: Frances Marion
Photography: Charles Rosher

Suds (June 27, 1920)
Producer: Mary Pickford Company
Director: Jack Dillon
Photography: Charles Rosher, L.W. O'Connell

The Love Light (January 9, 1921)
Producer: Mary Pickford Company
Director: Frances Marion
Scenario: Frances Marion
Photography: Charles Rosher, Henry Cronjager

Through the Back Door (May 17, 1921)
Producer: Mary Pickford Company
Directors: Alfred E. Green, Jack Pickford
Photography: Charles Rosher
Pickford's character, Jeanne Beaudemère, shares a surname with her personal maid.

Little Lord Fauntleroy (September 11, 1921)
Producer: Mary Pickford Company
Directors: Alfred E. Green, Jack Pickford
Photography: Charles Rosher
Based on the book by Frances Hodgson Burnett. Beaudemère, Mary Pickford's maid at Pickfair, was included in the cast.

Tess of the Storm Country (November 12, 1922)
Producer: Mary Pickford Company
Director: John S. Robertson
Photography: Charles Rosher
Beaudemère, Mary Pickford's maid at Pickfair, was included in the cast.

Rosita (September 3, 1923)
Producer: Mary Pickford Company
Director: Ernst Lubitsch
Photography: Charles Rosher
Beaudemère, Mary Pickford's maid at Pickfair, was included in the cast.

Dorothy Vernon of Haddon Hall (March 15, 1924)
Producer: Mary Pickford Company
Director: Marshall Neilan
Photography: Charles Rosher
With Lottie Pickford and her husband, Allan Forrest (the male romantic lead), among the cast.

Little Annie Rooney (October 18, 1925)
Producer: Mary Pickford Company
Director: William Beaudine
Photography: Charles Rosher, Hal Mohr
Pickford wrote the scenario under the name of her maternal grandmother, Catherine Hennessey.

Sparrows (September 19, 1926)
Producer: Mary Pickford Company
Director: William Beaudine
Photography: Charles Rosher, Karl Struss, Hal Mohr

My Best Girl (October 31, 1927)
Producer: Mary Pickford Company
Director: Sam Taylor
Photography: Charles Rosher
With Charles (Buddy) Rogers as the male romantic lead.

Coquette (April 12, 1929)
Producer: Mary Pickford
Director: Sam Taylor
Photography: Karl Struss
Mary Pickford dismissed her regular cameraman, Charles Rosher, on this production. Matt Moore, Owen Moore's brother, had a leading role.

The Taming of the Shrew (October 26, 1929)
Producer: Mary Pickford Company, The Elton Company
Director: Sam Taylor
With Douglas Fairbanks as Petruchio. The Elton Company was Fairbanks's producing company.

Kiki (March 14, 1931)
Producer: Art Cinema
Director: Sam Taylor
Based on the play *Kiki*, by André Picard, as adapted by David Belasco.

Secrets (March 1933)
Producer: Pickford Corporation
Director: Frank Borzage
Screenplay: Frances Marion

MISCELLANEOUS APPEARANCES

All-Star Production of Patriotic Episodes for the Second Liberty Loan
(also known as *War Relief*) (1917)
Producer: National Association of the Motion Picture Industry
Douglas Fairbanks was among the cast.

100% American (1918)
Producer: Famous Players–Lasky
Director: Arthur Rosson

Mary Pickford also made a brief, unbilled appearance as the Virgin Mary in *The Gaucho*, starring Douglas Fairbanks, in 1927.

PHOTOGRAPHY
CREDITS

Photographs in the two insert sections are from the **Academy of Motion Picture Arts and Sciences**, Los Angeles, except for the following.

Author's collection: A6 (section A, page 6), bottom left and right; A7; A9, bottom; A14, bottom left; B5, bottom; B6, top, bottom left; B9
Robert S. Birchard: B5, top; B13, top left, top right
Bison Archives, Los Angeles: A14, bottom right; A16, both; B2, both; B3; B4, bottom left; B10, bottom right; B12, bottom; B13, bottom; B15, top left
Malcolm Boyd: B15, top right
Culver Pictures, New York: A13, bottom; A14, top; B8
George Eastman House, Rochester, New York: B4, bottom right; B6, bottom right
Library of Congress, Washington: A4, bottom
Museum of Modern Art, New York: A5, top, bottom; B12, top
Toronto Star: B16, top

INDEX

The text in this book is set in Bembo, a typeface produced
by Stanley Morison of Monotype in 1929.
Bembo is based on a roman typeface cut by Francesco
Griffo in 1495; the companion italic is based on
a font designed by Giovanni Tagliente in the 1520s.

The display face is set in Trajan, which was designed in 1988
by Carol Twombly. This typeface is based on the inscription
at the base of Trajan's Column in Rome (AD 113).

Book design and typesetting by
James Ireland Design Inc., Toronto

B   Whitfield, Eileen,
PICKFORD   1951-

         Pickford.

$25.00

DATE			